The Pigeon P(

A Popular History of Elgin High School

Jeff Dugdale

With Forewords by Bill Hope and Gary Robertson

And with personal contributions from Richard Bennett, Bill Hope, Andrew Simpson, Hugh McCulloch, Sheena Ledingham, Anne Duncan, Aileen Marshall and over 175 former pupils

Complementary website pigeonpost.info curated by Leon G. Lumsden

Edited by Andrew G. Cowie

Formerly Editor with Clyde & Forth Press

This book is dedicated to all the pupils and staff, past and present of Elgin High School

LECTOR SI MONUMENTUM REQUIRIS HOC LEGERE

Published in Great Britain by Lunamoon Solaris. All profits from the sale of this book will be donated to the Elgin High School fund.

Email : jefforbited@aol.com and admin.elginhigh@moray-edunet.gov.uk

ISBN 978-0-9933884-1-5

First published 2018

A catalogue record of this book is available from the British Library

Printed in Keith, Banffshire by MMS Almac Ltd.

instance and carpets had appeared in many of the classrooms - but it was clear for all to see that the building itself had seen better days and fallen into a state of some disrepair.

In December I was fortunate to receive another tour - this time of the new building - which by contrast was all shiny new, dressed in pristine white and equipped with the latest state-of-the-art facilities. But what impressed me most during my tours of both the old school and the new was not the buildings themselves but the calibre of the senior pupils who conducted the tours and did so with an uplifting confidence, good humour and a genuine enthusiasm and pride for their school which was a delight to behold. I was reminded of the old saying that a church is the people, not the building. The same is surely true of a school - it's the pupils and staff who make a school what it is, not mere bricks and mortar. If this is the calibre of pupils being produced by the new EHS under the leadership of Hugh McCulloch and his senior management team, then I'm confident the future is in excellent hands indeed.

So let's not be sad over the demise of the original building. They might have knocked down the structure but, as this book proves, they'll never destroy our memories. Let's instead look ahead to the future and share in the excitement of the current crop of pupils as EHS embarks on a new era, regenerated, reinvigorated and ready to face the challenges of the next forty years. On behalf of FPs, I wish the present cohort of staff and pupils every success in their splendid new building and for the wider future beyond. Long live EHS!   A.G.C. 27.3.18

And it's Goodbye From them!!

What a picture!!

(Where's Nick?)

About The Author

Jeff Dugdale began his teaching career at Forfar Academy where he served from 1971-75. He was then Assistant Principal Teacher of English at Banff Academy from 1975-78 and at Elgin High School was Head of English 1978-85, Assistant Rector 1985—2003 and Depute Head 2003—2008. On retirement he taught English on supply for extended periods in many local schools, finally leaving the profession at Summer 2016.

He founded and edited the Banff Academy newspaper *Vivat* from 1975-78 and founded and edited Elgin High's *Pigeon Post* from 1978-2009.

Additionally he has been editor of *Orbit* the quarterly journal of The Astro Space Stamp Society since July 1995, and has written many articles on stamps related to spaceflight within its pages.

He has written occasional articles for *STAMP Magazine* since 1997, has had a regular two page column since 2016 and many other of his articles have appeared in several European and American general and thematic philatelic journals.

Acknowledgements

In addition to all the contributors of material for *Pigeon Post* between 1978 -2009 which I have drawn on freely, I should like to thank the following people for their contributions to the completion of this complicated assemblage of recent history

John Aitken, Richard Bennett, Alec Cadenhead, Anne Duncan, Alistair Farquhar, Martin Graham, Bill Hope, Donna Innes, James Hamilton, Janice Hyndman, Hamish Hyndman, Nick Ledingham, Sheena Ledingham, Hugh McCulloch, Neil McDonald, Eilidh McLean, Angela Matchett, Gregor Milne, Derek Ross, Andy Simpson, Anne Smith, Conal Smith,

And in particular......

My editor, Andrew G. Cowie

Eve Archer, my wife, who designed the covers and the look of chapter title pages and whose critiques of some of my dafter ideas shown to her in draft form, were invaluable

Leon G Lumsden, who initiated and curates pigeonpost.info.

Gary McKinney who started the former pupil Facebook site which I simply did not know about

Aileen Marshall who first said "You should write a book" and was a major player in proof reading and former pupil Claire Cameron who inadvertently suggested the title "The *Pigeon Post* Years"

Allan Robertson & Colin Brown of MMS Almac

James Nock, Sharon Slater and Scott Reid of the Elgin Library Heritage Centre

And many of the 2,600+ members of the Facebook site Former Elgin High School Students whose contributions inspired and guided me as I worked my way through this idea.

CONTENTS

Part One : Narrative and Commentary

Part Two: Compendium : Lists –Tables-Records

Foreword I

By Bill Hope, Rector 1978—2003

I am delighted to be asked to contribute some opening remarks to this history of Elgin High. I can tell already it is going to be good as there are not one but two Forewords, an Epilogue and an Afterword—Jeff Dugdale never did anything by half measures!

Launched in August 1978, Elgin High always had the advantage of being an attractive building. Rather than being of traditional north-east design, with its mansard roof it had the looks of a modern hotel.

However the building maketh not the school and from the start there was a determination to be truly comprehensive. We hoped it would become a community where every pupil felt of equal value and every achievement was recognised—small and great. Accordingly it has been a privilege to see so many pupils prosper in so many ways.

Nikki Grant played football 99 times for Scotland : news of her exploits as a schoolgirl star peppers issue after issue of *Pigeon Post* during her six years with us (and later). Now she is treading the new school's corridors as one of its Depute Heads.

We awake every day to the dulcet tones of former pupil Gary Robertson anchoring the morning programme *Good Morning Scotland* on BBC Radio Scotland and we will never forget former pupil Michael Gray M.B.E. being the lone piper on the castle battlements bringing an end to the Edinburgh Military Tattoo each night throughout August 2002.

Being succeeded by the dream team of Andy Simpson and then Hugh McCulloch was very rewarding as both fully embrace the school aim of achievement for all. Under their guidance Elgin High also developed an international dimension with the African links which have benefitted so many pupils there and here.

The old lady creaked (and leaked) as a building but she never lost her welcoming atmosphere and I am certain that EHS2 will be a seamless progression.

I wish much luck, much achievement and much fun to all who pass along her wide new corridors and I trust that those of you who read this book will have many happy memories stirred—and perhaps even learn something about the school sessions, pupils and staff you personally did not know about whilst it stood.

I commend it to you.

Foreword II

By Gary Robertson,

former pupil and BBC broadcaster and journalist

I am honoured to be asked by Jeff Dugdale to write a forward to this excellent book and be in the esteemed company of Bill Hope in doing so.

The passage of time allows you to reflect on, and appreciate, defining moments in life and my time at Elgin High School was certainly one such. I remember being a nervous 11 year old attending the 'big school' for the first time. The usual rumours did the rounds of Greenwards Primary before the start date about how the older pupils liked to carry out initiations on the new intake. There were grisly tales of first year students having their heads flushed down toilets. Thankfully these stories were no more than urban myths. The reality was a welcoming environment, personified each morning by the friendly face of Mr Hope as he stood at the main entrance greeting staff and pupils by name, a rollcall he learned remarkably quickly.

For me the school building always loomed large as it was opposite my parents' house and I remember watching its construction knowing that I would one day be a pupil. Although now entirely rebuilt – sadly deemed no longer fit for purpose - it was, for its time, a very modern looking building when I first arrived in 1979.

When I look back on how formative those years at EHS were, I appreciate the dedication of the staff, the friends I made, the academic knowledge I gained, and the extra curricular activities such as drama and debating which helped me in my future career.

As the years pass, it is interesting and enjoyable to reconnect with those school days and I think a huge vote of thanks is due to Jeff Dugdale for the effort he has made over the years to keep in contact with so many former pupils and to bring them together, both online and through his endeavours with this book.

I hope the current pupils of EHS enjoy their experience as much as I did.

1

INTRODUCTION

What's 99% of 4,000 ?

Welcome to *The Pigeon Post Years* – and thanks for your interest in this popular history of Elgin High School. Though your author did not know it at the time, this book has been maturing for 40 years, has 430+ pages, could have had 4,500 pages – and in a sense has !!

Elgin High claims to be unique in many ways, one of them being its school newspaper (*not* magazine) *Pigeon Post* which over 30 years of regular publication (between 5 and 8 times a year) <u>reported on or at the very least recorded every significant event in the school's history</u>. More than that, its pages contain at least one photograph and typically 40 or so words relating to over 99% of our pupils and staff between 1978 and 2008. Taking each year cohort of pupils to be around 110, that's roughly 3,500 pupils and, allowing for turn over, a staff of 400+.

So with the aid of this book, access to the internet and a good idea of when a certain pupil or member of staff was at the school you have *a portal* to a reference (often substantial) to and/or a photograph of

Every single prize winner

Every single athletics champion

Every single swimming champion

Every principal in a school play or show

Every member of a registration class, as photographed on their first day in S1

Every member of a house or pupil council

Every member of a sports team like football, hockey, rugby, badminton, athletics etc

Every staff member (teaching, non-teaching and guest or associated staff)

Really? Yes, you will find the text of this history of the school peppered with "PP…" parentheses identifying where further information about any topic may be found in a *Pigeon Post* article. All that is available to you via any internet device at **pigeonpost.info.**

Here you will find scanned (occasionally not very crisply, alas) every material page, some four and a half thousand of them, of every issue of our newspaper.

So that's pretty much unique. Yes, in the early days, when *Pigeon Post* was created using manual typewriters and cyclostyling machines, the quality of pages was relatively primitive but it improves steadily over three decades. And if you are frustrated by poor reproduction of certain pages, get up into your grandparents' loft and look for your original copies of *PP*.

You didn't throw them away, did you?

2 The Summer of 78 :
Beginnings at The Haugh

To most people The Mansion House Hotel has presented an option for a fine dining experience and "the perfect destination for business pleasure or a special celebration" according to their website. However in the Spring of 1978 parts of the 19th century country mansion known as The Haugh – an old Scots word for a flat field subject to flooding!! - were being used to house the Music and Classics Departments of the crowded Elgin Academy buildings, then catering for more than 1,700 pupils. Teaching Latin and "a little Greek" and instrumental instruction filled only a few rooms, so it was in a handful of run down adjacent facilities owned by Grampian Regional Council (GRC) that the first staff of Elgin High School gathered in the week beginning 5th June.

Most of those who came together then had been appointed in the first two weeks of April, before panels comprising Elgin High's new Rector, Bill Hope, legendary Divisional Education Officer John Cruickshanks, a GRC subject adviser (like Charles King in English) and a local councillor. I was one of the first two Principal Teachers (PTs) appointed, with my interview and that of PT History Mr James Hamilton conducted on the 4th April in the GRC's Education Department buildings in Academy Street, which a century before had housed The Girls' Technical School.

The Rector, the Depute (Alistair MacLachlan) and the Assistant Rector (Douglas Campbell) who formed "The Board of Studies" had been selected a few months earlier—the latter after a re-advertisement—and were now joined by a dozen or so male* colleagues, all but one in their early 30s. They were all very excited indeed to

3

be given the opportunity not only to run a department, but to create one in a brand new school, a rare privilege indeed.

Bill Hope had always been in favour of cross-fertilisation of ideas and those who had been appointed as Principal Teachers had come from all over Scotland as the table below shows. One measure of the calibre of the first senior appointments to EHS was the later promotion to Headteacher of four of this group, to Depute of a further handful whilst amongst the others were a future Director of Education, an SQA official, a Moray Councillor, an Education Adviser and a College Professor.

Teacher	Subject	Immediately previous school
Bill Hope	Rector	Lochaber High, Fort William
Alistair MacLachlan	Depute /	
	PT Business Studies	Keith Grammar School
Douglas Campbell	Asst Rector/PT Guidance	Trinity Academy, Edinburgh
Maurice Jackson	Art & Design	Forres Academy
Jeff Dugdale	English	Banff Academy
Alister Hendrie	Geography	Alloa Academy
David Cameron	Guidance	Forres Academy
James Hamilton	History	Robert Gordon's, Aberdeen
Sylvia Campbell	Home Economics	Plockton High
Judy Ross*	Modern Languages	Galashiels Academy
Alec Mackay	Mathematics	Ellon Academy
Donnie Macleod	Remedial	Elgin Academy
Sheena Cowan*	Music	Galashiels Academy
David Carstairs	P.E.	Carnoustie High
Nick Ledingham	Science	Kelso High
Alasdair Urquhart	Technical	Elgin Academy
Nancy Prentice	Admin/The Office	

*Because of other commitments, neither Judy Ross nor Sheena Cowan were able to enjoy the full Haugh experience, arriving on the Elgin High campus only in mid-August. Aileen Marshall, our Library Assistant, worked alongside Margaret McPherson the Elgin Academy Librarian until the end of term.

The first photograph of the first staff, taken by Nick Ledingham early on the morning of 13th August 1978

Back (-r) Mrs Constance Angus, Mr Jeff Dugdale, Mr George McKenzie, Mr Donnie Macleod, Mr Martin Cook, Mr Jim Hamilton, Mr Derek Ross, Mrs Penny McQuillan, Mrs Nancy Prentice, Mrs Maryann Dimmer, Mrs Mary Stewart

Middle: Miss Sylvia Campbell, Mrs Linda McPherson, Miss Sheena Cowan, Miss Judith Ross, Mr Douglas Campbell, Rector William Hope, Mr Alistair MacLachlan, Miss Pat Brown, Miss Isobel Wasilenska, Mrs Avril Clark, Mrs Alison Brown.

Front: Mr Maurice Jackson, Mr Alec McKay, Mr Alasdair Urquhart, Mr Nick Ledingham, Mr Alister Hendrie, Mr David Carstairs, Mr David Cameron.

On appointment, each of the new PTs had been asked to provide the Rector with their first annual "requisition" – a comprehensive list of the teaching resources they needed - within a budget and inside a daunting month! In those first few weeks our days were filled checking against our lists what books, jotters and equipment had by then been delivered (to the dilapidated, Spartan rooms of The Haugh). Whilst the Heads of Department were doing that, the Board of Studies triumvirate were developing a staff manual and policies, from scratch, literally *carte blanche*! We got to know our new colleagues in formal and informal meetings, debating education and socialising to build an easy camaraderie. We visited Elgin Academy to liaise with our subject colleagues, and were inducted in management according to the ways of GRC's formidable Director of Education James Michie and his depute Bill Fordyce[1]. Oh and we watched the Scottish Football team disappoint yet again in the World Cup in Argentina.

Having produced two dozen editions of a school newspaper, *Vivat*, at Banff Academy I was keen to suggest that I start a similar newspaper for Elgin High, and amidst collegiate enthusiasm (and scepticism that it would not last through the other pressures) I began to plan the first issue of *Pigeon Post* by chatting with each of my new colleagues, writing pen portraits of them for it and sketching out what would go into a further 20 pages. Little did I suspect then that I would still be doing that thirty years later!

However it was clear that having done quickly and with energy all that could be done, most of the new team had quite a lot of empty, wasteful days ahead before the scheduled Summer Holidays came along, and as a group we proposed we be allowed to go on holiday a week early. In exchange for this accommodation we would return to work a week early in August when the new school buildings in New Elgin were available to us. And after some humming and hawing from GRC this concession was agreed and we departed The Haugh on the 23rd of June.

Returning to Elgin to move into EHS on August 14th we found that there was a problem with the building warrant for the new school which had not yet been "signed off" by the contractors, Bardolin Scotia – staff had access to most but not quite all of the school, some other areas being out of bounds for Health & Safety reasons. Indeed there was speculation that the facilities might not be available to pupils in time for their scheduled arrival a week later! The buildings were still being finished off by tradesmen and what most of us found in our departmental areas was pretty chaotic. Much of that week was spent ferrying materials from The Haugh, then relocating them within our subject area classrooms and repetitive tasks like numbering textbooks and marking them with an "Elgin High School" rubber stamp. Staff even carried in many of the desks to their own classrooms.

All of the staff including a further dozen or so young[2] departmental colleagues arrived to join their PTs on Monday August 21st and the following day the first 216 pupils of the new Elgin High School arrived, having been summoned in by Bill Hope himself pressing the electric bell from the Janitor's office, a truly historic moment.

They comprised First and Second Years in four "teaching" and six "practical" [3] sets for each year - to be described as every cohort thereafter would be by Bill — "bright eyed and bushy tailed" as suggested by the photo below from *The Northern Scot* of Saturday 26th August 1978—retrieved from microfiche at Elgin Library Heritage Centre!

Obviously happy with their new school are pupils of Class 1B of the new Elgin High School, pictured on its opening day
[NS Photo]

[1]These two gentlemen each gave advice that few would forget. In particular, James Michie advised us there was no place for timidity and that "If you don't ask—you don't get" and Bill Fordyce cautioned against complacency with "No matter how well you are doing something today, you must consider how you can do it better tomorrow".

[2]On opening day the average age of the staff was 28.

[3]A "teaching" set could be up to 33 strong and was for classroom subjects like English, Maths, Geography etc. "Practical" sets had a legal maximum of 20 and were for hands-on subjects like Technical, Home Economics, Art & Design etc.

Press Reaction to the Opening

FIRST INTAKE AT NEW ELGIN HIGH

SCHOOLS throughout Moray District resume on Tuesday after the summer holidays. And on that day Elgin becomes the first centre in Grampian Region — with the exception of Aberdeen — to have two operational secondary schools.

Some 220 pupils in the first and second years will be settling down to studies in the classrooms of the new Elgin High School at The Wards, which within four years will be a complete six-year school, working to full capacity.

"The school will take pupils mainly from the New Elgin and Mosstowie catchment areas," said divisional education officer, Mr John Cruickshanks.

"First and second year classes are being taken in initially, with a new first-year intake at the beginning of each new session. This will finally lead to a full six-year school."

High School, which has taken 18 months to build, will help ease the congestion at Elgin Academy where the roll at the start of the session is expected to be around the 1550 mark — about 180 down on August last year.

REDUCTION

First-year intakes to the academy should also be considerably down in future years since 12-year-olds from the New Elgin area will now go on to the High School.

Mr Cruickshanks said the High School roll would gradually increase by 100-120 a year until it reached its capacity level of 500-plus.

Initially some 20 teachers will be employed, with a principal in each subject.

Work on the building has not quite been completed, but there will be very little inconvenience to staff and pupils.

Pictured in the library of the new Elgin High School is headmaster Mr William Hope, who until last January was assistant head of Lochaber High School, Fort William. A married man, Mr Hope is a native of Galloway, and a keen sportsman. He is a qualified hockey coach and also umpires cricket matches.

The Elgin High School staff who will meet their new pupils for the first time on Tuesday   INS Photo

The Northern Scot
AND
Moray and Nairn Express

ELGIN, SATURDAY, AUGUST 19, 1978.

NEW ERA IN EDUCATION

ELGIN has for long enjoyed a high reputation in the field of secondary education, producing a steady stream of young "Academicians" eager to pursue their studies at the universities of Scotland and further afield.

And that reputation as a centre of learning will be further enhanced next week with the opening of the town's new High School, ample evidence of Elgin's role as Grampian Region's most important growth point outside Aberdeen.

Elgin Academy's new home at Morriston was opened officially in 1969 amidst much ceremony. However, it soon became apparent that the building was incapable of handling the rapidly increasing secondary population. The hope must now be that the new school will relieve for a reasonable time the chronic overcrowding which has beset the Academy.

The High School, designed to accommodate eventually more than 500 pupils, provides its students with all the benefits accruing from a comparatively small school. The staff and pupils have a lot to live up to, but with the passing of time the empty building that now awaits its first occupants will come alive, assuming its identity and creating its own special place in the community it serves.

The article above appeared beneath a panorama of the North end of the school in *The Northern Scot* for Saturday 19th August, 1978 with the leader column (right) on a different page.

Amongst the male staff (back l-r): Messrs Ledingham, Cameron, Jackson, Hendrie, Carstairs and Macleod and front McKay, MacLachlan, Hope, Campbell and Hamilton are sandwiched Miss Ross and two non-teaching colleagues Mrs Alison Brown (centre) and Mrs Pat Brown. See photo earlier in this chapter.

3 Elgin Schools 1224 to 1978

by Richard Bennett

Head of English at Elgin Academy (1976—2002) and author

of *Elgin Academy 1801-2001*

Think of your own schooldays. You remember the buildings, beginnings and endings, your mates, your favourite subjects, good choices you made and bad, teachers you loathed and ones you loved, school dinners, playground games, parties and Proms, sweethearts and broken hearts ...

But what was it like to be a school pupil in Elgin, say, 400 years ago?

For a start, you – and you would be a boy – were lucky in two important ways: you'd survived childbirth – in those days 30% of children died before they were two; and you were one of the 10% of boys in Elgin whose father could afford to send him to school to train for the Church, Law, Army, or Commerce.

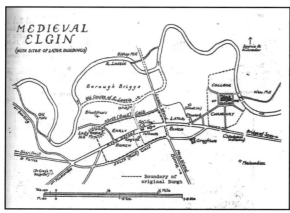

The school comprised a single room with one Master in charge of all pupils, aged from six to sixteen. You attended six days a week, for twelve hours a day. The focus of teaching was Latin, with some mathematics, and the Scriptures. You probably had no books.

In those days, the status of a child was low. There was no sense of childhood being 'special'. Children were imperfect adults, deficient in strength and wisdom, and clearly subordinate. By the age of ten the vast majority of children in Elgin would have been at work – fetching water from the Lossie, picking stones from the fields, frightening crows from the crops. Thereafter, they would be pulled into whatever occupation their parents followed.

A school for girls did not begin in Elgin till the middle years of the eighteenth century – and that was for learning of an entirely practical kind. Universal education for children did not become law in Scotland, until 1872.

The First Phase:

From the Founding of the Cathedral to the Reformation

In the Middle Ages, Elgin was a very important religious centre and a place of wealth and standing. After the Wolf of Badenoch burnt down the Cathedral in 1390, the Bishop of Moray wrote to the King, the Wolf's uncle, asking for compensation:

My church, he wrote, was the particular ornament of the fatherland, the glory of the kingdom, the joy of strangers and incoming guests, the object of praise and exaltation in other kingdoms because of the numbers of those serving it and of the beauty of its decoration, by which it is believed that God was properly worshipped; not to mention its high bell towers, its venerable furnishings and uncountable jewels.

As well as burning down the Cathedral, the Wolf's band of 'wikkid, wild, Heilandmen' torched the homes of the people and destroyed all the buildings within the walls of the Chanonry, including the manses of eighteen priests of high importance, and, presumably, the school. The Cathedral had been founded in 1224. The first school, the **Grammar School,** was established by and for the Church. The Church was completely dominant in all aspects of life and it offered great career opportunities for the sons of better-off citizens.

The Church remained solely responsible for education in the town until 1494. In that year, in the reign of James IV, an Act of Parliament was passed, requiring that all 'Barrones and Freihalders … put their elder sonnes and aires to the schuls from six or nine yeires and they remain there until they have perfect Latin … Art and Jure (Law)'. This Act required the removal of responsibility for schools from the Church to the 'heritors' or property-owners, as represented by the Town Council. That edict seems clear enough, but a battle for control of Elgin's schools between Church (and later Kirk) and Council began and continued, often bitterly, for another four centuries.

Education became popular among the 'heritors'. Some gentlemen were happy to keep on sending their sons to the Grammar School that continued to be run by the Church. Others patronised private schools.

In 1540, the Town Council established a 'public' – as opposed to Church-run – **Grammar School** and ordered that all rival schools be closed down.

The Second Phase:

The Reformation to the Founding of the Academy

Following the Reformation of 1560, Moray suffered constant harassment by Royalists and Covenanters for the next century and a half. Wars affect education. How did the boys react to seeing Cromwell's soldiers using the Cathedral walls for target practice?

Educational progress was slow. Former Church buildings passed into Council ownership. The Hospice of Maisondieu was used for the **Sang School** (or Music School). The schoolmaster was employed as Precentor and choirmaster at St Giles. In 1659, the Sang School became the **English School**, thus shedding the Roman associations and differentiating it from the Latin-dominant Grammar School.

These two schools operated in a variety of private houses and some odd locations, including a malt kiln. No dedicated school buildings were erected until 1676. In that year, the Town Council located the English School in a new building in Moss Wynd (near the top of Commerce Street). In 1694, they built a new Grammar School next door.

Wood's Map of Elgin: 1822 Reprinted here courtesy of Elgin Library

At the end of the seventeenth century, the original, medieval building of St Giles stood on the Plainstones and the Tolbooth – Jail and Town House combined – occupied the spot where the fountain now stands. According to town records, very few men holding seats on the Town Council in the 1690s could read or write or sign their names.

Maps of the time show a single street with closes running off it, in classic fishbone pattern. At the street end of each close stood a merchant's or burgess's house, and, behind that, maybe ten buildings, housing up to thirty families. An open drain ran down one side of each close, leading to an open sewer on the High Street. Town wells were notoriously unhealthy. Most people collected their water directly from the Lossie.

Poverty was desperate; diseases – scrofula, smallpox, typhoid, diphtheria, tuberculosis – were rife.

There was no school for the children from the depths of the closes

There was, now, some degree of educational stability in Elgin in that there were two specially constructed school buildings. However, the struggle between Kirk and Council for control of these schools flared up at times into open conflict. They were 'public schools', but the Kirk demanded rights with regard to the appointment of teachers and in the annual examinations. The relationship was, at the best of times, uneasy.

A record of 1649 details a code of discipline for Elgin Grammar School boys. It defines 'positive duties' – to seek God in the morning before coming to school, to come to school with washed hands, combed hair and neat clothes, and to obey and respect the Masters; and 'negative duties' – lateness, absence, and truancy were forbidden, as were gambling, carrying hurtful weapons, wandering, beggary, bullying, swearing or cursing, and speaking English – Latin was the only permitted language in school and in the streets. Punishment was limited to the cane or the strap and was at the Master's discretion.

．　　．　　．

Masters of the Grammar School left with alarming frequency. From its establishment as a 'public' school in 1550 to its closure in 1801, masters averaged about four years of service. It may be that salaries and conditions of service at the Grammar School were not sufficient to attract high quality candidates. Over these 250 years, the length of service of masters of the Sang, or English, School averaged more than double that of Grammar School masters.

The demands of the Grammar School contract were strict. The school day ran from 6am to 6pm, with two breaks for lunch and recreation; on Saturdays, the day ran from 6am to 2pm; on Sundays, the master was required to attend, with his pupils, morning and afternoon, services in St Giles Kirk. He then had to take the boys back to school to reflect and to talk about what they had heard.

．　　．　　．

Masters were often dismissed – for neglecting their duties, for rioting, drunkenness, swearing, gambling, fornication, 'merchandising', and other unspecified offences. In 1653, one master was sacked for failing to accompany his pupils to Spynie Loch on an expedition to gather 'bents' or rushes for mending the thatch on the school roof. One significant reason for masters leaving their post was to become a minister. School-mastering was a common 'way-in' to the clergy for educated men. At least two masters were sacked for preaching sermons when their contract expressly forbade them doing so.

．　　．　　．

The only school sport that we have any record of is cock-fighting. In the eighteenth century, this sport, popular with rich and poor, went on throughout the year. The climax of the season for Elgin Grammar School pupils was the fight that took place on *Fastern's E'en*, or Shrove Tuesday. The schoolmaster had a role in the process. Apparently, he either owned or was involved in the rearing and training of the birds. On the day of the fight, which took place in the schoolroom, the pupils, divided into two teams supporting different sides, met at the Muckle Cross in the High Street and marched in a body to the school, carrying a flag and chanting specially composed songs. At the school, the master greeted them and collected their 'cock pennies' — a charge for entry. All pupils were expected to attend — absentees were later fined the charge agreed for that year. The birds had been trained, fed a special diet, and armoured with long steel spurs to inflict damage. There was a series of 'knock-out' rounds to produce the pair that contested the final. There was enormous excitement. The master was the sole referee and when he declared the winner, the winning 'team' marched in triumph through the town, carrying  the flag and singing their songs. The boys were then invited, at the price of two-pence a shy, to throw stones at the surviving birds. The master then had the privilege of disposing of the carcases.

The flag, presumably the last one in use, is in Elgin Museum: see photos opposite. It was found when the old Grammar School building in Commerce Street was being demolished. One side carries a large Scots thistle with a crown and the motto *Nemo Me Impune Lacessit*. On the other side is a Lion Rampant between the letters G R, and the motto *Hold Fast*. It carries the date 1746 — the year of Culloden.

Right, an interpretation based on written evidence of the 1694 Grammar School buildings in Commerce Street, formerly School Wynd. Impression by artist/ architect Bill Bartlam

In the seventeenth and eighteenth centuries, the daughters of well-off parents may have received some limited education from private governesses, but the first reference to the education of girls in the Elgin Town Council records is on 12 March, 1722, and refers to the appointment of a 'woman school mistress capable to teach white seam, pastrie and other matters proper for women to learn ...' A 'Mris Ramsay, a schoolmistress skillfull in the aforesaid matters,' was duly appointed at the salary of '£20 Scots' for one year. In 1733, Miss Cheyne was appointed to teach girls how to spin, at an annual salary of £18 a year. Before the widespread use of the spinning wheel, fibres of wool or flax were attached to a spindle – a thin rod weighted at one end – and spun by a process of dangling and twisting to produce as fine a thread as possible. A Spinning School for little girls from two years old to seven was opened in 1742, specifically to make fishing tackle. Within ten years, however, the spinning wheel was in general use, and no further spinning schools are recorded.

For a further forty years, the education of girls had little priority in Elgin. In 1753, Mrs Hutton, from Edinburgh, was appointed to teach 'females'. In 1755, Miss Janet Christie was employed at £7 a year – described in Council records as a 'handsome salary'. In 1780, a Ladies' Boarding and Day School was set up by the Town Council under the Misses Elizabeth and Helen Duff in Elchies House, a rather grand building that stood next to where the White Horse pub stands, today.

Years of Change: 1801 to 1872

The late-eighteenth and early nineteenth centuries were a period of improvement and expansion for Elgin and the surrounding area. The Loch of Spynie was drained under the plans of Thomas Telford. A port was created at Stotfield to provide access to wider markets. The development of a woollen industry and improvements in agriculture brought money to the town. The frontages of buildings on the High Street were modernised; the medieval building of St Giles was replaced by the neo-classical building that we know today; the 'unseemly' old Tolbooth was demolished, and a new jail and Town House erected at the east end of the High Street; a fashionable gathering place – the Assembly Rooms – was constructed on the corner of North Street and High Street; a new hospital was erected – the magnificent gift of a native son. The growing village of Bishopmill was incorporated into the town. Gracious suburbs began to develop to the South and West of the centre. There was growing confidence and ambition in the community and a hunger for education.

.   .   .

Plans for a new burgh school – an **Elgin Academy**, to replace the Grammar and English Schools – began to form as early as 1790, and were, partly, the result of a Scotland-wide 'Academy movement' to modernise education by widening opportunities and expanding the curriculum. However, it took ten years to find the money to build and resource the school. The total cost was £505.12.6d, raised entirely by public subscription. The Town Council contributed nothing to the construction; they undertook to pay masters' salaries 'amounting to £42 sterling a-year'. Stone for the buildings, on the corner of Academy Street and Francis Place, was taken mainly from the 'Little Kirk', an extension of the old St Giles, and from the ruins of the Cathedral.

The Academy was divided into three schools – the Latin School, the English School, and the Mathematical School. In 1802, the Masters of the three schools were expected to teach the following subjects:

Latin School: Latin, Greek, Writing;

English School: Reading, English Grammar, Writing, Church Music;

Mathematical School: Arithmetic, Book-keeping, Euclid's Elements, Trigonometry, Geometry, the theory and practice of Land Surveying, Navigation, Fortification, Gunnery, Architecture, Algebra, Perspective Drawing, Geography, French.

We can assume that the Bible and the Shorter Catechism were in every schoolbag.

The school hours, from the start, were:

7am till 9am	Breakfast hour	9am till 10am
10am till 1pm	Dinner time	1pm till 3pm
3pm till 6pm.		

Fees, which formed an important part of each teacher's income, were charged quarterly, as follows:

Grammar School		English School		Mathematical School	
Latin	5/-	English	2/6	Arithmetic	3/-
Greek	5/-	Writing	2/6	Book-keeping	21/-
Latin & Greek	7/6			Drawing	10/6
				French	21/-

Low salaries and fees allowed to teachers at the Academy were a constant matter of complaint. Turnover of Masters was rapid. In 1824, one prominent Master of the Mathematical School, Peter Merson, made public his view of the Council:

'They act by their teachers more unfairly than even the West Indian planters to their slaves'.

The earliest known photograph of Elgin Academy, taken in 1879.

The above photo quoted at p 21 of Richard Bennett's book on Elgin Academy. On the other side of the fascia you see lies Francis Place and top right Moss Street U.F. Church.

Reproduced with permission from Elgin Academy archives

It is salutary to remember that the Academy, the only school in Elgin owned by the Town Council, existed only for those who could afford its fees, and, despite the thrust for improvement, expansion and investment, for the vast majority, living conditions were still desperate. The *Elgin Courant* of 1867 published an official report on sanitation by Dr Littlejohn:

'In Elgin, with its 8000 inhabitants, the number of middens is very large. In High Street alone I inspected 170; of these 90 existed in closes to the north of that street, while on the south side there were 80. No one can enter the closes without being disgusted with the sight of so much decaying material tainting the air, and, in a large proportion of cases, so placed as to be heaped against the nearest house. Associated with these middens were pigstyes, which, from their number, situation, and the manner in which they were kept, must be looked upon as a nuisance of no ordinary magnitude in Elgin. In the High Street there were no fewer than 129 pigstyes, and on average these contained four pigs each. Another nuisance, which at once arrested attention, was the state of the privies in those closes. In close connection with each midden and pigsty there was a privy, which of a general rule, admitting of remarkably few exceptions, was kept in a disgusting state, and gave little evidence of cleanly habits among the poor. Close after close exhibited ranges of middens, pigstyes and privies in front of the houses'.

Some personal reminiscences of Academy life in the 1840s:

'Every newcomer to the Academy had to be initiated or "Brothered". It was a time-honoured custom for centuries. The lad was seized, his arms pinioned and his legs tied. He was then borne to the ashpit. Two scholars stood on the parapet and grasped a foot each, others supported his body, while his posterior received three bumps against the parapet wall, and the fourth heavy bump landed him on top of the wall. Where his fastenings were unloosed, his breeks pulled down and he was fully exposed and duly initiated into all the rights and privileges pertaining to an Academician. He was, thereafter, as keen to "Brother" others as he was reluctant to have it done to himself.'

Another former pupil finishes a vivid description of his 'brothering' as follows:

'The dismay and humiliation I felt were of a kind I cannot describe, and the shock to my modesty was aggravated by the fact that there were girls in the laughing crowd'.

This boy, who had come from England, was mercilessly bullied:

'They worried me for my accent and laughed and jeered at me for my peculiar pronunciation of Scotch words'.

He describes a period during which 'open insubordination was rife'. He describes a school assembly being addressed by the Lord Provost at which a riot takes place. Books, slates, inkpots are thrown at the speaker, senior boys rush the stage and escape to the street through open windows. On another occasion, senior boys lock the school door and hide the key 'of large size' in a hole in the playground wall. The writer is standing near the spot when the Master – the *Reverend* John Allan – finds the key and, in a moment of furious rage, brings it down on the innocent boy's head, stunning him to the ground and leaving 'a swelling as big as a pigeon's egg'. The incident that ended this boy's unhappy experience of Elgin Academy is described as follows:

'A straw beehive was turned into a target by turning it onto its side, and this bully ... a big West Indian half-caste whose name was Quelch ... bethought him of a method of amusing himself at the cost of the smaller boys. He said he was William Tell, and so good a shot that, if we sat stride legs on the beehive, he could shoot his arrows through the hole in the centre without injuring us. I was the first one he selected ... I heard the whiz of the arrow and simultaneously felt its thud, and I tumbled off the beehive with several inches of the shaft sticking in my thigh'.

The boy's relations removed him almost immediately to a private boarding school in Dyke – for the 'sons of good families'.

Some random recollections of old Academy days:

'the sanitation in the old Academy was sheer horror. There was an open midden and structures of the most primitive type';

Masters used to burn the tongues of their straps in order to harden them; strokes of the tawse were called 'pandies';

unofficial fist fights against, first, the Trades School and later, 'the West Enders' were a regular feature of school life;

one annual event was the bitter battle between the boys of Elgin and Lossiemouth held at Spynie Castle. Weapons were cudgels and stones: the results often broken bones and concussion;

the first Academy School Sports Day took place in 1888, but cricket matches against Milne's Institution, Fochabers, are recorded earlier.

.   .   .

By the mid 1830s, the number of schools in Elgin had grown to eight. Of new schools, the most remarkable was the **'Elgin Institution for the support of old age and the Education of Youth'** – the set of buildings we know now as 'Anderson's'. The story of George Anderson's birth in the Cathedral ruins in desperate poverty and his rise in the East India Company to the rank of Major General is well-known. In his will, he left about £70 000 for the establishment of:

'an hospital for the support and maintenance of indigent men and women, not under fifty-five years of age, of decent, godly and respectable character;

'a school of industry for the support, maintenance, clothing, and education of male and female children of the labouring class whose parents are unable to maintain and educate them;

'an establishment of a master and mistress, properly qualified to conduct a free school for the education *only* of such male and female children whose parents may be in narrow circumstances, but still able to maintain and clothe their children'.

The Institution was opened in 1831. By today's values, we can make a very conservative estimate of General Anderson's endowment at about £6 million. By the mid 1830s about 230 pupils were receiving a free education 'suited to their station'. Classes at Anderson's were, at first, conducted on the Bell-Lancaster principle, which involved very large classes being taught by a single teacher, supported by senior pupils, or monitors. The boys wore a blue suit with an

Eton jacket. Their uniform made them objects of mockery to local lads. The girls were trained to find positions as domestic servants. Despite the obvious limitations of the system – it is pretty well damned in the opening chapter of Charles Dickens's *Hard Times* (1854) – it persisted well into the second half of the century, probably because it was cheap to run.

.   .   .

Near the beginning of the nineteenth century, the Incorporated Trades of Elgin started a school to provide elementary education for the sons of tradesmen in a house on the High Street. In 1837, the **Trades School** moved to a substantial property on the corner of Moss Street and Institution Road. The new school opened with 210 pupils; when the school closed, following the Education Act of 1872, the roll was 140.

In 1833, the **Infants' School** was opened on Academy Street, across the road from Elgin Academy, in buildings that, eventually, became the Education Offices. At first, children from three to six were admitted at a fee of one penny a week, with an extra penny a month for coals. The Duchess of Gordon was patron. In the late 1850s, the name changed to the **Girls' School,** although younger children of both sexes still attended. By 1871, the roll was 350 and, by 1888, had risen to nearly 500. In 1876, Miss Margaret Stephen, an Elgin woman, brought up in Lady Lane, was appointed Head Mistress. She soon became a nationally important force in the development of girls' education. Despite very limited resources, she strenuously promoted the teaching of domestic subjects and nutrition as means of improving the nation's health. HMI reports were unwaveringly positive and supportive of Miss Stephen's efforts. In 1905, the school became the **Elgin Girls' Technical School**, providing home economics classes for all schools in the town and a full range of day and evening 'Continuation' classes for girls and women.

Francis Place fascia of the first Elgin Academy with The Girls Technical School building at the top of the picture.

Photo Eve Archer 2.2018

.   .   .

In 1837, a school was established in Bishopmill in a granary that still stands at the corner of East High Street. It is now part of a plumber's premises. It was converted to a Mission Hall after the **Bishopmill School** was built on Balmoral Terrace in 1857 where it remained until succeeded, in 1936, by the school on Morriston Road.

.   .   .

Black's Morayshire Directory of 1863, refers to the **Trinity Episcopal Church Girls' School,** (established in 1853 and held in what is now the Holy Trinity Hall. *Teacher – Miss EM Anderson, assisted by three pupil teachers*), and five **Ladies' Seminaries,** all operating within private houses.

.   .   .

By 1873, the list of schools included **St Sylvester's Roman Catholic School** and two **'Ragged Schools'** – a Boys' school and a Girls' school – located in Lady Lane. The Ragged Schools provided an elementary education for children whose parents were too poor to provide suitable clothing. They also performed – with almost no support from the Council – a very important reformatory function in the days before compulsory education. They took children, who could easily have fallen into crime or vagrancy, off the streets and provided them with occasional meals. The records for 1873 show over 100 pupils attending the two Ragged Schools.

.   .   .

During the middle years of the century, life at Elgin Academy was turbulent; its reputation rose and fell. There were first-rate teachers – William Duguid, Peter Merson, and Donald Morrison are three who brought great credit to the school through their pupils' successes at the University Competitions and who were spoken of very warmly by former pupils. However, a succession of Masters left because of their failure to handle the boys' 'open insubordination'. In 1859, Donald Morrison, Master of the Latin School defected to **Weston House**, a private boarding and day school, at the corner of South Street and Hay Street. He took forty of his pupils with him. Weston House offered 'a complete preparation for the Universities, the Learned Professions, and for Commercial life'. Its most famous pupil was Alexander Graham Bell, who also served there for a short spell as a teacher of music and elocution. In 1874, Weston House became a Ladies' School. It finally closed in 1914.

.   .   .

The Academy was still subject to the dual control of the Magistrates and Presbytery. The conflict that had rumbled on since the Reformation, now, in Elgin, following the Disruption of 1843, grew to open discord and division.

A key figure in the hostile climate of those days was the Mathematical Master, Peter Merson, who also happened to be Clerk to the Presbytery. He was vehemently antagonistic to the predominantly Free Church Town Council. He took every measure he could to place obstacles in the way of the Council's running of the school until, in 1849, he was dismissed. He fought his dismissal – tooth, nail, and letters to the *Courant* – through the courts, arguing that the Council did not have the right to sack him, until, in 1861, decision was made in his favour. What became known, nationally, as 'The Elgin Academy Case' was the beginning of the final round in the seemingly endless battle for control of Scotland's burgh schools. Peter Merson and the Kirk had won – apparently.

Mr Merson was so highly thought of by his former pupils that, on his retiral, they raised enough money for him to build a house on Abbey Street.

The Argyll Commission, set up in 1864, conducted a wide-ranging investigation into school education and the condition of the school estate in Scotland. It discovered the following facts:

of about 500,000 children between four and fourteen only 400,000 were on the roll of any school;

the proportion of young people receiving higher grade schooling in Scotland was 1 in 205, compared with 1 in 1,300 in England and 1in 1,600 in France;

the North-East of Scotland had the highest level of illegitimate births in Europe.

The results of the Commission's findings were enacted in the Education (Scotland) Act of 1872. This Act transformed education in Scotland, making education compulsory for all children between 5 and 13, initiating a huge programme of school building, and passing the management of schools in parish and burgh to an elected School Board. Thus, ironically, Peter Merson's victory in 1861 signalled the end of the Church's control of schools.

Towards the Modern

Problems at the Academy continued, mainly as a result of the character and actions of one man – John Mitchell, the English Master, from 1867 until 1883, when he was finally dismissed. That he was a difficult character is attested by the following extract from a letter to the *Courant* in 1882: 'Mr Mitchell [has been] conspicuously notorious since his most unfortunate advent amongst us … he surpassed himself in unblushing effrontery, self-assertion, and unmitigated egotism'. During his tenure in the English School, the numbers of pupils dropped from 147 to 21. The numbers of pupils in the Mathematical and Latin Schools inevitably suffered.

One feature of the 1872 Act was the transfer of school inspections to the four Universities. In 1881, Professor William Duguid Geddes of the University of Aberdeen (a former pupil of the school, and, later, Principal of the University) wrote: 'Besides the general languidness which is both the cause and effect of the school's inadequacy there is a lack of concentration in the absence of harmonious working towards a combined result'. The 1882 inspection reads: 'it thus appears that the town of Elgin has suffered and is still suffering serious disadvantage from the failure of the English part of the Academy. Mr John Mitchell is responsible for the unsatisfactory state of the English School. I declare him to be unfit, incompetent, and inefficient …' One of Professor Geddes's recommendations for the better management of the Academy was for the appointment of a 'supreme Rector'. That position was created in 1883 with the appointment of John Mackenzie, head of the Latin School. Mr Mitchell fought his dismissal as far as the Court of Session but was dismissed in 1883. Why did he last so long? Partly, because he had been, in the Academy, his own master, and partly because he was a politician – he served on the Town Council for a number of years and had important friends. By the end, though, he had completely alienated the School Board, and his friends had deserted him.

Results of the damage caused to the Academy by John Mitchell were the establishment of private schools, set up and promoted by influential parents. From 1874 to 1879, the **Educational Institute of Elgin** operated as a boys' boarding school

in the Station Hotel, (as seen on this old postcard) now the Laich-Moray. The buildings to the East of the main block were erected to house classrooms and dormitories. The main building was the teachers' accommodation. In 1881, at the height of confusion and dissatisfaction, the first **Elgin High School** was established in an Evangelical Hall on South Street – later to be the Salvation Army Hall, and, latterly, *Sign of the Times* furniture store. This school lasted until 1883 when, on Mitchell's dismissal, pupils returned to the Academy, where every effort was being made to restore the school's prestige.

Photo Eve Archer 2.2018

New schools were built to fulfil the requirements of the 1872 Act: **New Elgin School** and the **West End** opened in 1875; and the accommodation at Anderson's Institution was increased and re-constituted as the **East End School** in 1891.

It took time for the Academy's reputation to be re-established. For a number of years, the West End, the East End, and Bishopmill offered secondary classes, including an 'Advanced' or 'Senior Secondary' division. The West End, because of its location became a serious rival to the Academy among the better-off parents of the town, even after the **'New' Academy** in Moray Street was opened in 1886. Built to accommodate 350 pupils, the Academy's roll in 1892 was 181; by 1900 it had risen to 253.

Photo courtesy Elgin Library Heritage Centre

.   .   .

The West End catered for the children of the stately homes of Mayne Road and Rose Avenue but it also had in its catchment the worst slums in Elgin. The clutter of closes at the foot of Ladyhill – the setting of Jessie Kesson's classic novel, *The White Bird Passes* (1958) – were seen as home to idleness, debauchery, and prostitution as well as whooping cough, dysentery, impetigo, ringworm and nits. Jessie recalled being called 'Beastie Heid' at school.

.   .   .

After 1872, the payment of fees was still a significant part of the School Board's income and the teacher's salary, but, in 1889, the Scottish Education Department abolished fees for all schools. The Academy, however, under the Act, retained the right to charge fees for another 40 years or so.   The establishment of free secondary education for all for 'as long as a child's abilities entitle him (*sic*)' did not come until the 1945 Education Act of the post-War Labour government. Meanwhile, in 1924, the Academy had opened a private, fee-paying 'prep' school, **Springfield**, in a mansion house close to the school in Moray Street. Springfield closed in 1955.

In 1891, **The Victoria School of Science and Art**, (*left*) on the corner of Moray Street and Gordon Street, was opened, as a result of public subscription, as memorial to Queen Victoria's Jubilee (of 1887). It was opened as an independent school, organised under the Technical Schools (Scotland) Act. It became a part of the Academy in 1915.

Photos this page Eve Archer 2.2018

A second **Elgin High School** opened in 'Southbank' (now a guest house, *right*) in Academy Street. The school, for boarders and day pupils, first started in the early 1880s, continued until about 1920.

There had been, for years, a growing tendency towards the idea of passing the organisation of schools in Scotland into local authority control. The Education Act of 1918 saw the end of the School Board. Management of education passed from 947 Parish Boards to 37 Local Education Authorities. The counties of Moray and Nairn joined together for the administration of education.

.   .   .

The two World Wars of the twentieth century had enormously disruptive effects on the schools and on the education of the children.

A significant number (about 20%) of male teachers joined the armed forces in the first few months of each War; those on reserve, numbering 800 in 1914, left immediately. Schools were taken over for billeting troops. Schools were combined – for example, the East End and the West End shared the same premises, each coming for a half-day shift. In the first three days of the Second World War, hundreds of evacuees came with their teachers, from Edinburgh mainly, and accommodation had to be found for them. About 90% returned to Edinburgh within six months to find their schools closed. School playing fields held military encampments or were dug up and planted with vegetables. Many children left school early – there was exemption for some occupations, notably in agriculture, and the pay was good. Fully qualified teachers were replaced by retirees or by unqualified people deemed to have 'an appropriate level of education'. Standards fell drastically. Delinquency increased.

Children had to adjust to rationing, to the absence of street-lighting, to working at weekends, on farms or in building obstacles to invasion along the coast. Later, they had to get used to the presence of German and Italian prisoners-of-war.

Primarily, of course, children had to cope with the constant absence – and the loss – of fathers, brothers, sisters, friends.

The Academy's First World War Roll of Honour lists 84 names of former pupils lost; the Second World War Roll lists 42. The West End's memorial tablet for the First World War lists 123 names. The West End's memorial tablet for the First World War lists 123 names; that of the East End lists 92. We do not have figures for Bishopmill and New Elgin.

.   .   .

Changes at national level saw the regularising of patterns of education across the country. New schools were built and were better funded, more teachers were employed, the number of subjects taught multiplied, much more attention was given to the education of girls. Education was coming closer to a pattern that we can recognise today. In 1936, in Elgin, the process of 'Centralisation' saw the location of all Senior Secondary subjects, leading to nationally recognised certification ('Lowers' and 'Highers'), in the Academy. Pupils who passed the 'Qualifying Exam' in Primary 7 went straight to the Academy. The other four schools had 'Junior Secondary' status, teaching pupils up to the age of 14. After the War, within the burgh, other schools were reduced to Primary status, and all pupils attended the Academy from the age of 12. Pupils from outlying communities, on the coast and on Speyside, continued to come to Elgin Academy for Senior Secondary education until the development of Lossiemouth High School and the opening of Speyside High School, well into the 1970s.

During the 1950s, 1960s and 1970s, the population of Elgin grew rapidly, as a result of changes in farming, mainly due to mechanisation and the amalgamation of farms, the growth of old industry, and the introduction of new industries, in part related to the discovery of North Sea oil. There were major housing developments in Bishopmill and New Elgin. **Seafield Primary School** opened in 1955. The Academy was hopelessly overcrowded.

The **third Academy,** pictured above, opened in 1969 on a spectacular site on Morriston Road. Built to accommodate 1400 pupils, by 1975 the roll was 1750, and the Academy was one of the biggest schools in Scotland. (£800,000 was spent in 1971 converting the second academy into Elgin Technical College, the precursor of Moray College).

Time for a new school, perhaps.

The fascia of the fourth Elgin Academy, which opened in 2012 at a cost of £30m, taken from Morriston Road and below an aerial view showing the asymmetric design of this beautiful and spectacular building — "the iPhone of modern schools"

4 The Need for a Second Secondary School

2nd?

A Little Background to the Situation in Elgin

Writing a substantial contribution to "Elgin Academy 1801-2001"[1] compiled by Richard Bennett, the Head of English at the Academy when the High School opened, A.J. Glashan (Rector from 1964-1987) explains how the new Academy came to be built...

"When I came to Elgin Academy in May, 1964, the 1886 building in Moray Street, extended though it had been to cope with the centralisation of local secondary education in the Academy, was inadequate in nature and also required pupils to travel to playing fields at Morriston, Home Economics Lessons in the Girls' Technical School in Academy Street and in the West End School and even for a mercifully short time in 1968, academic lessons in the High Church Halls, not to mention language classes in Springfield House which had been declared unsuitable for primary education in the 1950s.

"The Education Committee had wisely rejected a proposal to further amend and extend the existing building on its restricted site and had decided on a completely new building at Morriston Farm, and the planning commenced in 1964. While many different educational and, indeed, financial interests were involved in the planning, an unusual and very welcome feature was the degree of consultation afforded to the teaching staff, which resulted not merely in our avoiding a school constructed physically on the house system which would have inhibited its future flexibility but enabled each subject department to incorporate, within reason, the best features of professional thinking as well as to leave room for subsequent development. The planning and building was a long process, which required great effort from many people and this effort did not stop when we occupied the new premises on 12th December 1968..."

Some of the buildings on the south and north sides of Moray Street, comprising Elgin Academy in the 1960s had first been occupied in 1886. Immediately prior to that, as Richard Bennett reminds us at p 21ff of his book[1] and in the previous chapter, the school's location was in Academy Street/Francis Place, some 500

yards to the East of the new site. Some of those buildings today are occupied as as the yard of the Kilmollymock Masonic Hall and The Elgin Youth Café (The Inkwell) but for almost a century after being sold off by the Elgin Town Council they were used as a warehouse before being transformed into the Elgin Youth Café/Music Centre in the Spring of 2001.

The original heart of the new (1886) Elgin Academy was the Palatine style building opposite the old Victoria School at the West End of Moray Street, shown in the photograph above, courtesy of the Local Heritage Centre at Elgin Library. These two buildings now house The Moray School of Art, as part of UHI Moray College. This consisted of an imposing main hall off which could be accessed seven classrooms and various school offices[2]. In the 1930's a large two storey building with gymnasium was erected 30 yards to the south (just in sight to the left of the above photo) as the curriculum expanded and all of this formed the basis of Moray College when Elgin Academy was relocated to Morriston in the late 1960's.

However, by the mid-1970's it was becoming clear that the *new* Elgin Academy being such an attractive school in so many different ways was by no means big enough for all those who wanted to attend. The Academy was then one of the biggest schools in Scotland, attracting pupils from all over Moray, some by selection and fee-paying. With its roll edging towards 1,750—and for example *seventeen* teachers in the English department alone—extra accommodation had been constructed in the form of huts between the school building and the rugby field. Two subjects (Music and Classics) were being taught at the Haugh on the banks of The Lossie, no doubt a *very* leisurely ten minute pupil walk from the main buildings. Staff there at the time experienced little sense of the school bursting with pupils because of its large and airy corridors but some sort of change was being called for, for everyone's comfort.

The decision *in principle* to build a new secondary school had been taken by the Education Committee of Moray and Nairn Joint County Council (MNJCC) in the first week of March 1971: see article in *The Northern Scot* of 6.3.71 on a following page. However, at this point no decision had been made regarding the building a replacement secondary school in Fochabers. Construction of the new Elgin secondary would not start "before 1975" and it might be designed to accommodate 1,000 pupils if it was decided to rezone pupils in Fochabers to this projected new school.

However the Council was keeping its options open and as well as acquiring the 15 acre site of Bibohall Farm, 10 acres of the Glebe at Fochabers was to be purchased for a possible new secondary there. There had even been serious consideration given to building a new secondary in or near the equidistant Lhanbryde to accommodate the overspill from Elgin Academy and Milne's High. However other reports were suggesting that a sufficient new population might well be attracted to Fochabers to justify a new secondary being built there. The wait of a further four years would clarify matters.

Indeed by the end of 1973—see article in *The Northern Scot* of 8.12.73 on a following page- the decision had been made to build Elgin High School in the Bilbohall area of south Elgin and according to the MNJCC it was to be operational by August 1976. The catchment area was to include all houses south of the Aberdeen-Inverness railway line, much of Rothes, all of Alves and the area in between.

The Director of Education Mr W.F.Lindsay speculated that the new Elgin High School would open with a roll of 410, with S1-3 pupils attending and in due course "it would become a full secondary, although not with the same choice of subjects as at Elgin Academy".

NEW SECONDARY SCHOOL TO BE BUILT AT ELGIN

A NEW senior secondary school is to be built in Elgin on a 15-acre site to the south of Bilbohall Farm. This decision was agreed in principle by Moray and Nairn Education Committee at their meeting in Elgin on Wednesday.

From

The Northern Scot

6th March 1971

It follows lengthy consideration of the wider problem of a new secondary school for the east of Moray.

Still hanging in the balance is the question of whether a new secondary school should be provided at Fochabers. This matter will be looked at again in a few years' time.

The new Elgin school will not begin before 1975 and it will accommodate up to 1000 pupils — including the secondary pupils from Milne's High School, Fochabers, if this is decided upon later.

SUITABLE SITE

In order to keep the option open for providing a new secondary school at Fochabers, arrangements are to be made to acquire a suitable site forming part of the Glebe at Fochabers on the understanding that pending a decision about a secondary school in the village, the land should be let for agricultural purposes.

These various recommendations—made by a special sub-committee — followed consideration of a memorandum on the matter prepared by the county planning officer, Mr N. D. Couper, in consultation with the other technical officials concerned.

The special sub-committee minute stated that there had been a long discussion during which the merits of two schools, one at Fochabers and one at Elgin, were compared with the desirability of erecting only one school at either Elgin or Lhanbryd.

It continued: "The meeting thereafter arrived at the conclusion that in view of the substantial increase of secondary pupils which was likely to take place in the Elgin area over the next 20 years there was a clear case for the provision of a new secondary school within the burgh and that the best location for this would be a site on the south side, possibly in the New Elgin area.

"As regards Fochabers, it was noted that Milne's High School presently provides secondary and primary accommodation and that in due course it will be necessary to provide improved primary accommodation in Fochabers and that, if other accommodation could be obtained for the secondary pupils, the best of the accommodation at Milne's would provide satisfactory primary accommodation to meet the needs of the Fochabers area.

"Members were in agreement with the views expressed by the county planning officer in his report that the only factor against the retention of a secondary school in Fochabers is the limited numbers presently attending the school and the doubt about whether there will be any increase in secondary pupils in the foreseeable future.

"In this connection it was noted the Gaskin Report contemplated that as a result of industrial expansion in the Fochabers/Mosstodloch area there might be a fairly substantial increase of population in that area. The meeting were of opinion that in that event it was possible that a case might be made out for the maintenance of a secondary school in Fochabers.

"The meeting further noted that on the basis of the authority's projected school building programme for the next few years, it was unlikely that a new secondary school for Elgin would be approved sooner than about 1975. By that date some indication of industrial expansion and population trends in the Fochabers/Mosstodloch area might have become more apparent and would enable the authority to arrive at a firm decision about the desirability of maintaining a secondary school in Fochabers."

The recommendations were approved without comment.

Subsequently a further meeting of the Staffing and Studies Sub-committee approved recommendations that an area of 15 acres to the south of Bilbohall Farm be acquired for Elgin's new senior secondary school and that 10 acres of land be acquired at the Glebe, Fochabers, in case this should be required for a new senior secondary school.

ELGIN "HIGH SCHOOL" OPERATIONAL BY 1976

THE new secondary school to be built in south Elgin in the Bibohall area is to be known as Elgin High.

It is hoped to have it operational by August, 1976, and on Wednesday Moray and Nairn Education Committee approved its catchment area in principle.

Broadly speaking the school will serve all secondary pupils in the burgh south of the railway line, as well as Rothes and Alves and the areas in between.

Mr W. F. Lindsay, director of education, in a memorandum on the proposed school, envisages it having a roll of 410 in 1976, rising to 500 in the next two years, and possibly to over 600 in the future.

"It is obvious that this small number could create difficulties for the first few years," Mr Lindsay points out, "and probably the new school would start off as a unit for Classes 1-3, the older pupils continuing at Elgin Academy. As numbers justified it, it would become, in time, a full secondary school, although not with the same choice of subjects as at Elgin Academy.

"As the present accommodation at the Academy is overtaxed, and the accommodation available at The Haugh is not very satisfactory, an early start on phase one of a new school is imperative. Flexibility in planning would ensure that the school could later be adapted and enlarged to suit future needs in the area."

Lhanbryd. In presenting his memorandum Mr Lindsay has decided that no change be made to secondary schooling for Lhanbryd pupils, but that those pupils from west and south of the village, (Sheriffston cross roads, Cranloch and Clackmarras), who presently go to Elgin Academy, will go to the new school.

Speyside. Mr Lindsay also acted on the assumption that the new Speyside school would be ready in two years, and that all pupils in the Archiestown-Knockando area would go to Aberlour High School and that not less than half of the pupils in Rothes would go to the new school in Elgin.

Alves. The transfer of some 30 Alves pupils to Elgin from Forres Academy would alleviate the position there where numbers were increasing rapidly.

From

The Northern Scot

8th December 1983

35

Mr Lindsay's throwaway line in retrospect can be interpreted in several ways, perhaps merely indicating that for example no Russian or would be taught in Elgin High…. or that it might have the mind-set of a junior secondary school. It was also suggested that "not less than half of the pupils in Rothes would go to the new school" in the south of Elgin as would some from Cranloch and Clackmarras.

As we now know all such large building projects are subject to inevitable delay and plans mature and change but when Elgin High did open in August 1978 it carried S1 and S2 only and pupils from neither Fochabers nor Rothes travelled to it.

Yes, Elgin required another secondary - on the southern side of the railway lines to serve New Elgin and rural settlements to the south, east and west. Despite the building of Greenwards Primary School, opened in 1976 on a green-field site in New Elgin, the roll of New Elgin Primary itself was around 750, recalls Alistair Farquhar, then its Assistant Head and latterly Head of Educational Resource Service at The Moray Council. Such a size made that primary's roll bigger than many Scottish secondary schools. Education facilities across Elgin were very much stretched.

 The green-field site on the plain between Greenwards Primary and the rolling hills of Mayne Farm was an obvious choice for the second secondary, which was to be called "Elgin High School", - not the first use of the term, as Richard Bennett's book informs us[3] - though the term "Bilbohall" had been considered for both Greenwards and Elgin High but quickly dismissed on account of its connotations!

Proposals that in addition to the associated Primaries of New Elgin and Greenwards, Elgin High School should receive pupils from both Mosstowie Primary and from the West End Primary, both of which lay to the north of the railway lines were extremely controversial. Numerically this seemed to make good sense because it would help in time to balance the rolls of the two secondaries, but the School Boards (comprising parents, teachers and Grampian Region officials) concerned expressed strong opinions against these proposals and letters to *The Northern Scot* at the time showed lively debate on this matter. In the minds of some there seemed to be a distinct feeling that the new school to the south could not and never would match the academic cachet of its well established neighbour with a history stretching back over 200 years[1] and therefore was a more desirable place to send children.

So, in the end, the decision was made that the pupils of Mosstowie Primary only would be zoned for Elgin High School with the usual provisos giving parents rights to have their children sent to the Academy. All parents from the zoned associated primaries had a continuing choice for a number of years and siblings were to be kept together in the same school if they wished to be. This meant that when the second secondary opened it would have around 110 pupils in each of two years only, the First Year cohort coming from the officially zoned primaries with the Second Year cohort, who had spent their First Year (session 1977-78) at the Academy, having the choice of remaining there or going to Elgin High.

Alistair Farquhar, however, recalls the great excitement felt by the primary pupils of New Elgin that they were going to get *their own school* on their doorstep, which meant less travel, fewer traffic dangers on winter mornings and nights and quite literally - novelty. These understandable feelings were much enhanced when the Rector designate of Elgin High School, Bill Hope began to make evangelical visits to the associated primary schools. Being naturally ebullient and irrepressibly enthusiastic, Bill (coming from a family of business people) "sold" prospective life at Elgin High to most doubters. This was to be not so much a secondary school as a community education centre which would have musak, juke boxes, lemonade machines, pool and table tennis tables within its purpose-built community area. The school team strip was to be bright blue (like Manchester City's), there was to be no broad banding of classes on ability as in the pupils' alternative choice of secondary school but there'd be four teaching classes to be called A, B, C and D – well you had to call them something –and half a dozen practical size sets, of mixed ability pupils.

The school motif was to be a dove because of the old dovecot in the main recreation park in New Elgin. Keen sporting rivalry would be encouraged by pupils, formed into four houses, named not after local places, rivers or famous people – but after Scottish native birds of prey – Eagles (the yellow house) Falcons (blue), Kestrels (red) and Ospreys (green). There would be family connections, so that siblings were all to be in the same house, so avoiding any uncalled for rivalry and unpleasantness. And there was to be a school newspaper that pupils both in primary and secondary would contribute to, so helping to establish a continuity and permitting pupils to get to know aspects of the big school before they would come up in the following year.

In fact, many of Bill Hope's visionary promises were realised by his staff in the first 30 years – mainly through the consensual ethos created with some of following characteristics contributing…..

> Whilst striving for excellence, the school would eschew elitism, always aiming to avoid the "them and us" phenomenon.
> there'd be no "Head Boy, Head Girl" with braided blazer and badges – but many senior pupils with responsibilities to junior ones,
> there'd be no "top" or clever class in each year – the school would aim to be truly comprehensive.
> Any pupil could contribute to *Pigeon Post,* not just those doing, say, Higher English
> The choice of presenters at our prize giving, until we had old and famous enough former pupils to invite to do it would be by local heroes not local or national celebrities, with little if any connection to the school –
> our primary schools would be regarded as "associated" not "feeders" to the big school.
> A sense of community would be fostered in as many ways as possible with parents and friends through EHSA playing a role.

Bill Hope was to gain the reputation of a man who indulged in an occasional bit of hyperbole but who "could sell snow to the Eskimos". However after describing what life at Elgin High would be like in his speeches he had three aces still to play : the school would be open *really early* e.g. from 7.45 a.m. so pupils could come into use the sports facilities in the Community Centre, eat a first (or second!) breakfast – and the school would be open *at night* in the form of The Centre Elgin High. This would be staffed by community workers and volunteers and PE facilities like the Games Hall would be available for different sports each night, for football, circuit training, archery etc. adjacent to a convivial café atmosphere in the community area. Older members of the community would be encouraged to come in for more sedentary interests like Art, Conversational German, hands-on Craft etc classes.

Many of these ideas were revolutionary to those who heard them, though Bill Hope was just talking about what had been so familiar to him under his direction in Lochaber for years. Oh and the final ace? The school would *run monthly evening discos* with light catering!

And pupils had a choice to come to Elgin High or go to the other place? Well, technically there still was one.

It was not only that all this information in itself was attractive to the potential pupils from New Elgin, Greenwards, Mosstowie and a few from St Sylvesters R.C. Primary. It was the way it was put over by Bill Hope, later assisted by enthusiastic henchmen Depute Alistair MacLachlan and Assistant Rector Douglas Campbell, completing a triumvirate of ambitious and charismatic young men who'd been given the rare opportunity to play major parts in creating their own school. Most importantly they were all young men who *could connect* with pupils, a facet that the school would major on as it grew.

On page 40 a tribute to our first Depute Rector Alistair MacLachlan written by Jeff Dugdale and published in *Pigeon Post* no 125

[1] **Richard Bennett's scholarly and meticulously researched book (Moravian Press 2001) "is not a history of Elgin** Academy" but "a series of essays and personal recollections" about the school.

[2] For more detail see Richard Bennett's book at p22 and photo of the hall at p28

Alistair Maclachlan
Depute Rector, Elgin High School 1978-1982
Rector, Forres Academy 1983-1999

The school was very greatly saddened to learn of the death of Mr Maclachlan, Rector of Forres Academy and husband of Mrs Alison Maclachlan of our Business Studies Department. Mr Maclachlan who was 53 died at home in the early hours of Thursday 17th June, having learned only in February he was suffering from cancer.

Mr Maclachlan was well known socially to many of our staff but several of the present staff also knew him professionally as he had been our first Depute Rector when the school opened in August 1978. He was a close personal friend of our Rector, and Mr Hope spoke movingly of his former colleague at the Memorial Service held in a Forres church last Thursday and attended by more than 800 colleagues, friends, and present and former pupils of Forres Academy.

Mr Maclachlan was a native of Perth, keen on football at primary school whilst rugby and ballroom dancing were other interests at secondary school. At first thinking he wanted to be a journalist he changed his mind and took an honours degree in Economics from Strathclyde University and began teaching in a post shared between Carnoustie High School and Webster's Seminary (in Kirriemuir). He became Head of Business Studies at Keith Grammar School in 1974 and whilst there was for several years Secretary of The Keith Show. He later served as Assistant Rector there.

In his early days at Elgin High where he was for a while Head of Business Studies as well as Depute, he would arrive on his Suzuki 100 motorbike in full leather gear, which he said he rode for "economic" reasons" ! Apart from curricular duties at Elgin High he was keenly involved in teaching guitar and running a circuit training club as he was a fitness fanatic and keen squash player. He also enjoyed music of all sorts and played a number of instruments in the Moray Swing Band.

Mr Maclachlan was appointed to Forres Academy at interview on 26th November 1982 and began there in January of the following year. In his 17 years as Rector he gained the admiration of all who encountered him professionally. He was featured on a early 90s TV programme about Management fronted by Sir John Harvey-Jones, the management consultant in which Mr Maclachlan and his Depute Mr Allanach were jokingly referred to as "Batman and Robin". He was a great innovator educationally and in particular saw Forres Academy established with a very large Enrichment Fund to support the school. Under his leadership Forres Academy became the first school in Scotland to be quality approved by SCOTVEC and the school also gained the Investors in People marque. His talents were noted nationally and he became an influential member of the Scottish Consultative Committee on the Curriculum and represented Scotland at a number of international conferences. His latest initiative was to introduce "Cooperative Learning" into Forres following his appreciation of it whilst on an educational visit to Canada in 1998.

Tributes have flowed in from all quarters. Mr Maclachlan was quite simply an exceptional educationalist, one of the brightest and most able of his generation. His loss to his family, friends, colleagues and pupils past and present is immeasurable. Our Rector summed up Ally's approach to education very simply with the words: "To him every kid mattered"

Education in Scotland is greatly impoverished with this "early closure". J.D.

5   THE DESIGN, CONSTRUCTION EXTENSIONS

40 Years: Design, Build, Extend, Replace

Design and Build

From the day the first turf was cut into the green field site at Bilbohall[1] Estate to the opening of the school in mid-August 1978 roughly 24 months passed.

The main contractor for the build was a now defunct firm called Bardolin Scotia working to a design by a Grampian Regional Council (GRC) team comprising Senior Architect John McBoyle, Architectural Assistant Martin Graham (whose daughter Isla later attended the school) and Chris Griffin, a post grad Architectural student on his "year out".   Naturally there was input from the Advisor team and other Education and Architectural officials based in Woodhill House, Aberdeen.

Originally the school alongside its large spread of playing fields was to have been located several hundred yards to the south of where it was built. This was because the site which eventually did become the playing fields was affected by running sand and would have provided poor foundations for a housing estate. Ironically this fact had to be relearned when the replacement Elgin High was being planned in 2015.   At that time there were no houses to the west of High School Drive or the south of Springfield Road once you passed Sandy Road, though the Bilbohall estate was quite well established and indeed part of the need for the existence of Greenwards Primary and Elgin High.

1 See page 303/4

41

A view of the school taken from the bus turning circle. The Moray Council sign, the technical block extension and the maturity of the flowering cherry trees in the quadrangle place this photo in the mid 1990's. Reproduced courtesy of *The Northern Scot*

A view of the back of the school taken from the playing fields embankment in the late 1970's looking South, showing the fascia of the academic block which would be extended first. Pupils in shot are counting worms and other biota within a measured square yard, for a science experiment. Photo: Nick Ledingham.

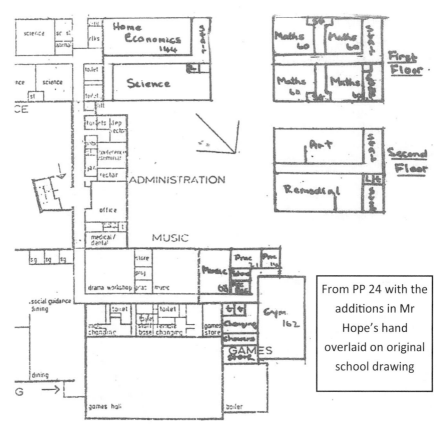

From PP 24 with the additions in Mr Hope's hand overlaid on original school drawing

With its mansard roof, Elgin High, influenced by design elements from other GRC schools of the time, and costing around £1.5M looked more like a modern hotel complex than a traditional learning centre.

Extend

Elgin High was built to be extended and within a few months of its opening, plans were in hand for that, as The Rector explained in an article in PP 24 (for January 1981—see below). Throughout the building's 40 year history it would undergo alterations on a regular basis.

The first major extension was to cost around £700,000 - the contract being awarded to Robertson of Elgin - and was planned to be completed within a year from Easter 1981. The main part of the extension was the building on three floors to the North of the school, providing on the ground floor new Home Economics

(144 metres^2) and Science (157 metres^2) facilities, four 30 pupil Maths classrooms on the first floor and on the second floor new facilities for Art, and Remedial (144 metres^2 each) .

Elsewhere on campus a second Music classroom (70 metres^2) and two practice rooms were to be built, and nearby a gymnasium (166 metres^2) with changing room facilities. The provision of a new lift in the academic block extension and other minor changes e.g an easily accessible toilet meant that the school would be fully able to cater for physically handicapped children, the only secondary school in Elgin ready to do so.

1.5.81. Y floor laid

Photographs of and reports on the progress of extension with staff reaction can be seen in PP33 for February 1982 (external dated photo diary by Ian Wallace as exemplified here) and in PP34 for March 1982 (internal changes).

In March 1983 our Technical Department was extended as The Rector explained in PP 43. At the original design stage of the school there was no expectancy that the Equal Opportunities Act would require boys and girls to have exactly the same learning experiences. Now, however, pupils were going to practical subjects like Technical and H.E. in mixed gender groups. Academic qualifications in some of the traditionally perceived subjects seemed to carry little clout with local employers, but they did want to see pupils leaving with practical skills. Furthermore, because of CSEm3 (see Chapter on Curricular Innovation.) the department was now offering a variety of attractive and popular courses such as Motor Vehicle Studies and Integrated Craft in addition to what you might expect. As a result, it was said to be "bursting at its seams" so GRC had agreed that one large multi-purpose facility would be built, extending the departmental area towards the bus turning circle.

In the October 1990 edition of *PP*, #81 it was announced that the Staffroom and Main Office were to be given a major refurbishment—during the October break—some dozen years after the school's opening. The staffroom was legally required to be partitioned because of regulations regarding the need for a non-smoking area. Staff who wished to sit in a smoking area would be accommodated at the end nearer the Lecture Room. (This wall would be removed late in 2005 when smoking was totally banned on school premises: PP 156.) Other minor changes would happen at the same time including a porch-type door so no one could look directly into the staff room *en passant*. Major structural changes to our Office included the construction of a photocopying room, a new Janitor's store and a waiting area for visitors. The Administrative Assistant (Mrs Nancy Prentice at the time) would have a new office created for her within the original open plan space.

Five years later, in February 1995, in PP 103 came enormous news. Elgin High was to absorb another school......

Hamilton Drive Comes to Elgin High

In his article in this edition, The Rector reminds his readers that the original intention of the school when opened in 1978 was to become "an educational centre", available to the community at large and he shows how this in fact has been realised with many youth groups, academic and recreational evening classes and other outside lets using our facilities since we opened. However, it was also the school's long term aim to be "available to all including those who suffer from handicaps of any kind". We are then reminded of the changes made to the original building in 1981 to accommodate this—installation of a new lift, ramping, handicapped toilet etc. and that a handful of wheelchair children had been educated in our mainstream classes across the years.

However, Mr Hope goes on to inform us that the GRC Education Committee now wanted to replace Hamilton Drive School, which catered for youngsters with severe handicaps—currently housed in an old and remote ex-fever hospital—with a brand new purpose built facility. This is now to become a new *wing* of Elgin

Our Extension Takes Shape

Pigeon Post 106

Extension Progressing to Conclusion

Extension's Finishing Touches

Pigeon Post 108

High, as the impression by our Art teacher Mrs Iris Wright on the above cover suggests. This new facility was not to be located "round the back" in any sense and would be built right next to our Community/Dining Area. Giving further details of related refurbishments, Mr Hope reminds us that Hamilton Drive pupils are already becoming well known faces as they lunch in school every Thursday as part of an acclimatisation process.

The target for the completion of the new facility was given as August 1996. PP 105 (June 1995) reports on progress with evidence of the foundation being laid of what would be called Kestrel House.

The cover of the first edition of session 1995-96 (top left) shows three pictures of the progress made by local building firm Gordon Forbes on the Kestrel House wing and on the garages being constructed at the rear of the school to house its related transport. The next edition (PP 107, above centre) shows the wing taking on the shape we would come to associate with the new build, which looks pretty much complete on the cover of PP 108, top right.

ACTIVITIES WEEK IS COMING

Pigeon Post 109

Our New £0.5m Extension Formally Opened

Hamilton Drive Pupils Set to Join us on June 18th - see pages 3, & 10-12

Then very much on time the new facility is declared open, just before the Easter holidays —on the cover of PP 109— making Elgin High the first school to be built by GRC and the last school to be extended by GRC before the latest reorganisation of local government. Pupils from Hamilton Drive were to first attend in mid-June.

Over the next few years, minor improvements are regularly made to various parts of the school with, for example, departments formally on Y and Z floors in the main block being reorganised, but the next major significant change is the arrival of a large amount of carpeting, as referred to on the front of PP 123 in February 1999.

This we learn fulfilled a long held ambition of Mr Hope's that every department in the Academic Block that wanted carpeted classroom would have them. The first carpeted room (Y13) had been treated thus, as it was the Remedial classroom in 1980 and a soft finish was held to promote a pleasant atmosphere. Other rooms had been carpeted here and there as funds allowed.

Rather more exciting was the news that the Workplace technologies/ICL technicians based in Z1-A would soon been installing just under 50 new computers, including in the Main Office and in the offices of Board of Studies members and redoing the telephone network within the school.

The first major changes in the new Millennium reported on in PP 138 (Feb 2002) are the reconstruction of the 15-year old Guidance base in the Community Area. It is expanded to include a new interview room and given new carpets and furniture. Community storage facilities are moved to beside the Tuck Shop. At the same time PSE classrooms X13 and X15 and Art facilities Z6, Z7 and Z14 were remodelled.

A couple of years into Mr Andy Simpson's Headship—Mr Bill Hope had retired in 2003—the future of education in Elgin is being debated seriously by The Moray Council and the issue of Elgin High School (and Elgin Academy) being closed to make away for one "Super School" is first mentioned. In PP 156 (October 2005) we reprint two newspaper articles published early in the school Summer holidays under the banner **"ELGIN HIGH TO CLOSE WITHIN 4/5 YEARS?"** We also note that the Council is planning a major consultation exercise

One high school to replace Elgin's two

by Tommy Smith

From The Press & Journal for 7th July

Extensive

The initial £40million public-private partnership proposal involved building new schools on the sites of Elgin Academy and Keith and Kinloss primaries, with an extensive refurbishment of Elgin High School.

A full meeting of Moray Council was presented yesterday with a range of options to take

and that a decision will be made early in 2006. This is a very hot topic indeed, particularly with the school's having just become the BBC SoundTown School for 2005/6 and therefore very much in national focus!! However the decision is delayed and postponed and then, as reported in PP 159, the idea of amalgamating Elgin's two secondary schools is dropped altogether.

However that is far too trite a summary of what really happened. So now do read the following italicised paragraphs by Andy Simpson for a local publication which crisply sum up the to-ings and fro-ings the stake holders underwent in considering the issues during these difficult years and those that followed before EHS2 was begun.

The Journey to the new build

The story starts in 2001/2 when Moray Council started looking at a Pubic Private Partnership (PPP) project to finance increasingly urgent construction work on school buildings. EHS was identified as needing major works due to suitability and was initially included as a significant refurbishment.

This went public in December 2002. Subsequent discussions identified that the council would get a better deal with a new build rather than refurbishment. Ground survey work was done and draft plans were prepared.

In parallel with this, members of the community had recognized the need for significant enhancement of sports opportunities in Moray. They prepared plans for sports facilities that could be based in South Elgin. This was called "The heart of Moray" and involved a wide range of groups who would sell existing resources to invest in the EHS campus. The potential for PPP funding stalled the progress of this initiative.

In March 2003, shortly after my appointment, Donald Duncan as Director told me "not to do anything to the building as we would be getting a new one." This meant that EHS was taken off the Moray Council capital plans for refurbishment and ongoing improvement work - other schools took our place in the order of priority and EHS was a maintenance only spend.

The 2004 inspection confirmed the need for major expenditure and identified serious weaknesses in the building and resources.

In 2005/6 Moray Council opened up the debate on a single secondary school for Elgin. A year long extensive public consultation followed and came to a conclusion in favour of two schools. The Council reviewed the PPP project and decided that they could only afford two schools (Elgin Academy and Keith Primary). The EHS School Board decided that they would not fight the decision as they recognised that the old Elgin Academy building was in a worse condition than EHS.

Nothing further happened, and fearing that EHS was being sidelined and the issues not tackled (as well as being leapfrogged by other schools onto the capital plan) the Parent Council decided to take up the fight.

The next stage by Moray Council was an attempt to attract money for a regional sports facility on the site. This would address some of the shortfall of resources and allow other issues to be tackled on the back of the construction work. Plans were drawn up and consultation started. This initiative stalled when the various funding schemes failed to materialize (e.g. Europe, Sport Scotland, etc.)

Following this the Parent Council started some serious lobbying involving Pupil Council, politicians, videos, etc. etc. Politicians and council officials were invited to tour the current building and see for themselves the challenges being faced by pupils and staff. A pupil group made a DVD highlighting the need for investment in EHS. Copies were sent to politicians in the Scottish Government in Holyrood as well as locally. And in 2012 we gained Scottish Futures Trust funding. Progress was further delayed due to the discovery of peat on the initial site, change in predicted pupil rolls, and, changes to European regulations.

However, after much discussion, the turf of the new build was finally cut on Wednesday 16th March 2016. Pupils from Greenwards, Mosstowie and New Elgin Primary Schools as well as EHS were involved to signify the place of the school in the local community.

Demolition Diaries

The photos below were posted (along with many others) on the Former Elgin High School Students Facebook site by former pupil Fiona Norrie (FN), former pupil and current staff member Roy Young (RY) and current pupil Ethan Gray (EG).

The school building was abandoned in mid-October 2017 but destruction did not start till January 2018 and it was all to be landscaped in time for an official opening later in 2018.

The first parts to be deconstructed were the Technical Classrooms: FN 8.1.18

Then down came other one storey elements: Kestrel House, Canteen and Community Area RY 15.1.18

The destruction of Kestrel House photographed from the new school: EG 15.1.18

Below the Drama Studio disintegrating in a shot taken from the playing fields

RY 22.1.18

All one storey elements down and most of the admin/staffroom/library block :

RY 29.1.18

The same area a day later eerily showing the remains of the staffroom and above it the library: RY 30.1.18

The beginning of the end for the academic block: EG 29.1.18

Only most of the academic block now resembles a school: RY 6.2.18

Phoenix-like, a new school seems to emerge from the ruins of the old: FN 6.2.18

An aerial view of the site © Andy Innes Aerial Photography, showing the two grey and black structures of the new academic block and *right* the PE facilities, a temporary staff car park and scope for a 300 metre running track within the playing fields.

January 2018—Reprinted with permission © Andy Innes Aerial Photography

Above Jamie Rollo's FB post on the morning of 23.2.18

Now only part of the gable end of the 1981 extension remains. None of the debris of the demolition has been removed at this point. It's all there, just in a different order! The PE block can now be seen behind the old academic block. RY pm 23.2.18

Above : just a pile of rubble now. EG 2.3.18

Below—a quirky photo blending the old and the new. EG 2.3.18

6 Leadership: Three Heads

In its 40 years of existence, Elgin High has, quite remarkably, had only three head teachers, or strictly speaking, because the titling of school leadership officially changed across Scotland in 2003, two "Headteachers" and one "Rector". Curiously until that year the school also had had only two Deputes.[1]

"Rector" is a traditional term, confusable by those who don't know with the person in charge of an English church, but in Scotland the word, deriving from the Latin for "ruler", was given to the person in charge of the local "high" or grammar school.

More often than not the new Rector of any school would be appointed having been a Depute in a school of similar size. However our first Rector came to us from the ranks of Assistant Rector (Guidance) and in his ten years of teaching History and in Guidance before coming to Elgin had not been in charge of any subject department.

Bill Hope (1978 – 2003) *

Mr William Hope was appointed Rector of the new secondary school in New Elgin late in 1977 when he was Assistant Rector at Lochaber High School, Fort William.

The Lochaber High School badge showing the famous Lochaber axes, carried by Highland foot soldiers

He is "A Doonhamer" - a native of Dumfries, and attended a variety of primaries in Beattock, Moffat, Castle Douglas and Dalbeattie. He admits he didn't try very hard at school – yes, "I was lazy" - until confronted by a fearful Primary 5 teacher, whom the pupils called "Ma Gann". On the wall of her classroom was a chart listing the names of children in the class and opposite each name – no doubt as an *aide memoire* - a little sketch of the child as seen by that teacher. Beside "W.Hope" was a drawing of a figure – curled

1979

2002

up, asleep. Ma Gann set out to uncurl that dozing figure with a daily dose of the strap. Rigorous and barbaric it may have been but it was certainly effective and by the end of the year W.Hope had moved from 36th to 5th position in class.

After this he didn't look back and left Primary School for Kirkcudbright High as Dux. He enjoyed his secondary schooling but regretted that as he had been put in an academic stream he was unable to take such hands-on subjects as woodwork, technical drawing etc. He also hated being one of only two boys in a class of 24. Though not enjoying many aspects of his schooling he applied himself, thinking, "If you're going to do something you might as well enjoy it".

His favourite subject at school had been History and growing up in the Border regions of Dumfries and Galloway he says that this was inevitable. His imagination was caught by tales of the Border reivers and ever-present reminders of the past around him. In fact for several years as a lad he had lived close by a ruined castle and like many Doonhamers and Gallovidians he took great pride in the stories of the dreadfulness of his ancestors!

At school, too, he had enjoyed all kinds of sport including football, rugby and athletics. He was a prominent member of the debating society and speaks highly of the training he received in the arts of public speaking In fact he believes that his ability to speak out loudly and to speak his mind helped him throughout his career.

He pursued his interest in History at Edinburgh University where he took an Honours degree and on leaving he faced the dilemma of what to do with it. Coming from a family of businessmen he contemplated industry and was offered several jobs including ones with large national firms like Proctor & Gamble and Ranks Hovis Macdougall but he rejected them in favour of a career in education and found himself in his first teaching post at Alloa Academy in Clackmannanshire. Here met the man who was to shape and influence his teaching style, Rector and international rugby referee A.I. (Sandy) Dickie OBE, whose motto was, "Not tomorrow – yesterday will do!", an approach which he adopted himself. He freely admits he always wanted to run school on smart, business-like lines.

At Alloa Academy Mr Hope got involved in hockey. Little did he think his agreement to take on coaching the hockey team would result in his becoming a selector for Scottish Schools and umpiring in the National League, taking him to the verge of selection as an international match official.

From Alloa he went to Lochaber High, Fort William as Assistant Rector and here he was remembered chiefly as "the mannie who introduced the discos". There he succeeded in making the school less of an institution and more of a community in which pupils felt "at home". And that was the central philosophy which he brought to Elgin High School when invited to be the Rector who would build the school's approach to learning.

School in general and hockey and cricket in particular would take up a considerable proportion of his Mr Hope's time as our first Rector but he still found time to do a bit of fishing on the Spey. When he arrived he thought, "Yes, I will give this place ten of my best years – and move on". He felt when he started that you could be an innovator for only so long and then your ideas dry up. Well, despite flirting with the idea of being in the Directorate of Grampian Region (as it was then) Mr Hope found out that fate didn't turn out that way and a welter of new ideas came thick and fast over his twenty-five years in charge.

As Rector, Bill Hope proved to be one of a dying breed, for whilst having led a modern comprehensive second school for quarter of a century he brought an old-fashioned dedication to the task which regularly saw him in school by 7 a.m. and not going home until 10.30 p.m. Additionally, many of his weekends throughout his time in EHS were devoted to school matters, curricular or extra-curricular. He never seemed to understand what "taking a rest" meant.

Within school he developed a reputation as a leader who was out and about its corridors and classrooms. Every pupil knew who he was and he knew instantly by name a very high percentage of each cohort which went through the school. He also deserved the reputation of always being willing to "go the extra mile" where a pupil was concerned or to give a pupil in trouble the benefit of the doubt. Fairness was his trademark.

Under his leadership as founding Rector, EHS became and remains to this day a vibrant school at the heart of the New Elgin community in contrast to some of the more traditional Scottish Schools. Bill Hope always sought to be at the forefront of educational initiatives and in the course of his time in charge he saw the school implement CSE, Standard Grade, TVEI, TVE, 5-14, Higher Still, a local PFI, Cooperative Learning, Promoting Positive Behaviour, and Managing Challenging Behaviour. In his time SCE and then SQA exam results were always on an upward trend. He was particularly proud of how many pupils of his school were the first in their family to attend university and how many went on to make a positive impression in public life. But whether they were of academic bent or not, Bill's ambition was for every pupil in school to be a rounded human being, confident and responsible.

His judgement of people was of a high order. Almost every promoted person he appointed was a great success in their new role and over a dozen went on to become Rectors in their own right. The school established and maintained a reputation for consistently high quality promoted staff.

Bill also devotedly supported extra-curricular activities. Even as he approached retirement at 60 it was he who saw that the school fielded four football teams on Saturdays, organised the booking of pitches, the strips, the putting up of nets and the parent managers. He became in addition to everything else *de facto* the School's Sports Coordinator.

Changing of the Guard: Andy Simpson visits the then current Board of Studies in April '03.

Back (l-r) : Deputes Finnie, Cadenhead and Dugdale

Away from sport throughout the life of the school Bill personally attended and proposed memorable votes of thanks – given his special skills as raconteur and wit – at 99% of our extra-curricular events such as concerts, musical shows, drama productions, quiz nights, debates and public speaking events (one of his particular personal interests). He contributed a page of comment on school events to every edition of *Pigeon Post,* which appeared 145 times between 1978 and 2003 and also wrote regular football reports for its pages. With regard to foreign trips and theatre outings by coach to London etc., Bill rose with the lark to see the tour bus away and was invariably there to welcome the pupils back no matter how late the hour of their return might have been.

Bill was a mainstay of EHSA, the parent teacher association and was involved every year in their programme of activities, putting together Treasure Hunts, Fashion Shows, Race Nights, Tea & Competitions - oh yes and Whist Nights - although he rarely won a prize at any of those. Later he played a vital role in the creation of the new School Board.

"And finally…." - to coin a phrase (!) - as well as being their boss, Bill Hope was a warm, personal friend and adviser to a large number of colleagues and his legacy is that in his time as Rector he made a unique contribution to the lives and education of thousands of citizens of Elgin and Moray.

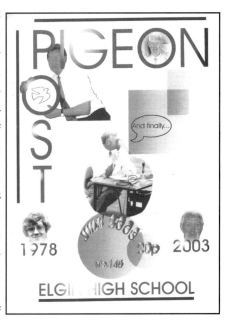

Andy Simpson (2003—2016)**

2003

2016

Our second head teacher[1], appointed on Monday 17th March 2003, was born and brought up in Enfield, a metropolitan borough in the North of London. At the independently run University College School (known for its focus on individuals and educating the "whole person"[2] — not that dissimilar from EHS) Mr Simpson's interests lay in History, English and Economics. He made a little pocket money at weekends picking and meticulously preparing carnations for local florists and doing a paper round.

On leaving school Mr Simpson took a gap year in Canada. There he worked with the International Grenfell Association as a radio operator for the air ambulance services in Newfoundland and Labrador. Based on this experience he recognized the value for some pupils of taking a year out before going to college or university as it also confirmed the travel bug in him. After this year he came North to do a degree in Divinity at Aberdeen University, initially thinking of becoming a social worker, but it gradually dawned on him that teaching was his true calling.

His first post as teacher of Religious and Moral Education was at Turriff Academy in deepest Aberdeenshire. In 1991 he was seconded to the post of Staff Tutor with Grampian Region. It was during this year that he enjoyed one of his first visits to EHS. One of his duties was to escort a Sikh theatre group around the area and EHS was chosen for the Moray venue. The cast included an actor from *Eastenders* which helped create much interest. He then became Assistant Head Teacher at Mintlaw Academy before becoming Deputy Head Teacher at Keith Grammar School. He recalls arriving very red faced at KGS on a Monday morning when his flight had been delayed following the rugby international against Italy in Rome. Much to his chagrin nobody seemed to have noticed he hadn't been there all morning and had simply assumed he was at a meeting in Elgin.

Apart from following the international rugby team, Mr Simpson's interests lay in hill walking – he is a Munro-bagger[3], swimming and travelling – enjoying Italy and Middle Eastern countries in particular. Perhaps he was a frustrated travel journalist like the award winning Scottish writer William Dalrymple. But he is also interested in music, his father having been a university lecturer in music education. He has a catholic taste in music enjoying in particular Black Gospel Music.

On arrival at EHS Mr Simpson was particularly impressed by how he was accepted with all those around him fitting back into their roles seamlessly. He also liked the fact that the pupils walked about the school without fuss and did not jostle so much in the corridors – despite being so narrow compared to those in the older KGS building.

At the start of his spell as Head Teacher Mr Simpson assumed that his career would see the new building completed and everyone settled in! He set out to ensure that the school curriculum met the needs of the pupils in the new century and to build on the friendly and positive atmosphere and sense of community that he found here. He wanted, however, to encourage pupils to become more involved in the school by promoting ideas for new clubs and new support groups so that fellow pupils could help each other. At Mintlaw Academy he had helped establish a system where Sixth Years held drop-in sessions for younger pupils with problems – lending them their shoulder and providing advice.

During his time a number of initiatives were started. One of particular note was the Solution Oriented School initiative. Working with the Educational Psychology Service and staff from one of the universities in Wales, EHS was amongst the very first schools in Moray to embrace the ideas that helped ensure that pupils were given the support that would make a difference to them. From the experiences in EHS this approach now underpins the approach to supporting pupils throughout Moray.

One of the highlights of Mr Simpson's time as Head Teacher was the choosing of the school as the BBC Soundtown, resulting in considerable media exposure for the whole of session 2005-6. Being the "BBC Soundtown" meant that a fully working radio station was installed in the school, manned by staff and pupils with professional BBC Scotland support and the broadcasting of almost all of their popular programmes at least once from the school campus. The experience did much to raise the profile of EHS not just locally but also presented a very positive image of the school across Scotland. (See Chapter 13 and finer detail within PPs numbers 155-161 at **pigeonpost.info)**

During his time as Head Teacher Mr Simpson was particularly proud of the connections formed between Elgin High School and pupils in a number of African schools including Mukonchi in Zambia and Mbeya in Tanzania. Several visits took place of EHS pupils to Africa and Zambian pupils to EHS and its associated primaries. Supported by the British Council through their "Connecting Classrooms" project, he set out to promote the theme of "Umoja" a Swahili word for working together which - as "Working Together for Success" - had become a new mission catchphrase in EHS.

Andy Simpson with a group of EHS staff holding certificates for long service with the local authority (in November 2010)

Back (l-r) Mr Eoin Mackenzie (Evening caretaker), Mrs Karen Highmore (PT Geography), Mr Ken Simpson (Science and Kestrel House), Mrs Cath Donaldson (Chief Cook), Mrs Moira Watson (PT Maths), Miss Linda Duncan (Maths) Mr John Farquhar (Technical) and Mrs Maureen Duncan (Kestrel House auxiliary)

Hugh McCulloch (2016 -)***

Our third head teacher, Hugh McCulloch, is originally from Fortrose on the Black Isle. After graduating with a B.Sc (Hons) degree in Biology – his favourite school subject - at Paisley University he began his teaching career in Oswestry, a town a little smaller than Elgin in Shropshire on the Welsh/ English border.

During his university years Mr McCulloch had travelled widely in the USA taking on a number of varied jobs like selling ice-cream in Denver, being a bouncer at a night club in Denver, Texas and undergoing training at the Texas Police Academy, which later gave him much kudos when he worked as a security guard in Glasgow for Group4. These experiences led him to entertain the idea of becoming a policeman but this did not materialise. In 2000 he was appointed Head of Biology in Worcester and later Deputy Head of Science which gave him a lot of management experience. Yearning to return to the area he was brought up in Mr McCulloch applied to join the staff as Head of Biology and joined us in August 2006. Away from the classroom he showed considerable interest in sport, particularly in distance running and football refereeing.

On Mr Dugdale's retiral in July 2008, Mr McCulloch was appointed in his place as Deputy Head and took on most of his curriculum and administrative responsibilities, later being given responsibility for the development and contractor liaison for the building of the new school and for the school's African links, which allowed him to travel to Africa a few times in the last decade.

Mr McCulloch was appointed to the post of Headteacher a couple of months before Mr Andy Simpson's departure in October 2016 and was in effect Headteacher Designate for an extended period. Needless to say his main responsibilities since becoming head were to do with the completion and opening of the new buildings which the school officially took over after the October holiday in 2017.

6A "It Shouldn't Happen to a Rector" by Andrew Cowie

PIGEON POST

1978   2003

ELGIN HIGH SCHOOL

"A Guidance teacher masquerading as a Headteacher" - that's how Elgin High School's founding Rector, Bill Hope, describes his 25-year tenure at the helm of the juggernaut he helped to create. It's a typically self-deprecating description but one which also sums up the exceptional level of interest he took in the vocational development of his pupils, striving to ensure each maximised their full potential in whatever sphere they were best suited to.

Nobody associated with EHS during its first quarter of a century will ever forget Mr Hope's distinctive claxon of a voice, nor the sight of this iconic red-haired figure patrolling the corridors and community area at intervals and lunchtimes, interacting with pupils, addressing them each by name and bristling with seemingly limitless reserves of energy and enthusiasm - attributes which have become the stuff of legend.

To have been tasked with launching a brand new secondary school in 1978 and building it from the ground up must surely have seemed a daunting challenge but,

if so, it was one from which the then 34-year-old Mr Hope didn't flinch. Appointed to the Rector's post from his previous position as Assistant Head at Lochaber High School in Fort William, he seized the opportunity with both hands

photo :Nick Ledingham : 1978

66

and ran with it, relishing the chance to create a school which was radically new and different and, in many respects, years ahead of its time.

"It was a privilege to have the challenge of starting a new school absolutely from scratch," he recalls. "And it was an exciting time in education. Grampian Regional Council gave me a blank sheet of paper to do things however I wanted, so it really gave me the opportunity to think about what was going to serve the pupils best."

A staunch believer in equal opportunities, Mr Hope took the ground-breaking step of introducing mixed-ability classes in S1 and S2 - something which had never been practised in Elgin before but which eventually became the norm.

"It meant that kids weren't being marked out at 10, 11 or 12," he explains. "I felt that with a new school we wanted to give everyone an equal opportunity. That's how we set up and I think that's how the High School has always been. We always tried to take the policy that the achievement of every pupil was important, that it didn't matter how great the achievement was as long as it was their best achievement, and I think the High School has really stayed true to that maxim all its days. I always felt it didn't have a feel that certain kids mattered and certain kids didn't."

Mr Hope believed passionately in treating pupils as individuals and that the pursuit of academic success should not come at the price of failing to match young people to their own unique skills sets. It was a philosophy forged at the coalface of his first ever teaching post in Alloa Academy (*badge shown right*) where many of his pupils came from challenging backgrounds and from families which had been plunged below the breadline by savage cuts to the mining industry. Two experiences in particular from his time at Alloa made a lasting impression on him - one in which he persuaded the school to stump up cash to enable those pupils whose families had been hit financially by the miners strike to join their  classmates on a Baltic cruise, and another occasion when he was dispatched to speak to an unruly boy's mother at the family home, only to find the woman was on the game and running her business out of the back of a van at the kerbside! Experiences such as these forged an awareness of the need to take account of pupils' individual backgrounds and circumstances - a philosophy which became a cornerstone of his approach to running EHS.

It was an approach, however, which brought him into conflict with HM Inspectorate who, with their preoccupation with league tables and other so-called "performance indicators", didn't necessarily share his ethos.

"It really was very difficult because the Inspectorate put you under pressure," he admits. "One of the ways you're measured is the number of your S1 intake who go on to achieve three Highers. Now I would have pupils coming to me at the end of 4th year or the beginning of 5th Year and telling me they'd been given the opportunity to serve an apprenticeship with the promise of a permanent placement. And I would think, 'Oh Lord, here's another pupil who's going to leave early!'

"You got about a thousand pounds per capita for each pupil and your staffing is also determined by the number of students, so it's really not in the school's funding or staffing interests for pupils to leave early, but you really have to be fair to the kids and put all these other things aside. So almost without exception I would tell them to take the offer of an apprenticeship because it was the right thing for them.

"I always argued with the Inspectorate and said we should be measured not just against the number of pupils who go on to do three Highers. We should be measured against the number who go on to meaningful employment, who go into the job or vocation that really suits them. I never agreed with some of the performance indicators that they use in Scottish education and with hindsight I wish I had stood up to the Inspectorate even more."

He might have had his disagreements with HMIs over the years, but the local Education Authority at the then Grampian Regional Council couldn't have been more supportive, giving the young Rector *carte blanche* to create a school in accordance with his own vision, including areas such as uniform policy and design. Mr Hope initially toyed with the idea of having a bee as the school logo to symbolise "the busy worker", before eventually settling upon the distinctive white dove to tie-in with the dovecot emblem of New Elgin Primary - the high school's largest associated primary. But it was another of his uniform decisions which would spark the greatest controversy in the lead-up to the school's launch.

"The first parents night I went to was at New Elgin Primary," he recalls. "I told them the High School was going to be mixed ability, which was quite radical for

here, and that we were going to have the dove for the uniform and so on. And then I told them that the girls would be allowed to wear *trousers!* Well, there was absolute uproar! We had to disband the meeting for five minutes so they could discuss it!"

His opposite number at Elgin Academy, Alastair Glashan, also disapproved of the decision, believing it would make it harder to ensure pupils were using the correct toilets if their genders were not so easily identifiable and even claiming there were "very obvious hygiene issues" associated with girls wearing trousers!

"I never quite discovered what those issues were!" muses Mr Hope.

As the man in charge of the new school, Mr Hope was given the choice to have the title of either "Rector" or "Headmaster" and decided on the former as it was the title also used by Alastair Glashan at the Academy. It was a decision he later regretted, however, as many people mistook him for a minister of the church!

Shock and awe !

His comparative youth would also cause some identification problems in the early days. When a *Press and Journal* journalist turned up at the school to interview Mr Hope, whom he'd never met before, and was confronted by a long-haired 34-year-old, he duly apologised for being late and explained he was annoyed to have missed the Rector!

Despite some reservations by parents in the Pluscarden area who were initially resistant to being zoned with the High School, any doubters were soon won over once the new school was up and running. Starting out as a small school of 220 pupils, but in a building with the facilities for 800, it provided a unique opportunity for staff and pupils alike to create something unique and special. The school received an early stamp of approval from parents when, after its first year, only one family out of 100 ended up taking advantage of the extinguishing principle - a rule which stated that those with children already at the Academy could continue to send their other children there so as not to split-up families.

One of Mr Hope's hallmark qualities was that of knowing his pupils by name - a trait which he says stems from his father having been a shopkeeper. "If you work in a family business it's your livelihood to know your clients," he says. "I spent a lot of time amongst the pupils. I spent every morning in the community area before school started, every interval in the community area, every lunchtime and I accompanied the football teams at weekends. I don't think that I necessarily knew every pupil and the ones that I possibly didn't know were the kids in the absolute middle who were non-doers. But if they were in a football team or were in trouble or were achieving then I would know them. If you immediately knew a pupil's name then that gave you a head start when it came to dealing with difficulty or a problem."

Mr Hope was also a legendary workaholic. He never missed a single day through illness in the whole of his working life, devoted many of his weekends to refereeing football, hockey and cricket matches, was first into the school every morning and invariably the last to leave at night, though he insists there is no truth in the rumour that he even used to go in on Christmas Day!

"Some of these stories are just overnight legends!" he snorts. "And in a sense it wasn't as epic as it sounds. If you're first in, you sometimes intercept problems before they start, such as being able to cancel the buses if it's snowing. Also, it's amazing how many parents would phone in to complain about something between 4.00 and 5.30 and you were far better to be there to deal with it then because you could often head things off at the pass. I would often get an irate mother phoning up to say her son's bag had been stolen and within fifteen minutes I would be able to get back to her and tell her that the bag was exactly where they'd said it wasn't! If you could phone somebody back within quarter of an hour and say 'problem solved' it was a plus for the school."

A tireless supporter of the school's sports teams, he took personal responsibility for ensuring the school fielded four football teams every Saturday morning. He also organised the booking of pitches, the strips, the putting up of nets and the parent managers. His contribution was recognised by an international award from the Scottish Football Association in recognition of his involvement in refereeing and coaching throughout his 25 years at EHS.

Under his Rectorship, EHS established itself as a school at the very heart of the local community. The Elgin City squad would use its facilities to train for cup matches if Borough Briggs was frozen over in winter, Moray's football referees met in EHS and the Moray Swing Band was born in the school and met there every night for 20 years.

Perhaps most significantly, the school would be used as an emergency refuge for families evacuated from their homes by the devastating floods which wreaked havoc in Elgin on no fewer than three separate occasions in 1997, 2000 and 2002.

"Nobody had ever even told me that we were on the list to be a rest centre!" Mr Hope recalls. "Top of the list was Elgin Community Centre but of course it was the first place that was flooded! Typical planning! So Moray Council phoned me up and said the school was second on the list and I said 'What?!'"

Once he'd recovered from the initial shock, however, Mr Hope threw himself into this latest mercy mission with his customary aplomb, converting the staff room into sleeping accommodation for the flood refugees, making regular runs to Asda to collect industrial quantities of sandwiches to feed them with and providing statements to the local and national press and TV crews who had descended on Elgin in their droves to cover the unfolding story. A personal highlight of the whole experience for Mr Hope was an invitation to appear on Edwina Currie's radio show!

EHS Used Again As "Rest Centre" for Elgin Flood Victims

Above, the Rector accompanied by Mr Alistair Keddie, Chief Executive of Moray Council prepare for a live interview on Moray Firth Radio on a bitterly cold morning on Monday 18th November.

From a *Pigeon Post* in 2002

"The BBC and ITV would phone up and I'd quite happily blether away to them, telling them what a great job Moray Council were doing to help people," he recalls. "Eventually it got to the point where I was inviting all the television crews into the school and we were feeding them and wining and dining them. And then I got this request to appear on the Edwina Show (*Edwina Currie, former Tory MP shown next page*) and I thought

71

- *'Ooh, Edwina!'* - but that I'd maybe better clear that one with Headquarters first. "So I phoned up the hub at Moray Council and asked if it would be okay with policy for me to appear on Edwina's show. And they said, *'Why stop now? You've been breaking policy all day!'* It transpired that the council's official policy was to make no comment at all on the situation! Anyway, they said I might as well go ahead since I'd been speaking to the media all

day anyway and wasn't saying anything that wasn't positive about Moray Council. But after all that, it turned out Edwina was on holiday and I only got to speak to a researcher in London, so that was a bit of a let-down!

"The floods were an interesting experience though. The first time there was a wonderful camaraderie but by the second time there was a real bitterness amongst people when they were coming into the school because they felt nothing had been done about the flooding issue in between. The anger wasn't aimed at me but you could tell it was there."

His determination to make Elgin High a "community school" rather than an institution also influenced his approach to staff recruitment. When the school suddenly found itself in need of a temporary groundsman to cover for an illness, Mr Hope immediately offered the position to a former pupil, Colin Grant, who he knew had just been laid off by the painting firm he'd worked for. The groundsman position soon became a permanent one and in due course Colin went on to become the school's Janitor - a post he still holds to this day. In a heart-warming twist to the tale, Colin would also wind up marrying Karen Gordon, then the school's Principal Teacher of Home Economics and now Depute Head at Elgin Academy.

"I often laugh when I see Colin and Karen," chuckles Mr Hope, "Because I know there's no way they would ever have got together had I not offered Colin that job! And that came about because instead of going through a long list of job applicants who I didn't know, I went for somebody who already had links to the school. Colin was a former pupil, his dad took the badminton club and his mum had been on the school board. Whenever I had a vacancy for a temporary position, I would always ask myself if it could be filled by somebody who was already a part of the school community. I always took the view that it wasn't *my* school, it was the community's school."

Running a school for 25 years wasn't without its challenges, as one would expect. He freely admits that staff meetings were the bane of his life - something which will probably come as little surprise to former colleagues who recall his propensity for snapping pencils in moments of pique during heated discussions.

"I'd rather have stood in front of an audience of 400 people than chaired a staff meeting," he admits. "Teachers can be argumentative as hell, and every one of them a graduate and fighting for their own subject!

"The biggest difficulty was trying to maintain an enthusiasm for 25 years and realising when you were speaking to Primary 7 parents that each year was equally important to the school and to the staff. You couldn't say, 'Oh, I've done this before'".

He's never forgotten a speech given by Lord Bullock at a meeting of the Headteachers Federation of Scotland at St Andrews one year. Bullock was just back from a trip to China where he'd seen schools that were bursting at the seams with class sizes of 60 and he told the assembled throng that they had little to complain about compared to many other countries. "Very few people had a real influence on me but that speech by Lord Bullock did," Mr Hope admits. "It reminded me that if I went into school on Monday morning with my head down and saying *'Oh my God, why am I here?'* then the staff would also say *'Oh my God, why am I here?'*, and the pupils would say *'Oh my God, why am I here'*?

"Of course you had ups and downs. You had problem issues with pupils that were delicate and difficult but that was part and parcel of the job. Fortunately, I think I was always a Guidance teacher masquerading as a Headteacher, which was both a strength and a weakness. It was a weakness because it meant you were always hands-on but I wouldn't have done it any other way."

One of the biggest frustrations he faced was the number of pupils who were forced by curriculum and timetable demands to take subjects to which they weren't really suited and for which they would never have any lasting use - a sore point which rankles with him to this day.

"I still wonder about how many pupils are doing subjects which they don't actually see as important in terms of their real life skills," he says. "The phrase that would turn my blood cold if I was dealing with a disciplinary issue was *'I never wanted to take this subject'.*

"You sometimes wonder if in fact kids should be made to spend their time doing something that is never going to be of any relevance to them and if some radical package didn't exist for it to be otherwise. I still wonder whether somehow or other there could be more individualisation of the educational experience so that we don't get this *'I never wanted to take it. Why am I doing it?'*"

Witnessing the demolition of the old school building and the opening of the new EHS must inevitably have been a bittersweet experience for the school's founding rector but one about which he is characteristically philosophical.

"I liked the old building," he says. "I often said it looked more like a hotel than a school. I liked the smell of the school. So many schools smell of disinfectant but

Photo by Roy Young : 22.1.18

the High School never smelt like a school. But the heating system was not up to the job and there was no air conditioning whatsoever - I had to put that into Business Studies because computers heat the atmosphere. But it was a school of its time, just as the new building is a building for *its* time and will I'm sure be much more airy and suitable for modern requirements. Everything has to move forward. You can't be sentimental about these things."

Upon accepting the Rector's position, Mr Hope intended to give the role 10 of the best years of his life before moving on, but he ended up retiring from the post in 2003 after a marathon stint of 25 years. Looking back, he clearly has few regrets. (*Opposite a page from PP145, just before Mr Hope left us*).

"It was a privilege and I think that looking back on it, it was probably a community that suited me," he says. "It suited my personality in as much as style has never been my thing. In all the reunions I've gone to it's amazing how people will come up to you and mention something you did that meant something to them.

"You always have to be thinking about how you handle young people because it's amazing how rejection can leave a lasting effect. I can meet people who can't remember what they had for breakfast that morning but they remember in detail how they were badly treated by somebody when they were at school.

"I sometimes think we do not appreciate how much, either one way or the other, we affect kids during the day. I sometimes used to stand in the community area and think, 'My God, these bloody kids are terrible! And then I'd think *Actually, is it them or me?'"*

Friday June 27th
A Dinner for Bill

Scores of staff past and present celebrated 25 years of the Rector's Headship at a dinner held in his honour at the Mansfield Hotel last Friday.. He was presented with serious and frivolous gifts including a painting by local artist John Todd and clockwise from left top a "fair dinkum" hat for his trip to Australia, a football manager's jacket and a model broken pencil (!) Later he addressed the company from the new lectern which he has gifted the school.

From PP 145

Bill Hope's Final Staff Photograph : October 2002

Front (l-r) : Mrs Hilary Adamson, Mrs Aileen Marshall, Mrs Fiona Davidson, Mrs Fay Watt, Mr Willie Finnie, Mr Alec Cadenhead, Mr Bill Hope, Mr Jeff Dugdale, Mrs Margaret Goodlet, Mrs Meredith Hyde, Miss Vicky Taylor, Miss Judy Ross.

2nd row: Mrs Maureen Fraser, Mrs Pam Kneen, Mrs Hellen Fleming, Mrs Debbie McDonald, Miss Norma Neish, Mrs Shona Grant, Mrs Clare Rhind, Mrs Isobel Robertson, Miss Jessie Farquhar, Mrs Alison MacLachlan, Miss Celia Hawco, Mrs Kathleen Alexander

3rd row:: Mr Iain Hamilton, Mr Bruce Downie, Mrs Jo Little, Mrs Eileen Flett, Mr Mike Stewart, Mr Roy Young, Mr Neil Munro, Mrs Maureen Gravener, Miss Linda Duncan, Mrs Kay Hamilton, Mr Sigi Spence, Miss Karen Gordon

4th Row: Dr Steve Wilkinson, Mr Douglas Watt, Mr Colin Grant, Mrs Joyce Marriott, Mr Miles Stubbs, Mr David Allan, Mr John Farquhar, Mr Ken Simpson, Mr Brian Johnston, Mr Ian Walker.

*based on the article in PP10 by Mrs Linda McPherson, revised for a PP65 feature by Mr Dugdale

based on the article in PP146 by Claire Cameron   * based on the article in PP164 by Callum Reid

[1]As a result of the Scottish Executive's 2001 document *A Teaching Profession for the 21st Century* affecting all schools in Scotland the term "Rector" was replaced by "Headteacher" (sic) and the post of Assistant Rector abolished. [2] The *Good Schools Guide*, quoted in Wikipedia [3] A Munro is a mountain in Scotland with a height over 3,000 feet (914m). Munros are named after Sir Hugh Munro (1856-1919) who produced the first list of such hills, known as *Munro's Tables.*

INTERLUDE No.1

Random Recollections

Through the Facebook site "Former Elgin High School Students" fps and staff were invited to send in stories for publication that might not have made it into *Pigeon Post*. Where these stories refer to events that we did record the reference is given.

Tales from Europe

Back in 1989/90 when I was Aylsa Lumsden of 1C, we were fortunate to have Mr Ian Ferguson (*right*) for French. He was a great teacher but in our class he faced some "challenging" individuals. On one occasion I recall, a particularly chatty half hour, all *en français* obviously. But when the class was called to order, there was little response and the din continued. Mr Ferguson asked again for quiet, and again he got little response then finally he got so annoyed he slammed his hand down upon the  overhead projector to get people's attention. Which he did because he had hit it so hard he smashed the glass and we all burst out laughing, which didn't help his mood.. or the projector!

(Aylsa J. Kennedy via email 10.10.17)

Mrs Linda McPherson, English teacher, also taught Latin, and I was one of a class of four who wanted to learn it. I loved it, and was a very enthusiastic student, but possibly not for the reasons Mrs McPherson thought. Everything I learned, I taught my sister. We used to spend evenings hanging out in the swing park and so with apologies to Kevin Ogg, Chrissie Steel and the others....when we wanted to say things to each other that we didn't want you to know, we would speak to each other in Latin. *(Teenie Cottam)*

Miss Judy Ross (*right*) always expressed a particular form of body language to indicate she was getting angry. She used to start by bouncing up and down on her heels while writing on the blackboard. Once she did this, it was only a matter of time till the blackboard duster would fly across the room and bounce off the back wall. (Anon)

Miss Ross swears that what follows is apocryphal but it is a legendary tale nevertheless. In the early days of the school Mr Hope and his Depute Mr MacLachlan were observing a typical S1 French lesson. Mr MacLachlan, no doubt trying to impress with his knowledge of the language said loudly on seeing a bluebottle fly buzzing around the classroom, "Mon dieu – regardez le mouche !". Miss Ross turned on him testily saying, "Mr MacLachlan "the fly is feminine" (i.e. he should have said "**La** Mouche"). To which Mr Hope quipped, "My goodness, Miss Ross must have really good eyesight." *(Percy)*

The Goldfish Incident

In the early days, the annual summer fete (held in the Doocot Park on a Saturday in June) included "Win a goldfish!" pin-a-card-with-a-dart stall run by Mr Hope, with me as his assistant, *recalls Teenie Cottam* (22.10.17). The fish were sale or return from Birnie's Pet Shop in the High Street and Mr Hope would collect them in giant plastic bags on the Saturday morning and return the ones that weren't won at the fete on the Monday. See report in PP 9

The first year, all went well. After the fete, I took the goldfish that were left back to the science room, which had big blue buckets with plenty of swimming space for fish. I stuck in a pipe to blow air bubbles into the bucket, and job done. Back to

Birnie's Monday morning.

Year 2 didn't go so well. Unbeknown to me, the science room buckets had been enthusiastically cleaned (with bleach, perhaps ?) the week of the fete, and whatever it was that was used, it wasn't good for goldfish.

I wasn't asked to help the following year.

"It's Behind You!"

I was in "The Monkey's Paw" at Easter - 1984 or thereabouts - as the mother.

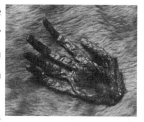

Robert Blyth from the year below me was the dad. I've completely forgotten who else was in it, but Mr Hamilton directed. I'll never forget the dress rehearsal in front of the local brownies: Robert crawling around in what should have been an atmosphere of high suspense, looking in panic for the paw to drive his zombie son from the door, and the helpful brownies chorusing "It's behind you!"

(Abiy Orr on FB site 25.10.17. See details in our chapter on School Shows).

The Writing is on The Wall

My sister Karen and I had been given some fab silver and gold marker pens and were using them at every opportunity. We lived really close to the school and used to hang out by the steps to what I guess was a fire exit door from the gym block. That door was a blank canvas, and one weekend we just couldn't help ourselves and the gold and silver markers were put to good use marking that "K and K woz 'ere" and the like.

Come Monday, I got summoned to Mr Hope's office to discuss graffiti. Instead of the rant I was expecting, he said something along the lines of..."I know you live close to the school, and know the people round here. Someone has been putting graffiti on the school, and it's a shame as it spoils the look of it.   I am trusting you to find the person or persons responsible, and to ask them to remove the graffiti. We'll then say no more about it".

Karen and I sneaked out late that night with a bucket and sponge and cleaned the door. (Teenie Cottam)

Mr Alec Cadenhead (*right, dressed as "Smart Alec" on a dress-as-a-character day*) always received the greatest of respect from pupils, and because of his gait and general laid back demeanour acquired the nickname "Clint" (as in Eastwood). A measure of the awe he inspired was seen in a famous graffito in the Y floor Boys toilets, Golf course end) which read, "**Mr** Cadenhead is a Bxxxxxd" (Percy)

On another occasion, *as an anonymous contributor confessed by email* he overhead two senior members of staff discussing a graffito in another toilet, in which the "c" of a common four letter insult directed at a member of staff was misspelled, with a "k". "Oh" said one of them, "Clearly this" – and then he spelled out the four letter word in capitals "has problems with authority – and spelling".

Odd Room Numbering

Why was Y18 next to Y2? Why did Y3 share a wall with Y9. Well apparently it was all to do with the mysteries of "Phase Two", the planned extension which on the cards from the moment the school opened. It would add another dozen classrooms to the North of the school, i.e. nearer the playing fields: see Chapter on Extensions..   So in order to accommodate the room numbering of those prospective classrooms, for years confused pupils had to tolerate a really weird system, which actually confused staff as well. (Percy see DoosNews p22 of #1)

And a Host of Others

The blue book of school rules which we were given on the first day, which included maximum acceptable widths for flared trousers.

Mr Hope standing in the corridor near the school office saying good morning to us all by name (and confiscating football scarves) as we walked up from the Community Area.

Miss Linda Duncan (Maths teacher) bringing her ferret to school.

Doing computing in maths, when the lesson would be spent colouring in boxes on a huge stack of programming instruction cards that looked like pools coupons. They would be fed into the computer to run overnight, and we'd get the results of our labours the next day. My list of instructions inevitably 'fell over' on about line 2.

Sewing class, when you weren't allowed to start making your garment until you'd passed your sewing machine 'driving test'. This involved thread-less sewing following a series of lines and patterns on paper cards. By the end of term, I'd got as far as cutting out the pattern on my material, and that gypsy skirt never got made.

Cookery class…learning to cook sponge cakes using a microwave. My effort was offered to the neighbours with the line 'Teenie's made *lovely rock cakes* at school today…would you like one'

Forging the parental consent form every month so I could go hillwalking with the school club. I had borrowed boots (Mr Birnie kept a supply of various sizes in the biology cupboard) and no decent waterproofs but I didn't care. It sparked a love of hillwalking in me which has since taken me up Kilmanjaro, mostly up Cerro Plomo in Chile (high winds, a storm, and a partner with AMS stopped play), and Mera Peak in the Himalayas. Thanks Mr Birnie!

Mr Jim Hamilton (*History, right*) telling our class (1A) that we were his best class. He also told 1B, 1C and 1D that they were his best class….. He was the best history teacher though.

Hiding a stash of soft drinks and chewing gum part way along the cross country course, to collect during the 'run', and walking the whole part of the route that was out of sight of the school. Hated Cross Country.

Making puff candy in science class on the last day of term, using golden syrup, bicarbonate of soda (I think!) and Bunsen burners. Unfortunately, one year the lid came off my syrup tin in my schoolbag.

The long silver streamers with round holes which were used to decorate the Community Area for the Christmas Party, which were what was left after Allarburn Dairy had made their milk bottle tops.

Euan Ogilvie recalls some of his favourite teachers…

I was taught English by **Mr James (Jocky) Fyfe**, (*right*) who used to say to me if I was talking too much or mucking around, "When was the last time you had the strap Ogilvie, perhaps I"ll have to refresh your memory" and "less o the comedy capers!"

I shared a house in Aberdeen with one of his sons, Graeme, and the day Scotland won the rugby Grand slam against England in 1990 Mr Fyfe turned up at our door so we took him for lunch then back to the house to watch the Rugby and have a few drinks. He was in great form and he laughed when I reminded him of what he used to say to me in class.

Another great teacher I had was **Mr Bill Leslie** (PT Physics, *right*) who was always surprising us with the bouncing ball and astonishing folk by a standing jump onto his high desk and then running across the desks. He kept his strap in a drawer on a plank of wood, to keep the plank of wood straight. I feared I might have had to get strapped one day in class when I blurted out a remark without thinking. You see Mr Leslie would always run to the window when an RAF plane was heard going past to see which one it was. One day after checking what plane had gone past he proudly turned to the class with both hands on the lapels of his white coat and announced to us the he used to work in the place that built those planes. So…. I asked "Where was that? Airfix?" There was a gasp from the class and a couple of chuckles but luckily for me Mr

Leslie took it very well and even had a smile and a chuckle as he leaned across the desk and took me by the collar of my shirt and said "very good Mr Ogilvie" My friend and classmate, Scott Johnston and I always laugh about it when we meet up.

Mr Sigi Spence *(right)* taught me Engineering Science and I remember Mr Leslie getting slightly cross with me when in Physics periods I used to contradict him on certain things that Mr Spence had taught us in Eng Sc. It was a bit funny to see him get a little annoyed, but not in a bad way. However, Mr Spence just used to laugh about it. Both very good teachers that I have much respect for.

In S5 I was part of a team, guided by **Mr Ken Duncan**, who won the Hawco Award that got us a trip to the Volkswagen factory in Wolfsburg, Germany. I was with Peter Moffat, Mark Bruce and David Fraser. I don't think we got into *Pigeon Post* as it was at the time when there was a lot of industrial action but see full story with newspaper clipping in "What Elgin High Did for Me".

There was one other story I have that—maybe not for the book— regarding one very **good looking PE teacher**. Kevin MacLennan and I were walking behind her in the corridor and I made a gesture with my hands, as teenage boys might do about an attractive girl, and I was caught by a male PE teacher who was walking behind us ! He pulled me up and

gave me a telling off for being rude or disrespectful and gave me a long stare eye to eye. When Kevin and I got into the changing room we just cracked up laughing at being caught. I always got caught doing something I shouldn't have.

Lastly I believe I came up with the conundrum "What would Elgin High School be without a headmaster?" .... Hopeless! (Boom ....)

A typical page of school gossip from Doos' News (PP 136—Oct 2001)

Doos News

Staff News

Congratulations to **Mrs Debbie McDonald** our long serving P. E. teacher who was appointed Principal Teacher of P.E. succeeding Mr David Carstairs, on Friday 24th August, having held the post on an Acting basis for a year or so.

Mrs McDonald joined the staff as Miss Debbie Abel, in August 1983 having been a pupil at Banff Academy, where Mr Dugdale was her Higher English teacher. Throughout her 18 years in Elgin High she has been active in promoting various sports, notably hockey in the early days. (One sport you might be surprised to learn that she excels at is snooker).

We say goodbye at the October break to **Mr David Vaughan** who is moving to become Head of Biology at Nairn Academy which is much closer to his home in Cawdor than Elgin High to which he make a daily round trip of 50 miles. Mr Vaughan has been with us for 14 years and we know that he leaves us with very mixed feelings.

We wish Mrs McDonald and Mr Vaughan all the best in their new roles as Head of Department.

Replacing Mr Vaughan as Acting Head of Biology is **Dr Stephen Wilkinson** currently teaching Biology and Chemistry on the staff of Buckie High School. Dr Wilkinson was appointed on Tuesday 25th September and will join us in early November.

Joining our Modern Languages Dept to cover the timetable currently shared by Mrs Drysdale and Mrs Cameron will be **Mrs Hilary Adamson** who is APT Guidance at Nairn Academy. Mrs Adamson was appointed on 14th September but will not be joining us until the first week in December.

Moving Messages

An important addition to our communications arrived during the summer courtesy of funding from E.H.S.A. in the form of a moving LCD display in the foyer which allows the office staff to highlight short messages for the attention of staff and pupils.

We are also grateful to the Association for the funding which allowed us to install new wall mounted monitors

Additional Dates for your Calendar

Now determined following a staff meeting in early September are the following dates:

Prelim Exams and Study leave for S4 begin on Tuesday 5th Feb

For S5/6 they begin on Friday 8th when the English exams will be held.

The last day of the prelims will be Tuesday 26th and all pupils return to normal classes the next day.

S4/5/6 Parents evening is therefore Tues 12th March

S3 Parents evening is Mon 25th March

and video players in each of the six English classroom which now permits very quick access to video recordings without resort to booking TV trolleys in advance and having to manoeuvre them down the corridor, sometimes endangering life and limb !

Other new IT equipment has appeared in Y3 over the holidays which now looks very smart indeed "thanks" in a sense to our flood during the early Summer which actually necessitated refurbishment of this large IT room.

Respect Paid

A sizeable proportion of the school gathered in the Library just before 11 a.m. on Friday 14th September for a three minute silence to pay their respects to the memory of the thousands of people killed in the terrorist atrocities in America on Tuesday 11th. A former pupil of the school Dawn Bachelor had been due to start a new job in the World Trade Centre on that fateful day but had delayed her start because her parents had come across to see her.

New Elgin Mart Stall

A group of enterprising S4 Business Management pupils, supported by a series of staff members, ran a stall at New Elgin Mart selling Elgin High products on the last Saturday of September to raise money for school funds. On sale were our academic year calendar, our 2002 calendar, our school pen, diary, Elgin Scenes notelets, polo shirts and sweat shirts.

STAMP of approval

For the second time in 2001 **Mr Jeff Dugdale**, the Editor of *Pigeon Post* has had an article published in *STAMP* the leading British glossy magazine for philatelists. The September edition contained a four page article on The Moon Walkers whilst earlier in the year Mr Dugdale had an item published on stamps commemorating the achievements of Yuri Gagarin, the Soviet cosmonaut and first man in space. Mr Dugdale, who is currently President of Moray Philatelic Society, is now working on an article for *STAMP* to be published next year on the first Chinese manned space flight launch.

18

84

7 Curricular Innovation No.1

1978 to 2008

Many parents and most grandparents will remember their own schooldays as quite different from those of the pupils who attended Elgin High which opened in 1978. "When I was at school…." pupils were taught in classes of over 40, set out in strict rows, addressed by a black gown-wearing teacher, possibly raised on a dais. He or she would often impart information by stern dictation or copying from the blackboard and promote rote learning in many subjects, supporting it with the tawse as necessary. The wearing of the gown, which often housed the tawse in one of its commodious wings or disguised its location over a right handed teacher's left shoulder, was symbolic of authority and TALKING IS NOT ALLOWED.

This air of superiority, which was not all that far removed from the behaviour of Dickens' Wackford Squeers in *Nicholas Nickleby* or Thomas Gradgrind[1] in *Hard Times* – "pupils are pitchers to be filled to the brim" was accompanied by varying attitudes to different kinds of learners. Pupils had been selected for secondary schooling after a formal primary school assessment known as the "Qualifying Exam" (colloquially the "Quali" and 11+ in England) taken on one particular day and without allowance for feeling unwell or being nervous etc. This might be an IQ test, success or failure at which would lead to attendance at a Secondary, a Junior Secondary or a Junior Modified school, for the scholars and the "non-certificate" pupils and "the others" respectively.

Even within the Secondary School, classes might be formed via "streaming" whereby a class of really bright pupils attended all subjects as a discrete group irrespective of their ability in any particular one. Alternatively pupils could be "set" within subjects, meaning that a whole year or half-year would attend a subject like English or Maths simultaneously and then be sorted on ability within that subject. This might be thought appropriate if linear learning was considered necessary as it was then in many subjects beyond the Mathematics corridor. Note that the naming of the department designed to support those who were the least talented as "Remedial" speaks volumes about how we regarded such pupils in those days.

Attitudes were changing however with the publication of the SED "Orange Paper" in 1968 which outlined an innovative Guidance System for Scottish schools. More and more young adults were coming into schools as teachers, replacing those appointed just after the end of the Second World War, many of whom had seen the imposition of a "lite" form of military discipline as an important part of their approach to classroom ambience. Education, like many other fields, has endured constant change in emphasis and the surfacing and disappearing of buzz words and phrases, one of the most important of which in the mid-1970's was "experiential learning". The young staff appointed to create Elgin High were all selected on the basis that the old traditional methods alluded to above were very much passé and that learning *by doing* was the coming thing.

Traditional attitudes had also meant that assessment for qualifications was regarded differently for "the clever eens" and the others. In Scotland the "Lowers" gave way to "O-grades" and the achievement of the latter meant doing your "Highers" in the following session(s). But if you were a non-certificate pupil at a Junior secondary you were glad to escape to the real world of work as soon as possible without much in the way of formal qualifications and so the arrival of RSLA[2] in the early 1970s was definitely "a bad thing". This atmosphere understandably led to a classic "them and us" feeling within the pupil cohort and consequently a feeling that many were second class.

"The problem with O-grades" as Bill Hope would often remind his staff was that success in them was likely for the "top 30%" of pupils only and for the rest there was little formal recognition of four years at school. Which is to say in a typical school of 700 pupils, the education of 270 was the staff's highest priority. Elgin High serving New Elgin and its catchment area would have to surmount major challenges to be accepted as a credible academic establishment.

Bill Hope had arrived in Elgin High School in August 1978 determined to make EHS different from any other school he had worked in and in the following years the school would be in the forefront of taking innovative approaches to learning best suited to the needs of "our" pupils.

The Certificate of Secondary Education mode 3 (CSEm3)

As early as issue #3 of *Pigeon Post* (November 1978), the Rector announced that he would be addressing this challenge head on, by considering what the options for our first cohorts would be in the school's second session (1979-80)...

"In most Scottish schools (there are) serious problems as there is only one national certificate awarded to fourth year pupils – the SCE "O" grade. Unfortunately the "O" grade was originally designed for only the top 30% of pupils.... (however) many Scottish schools have chosen to enter the vast majority of their third and fourth year pupils for (these exams). The result of this has been that many pupils are following courses which are in no way suited to their needs or abilities and find themselves struggling......

"Elgin High School fully recognises the importance of providing its pupils with the opportunity of gaining qualifications but at the same time wishes to ensure that the courses taught are relevant and practical, especially for those for whom academic subjects are unsuitable..."

Bill Hope then goes on to describe a radically different approach. All the usual courses would be offered at "O" grade level – English...Arithmetic...Home Economics etc. But for those pupils who staff from their knowledge of "O"-grade courses elsewhere thought might struggle, the school would put in place the English Certificate of Secondary Education mode3[3] (CSEm3), awarded by the Northern Region Examinations Board (NREB) based in Newcastle. The particular advantage of this – and an enormous amount of work for the departments involved – was that these courses were not to be laid down by the NREB but that the syllabus and methods of assessment were to be designed by Elgin High teachers, tailoring them to our pupils' needs with local Moderators[4] appointed by NREB to ensure standards. So, Mr Hope went on, "our school will not have a "them" and "us" situation between "O" grade pupils and "non-certificate" pupils.

In fact most pupils would take on a mixture of "O" grades and CSEs depending on their bent. Showing that advance thinking was already in hand, Mr Hope goes on to list names for some of the new-style CSE courses, created by his new Principal Teachers viz., Social Arithmetic, Rural Science, Home Management, Child Care, Theatre Arts, Commercial Practice and Social Studies, each of which as appropriate would be able to take on the demands of local industry and employment.

This was to be seen as a genuine attempt to ensure that older pupils saw their time well spent, purposeful and worthwhile and that their efforts were to be recognised not only in the form of a certificate but by the local community and employers.

In the following years, *Pigeon Post* regularly carried stories about the experiential learning opportunities of CSE. The Rural Studies pupils were involved, as PP14 for December 1979 explains, in preparing the ground for the school garden. Potatoes and tomatoes had already been produced and each pupil given a small area to themselves. Plans were in hand for a small henhouse and for planting trees at the back of the school. In English Language and Literature pupils were analysing TV programmes and pop lyrics such as "I Don't like Mondays" by The Boomtown Rats and involved in drama and improvisation. The Commercial Organisation group set out to cover many aspects of office work and with the help of the Drama department imagined being marooned on a desert island and having to make decisions to help them survive. In Social Arithmetic topics included understanding telephone bills, some aspects of arithmetic in The Post Office and using calculators. PP23 (December 1980) outlined pupil visits to Elgin Mart, to the local Police Station cells (where one pupil actually fainted because of its ambience), Baxters of Speyside factory, Aberdeen Airport etc in order to experience the world of work. See also e.g. PP30

This initiative was well ahead of its time, a real precursor to Standard Grade Social and Vocation Skills (SocVoc) and the SCOTVEC modules which would be offered in the mid-1980's to all pupils.

Raising the Standard

The by-then widespread agreement that O-grades were elitist and past their sell-by date, as exposed by the Munn and Dunning Reports of the late 1970's, was to be comprehensively addressed with the national introduction of the three-level Standard-Grade system of certification in August 1984, which pretty much provided certification for all.   PP 55 (June '84) recognised this with a front page story and cartoon, explaining that the introduction of the new post S1-2 courses with exams in the early Summer of S4 would be a gradual one.

In the first year (session 1984-5) English, Mathematics, Science and Social and Vocational Skills (SVS, see PP 38) would be offered at Credit (the most difficult), General and Foundation levels, following two years of preparatory work by staff across Scotland.

The second tranche of subjects would follow in session 1985-6, when pupils would select from Art, French, Home Economics, Integrated Craft, Craft, Latin, Contemporary Social Subjects and Health Studies. Elgin High with its six year experience of CSE subjects across the board was already well primed to take advantage of the new system which now would be certificated by the Scottish Education Dept (SED) in Dalkeith, Edinburgh and not from the North of England. A system of moderation known to our staff from CSE days also meant that local overview of courses and advice giving could be passed on to colleagues in other schools. For example, the new Assistant Rector, Dr Rob Kerr was the moderator for SVS for the whole of Grampian Region.

The general idea was to get away from the "them and us" of the traditional O-grades and to put in its place subjects which almost all pupils could take at levels appropriate to their abilities. And each would get two chances to shine, being presented for General and Credit or General and Foundation in S4, depending on their showing in S3. And pupils would take courses across subjects depending on their particular abilities, for example they could be doing Credit Geography but Foundation Maths or Credit Science and General Mod Studies. The other subjects not mentioned so far were to be phased in in Year Three of Implementation (1986-7).

Arguably the most revolutionary of the courses was SVS or as Elgin High called it "SocVoc" or "Soc & Voc". This subject offered pupils guidance and instruction in a myriad of practical contexts, blending aspects of many different narrow subjects and was taught in Core time (i.e. not subject specific periods) so almost everyone would take it. Here pupils would learn and later be examined on a range of cross – curricular courses under three broad themes – Community, Home, and Work. Necessary practical components to success in the subject (before the written exam) included pupils planning and running a community event, making an item or offering a service, taking part in a co-operative learning activity, taking at least one leisure activity and - the major ones - undertaking a Work Experience Placement and/or a Community Involvement Placement and/or a Residential. The

BRING AND BUY SALE RAISES £49

A hurriedly organised Bring and Buy sale, planned soon after industrial action came to an end produced a modest amount in terms of cash raised but a great deal of goodwill from many of the S3 and S4 pupils who participated in its organisation and execution.

A elected pupil committee of Paul McHardy, Gavin Henderson, Craig Christie and Debbie Slinn (S4) and Ross McHardy and Pamela Clark (S3) advised by Mr Crossland and tutors Mr Carstairs and Mr Dugdale met on four occasions before the event to determine what stalls were to be organised and who should do what.

The Sale was held in Elgin High Church Hall in North Guildry Street from 10.30 to 12 noon on the first Saturday of the Easter holidays (4th April) with such stalls as Bric a Brac, Toys, Name the Donkey, Daffodils, Cake and Candy, Books and Clothes. The daffodils were most kindly donated by Capt Lahore of Burgie House Estate and picked by Mr Carstairs and four rather wet pupils the afternoon before the event.

In addition to the cash raised, the unsold items were disposed of to other charities – OXFAM, UNICEF, and Barnardo's shop and unsold flowers went to old folk, and local hospitals. The main beneficiaries of the event were the residents of Winchester House, a home for mentally handicapped adults near the Cathedral and they intend to use it to help fund a holiday. (See photo opposite.)

A LESSON IN GIVING . . .

Elgin High School pupils taking social and vocational skills, Ross McHardy (left) and Pamela Clark (centre), present a cheque for £49 to Winchester House resident Mr Johnny Roy, watched by the resident social worker Mrs Lynne Harkins (right), Mrs Letty Smith (second right), a resident at the hostel, and Mr David Carstairs, the school's social and vocational group tutor. The money was raised by pupils at a bring and buy sale.
ex Midweek Extra 6/5/87 N.

last of these was optional, costing £12-£15 for a three day experience, but was phenomenally attractive. Ideally, pupils would pay for the residential by earlier activities for which they could charge, for example via a cake sale or mini-fête or local gardening or running errands or car-washing.

Throughout the following years Core Groups regularly contributed to issues of the school newspaper with accounts of their adventures: dip into "SocVocToc" features in the *Pigeon Post* Synopses tables in Section Two for a flavour, one example of which from PP 60 (5.87) "Bring and Buy Sale...." is given above.

Learning Outside the Box

Most teachers of the new Elgin High School had attended school in the 1960's in an environment of almost exclusively classroom learning, with nary a trip away. If such did occur it would be regarded as a bit of a "skive" or a jolly. Pupils in a top class would not typically have been taken, for example, to look around a local factory, business, or farm or zoo because book learning and preparation for exams was *the* priority.

But by the time those pupils had become teachers themselves in the mid-1970's, educational philosophy was changing and learning *by doing*, "heuristics" and "experiential learning" were in and are now embedded in our current approaches. Increasing numbers of teachers gradually realised there was more to learning than books, lessons and the occasional educational TV broadcast for which we were so excited to gather together.

The new approaches adopted many forms such as inter-department and cross-sector cooperation (with primaries and colleges), extra-mural ("field") trips, community involvement and work experience placements, careers convention attendance, receiving guest experts into school to talk at assemblies or in classrooms, trips to local sites (most often in Art and Geography), outings to Scotland's cities, London Theatre trips and excursions abroad. In due course these last mentioned elements would be incorporated into Activities Weeks (see dedicated paragraphs below) and in Equal Opportunity and Industrial Awareness days. Additionally there would be the occasional major events like "Oilstrike!" in May/June 1989 (PP 74) run under the aegis of TVEI and then TVE.

Such features would become so common that those of our pupils who went on to become teachers themselves would think it odd if such activities were *not* part of the curriculum or departmental syllabi.

Given Elgin High's relatively rural location, pupils' first out-of-classroom experiences would include using the playing fields, adjacent burns and the scrub land of The Wards as a source of water samples and insect nymphs. The visit to Mayne farm a quarter of an up-hill weary mile to the west of the school campus was the first logical extension. Bill Hope had established an excellent relationship with Mr Dean Anderson of Allarburn Dairy/Mayne Farm and well before the days of "risk assessment", "health and safety" prohibitions and helicopter parenting attitudes re children getting too close to farm beasts, pupils regularly spent an afternoon on the local farm: see a typical report in PP 14. Here they'd witness the workings of a milking parlour and learn about the various types of farming on their doorstep, which provided different types of food.

Being rich in history, Elgin also offered opportunities to other subject groups to visit such places as the Cathedral, Spynie Palace, Duffus Castle, local graveyards and Elgin Castle on Ladyhill. The department which probably took pupils out of the classroom more than any other was Geography with trips for example to Culbin Sands, Findhorn, Aviemore and the local RAF stations, but see also the section elsewhere on CSE and its extra mural trips described in detail in PP 23.

The school's first foreign trip at Easter 1979 was to the Dutch city of Valkenburg with pupil accounts and photographs given in PP 8 and 9. The town is a major tourist resort with two spectacular amusement parks nearby. The experience of such a foreign trip would provide learning in many forms not possible in the classroom, for example,

Coping with all aspects of a long bus journey including motion sickness

Making new friends out of previously unknown peers and seeing different sides to members of staff

Learning responsibility in meeting deadlines and respecting curfews

Getting away from Elgin and parents/guardians

Saving up for and spending your money responsibly when on holiday

And of course having a good time!

A comprehensive list of trips for example, La Plange, Italian Ski Trip in January 1984 in PP 51/52, Edinburgh Festival in August 1991 in PP 88, Lido di Jesolo, Italy Summer 1994 and in PP 101 (October 1994) etc etc and pupil reports on them can be found within Section Two, both in the "PP Content Summaries" and "Trip Advisor" pages.

These excursions were not uncontroversial however, as many involved parents and guardians finding sizeable amounts of money to support them. Sometimes their timing, overlapping with days when most of the school remained on campus, for example the annual trip to the Edinburgh Festivals in mid-August, often in the first week back after the Summer holidays was self-evidently a source of irritation to some parents and teachers.

"I survived TVEI* in Elgin High"

Immediately after two and half years of teacher industrial action (during sessions 1985/86, 1986/87) which changed so many aspects of the ethos of schools across Scotland and not always for the better, Elgin High was selected as one of the schools in Scotland—there were at that time only 50 of them in the whole of the United Kingdom—to be involved in the "Technical and Vocational Educational Initiative", more easily spoken of as "TVEI".

The TVEI website which is still live explains the thinking behind the scheme..

The Technical and Vocational Initiative (TVEI 1983-97) represented a dramatic departure from the education policy conducted by successive governments in Britain since the Second World War. It tried to address the deficiency in the school curriculum namely the absence of any meaningful vocational content*

The Moray pilot scheme was funded by the government to the tune of £2 million. Its headquarters were a suite of rooms in Elgin Academy, with the teacher in charge being paid at a Headteacher rate (but crucially lacking the same status or clout). It covered the two Elgin secondary schools, and later Moray College, Forres Academy and Milne's High School, Fochabers.

*   https://technicaleducationmatters.org/2011/11/12/the-technical-and-vocational-education-initiative-tvei-1983-1997/

Whatever was to be learned in the Moray pilot scheme was to be "cascaded" in the following decade to staff in all other Grampian schools. They were eventually expected to introduce aspects of TVEI type learning into their syllabuses with the guidance of Moray staff but controversially without the same enhanced level of funding. This second settled phase was to be called "TVE" (that is, with the "Initiative" dropped, because it was then normalised, presumably).

Special TVEI Course Development Officers, (CDOs) in Maths, Contemporary Social Studies, French, Science, Art and Computing seconded for up to two years and housed in the TVEI bases in the Academy from their own schools would do the ground preparation for these additional aspects of learning. Elgin High staff played a major part in the design of local TVEI courses in the subjects mentioned with the secondment of Guidance PT Mr Cameron Gibson and two members of the Board of Studies, Mr Alistair MacLachlan and Dr Robert Kerr, comprising two thirds of the team who wrote the original funding submission to the UK government. In school Mr Willie Finnie, our PT Geography was temporarily promoted to Assistant Head (Curriculum: TVEI) to become the School Coordinator for the five years of the scheme.

Over sixty S3 (1987/8) pupil "guinea-pigs" were timetabled for "TVEI Core" activities across the week, effectively taking a new subject. This was led by tutors teaching such topics as Life Skills, Organisation Skills, Enterprise, Keyboarding and Information Technology, Education for Health, and for Leisure and using Microprocessors in Science and in Technology. This group would also experience a Residential trip (in S3) and a placement in a local place of work (in S4). Pupils would be certificated for certain parts of what they had learned via S-grade SocVoc and/or via units assessed by the SED and by SCOTVEC.

Each edition of *Pigeon Post* for the following *five years* carried reports of TVEI activities, each identified with the cartouche *opposite* hinting at off-campus, out-door learning, though of course that was just a small part of it. The example opposite - "TVEI Lads Sample Gliding"- is from PP 66 (March 1988).

It goes without saying that five years of TVEI activities totally changed learning in Elgin High School, with a considerable percentage of each of five cohorts, those entering S3 in session 1987-88 through to 1991-92 experiencing news ways of

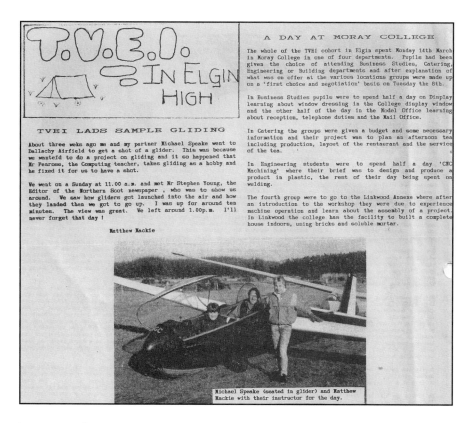

T.V.E.I. IN ELGIN HIGH

The whole of the TVEI cohort in Elgin spent Monday 14th March in Moray College in one of four departments. Pupils had been given the choice of attending Business Studies, Catering, Engineering or Building departments and after explanation of what was on offer at the various locations groups were made up on a 'first choice and negotiation' basis on Tuesday the 8th.

In Business Studies pupils were to spend half a day on Display learning about window dressing in the College display window and the other half of the day in the Model Office learning about reception, telephone duties and the Mail Office.

TVEI LADS SAMPLE GLIDING

About three weks ago me and my partner Michael Speake went to Dallachy Airfield to get a shot of a glider. This was because we wantefd to do a project on gliding and it so happened that Mr Penrose, the Computing teacher, takes gliding as a hobby and he fixed it for us to have a shot.

We went on a Sunday at 11.00 a.m. and met Mr Stephen Young, the Editor of the Northern Scot newspaper , who was to show us around. We saw how gliders got launched into the air and how they landed then we got to go up. I was up for around ten minutes. The view was great. We left around 1.00p.m. I'll never forget that day !

Matthew Mackie

In Catering the groups were given a budget and some necessary information and their project was to plan an afternoon tea including production, layout of the restaurant and the service of the tea.

In Engineering students were to spend half a day 'CNC Machining' where their brief was to design and produce a product in plastic, the rest of their day being spent on welding.

The fourth group were to go to the Linkwood Annexe where after an introduction to the workshop they were due to experience machine operation and learn about the assembly of a project. In Linkwood the college has the facility to built a complete house indoors, using bricks and soluble mortar.

Michael Speake (seated in glider) and Matthew Mackie with their instructor for the day.

learning. Of course those who came after them when the scheme had officially expired—and the extra funding was all spent—experienced teaching methodology forever changed by what had happened in that extended, concentrated spell.

Naturally during those five years, staff came and went and when TVEI eventually morphed into TVE for those schools in the scheme and all our partner schools in Grampian, those staff who were in at the start of it were proud to wear a badge of honour.

Some even went so far as to Tippex out "TVEI". Phew!!

Activities Weeks [5]

These began in May 1992 (PP 89) with all pupils in Year 1-3 who were not under SCE examination experiencing a "suspended timetable" shortly before the new session began in June which was being debugged for a few weeks before the Summer break.

The notion of abandoning normal classrooms to try out alternative scenarios for learning which had been around for many years was finally realised in EHS in 1992 and the occasion has continued ever since with one or two modifications. It was born out of a universal desire by EHS staff to enhance the ethos of the school by improving relations between pupils and staff, already perceived to be good. At the same time clear educational objectives were outlined based on the fundamental meaning of "Education" - the "leading out" of young (and older) minds towards new experiences and situations. In jargon terms this was putting into practice the theory behind "experiential learning": all staff were aware of the limitations of the classroom, books, worksheets, videos (as they were then) and the tiny number of now very chunky-looking computers to which the school had access.

What the school undertook was by far the biggest logistical exercise in its fourteen years, dwarfing very considerable achievements like school concerts, fêtes, auctions, pantomimes, musicals and reviews and industrial awareness days - by involving every pupil in S1-3, every teaching member of staff and several non-teaching for every day of a full five day school week.

The variety of experiences on offer to our pupils during May 18th-22nd - can be gauged by flicking through the 14 pages of PP90 which comprises scores of photographs and pupil reports on their experiences. The headings on these pages give just a flavour of what was on offer over those five days on and off campus: Foreign cooking, Tennis at Cooper Park, Edinburgh Theatres and Galleries, London Culture Vultures, Inverclyde Residential, Loch Morlich Camping, Biking, Outdoor Sketching, Ten Pin Bowling, Ice-Skating, Day Walk, Conservation, Jewellery making, Aberdeen Leisure Centre, Hockey Camp at Inverness Astroturf, Snooker, Video

Camera Skills, Motor Vehicle Studies, Tourist Trail, Golf, Creative Crafts, Aviation Society, Aviemore Sports, Computer Games, Card games, Sea Fishing, Water Activities, Horse Riding, Campus Sports etc etc.

Your author was privileged to lead the most talented and hard working group of professionals he had ever encountered through six months of meticulous planning with duties allocated as follows: Mr Bruce Downie (catalogue), Miss Norma Neish, now Mrs Watson (pupil allocation), Mr Sigi Spence (documentation), Mrs Karen Highmore and Mr Alan Sturrock (Parental Consent forms), Mr David Allan (Finances), Mr Alan Taylor (back up). Additionally of course all members of staff (including those just named) were planning their own activities.

This would prove to be the first of an annual occurrence in the school calendar, latterly reduced to three days, but it was much appreciated by pupils who found many teachers they did not know to be rather "good sorts" and provided many eye -opening occasions. Activities Week was reported on at length in the June edition of *Pigeon Post* each year, so if you would like to see other newly introduced activities, see any of the last editions of the academic session (e.g. PP 95 (6.93), PP100 (6.94) right up to PP 171 (6.09)

But no amount of that could prepare the school for dismay should the weather spoil our efforts. As it turned out, only Thursday disappointed, and all the planning was shown to be so worthwhile. Pupils, freed from their uniforms, behaved superbly, seeming to really enjoy and appreciate these new ways of learning (even if they did not *seem* to be doing that), as it was all so enjoyable.

S3 Industrial Awareness Day

The school's first I.A.Day, preceded by one held in Elgin Academy a month before occurred in the same session as that first Activities Week – on March 24th 1992. Involving all Third Year pupils working with over a dozen local "industrialists"* provided by the Moray, Badenoch & Strathspey Local Enterprise Company, it promised "an action packed day with lots of group activity and problem solving exercises" and "great fun" in "an informal atmosphere": see PP 89. Pupils were to be prepared in advance with some warm up exercises the week before in Core Groups but it was largely all to be a surprise.

As reported in PP 91 (June 1992) guests from "world of work" met senior pupils for a working breakfast to discuss with them career opportunities in their particular spheres of industry and commerce. Then each guest worked with a group of a dozen or so Third Year pupils in their home classroom, making posters

on the theme of "What is Industry?" They made advertising material for a new kind of pizza and finally designed and built a miniature oil-rig out of paper, string, sellotape and glue. The climax of the day in the Tuck Shop area was to be the testing via The Coke Can Challenge of the oil-rig's integral structure and the decision of the guest panel re which was the best oil rig. This is shown here on photos from PP115 for June 1997.

As a pilot scheme for all Moray schools this was judged a success and became a regular feature of the school year.

*Industrial advisers came from local organisations and companies like Boots the Chemist, Grampian Police, Elgin Community Council, Safeways Supermarket, The Army Careers Office, Moray District Council, the Hydro Board, M.B.& S. LEC etc

S2 Equal Opportunity Day

With S3's Industrial Awareness Day well bedded in, it was decided to organise a complementary but quite different experience for Second Year pupils to make them aware of other peoples "disabilities" as it was bluntly called first of all. First run in early May 1996 Equal Opportunities Day was intended to make our able-bodied pupils aware that not everyone was as lucky as them and was indirectly linked to the imminent arrival on campus of a sizeable number of differently abled pupils when Hamilton Drive School moved to our new Kestrel House extension.

On a day in May, normal timetabled classes were suspended and all S2 pupils in

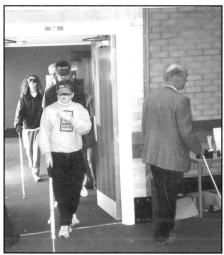 

small groups went round various stations across the school learning a little about what it was to be blind or partially sighted, confined to a wheelchair, having to walk with a stick for support or to be deaf or partially deaf and so on. This was done with the aid of props as the accompanying photos from PP 110 (June 1996) suggest. Also present were a number of local individuals from organisations like PHAB (Physically Handicapped Able Bodied). They generously volunteered to come into school to talk about coping with physical challenges, and managing tasks like dressing and having breakfast, all too often taken for granted by young people in rude health.

Once the initial excitement of these experiences passed, pupils in general began to talk about and later write down what they had realised throughout their day. Such comments as, "I didn't know it could be so hard to pour a cup of tea but now I know how blind people learn to do it", "I had never talked to a person with difficulties but I talked to Scot. He was a lot like me" and "It has made me feel how handicapped people must feel and we just take (our health) for granted" and so on. S2EO Day then became a firm fixture in the school calendar.

Promoting Positive Behaviour: The "Possie" System

In late September 2001 a new system of rewarding good behaviour was introduced, became very popular quickly and was immediately rechristened by the pupils. The school had been considering innovative ways of rewarding pupils, beyond the Annual Prize Giving and praise in formative assessment feedback on single pieces of work. Following an in-service day earlier in the year when the Head of Tynecastle High School, Edinburgh spoke to all staff about the system he had introduced in his school, it was decided to try something similar in Elgin High.

On display in each classroom two large bright posters entitled "Code of Behaviour" and "Consequences" summarised how pupils could gain Positive Behaviour nominations and the new system was explained repeatedly by registration and classroom teachers.

In short, instead of *just being expected* to behave well in class, deliver homework on time and apply themselves in general etc., pupils were to be rewarded via

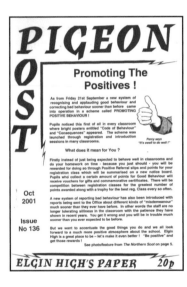 

Positive Behaviour slips and points for their registration class. Once pupils had accumulated a certain total of PPB slips they were to receive a certificate at special assemblies, with thresholds for Bronze, Silver, Gold, Super Gold and (very rarely) Platinum awards. Staff were encouraged to issue "possie" slips for outstanding single *ad hoc* achievement—and for accumulated good behaviour and endeavour at certain points in the year with tallies totalled by a member of the Senior Management Team. The registration class with most accumulated points for the session was to be rewarded by a day out for example to Landmark.

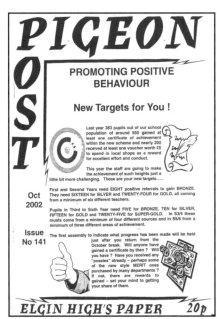

PIGEON POST

PROMOTING POSITIVE BEHAVIOUR

New Targets for You !

Last year 383 pupils out of our school population of around 550 gained at least one certificate of achievement within the new scheme and nearly 200 received at least one voucher worth £5 to spend in local shops as a reward for excellent effort and conduct.

This year the staff are going to make the achievement of such heights just a little bit more challenging. These are your new targets.....

Oct 2002

First and Second Years need EIGHT positive referrals to gain BRONZE. They need SIXTEEN for SILVER and TWENTY-FOUR for GOLD, all coming from a minimum of six different teachers.

Pupils in Third to Sixth Year need FIVE for BRONZE, TEN for SILVER, FIFTEEN for GOLD and TWENTY-FIVE for SUPER-GOLD. In S3/4 these musts come from a minimum of four different sources and in S5/6 from a minimum of three different areas of achievement.

Issue No 141

The first assembly to indicate what progress has been made will be held just after you return from the October break. Will anyone have gained a certificate by then ? Will you have ? Have you received any "possies" already – perhaps some of the new style MERIT ones purchased by many departments ? If not, there are rewards to gained – set your mind to getting your share of them.

ELGIN HIGH'S PAPER   20p

A new system of reporting unacceptable behaviour was also introduced via "misdemeanour" slips and staff were exhorted not to patiently tolerate and cajole unco-operative pupils. However, misdemeanour slips were not to cancel out any "Possies" that pupil had achieved. The front covers of consecutive issues of the first *Pigeon Posts* issued after the scheme's introduction further reinforced and explained the system, as shown opposite.

The specially designed Possie Certificates printed on special parchment-like paper were to become much treasured and displayed on the walls and trophy cabinets of many New Elgin homes and pupils having produced good work often asked, "Is that not worth a Possie, sir?"

The system was refreshed and revised regularly and was still in operation seven years later, by which time the collection of data had been made a lot simpler through IT.

See the cover of PP141 above and a page from an issue in 2008 right.

Connecting Classrooms – A Partnership[6]

The British Council was very clear in the application form. Connecting Classrooms was a partnership between schools in the UK and schools in countries sub-Saharan Africa. This was not a charitable arrangement between schools in the rich world and schools in underdeveloped countries. UK schools were expected to learn with and from the African schools as much as they would learn with and from us. And so it proved to be.

The idea of taking part in Connecting Classrooms occurred in 2008. The project would bring together Elgin High School with its local primary schools and provide an excellent context for developing global citizenship. The first years were a three way partnership between EHS, Greenwards and New Elgin with three schools in Mbeya, Tanzania and the Central Province of Zambia. From 2011 the focus turned to Elgin High School and Mukonchi Secondary School. While visits between the school have provided a focal point and life challenging experiences for all involved, the partnership has impacted on the wider life of the school. Activities in both schools have included: newsletters, website pages, essay competitions on the life of David Livingstone, video conferencing, cooking lessons, art work, assemblies, talks, food demonstrations, posters, surveys, penfriends and much more. In Zambia, pupils at Mukonchi Secondary School have had similar experiences. However, having a school in Scotland to communicate with has provided a focus for their development of ICT. They are now seen as one of the leaders in ICT in their area.

Boyd above right with friend

After each visit, pupils like Boyd Shimwense Jnr were asked to write a reflection on their experiences as either a host or a visitor. Their words provide an insight into what has been achieved by the partnership: but please remember that for Zambian students English is their second or third language….

Boyd Shimwense Junior, Mukonchi Secondary School, 2013

A visit of our partner school from Scotland, Elgin High School was one of the precious moments to the pupils and people of Mukonchi. We had been left with cherished memories. Our partner school, Elgin High School, and our school have made a good foster relationship which has also promoted international relationships. Both have shared experiences of the way of life which is here in Mukonchi and in Scotland.

The visit [in 2013] made pupils and people of Mukonchi learn different things from one another. And some of these that we learnt from one another is how to speak Zambian language and Scottish language. We also learnt how their classes and our classes are being conducted, how these two schools differ in agriculture and how to interact with different people form a different country or race. We also shared some experiences in academic work, and this really helped us to improve our schoolwork and in improving our grammar.

Starting with relationships, internally and externally which has promoted in developing our school and our country Zambia. This has made it possible for some to go and study in Scotland or from Scotland to Zambia if they so wishes and it enables our country to have access to sell its products countrywide freely.

And on 12th July 2013 we had a chance to have a quiz in school we really enjoyed the sharing of ideas and knowledge with our fellow pupils from Elgin High School. And we also shared a lot and even learnt from one another. We also taught one another about our great hero David Livingstone, who died in 1873 and was born in 1813. We discussed his life history from the time he was born until death. This really helped to understand his early life. During class we learnt things that were very important, we asked some questions about David Livingstone.

The visit also enabled us to share some life experiences in terms of weather and geographical features, especially on sunlight. There in Scotland sunshine is rare but they were surprised to find that here sunlight is always there. They were also surprised to find that there is no snow in Zambia. This again helped us to understand that in some countries snow is there and the way these people survive to live in these cold places.

We also taught one another about the disease that is at high risk in both countries here in Zambia and in Scotland, and how people who have this disease are being treated. We discussed the common disease which is here in Zambia which is HIV/AIDS and people who are found to have this disease are being supported by the government while there in Scotland HIV/AIDS is not a common disease. But for those who are caught with it, the treatment is the same. We also learnt from them that in their country gay practice is accepted but here in Zambia it is not. This helps us to know how some countries respond to such practice and the laws that they apply.

We also learnt from one another, how these two schools, Mukonchi and Elgin differ in agriculture and the importance of agriculture to the people in Mukonchi. We went around to find out the type of crops and how they grow them. We discussed some crops that are grown here, like maize our staple food, cotton, tobacco, groundnuts and soya beans. All these crops are grown here in Mukonchi in different amounts, but the most common crop is maize. Maize is one of the major crops which is grown here in Mukonchi. Maize is one of the major crops we have which is used as mealie meal. It also helps people to find money to buy their children school materials and other equipment, when they reap their maize and sell them. And not all can afford to buy mealie meal. Some would prefer to grind maize so that they can have mealie meal and it is also a source of income when the country sell the maize outside they can earn foreign exchange which enables the country to cover its debts and other financial problems.

Rose Kendall , Elgin High School pupil - 2015

A series of snapshots:

Rose face painting

Bumping along in the dark, in an unknown country, packed 5 people across 4 seats in the back of Mukonchi High school bus. Everybody is tired but, through the mumblings of conversation, Natasha [one of our new Zambian friends] starts to sing. It's a western song, John Legend I think, and we all know the words. Jane [another Zambian friend] joins in and within moments, the entire bus is singing. Different first language, relative strangers, different culture, a different continent, and yet, when two Zambian girls begin to sing, we're all together, just young people giggling together.

Standing in the bright morning sun in the dusty centre of Mukonchi Basic School, the excited chatter of children almost overpowered by the rhythm of stamping feet and the deep song of "Welcome to Mukonchi" of the school choir. We are swathed in children, head to toe in green uniform – fraying and unravelling around the edges but topped with grinning smiles, waving hands and dancing feet. A little girl skips by, dancing and shuffling her feet. She catches my eye and I copy her move. She giggles and does it again. Other children begin to notice and join in. I glance across to Caitlin who also has a growing group of children laughing and leaping around her. Laughter was my overriding memory of the Basic school .

It's about 9pm, right in the middle of a scheduled power cut. Some of the girls from the dormitories who had joined us for the evening to chat and play board games are about to make their way back from our guesthouse. We're outside and the sky has taken our breath away. We end up lying on the sand with two Zambian girls, discussing our aspirations (they wanted to be a nurse and a teacher) under the massive, twinkling African sky.

'Once in a life time opportunity', was the wrong phrase to use to describe the trip prior to going. I know that now. I truly think that someday (and pretty soon I hope), I will return and create yet more memories I will treasure. I'm glad that modern social networking is allowing me to stay in touch with the friends I made in Mukonchi and that the trip did not end when we got off the plane at Aberdeen. I carry forward with me friendships, revelations and memories and look forward to sharing our experiences with those in the community so that the link with Mukonchi spreads further than the dozen of us that travelled to Africa. Thank you for a wonderful, awe inspiring trip.

Ellen O'Hare, Elgin High School – 2016

On Tuesday 23rd August 2016 myself and 3 pupils, who visited Zambia back in 2015, went through to Aberdeen to welcome our Zambian visitors. Jhene was one of the Zambian pupils visiting who I had met last year on my trip where we became good friends and kept in touch since. She approached me with a hug and excitement in her voice as she was looking forward to staying with me and my family for the next 10 days. Before heading back to Elgin we took them to McDonald's for lunch where it was interesting to see that they were unsure on how to use the cups, as they just removed the lid instead of using the hole in the lid for the straw.

Ellen front right on new school inspection visit

The next 10 days were nothing like I had experienced before. It was an interesting experience as me and Jhene both have different cultures and ways of life which to begin with that was difficult for her to understand, but she was able to deal with within the first few days. Zambia being a landlocked country means that maybe Zambians have never seen a beach or know what it is. My family took Jhene along to Lossiemouth Beach on the Wednesday evening for a walk, where there was a lovely sunset but it didn't quite compare to an African sunset! After the walk of course we had to go Mieles ice cream shop, where Jhene had chocolate and vanilla. Although it was quite a cold evening, especially for her, she never *complained about the cold as she really enjoyed the beach and overall she said it was her favourite activity and feature about Moray.*

Showing Jhene and the other Zambian visitors around our school made me realise just how grateful we should be for our school, as it reminded me of their school and just how different they are. Yet there are so many children that don't attend school just because they don't want to, but there are millions of children across the world that don't have an education. My experience of being in Mukonchi and our Zambian friends being over here, have really just shown me that I shouldn't take school for granted for as simple as it seems many children see this as their way to achieve a better life.

Having this partnership with Mukonchi has made me realise the friendships that have come out of this and that even a year after seeing these friends we still remember each other, which is an amazing thing to have. From being over there myself in 2015 and making close friendships to them coming over this year and being so excited to meet again just made me realise how much of a difference a simple friendship can make to both our lives and theirs. Having Jhene over and staying with me has really strengthened and grown our bond as we had so much time to spend together, whether it was one on one or in group of other friends.

Although Jhene and our Zambians visitors are back safely in Mukonchi we still keep in very good touch through Facebook or WhatsApp. I hope to see Jhene again at some point in the future whether I go back to Zambia, which I hope to do, or if Jhene returns to Scotland. However even if that does not happen we will still remain friends and continue to keep each other up to date on our lives.

Charles Simenda, Mukonchi Secondary School - 2016

A visit to Spynie Palace - *We visited Spynie Palace with other pupils from Elgin High School, who were learning about History. I learned that this palace was a residence of bishops of Moray and the location of the palace was chosen because of the coast nearby. The palace was built in 1200.*

A visit to Johnston's Woolen Mill - *This visit was one of the most interesting places I visited in Scotland. When we were going round Johnston's I learned a lot of things. The building was built many centuries ago and has been making beautiful knitwear, clothing and accessories from*

Charles in an H.E. Lesson

Angus Lawson sharing musical experiences

A Social evening in Mukonchi 2013

A discussion group on the UN Charter on the Rights of the Child

Drumming workshop in Livingstone 2015

the most luxurious wools, since the building was made. This has contributed to the development of Elgin and Scotland.

***A visit to Primary Schools -** In all the Primary Schools we visited I have observed one thing about young pupils and that is they all have excellent behaviour when they were in class and outside class.*

***Activities -** There were many activities that we could do in Scotland and these activites were planned by members of staff in Elgin High School Thanks to them all the activities they planned were very interesting and made me learn something new. These are the list of activities: Ice skating,Ten-pin bowling, Edinburgh Castle and Edinburgh Dungeon*

***Elgin -** What I thought about when I visited Elgin High School is that, Scotland is a very clean country, a nice place to stay, has a good climate and good temperature and the most important thing is there is no noise pollution but where we are from there is loud pollution. There are also very beautiful houses, not to mention that Elgin High School is quite well planned and an organised school compared to Mukonchi High School.*

***Friends -** There is a lot of things that I learned from my friends at Elgin High School as follows: their cultures; how they learn in class; their way of life; how to socialise with others; how to count in French from 1-10; that phones are allowed in school but not in class time.*

The most important thing I have learned from my trip to Scotland is that it was a really great experience as it allowed me to learn about other people's cultures. In addition I learned that it is important to share good ideas with global partners such as between Mukonchi and Elgin High School and that sharing knowledge helps to build the relationships that we have. It is a way of providing guidance, support and counselling instead of testing others. It means acting like family, caring for one another and teaching each other how to be successful and productive.

Many other curricular innovations could be described in these pages in detail. like imaginative Induction experiences for the new S5 and S6 cohort each June (look for reports/photos in the first PP of any new session), how the school coped with the new Inclusion agenda which saw "Special" schools closed and 99.9% of pupils from our catchment areas schooled on campus (PP 112), or the Promoting Positive Behaviour agenda (PP 136) or Solution Oriented Approaches to Problem Solving (PP 156) or other aspects of Umoja (PP 166) but there isn't enough space to do each of these justice. Details of these and a handful of others, however may be found in the pages of *Pigeon Post* as indicated in the Highlights synopses, and in the General Index. However let's finish this section with something most unusual, the arrival in school of.....

An Artist in Residence

Many schools had invited onto their campus creative artists like poets, novelists and musicians to inspire pupils with an all-to-brief talk and Q&A session, before he or she moved onto a neighbouring school the next day and so on. Elgin High had welcomed both Ian Rankin and Mark McManus in recent memory. This was and is commonplace and has its own fascination of meeting "someone famous". However, largely because our Art Department had spare studio capacity we were able to receive onto our campus an artist who would join the department, Perthshire born sculptor Dr Alan Watson, (*left*) for *four months*— November 1992 to the following March, as reported in PP 93.

The artist-in-residence schemes were established in Scottish schools but relatively rare because of financial and resource considerations. Elgin High's experience was to be the third run under the auspices of GRC with previously successful schemes run at St Machar Academy and Westhill Academy in Aberdeen. Dr Watson moved into Z12 to continue his professional practice as a sculptor but with the difference that instead of concentrating solely on his own projects would engage, advise and inspire pupil artists and in general to raise the profile of Art within the school on a day to day basis as well as with one-of displays and exhibitions.

Writing in PP 94 (February 1993) Dr Watson explained that he had had settling in challenges, not having been in a school since he'd left Blairgowrie Academy in 1978. Naturally he found the period bell system unnerving and the masses of pupils who passed his door soon after each sounding. He explains there that he was working with three S3 classes on sculptural projects two using withies to "draw in space" and create humanlike figures whilst the third was producing cardboard relief constructions. Pupils were encouraged to visit the Z12 studio at lunchtimes to chat with him and ask "awkward questions" about the design and creative process.

Dr Watson with pupils.... Fiona Brands, Lisa Allan, Scott McKenzie Ilona Davies, Scott McKenzie and Gary Wright.

Finally as detailed in PP 95 (June 1993) Dr Watson held an exhibition to mark the end of his residency. On display at this were pieces created by the pupils he worked with and some structures he himself had created in his time with us.

A fitting conclusion to a section which has been very much about hands-on learning approaches.

There was a second, much shorter Artist in Residency experience, when Nairn based artist Sean McDonald spent eight days with pupils, spread over two months in May –June 2004. See details in PP 150 and the photo below.

Footnotes

[1] "Now, what I want is, Facts. Teach these boys and girls nothing but Facts. Facts alone are wanted in life. Plant nothing else, and root out everything else. You can only form the minds of reasoning animals upon Facts: nothing else will ever be of any service to them. This is the principle on which I bring up my own children, and this is the principle on which I bring up these children. Stick to Facts, sir!" (ex *Hard Times* Chapter 1)

[2] The Raising of the School Leaving Age (from 15-16), known by the more pronounceable "ROSLA" in England

[3] The Mode 3 version meant that for any school courses were D.I.Y. - to be entirely devised and crafted for your own local context.

[4] For example the local Moderator for English was Mr Gerry Haines of Keith Grammar School

[5] Based on the author's Post Script article in PP90 (June 92)

[6] *Connecting Classrooms* section contributed by Mr Andy Simpson

8 Curricular Innovation No.2
by Andy Simpson

2008 and beyond!

Our second Headteacher picks up the story of how the school kept in the forefront of curriculum development.

By 2008, times were changing in Scottish education (again). A new contract for teachers, a new Curriculum for Excellence and a new qualifications system looming on the horizon were all making an impact on schools. Elgin High School was not immune from the changes. Along with many schools, an expectation to raise attainment and aspirations was becoming a key driving force. When Judy Ross left in 2009, a landmark was reached and EHS moved into a future without any members of staff who had been appointed in1978 when the school opened.

Methods of communication were also changing. Previous generations of senior pupils had eagerly devoured the daily copy of *The Scotsman* newspaper. Around this time, as a money saving measure, this was stopped. No one complained. The digital age was taking over. Efforts to produce *Pigeon Post* – or a successor – were tried on several occasions, and each failed to develop into something sustainable. Instead the school website was becoming the preferred method for highlighting the achievements of pupils and the school. This allowed an immediacy for news stories as well as the extensive use of photographs and videos. However, if pupils and their families enjoyed seeing the pictures, the regular structure provided by *Pigeon Post* was not yet there. The systematic record of the school life could become lost in a plethora of files containing countless pictures that digital photography made so easy to take.

You Tube and Social Media Likes!

The world of social media also provided opportunities. YouTube proved to be an excellent medium for recording and publicizing films of key events. These ranged from class productions in Drama through to charity events and extracurricular activities. At the time of writing, (November 2017) the most viewed films included the Ice Bucket Challenge of 2014, PE department activities on the beach at Lossie, a tour of the school building dubbed into Polish, The Great British EHS Bake Off charity event in 2015, Goodbye to the 6th Year of 2016, and the Rights Respecting School Award pupil video. All these received well over

Agadoo—World Record attempt: December 2015

1000 views. However, the most viewed EHS video was the "Agadoo World Record Attempt" at Christmas 2015. Along with pupils from Greenwards, Mosstowie and New Elgin primary schools there were more than enough people to break the world record. Sadly, despite exceeding the required numbers of participants, and having local Rotary club members present as external checkers, the technicalities and lack of clarity of the Guinness verification procedures meant the official world record was not to come to EHS. However, over 7200 people have viewed the video. Not bad for a school of under 600 pupils as there were at the time.

However, when Moray Council relaxed its regulations on the school use of Twitter and Facebook, Elgin High School was one of the first to take advantage. Starting with a "Head Teacher" Twitter account it was not long before several departments were tweeting. Information and pictures of EHS successes were being followed by pupils, parents, colleagues in other schools, Moray Council staff and national educational bodies as well as the public in general. Facebook followed and the EHS pages became the normal method of celebrating the successes of the pupils as well as for disseminating news. The record for the highest number of "hits" on the Facebook was set on 23rd June 2016. The announcement of Hugh McCulloch's appointment as Head Teacher reached over 13,000 people by midnight! However, this figure was well overtaken by the invitation to view the old school building that was seen by over 45,000 people in September 2017.

Celebrity Speakers

EHS regularly welcomed speakers both to subject classes and to assemblies. These included a professor of science (as part of the Moray Science week), an astronaut, top chefs, best selling authors, politicians, medical students, a peer of the realm as well as successful sports personalities. However, one visitor stands out and deserves a separate mention for the impact that he had on not just the pupils and staff, but also the community. In 2008 EHS was awarded two places on a trip to Auschwitz organized by the Holocaust Educational Trust. The senior pupils returned deeply moved and keen to spread the messages they had learnt from their experiences. This became a regular trip and in 2011 the seniors were successful in inviting Zigi Shipper to Elgin. Zigi was born in Poland and spent time in Auschwitz as well as other concentration camps. He very quickly won the hearts and minds of EHS. As an 80+ year old he amazed everyone by being able to speak, without notes, for over an hour. All were held spellbound by his account of his experiences and were receptive to his final message to 21st century young people – "do not hate". The horrors and suffering that people had learnt about in the classroom, seen on television and in films, they now heard first hand for themselves. In 2013 Zigi addressed the annual prize giving ceremony – that year held in the Town Hall. As each prize winner received their award they had their photograph taken with Zigi. Hopefully, in years to come Zigi's story and message of "no hatred" will live on. When future generations of teachers are delivering lessons on the Holocaust to the children and grandchildren of the prizewinners, the pupils were challenged to allow these photos to be taken into class and shown off with the comment "my parent met a holocaust survivor".

AQA-tics!

Elgin High School has always prided itself in being a "truly comprehensive" school – catering for the needs of a wide range of pupils. Throughout this period, the school became a magnet for pupils arriving in the area from a variety of countries. On arrival, many of the young people spoke very little, if any, English. There could be a sense of justifiable pride from parents, teachers and the young people themselves as they gained confidence in the English language and then moved on to positive destinations, including several who gained entrance to university. To support these young people Elgin High School became one of the very few schools in Scotland to be a registered centre for AQA, the English based exam providers. This allowed pupils to sit A Level and GCSE Polish – with great success. One of the highlights of 2010 was when a group of Polish students prepared and delivered an assembly to  mark the death, in an air crash, of the Polish President, as pictured above. All EHS pupils were able to join them in paying their respects at a time of national tragedy.

The young people based in Kestrel House continued to receive a rich and varied education – including gaining a number of SQA awards at a variety of levels. This included making very good use of Riding for the Disabled, as well as the facilities at Cedarwood, the Leisure Centre and Gordonstoun School. One of their many highlights was a concert performed in front of the public in the St Giles Centre. This was to mark the publication of a music book by one of the teachers. For their talents the pupils received much praise from the shoppers who clearly enjoyed the performance.

During these years, Elgin High School continued to develop its standing in local and national activities. Pupils from the RME department regularly won national prizes in the Inspire Aspire competition. Teams from the Mathematics department frequently travelled to Glasgow to represent Moray in the Maths Enterprise competition. A few pupils successfully managed to reach the European stages of the Maths Challenge competition. Under the guidance of the librarians, pupils enjoyed great success in the Grampian Book Awards competition. Designing posters for the Edinburgh Fringe, Science Haiku, Space School at Stathclyde, Young Chef and Rotary are just a selection of the competitions where EHS pupils excelled and were able to display their talents against local and national standards. The English department also supported pupils having compositions published and had a winner of the prestigious national Pushkin Prize.

Young Citizen Awards

In 2010 Moray Council, along with Diageo and Grampian Police introduced the Moray Young Citizen of the Year awards. This provided an ideal platform for EHS pupils to shine and for the achievements of the school to be recognized by a wider body.

The first individual winner was Chloe Fraser, pictured at the ceremony, right. In 2012, she was followed by Holly McKenzie. Angus Lawson won in 2014 and Scott Fiske in 2015. Four individual winners in the first six years of the awards scheme is impressive by any standards and reflected the quality of the pupils in EHS, as well as the opportunities given by the school to allow them to show and develop their skills. This is particularly evident when the list of commended and highly commended individuals is added.   These included: Sarah   Fiske,   Sandra Zakrzewska, Kerrie Short, Sinead

Gray (in 2013 and 2015), Callum Jacklin, Ross Dethick, Siobhan Duncan, Chloe Sutherland, Lindsay Johnston, Michael Gates and Ryan Denoon. Each individual had an impressive story of success and achievements – often in the face of significant challenges. The Awards system also had categories for groups. The successive groups of pupils who visited Zambia won the international section several times in recognition of their work not only in Zambia but before and after the trips with their contributions to the school and wider community. The pupils who went to China in summer 2015 were also winners. In the local group section, EHS had success with the Skateboarders, SAMH supporters, S4 Participate class and the Events Management Team. Two of these individual winners, Siobhan Duncan and Sinead Gray, also won national recognition. In 2016 they were recognized with the Diana Awards for their volunteering work in school and the community. They are probably the only pupils in Moray to have received this highly prestigious achievement.

National Awards

Elgin High School also demonstrated its successes by gaining recognition from a number of national bodies. A silver Eco School award demonstrated a commitment by pupils and staff to saving energy and an awareness of environmental issues. The anticipation of the new building, prevented further progression that would have required longer term changes to the old building and grounds – much of which was included in the design for the new grounds. EHS was also the first secondary school in the area to achieve the silver level as a health promoting school. A folio of pupil and staff activities and policies was put together for a gold award, but the scheme was suspended while changes were introduced. Fair Aware status was gained by the inclusion in the life of the school a variety of Fair Trade activities - including using fairly traded ingredients to make home bakes for sale at the Elgin Big Breakfast organized by the community fair trade group. Success was also achieved in Social Enterprise competitions through groups organized by the Guidance team. EHS twice won the prestigious British Council International Schools Award. This reflected not just the Zambia partnership, but also a wide ranging of activities that promoted global citizenship. Included in this was (pictured on previous page) the International Day of Languages held in September. On these days, almost every department, through their own subject areas,

International Day of Languages activities

demonstrated the relevance of studying modern languages. Very recently EHS became the first secondary school in Moray to achieve level 1 of the Rights Respecting Schools Award. This is a demanding international standard and demonstrated that the principles of the United Nations Charter on the Rights of the Child is embedded within the life of the school.

In 2012, Elgin High School was one of the first schools in Moray to participate in the Youth Philanthropy Initiative (YPI). This involved teams of pupils competing to win £3000 for a local charity. The money and scheme came from The Wood Foundation. This was delivered through the RME department and found a very appropriate place in the third year curriculum, shortly before the pupils moved into the Senior Phase and exam preparation. This often provided an exciting climax to the third year. In small groups pupils had to make contact with a local charity and then convince a panel of judges that awarding their charity the £3000 would make a significant difference to a social issue. Many used the opportunity to find out more about a charity that supported a challenge faced by someone in their own family. Not only did pupils find out about what was happening in the community, but many ended up getting involved with charitable work – spending time fund raising and working in the evenings. On one occasion EHS became the first school in the area to welcome Therapets in to support pupils preparing for exams – a practice that has become common in many other schools across Scotland. The YPI final also gave the groups to demonstrate presentation skills learnt across the curriculum and an immense variety of powerpoints, drama, poetry, songs, videos as well as colourful teeshirts and cuddly mascots always impressed the judges.

Growing seeds for the ISS: 2016

The YPI activities also illustrated the links and partnerships that EHS developed with many groups and organisations in the community. Local businesses, the neighbouring primary schools, 39 Regiment of the Royal Engineers, RAF Lossiemouth, voluntary organisations, the health service and almost every aspect of life was brought into the pupil experience. EHS even had a partnership with the International Space Station. In the year when Tim Peake became the British representative on the ISS, Elgin High pupils were growing seeds that had been in space and comparing the results against seeds that had never left earth's gravity. The results from EHS (and the other schools taking part) will contribute to development of food supplies for future space missions.

Attempting to condense eight years of the life of a school into a few pages inevitably means that many important events will be omitted through lack of space. My most glaring omission to this point has been the day to day work in the classrooms and teaching practical areas of the school. On a regular basis my senior colleagues and I were able to spend a complete day following individual pupils from class to class. One of the abiding memories of these days was the rich variety of activities and learning experiences that pupils encountered in a six period day. The range of topics and skills that challenged the pupils was amazing. The dedication of staff in seeking to tailor the learning to meet the needs of pupils was impressive. It clearly demonstrated the success the school has had in preparing pupils for the next steps in their careers after leaving school. From professional rugby players to environmental researchers, from apprentice joiners to doctors, from actors to care workers the curriculum and wider experience of Elgin High successfully continued to set young people up for life after school.

"Working Together For Success"

A number of years ago, when asked to come up with a slogan that summed up the values and characteristics of EHS, a group of staff, working with pupils, chose the phrase "Working Together for Success". "Work" took different forms at different times – and often included great fun. "Together" involved countless people, including parents, staff and the community alongside the pupils. The word "for" points to a purpose in what was happening – preparing the young people for their futures. "Success" was found in a wide variety of forms for pupils of all ages and skills.

This motto will continue into the new build and provide an exciting and appropriate education for future generations of pupils at Elgin High School.

Calcultta Cup 2008-09

Badaguish Challenge April 2016

Donation made to mark the life of
Andy McIntosh

Moray Science
Festival, with Prof
Coustra from Heriott-
Watt University

Leah Stuart with Olympic torch

Moray Netball Champions:

May 2015

Moray Young Citizens' Award
Winners 2015

9 Pupil Voices :
Letters to the Editor,
Pupil Councils

Consistent with promoting a sense of community and the creation of a pupil-centred school, Elgin High's leadership team were always keen to consult pupils on various issues. They wanted the pupil voice to be heard in a variety of ways, such as writing to the Your Letters pages of the school's own monthly newspaper, meeting formally with House Council reps, Pupil Council reps and with The School Board, first elected in 1978 (names given in PP 1). This latter august sounding body comprised – in modern political jargon – representatives of the school's stake-holders - parents, teachers, pupils and outside agents.

Your Letters

Pigeon Post published many observational letters in its early days with pupil comments on some topics showing great righteous indignation. In fact very much as letters to *The Northern Scot*, for example, have done in recent years on the subject of local wind farms!

Two hot topics early on were the inclusion of Primary School material in *Pigeon Post* and then the access to and distribution of the newspaper itself, which was delivered to New Elgin Primary and Greenwards Primary on the evening of *the day before sale* in Elgin High. Because of this it quite possibly found its way into some homes via staff still in primary school office and staffroom after close of school! Each edition was keenly awaited, with a flurry of activity on the typical Friday publication morning when sold in our Community Area between 8.15 a.m. and Registration. A summary of the contents would already have been leaked to friends by the class of compilers and staplers the day before and broadcast in the daily bulletin in advance to promote sales.

PP#2 and #3 include letters of complaint and responses about this topic....

Dear Sir, My first impression of Elgin High is "Super!" I like all my teachers and like most of my subjects. The first Pigeon Post was really good and I hope it will be a good success. The only thing I object to, as do my friends, is the Primary School getting into our magazine. (PP#2)

Dear Sir, I was most disappointed to read in last month's PP that one of the High School pupils objected to other schools being allowed to subscribe to your magazine. We are all future pupils of Elgin High and find the magazine interesting and informative. When we hear of football hockey or rugby games it is Elgin High who get our support. So Elgin High objectors think back to not so long ago when you were primary sevens. Would you, if given the opportunity not have enjoyed taking part in a senior school's newspaper? (PP#3)

But there were other issues to grouse about....

Dear Editor, My friend and I have a complaint to make about rugby. Last week we asked to join the rugby club and were turned down. We find this appalling. There should be girls in the rugby club, or even a girls rugby club since the boys won't let us join theirs. We were told at the start of term that everything was fair for both and female, so what happened to RUGBY ? Two disappointed second year girls (PP#1)

Dear Sir, We are writing to you to complain about the lines on the football and Hockey and Rugby pitches. They are too hard to see at present because they blend in with the grass. We would like to see them in white because white is easier to see. (PP#2)

Dear Sir , After attending the introductory meeting of the Centre Elgin High, we were surprised and shocked to find that smoking would be allowed for 13 year olds and over. We think that this encouraging people to take up the DIRTY habit of smoking. (PP#2)

There were, more pleasingly of corse, plenty of positive opinions about the new school...

Dear Sir, I am writing to say how pleased I am with E.H.S. The first month has been great and I don't have a single complaint to make. There are so many activities and subjects that it took me a while to settle in but now I am even managing to memorise some of my timetable. I think EHS is great and the only thing that could be done in the way of improvement would be to abolish Maths and English. (PP#2)

Dear Sir, I think we are very privileged to have a Rector like Mr Hope who shows so much interest in our sport and setting up the Community Area like it is and organising disco's which so far are a great success. The machines which have been installed in the dinner area seem very popular and have not yet been mistreated or damaged so let hope it stays that way. At most hockey practices we have Mr Hope comes along to give us good coaching. I've never seen any other Rector take so much interest in Girls Hockey. One day he was out in his track suit all ready to do business while other Head masters just ignore us and bother about boys football.... (PP#2)

The Letters pages of *Pigeon Post* continued to be a source of interest and amusement for many editions to come.

The Pupils' Council

The first Pupils' Council comprising 12 First Year and 12 Second Year pupils had been elected by ballots held at morning interval and lunchtimes on Friday 15th September, 1978—that is within a month of the school's opening. Much canvassing preceded the elections with candidates addressing their peers in some registration classes. "I'll be available all day" claimed one girl. "That's what she thinks!" replied Mr Hope. Also elected were 16 House reps from the four Houses, Kestrels, Falcons, Ospreys and Eagles. No photo of this council was published but see page 6 of PP1 for names.

Our second 20+ strong pupil representative council was elected at the start of session 1979-90. Photos of this Council appear in PP19 (a good quality one reproduced below in the June '80 Summer Special) and on the cover along with a reclining Percy claiming "it's the Percy Council" on the cover of PP13 (Nov '79). As Bill Hope explained in his "Headlines" column in PP12, two pupils from the PC had been co-opted to the school Finance Committee which was already pleased about our purchasing better printing equipment for school worksheets (oh, and for *Pigeon Post*!)

In the first election (PP11) seven pupils in the new S1 plus six in our first S3 were elected unopposed, but in the S2 constituency there was competition and following ballots in registration on September 14th six pupils were chosen.

It's fair to say that several members of this first Council, chaired by Kevin Reid with Lynne Craib as Secretary, played leading roles as they progressed through school in public speaking, contributing to *PP*, plays and in sport, notably Neil Proven, Susan Sutherland, Iain Catto and Gary Robertson (S1), Sarah McGregor, Wendy MacGillivray, Teenie Cottam, Paula Aldin and Douglas Scott in S2 and S3s Roy Young, Shirley Moir, Lynne Beaton, Douglas Logan, Kevin Reid, Lynne Craib and Bryan Shortreed. Few of this group were "shrinking violets" and all left school as very confident individuals.

As the school grew councils representing each of the four Houses were formed, sending delegates to the full Pupils' Council meetings held during the school day in class time, requiring absence from lessons - sometimes a sore point with staff. Members of the House Councils were profiled each year in *PP* in order to publicise who reps were when pupils wanted issues raised.

Summaries of PC discussions and decisions were published regularly in *PP* and their role became an established one in the life of the school, being revised and refreshed from time to time (e.g. cf PP 63).

Our second Pupil Council elected at start of session 1979-80 Ex PP 19 (June 1980)

Back (l-r) : Bryan Shortreed, Douglas Logan, Kevin Reid (Chair), Roy Young, Lynne Beaton.

Front (seated): Gary Robertson, Shirley Moir, Neil Proven, Stuart Speake, Sarah McGregor, Elsie Geddes, Paula Aldin, Teenie Cottam, Sharon Duroe, Wendy MacGillivray and Iain Catto. (Absent from photo are Lynne Craib, Janette Brown, Susan Sutherland, Neil Shiach and Douglas Scott).

As the sessions passed pupils were given more and more responsibility. Organisation of the regular discos, the festive season celebrations, the organisation of Children in Need and other charity collections, the Talent Contest (see List of winners in Part 2) and some comedy sketch shows and concerts all fell to the Pupil Council.

PRC 2003/4 *right*

124

10 Parent Voices :
EHSA, The School Board
Community Involvement

The initials "E.H.S.A." (The Elgin High School Association), made with a primitive stencil, stand out in early editions of *Pigeon Post*. It was decided not to call the body a "PTA" (Parent—Teacher Association) as that seemed to exclude non-parents and we wanted to attract other "friends of the school". And as it turned out, it wasn't the only thing that was named using finessed vocabulary.

The purpose of a traditional PTA is to raise money for "extras" - for The School Fund, to purchase things a school needs but which cannot be afforded from its "per capita". *That* term refers to the money each school got for each head or pupil in the school, depending on which year they were in. For example, a school might get in any given year £35 for every First and Second Year, £60 for every Third and Fourth Year and so on, which when aggregated gave the school its main budget.

One of the main ways of raising money for The EHS School Fund was advertised in the local press and school bulletins as EHSA-organised "Tea & Competitions". There were indeed light refreshments at these events. However the competitions were rather familiar and went a bit like this…..Every person paying to take part was given a unique piece of paper, rather like the illustration *right* and there would be a caller out in front with a little ballot machine containing numbered balls. These were spun and taken out in turn and the first person to spot a pattern of achievement on their own piece of paper shouted out to claim a prize. This is probably ringing bells with you by now…. However this was a competition that dare not speak its name, because that would be "gambling".

The EHSA was formed on the evening of October 3rd 1978, when a few months after the school opened a look-around-the-school event was organised for parents and some from those attending a special meeting on the night were called upon to create a school support group. The first events it organised (PP 2) were a Beetle Drive (some of you may need to look that up), a quiz evening including a Staff v Parents event and an outing to Eden Court Theatre, Inverness to see Rikki Fulton and Walter Carr in "Cinderella". The Beetle Drive on Friday 10th November was attended by over 100 people, won by First Year pupil Gordon Duthie and had some bizarre prizes (see PP 3) including that for Best Grannie. The event offered refreshments, brought in by the public and so much food was donated that supper bags were offered for people to take home what they could not eat! A very good start then, if you recall that at this point the school had just over 200 pupils.

PP 4 carries the picture opposite showing the staff quiz team comprising Mr McKay, Miss Ross, Mrs McPherson and Mr Ledingham.   The text is too poorly reproduced in our extant copy to know who won, but you know—the Olympic spirit is the important thing!

Parents v Staff in Quiz Team Competition

Events continued on an almost monthly basis throughout the first academic session with a dance in February at the St Leonards Hotel ("Tickets £4   Dress optional..")   The last detail indicated the intended informality of the occasion and not that it was for naturists!

March saw the first of the euphemistically entitled …

E.H.S.A.

TEA AND COMPETITIONS
EVENING !!!
in Elgin High Community Area
at 7.30pm on Friday 9th March
Refreshments Provided

entertainment referred to above: intimation from PP 6. By now, bringing along sandwiches and cakes etc to share was an established practice. In May there was a Car Treasure Hunt followed by Staff v Parents Sports events on a warm (?) Summer's evening.

Friday 19th saw a double bill sponsored by Elgin High School Association – at 6.30 pm the Treasure Hunt was set in progress with 23 bewildered sets of passengers madly studying the 28 clues that had been set by Messrs Hendrie and Hope. What seemed to be a simple course really found people out and reports from the course constantly indicated that the staff were in difficulty – couples were seen arguing in the middle of the main road;   one couple were reported to be going in the opposite direction to everybody else, one member of staff ended up at Dr Gray's looking for "Tardis" and others ended up at the Cathedral looking for what St Giles said to the angels.   These reports caused some surprise when the competitors were never supposed to be in Elgin.

Despite these alarms, there were some very good scores and the first prize of a £5 voucher went to our Librarian, Aileen Marshall (John and family are still claiming that they helped), second prize went to the family Duthie and third prize to Mr and Mrs Hector.

The Car Treasure Hunt involved around two dozen sets of participants driving away from the school with the passenger clue spotter grasping a sheet of cryptic clues such as "Near the Aberdeen end of the A96 look out for a lot of elderly European gentlemen". (The solution to this was the row of white topped *poles* leading up to Barmuckity Farm!!) You were given a set time to complete the nearly two dozen plus clues and presumably some kind of warning to "drive carefully"! See part of report above from PP 9.

By now such a good spirit had been inculcated between the school and community that although it was officially run by staff, it was unthinkable that EHSA folk should not have a major input into the biggest event of the school's existence to date, as advertised on the cover of PP 9.

The Fête, coordinated by Music PT Sheena Cowan was a little rain-affected, as reported in PP 10, but attended by between 600 and 700 people and raised well over £1K for The School Fund. Stalls included cakes & candy, win a goldfish, lucky teddies, bottle stalls and Wheel of Fortune etc. Entertainment and displays came from our gymnasts, our majorettes, Moray Model Club, Elgin Silver Band and a local Pipe band.

Percy Pigeon chipped in by getting some of his mates from Arbroath to come to Elgin and invite people to pay to guess the time the best of them would take to return home. Apparently that journey, some 100 miles by road took just over 1 hour 52 mins for the fastest pigeon, named for the day "MacLachlan's Magician".

By the end of our first session, between them pupils, staff and EHSA together had created a great community spirit which was to be the hallmark of the school thereafter.

You will find accounts of activity under the aegis of EHSA for the next three decades in the pages of *Pigeon Post* but let's sample just one such report, from PP 60, for May 1987 (right).

Here you see the pattern established in the first year continuing with popular monthly events such as Cheese & Wine party, a Disco, Ten Pin Bowling, Whist Drives. However some events are proving less attractive though it shows an organisation confident enough to try new things.

The School Board

However, the government was by then encouraging the formation a new kind of parent-teacher support

E.H.S.A.

Session 1986/7's activities received very good support on the whole. The Cheese and Wine evening, Disco Dance, Ten Pin Bowling and three Whist Drives were very well supported, but for some reason attendances were low at the Beetle Drive and the evening with the Children's Panel. However those who did attend these last two events mentioned really enjoyed themselves.

The Association hope to conclude this session's activities on a high note with an Indoor Games Evening on **Friday June 26th**. It is hoped that this event will follow the format of the last hilarious occasion held in 1984, when each eight-person team competed in Fancy Dress. At that time each team consisted of a male and a female member of staff, a mum and a dad, a boy and a girl from the upper and from the lower school.

Those who saw it will long remember the costumes, the Babes team with Roy Young of Technical in a baby bonnet and nappy !! and Mrs Watt's team dressed as Greenwards pupils Remember Miss Judy Ross and the Sunflowers and the sight of Mr Donald Morrison dressed as Santa was enough to drive everyone to Lappland.

It is hoped that the format of this year's event will be similar with obstacle and novelty races, a tug-o-war contest and Beat the Goalie. So do make a date of it.

FRIDAY JUNE 26 Games Hall 7 p.m.

Admission Free - Light Refreshments on sale.

organisation, to complement a PTA type body—The (elected) School Board. But it took Elgin High some time to get one organised.

A formal photograph of our first such Board appears on the cover of PP 78, (for March 1990) shown on the next page...

Your School Board, pictured at their first meeting held in our
Learning Support Suite on Tuesday March 13th: (see page two:)

From left: Rev Gordon Cowie, Mr Ernie Pearson, Mrs Vera
Cruickshank, Mrs Angela McCalman, Mrs Ann Wiles, Mr Bill Hope,
Miss Martina Hickey, Mr Jim McDonald, Mr James Goodlet.

In the accompanying article, *Pigeon Post* Pupil Editor Andrew Cowie (then in S5) gave brief details of membership and purpose. The Board was comprised of voting members, elected after a ballot—five parents : Mrs Vera Cruickshank, Rev Gordon Cowie, Mr James Goodlet, Mr Ernie Pearson and Mrs Ann Wilson, two staff members : Mr Jim McDonald and Mrs Angela McCalman and two non-voting members, our Rector and Miss Martina Hickey the school's Community Education Officer.

The business of the first meeting including co-opting two additional members, (who would most likely come from willing members of local business or commerce), appointment of a clerk and as the Board was to have rolling membership, decisions on how long each of those present would serve, for four or for two years to allow later new blood. Board Meetings would normally be open to members of the public to observe.

Already you can see that this was quite a different type of body to the EHSA, one intended to represent the parent body on matters of more serious import.

Boards had been established by an Act of Parliament in 1988 but did not prove very popular, with apathy in many constituencies across Scotland when elections were organised. It was intended that once established Boards would offer views on school policies, objectives and ethos and act as a conduit between the school and its catchment area community and approve the way in which the Rector's annual budget was spent. Board members could also sit on interview panels when new staff were being appointed. Perhaps because of the success of the EHSA there was little enthusiasm from the parent body to elect a Board for Elgin High initially as we struggled to form one.

Changes were made to the composition of School Boards after ten years allowing for more co-option where elections were not attracting enough candidates and they were finally dispensed with via an Act of Parliament in Holyrood, in 2006.

From that date onwards parents were to be represented by Parent Forums and Parent Councils.

Reports on *EHSA* activities continue to be found in most editions of

E.H.S.A.

The recent visit to the pantomime at Eden Court was a success. The acting, scenery and costumes were excellent, but the band was considered to be too noisy and tended to drown out the voices of the singers.

Wednesday 13th Feb saw the Whist Drive take place in the Lecture Room. A warm welcome was extended to both new and experienced players.

This year's Tea & Competitions evening will take place on Wednesday March 20th at 7.30 p.m. Among the many attractive prizes on offer will be a butcher's voucher for £25 and a lucky winner will also be given £50 to spend on groceries.

Proceeds from these events are to be given to the school for the benefit of the pupils therefore prizes for the bingo and raffles would be most welcome. So too would donations of cakes or sandwiches.

If you would like to donate anything please let Mr Crossland or Hope know as it will aid them with their planning.

The **Whist Drives** organised monthly by the ladies who used to be on the Committee continue to be well attended and very popular. The average attendance means we can usually run nine tables. See your school calendar for notice of the next one.

Plans are at an advanced stage for the **Annual Quiz Night**, which will take place on Friday March 3rd – 7.30 p.m. for 8. There will be a Bar available. The format will be as in previous years – teams of up to four people and all questions will be team ones with answers being written down so no one need feel embarrassed if they don't know an answer.

The questions are of a standard that ensures most teams score highly making it a friendly enjoyable evening. Winners cannot consider them masterminds. A supper will be included in the price which is £3 per person, £12 a team. Last year 21 teams took part and we hope this number will be exceeded this year. Why not come along and surprise yourself ? You probably know a lot more than you realise !

Answer sheets will be provided so all you require is a pen and some cash .

Pigeon Post like the one *above* from PP 84 (for February 1991) and the one *left* from PP 128 (from February 2000), the detail of which is effectively interchangeable but you will find little in our pages about what School Boards did unless you scrutinise the Rector's regular *Headlines*, where was obliged to report on their contributions towards school decision making.

11   School Shows

Oh For a Stage!

For some of the most confident and talented individuals in a school, the chance to perform on a stage in front of their peers was both nerve wracking and irresistible. Shows in the form of short plays, sketch revues, full scale musical productions, musical concerts, dancing displays and the Talent Contest (see tables listing these last three forms of entertainment in Section Two) were highlights of each session and well publicised, recorded and reviewed in the pages of *PP*. As in many other schools certain productions involved pupils and staff interacting both back stage and on the boards, a challenging and rewarding experience for both.

However, there were always production difficulties, the school having been built without a traditional hall with a small curtained stage provided in most school buildings to date. Having to improvise in "a (*expletive*) café" as one member of staff notably remarked meant overcoming the challenges of raising the performance area to enhance sightlines and bringing through from the Drama Studio hundreds of metres of ugly electric cable spaghetti and spotlights, all gathered up and bolted to the roof in a kind of Heath Robinson way.

The main challenges that came with putting on productions on raised and cramped staging in the Community Area were - there was no Stage Left, but conversely a huge Stage Right in which those waiting to go on would be corralled waiting seldom quietly. So, many productions were punctuated by staff exhortations to "SSSHH!" and "Please be quiet!" to the excited thespians.

Nevertheless, in our first academic session there were five productions coached by four different staff stage directors held in three separate places, two of which were off campus for reasons as explained above.

Foiled Again!

This absurd Victorian melodrama by Paul Groves and Nigel Grimshaw was staged in a competitive drama festival in Elgin Town Hall on 17th January 1979. The director was Mr Derek Ross, who was also staging two players with Elgin Academy players in the same festival!! Adjudication came in the form of sympathetic comments from no less a personage than the veritable Mr James Scotland. (See report in PP 5)

The script was designed for hamming up and it's fair to say it was: it raised the roof, possibly for the wrong reasons. For one very enthusiastic but nervous performer Fraser Cluness, a mute role was specially created by Mr Ross. With scene changes going on, in front of the curtain, Fraser as a totally bored and dishevelled Stage Manager would spend two minutes (several times) meticulously sweeping the stage from right to left and then from left to right – you've got it.

His performance was regarded by many who witnessed the spectacle as the best thing in the show. This play would be staged three times in the school's history.

Photo from the 2005 Northern Scot production *Times Gone By* (reproduced with permission) .

Tam o' Shanter

Though not a stage production, there followed soon after a second hilarious dramatic event that first January – an enactment of the whole narrative of Burns' famous poem, directed by Mr Donnie MacLeod. As the various scenes unfolded our PT History Mr

Back (l-r) : Richard Anderson (as Uriah Creepe), Avril McKnockiter (Narrator), Robbie Allen (Constable Moses Plodington). Maureen Gow (Widow Frailbody), Heather Gerrard (Nelly Whortleberry) Andrew Edwards (the evil Sir Jasper Devenish) and Fraser Cluness (Stage Manager).

Kneeling in front: Brian MacGillivray (Enoch Strine), Kim Kerr (Lavinia Frailbody), Caroline Pirie (Scene Setter) and James Laird (Hector Sturdily).

James Hamilton recited the poem from memory – pausing for gusts of laughter from the audience at our first Burns Supper. This is depicted on the front cover and within PP 6, and in PP 10, where - as Tam, James Stuart – more Benny Hill than anything else - just manages to cling onto his pantomime horse, played by Hamish Hyndman and David Gardener.

Easter One Act Plays

Their first staging began a tradition with English teachers directing short plays, played in the Drama Studio before tiny paying audiences, usually of friends and relatives on raised seating.

At Easter 1979 Mr Jeff Dugdale produced two One Act Plays which seemed to have entertained S1 and S2 classes in classroom readings. However, these were quite dated and couthy Scottish pieces intended for adult actors : *The Pie in the Oven* by J.J.Bell and *The Centre Forward* by Neil Grant.

The first of these plays produced a notable moment when Richard Anderson, appropriately named P.C. Duff, occasionally forgetting his lines through nerves, had to be prompted by Mr Dugdale, from behind the scenery. The line he usually forgot was "It's a total disaster!" He was not far off the mark and it is fortunate that no video exists of this performance. (See Mr Hope's sympathetic review in PP 8).

Players (l-r): Sharoe Duroe (Flora McNab, the love interest of P.C. Duff) Richard Anderson (P.C.Duff, bashfully seeking permission to "walk out" with Flora), George Brandie (the stern Mr McNab, Flora's suspicious father), Carole Lawton (the weary Mrs McNab). Photo by Mr Ledingham - PP 10.

The second play was a little better and being about football possibly attracted more interest.

Players: Andrew Lowrey, as dashing Roy Gordon in the title role), Janice McKillop (Janet Leitch, his love interest), Gerald Craig (Mr Leitch), Angela Watt (Mrs Leitch) all target Gordon Duthie (Sandy Leitch) asking him "Why did ye dae it!" (Sandy had been impersonating Roy in order to get attention from the girls). Photo by Mr Ledingham - PP 10.

Pilgrim and *Tom Sawyer* (excerpts)

The final productions of the year were staged in New Elgin Primary School Hall in late June: "Pilgrim" by Michael Hall and Excerpts from "Tom Sawyer" by Charlesworth & Brown based on Mark Twain's novel. The producers of these two strongly moralistic dramas were respectively English teacher Mrs Linda McPherson and Remedial teacher Mr Donnie Macleod. Pilgrim and his wife were played by Julie Stephen and Lorna Alexander. Tom Sawyer was played by Geoffrey Lee on the Tuesday (and on Wednesday by Kenny Green) with Angela Watt as Aunt Polly and Richard Anderson giving us his Parson Dobbins. Photos and report in PP 10 .

Above left Aunt Polly (Angela Watt) and Parson Dobbins (Richard Anderson) reprimand Tom Sawyer (Geoffrey Lee). Above right Tom Sawyer (Kenny Green) is shown scheming with his gang

Photos by Mr Ledingham : left in PP 10. and right previously unpublished

Later Productions

Restrictions of space mean we can make only scant allusion to later productions but below is a comprehensive list with reference to the issues of *Pigeon Post* where you can read all about them in detail with reviews and many photographic illustrations. The complete archive of 171 *Pigeon Posts* is available through the Dropbox Archive curated by Leon Lumsden : see **pigeonpost.info**

1979 December : *Joseph and His Amazing Technicolor Dreamcoat*

by Andrew Lloyd Webber and Tim Rice

Musical Director: Mrs Sheena Ledingham   Stage Director: Mrs Anne Duncan

Featuring: Kenny Green (as Narrator), Neil Proven (as Joseph) Richard Anderson (as Jacob *and* Pharoah) Sarah McGregor (as Jacob's wife)   Sharon Duroe (as Mrs Potiphar) and Gary Robertson (as Napthali).

Lorna Alexander, one of the Adoring Girls (the others being Lynne Craib, Carole Lawton, Audrey Smart, Paula Aldin, Janice McKillop and Marie Young) recalled on the Facebook FP site in 2017 how Neil Proven used to get terribly embarrassed when the girls "adored" him *en role*. See PP 12 for full cast and PP 15 for reports and photos. The cover of PP 15 shows Neil and Richard (in both roles).

1980 Easter One Act Plays

The Bloaters by Ella Adkins directed by Mr Dugdale, Report and pictures in PP 18, PP 19

The Bloaters cast: Back (l-r) Sarah McGregor, Jill Ellwand, Douglas Pirie Front: Paula Aldin, Elizabeth Wheeler, Angela Watt, Janice McKillop, Michael Pirie. Photo by Mr. Ledingham

Ernie's Incredible Illucinations by Alan Ayckbourn directed by Mr I.Hamilton, featuring Gary Robertson as Ernie

Back (l-r) Iain Catto, Gary Robertson, Fraser Cluness, David Bremner, Benny Johnstone, Andrew Allan.

In front: Richard Anderson, David Gray, Jeb McLeish, Kevin Walker, Susan Scott, Ian Still, Carole Lawton, Lorraine Allan, Teenie Cottam, Elizabeth Wheeler, Marie Young. Kneeling: Marlyn Roy and Lorna Alexander. Photo by Mr Ledingham in PP19

1980 December *Babes in The Wood* pantomime

Principal Players: David Grey, Jeb McLeish, Angela Watt, Carole Lawton, Douglas Scott, Richard Sundalskliev, Richard Anderson, Stephen Campbell, Anna Hamilton and Douglas Logan.   Musical Director: Mrs Sheena Ledingham   Stage Director: Mrs Anne Duncan

See PP 23/24 for rather poorly reproduced pix

1981 Easter One Act Plays

The Dear Departed by Stanley Houghton produced by Mr Dugdale, featuring Sarah McGregor, Gary Robertson, Angela Watt, Douglas Pirie, Michael Pirie and Lisa Grant. (Original picture credit: Michael Pirie)

Hijack! by Charles Wells featuring Stuart Chambers, Teenie Cottam, Lorna Alexander, Jeb McNeish, Nigel Squair, Stuart Christine and Ian Edmonstone.

For Photos (as above) and review in PP27

1981 December : *The Wizard of Oz*   by Baum, Harburg and Arlen

Principal Players: Douglas Logan, Richard Anderson, Lorna Alexander, Anna Hamilton, Jill Ellwand, Stewart Christine, Lynne Reid and Brian Johnson.

Musical Director and Stage Director: Mrs Sheena Ledingham

For Photos and review See PP 32 and 33

1982 Easter One Act Plays

Billy Liar (Act I) produced by Mr Dugdale, featuring Douglas Pirie, Sarah McGregor, Angela Watt, Rodney Badenoch, Teenie Cottam and Gary Robertson.

Rory Aforesaid by John Brandane produced by Mr I. Hamilton, starring Ian Edmonstone, Iain Catto, Gary Sinclair, Michael Alexander and Lorna Alexander

For photos and report see PP 36, reprised in PP149 as an archive item

1982 December : *Puss in Boots* pantomime

Principal Players: Debbie Sinclair, Caroline Jefferies, Emma Garvie, Carole Lawton, Jacqueline Melrose, and Gary Robertson with Mr Dugdale as The Ogre.

See PP 41 and 42

Musical Director: Mrs Sheena Ledingham   Stage Director: Mr Phil McMillan

Choreographer: Mrs Carol Grant

1983 December : *Cinderella*

Principal Players: Debbie Sinclair, Emma Garvie, Agnes Gault and Brian McPherson with Mr Finnie, Mr Dugdale (*see photo above*) and Mr Stewart as The Ugly Sisters and their mum and with Mr McDonald, Mr Sturrock and Miss Abel as Superheroes

Musical Director: Mrs Sheena Ledingham   Stage Director: Mr Phil McMillan   See PP 49 ,50 and 51

1984: Easter One Act plays

The Monkey's Paw by W.W.Jacobs directed by Mr I. Hamilton, featured Robert Blyth, Jacqueline Taylor and Thomas Webster in a cast plagued by illness or "the curse"!! (Photo above left). See background story in PP 54.

Money Makes a Difference by F. Morton Howard directed by Mr Dugdale, featured one experienced actor in Brian McPherson, and a handful of novices— Karen McCallum, Charles Grigor, Andrew Pirie and Colin Greenslade.

(Photo above right shows The infamous Meal Scene). See PP 53 and 54

These two plays were prefaced by sketches from Mr McMillan's NEDS group, featuring Gary Robertson, Marie Young, Agnes Gault and Jacqueline Melrose (right).

1989 December : *Oliver!* by Lionel Bart

Principal Players: Leigh Collins in the title role shown on this PP cover), Anne Simmers, Jan Marshall, Jonathan Mackintosh, Richard Duroe and Graeme Roger with Mr Leiper as Mr Bumble and Mr McMillan himself as Mr Sowerberry

Musical Director: Mr Alan Taylor   Stage Director: Mr Phil McMillan.   See PP 76 and 77

1990 Easter One Act Plays

Werewolf in Town and *Little Nellie's Hovel* produced by Mr McMillan's S3 and S4 short course Drama Group

Werewolf – featuring Leigh Collins, Graeme Roger, Clare Anderson, Anne Simmers.

Little Nellie – featuring Jan Marshall, Brian Wheeler, Richard Duroe, James Davidson and Sheila Rowan. Reviewed in PP 79, but no good photos are available.

1990 *Robinson Crusoe* panto

Musical Director: Mr John Watson Stage Director: Mr John Aitken Producer : Miss Norma Neish

Principal Players: Claire Anderson, (shown centre in this photo) Kathryn McInnes, Gordon Thomson, James Davidson, Nicola Dodsworth, Ann Simmers   See PP 82 and 84

1991 June: *Grease*

Musical Director: Mr John Watson

Stage Director: Miss Norma Neish

Principal Players: Gordon Thomson, Claire Anderson, Brian Wheeler, Amanda Hutcheson, Ann Simmers, Richard Duroe, Graeme Roger . See PP86 (front cover opposite) for four pages of photos and review.

1991 December :*Christmas Crackers* revue

Songs, sketches and dance, featuring Suzanne Lynch, Ann Simmers, Graeme Roger, Amanda Hutcheon, Gavin Dunbar, Julie Webster, Yvonne Gregor and many more

Production by senior pupils.   See PP 89 for review, photos and names of all actors, musicians and support team. Photo above of a sketch called "Knickers"

1992 December: *Cinderella* pantomime

Producer and   Stage Director: Miss Norma Neish

Principal Players: Kathryn McInnes, Shonagh Fraser, Julie Webster, Faye Butterly, Ann Simmers Yvonne Gregor.   Roger Scott, Garry Collins, Mrs Ross and Mr Ferguson. Cameos by Mr Dugdale and Mr McDonald.

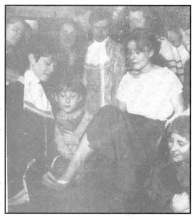

See PP93 for pages of photos and PP 94 review   Photo above showing Shonagh and Kathryn taken from *The P&J* of 12.12.92

1993 December: The Bi-ennial Revue

Produced by Messrs Aitken & Dugdale

Entertainers included: Lee Fawbush, Faye Butterly, Suzanne Lynch, Malcolm Walker, Pamela Lussier, Mark Gravener, Josephine Ho, Colin Reid, Tino Allan and Ryan Harrold.

See: PP 98 for revue review by Dougall Robertson and two pages of pics.

1994 December: *Body Parts* revue

Featuring… Julie Cruickshank, Jodi West, Faye Menzie, Lee Butterly, Rory Morrison, Garry Collins, Richard Gamba, Mark Smith, Liam McBride Pamela Lussier, Colin Reid.

Director and coach Mr Laezer Schlomkowitz, Music : led by two bands under direction by Ryan Harrold and Colin Reid (who is shown singing in "The Lumberjack" sketch).

See PP 103 for photos and review by Dougall Robertson

1995 June : *Fallen Angels* and *Old Comers* revue

Director and coach Mr Laezer Schlomkowitz, Musical Director Mr John Watson

Featuring…Donna Burns, Neil Malone, Jacki Henderson, Debbie Davidson, Neil Rhind, Kelly Slater, Pamela Lussier and many others

See PP 105 for review by Jody Curtis & 106 for photo. In the photo above Neil Rhind as Lazlo Woodbine continues to search for the truth, a running motif throughout the evening.

Alex, Alison, Stephen and Pamela dressed up to visit classes and tout for trade

1995 June *Ebolia* revue

Director: Neil Rhind (S6) See PP 106

1995 December *Avoid the Crush* S6 revue

Directed by Pamela Lussier and featuring Colin Reid

Emma Noble, Alison McCook, Lee Butterly, Tammy McCudden, Richard Gamba, Steven Cochrane and many others. See review by Mr Aitken in PP 108

1996 June: *Little Shop of Horrors*

Musical Director: Mr John Watson
Stage Director: Miss Norma Neish

Principal Players: Garry Collins (shown right on stage with Audrey I and II), Jacqueline Allan, Paul Fyvie, Neil Rhind, Neil Ware

See PPs 109, PP 110 & PP 111 for reviews and photos

1996 December Wall to wall *Cinderella*

Director and coach Ms Liz Turner : see PP 109

1997 June: *Return to the Forbidden Planet*

Musical Director: Mr John Watson   Stage Director: Miss Norma Neish

Principal Players: Neil Rhind, Garry Collins, Michael Duncan, Heather Lawrence, Paul Fyvie
See PP 114, PP 115 (Photos and Review by Mr Aitken)

1998 May : *Foiled Again!*

Featuring... Tracey Sievewright, Scott Thomson, Paul Fyvie, Ross Allan, David Waite, Gemma Hampson. See PP 119 for photos and report.

left : Widow Frailbody (Gemma Hampson) Nelly Wortleberry (Keri-jane Newlands) and Moses Ploddington (Alan Dodd) look in shock upon the corpse of the poisoned Uriah Creepe

2001 June : Nikki Darling's one woman show –

See report and photos PP 135

2004 June : *Dracula Spectacula*

Musical Director: Mrs Diane Pert   Stage Director: Mrs Ruth Ralph

Principal Players: Ben Mortimer, Mrs Joyce Marriott (shown in full flight in this production photo) See PP150

2008 June : *We Will Rock You*

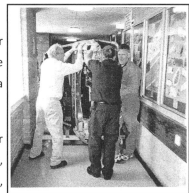

Musical Director: Mr John Watson   Stage Director: Miss Norma Neish

Principal Players: Mr Shaun Paul McGrath, Shelley McDonald, Claire Munro, Ryan Denoon, Fraser MacGillivray and Scot Munro

See PP 169 and 170. Production photos were prohibited by the contract terms but we can show staff struggling to get a real car into the Games Hall as a major prop for the show.

Music in Elgin High August 1978-March 1984

The first 6 years –almost!

So far, we have just recorded with a broad brush the musical activities of the early days of the school, but now a feature with a little more insight, penned by our first Head of Music, Sheena Cowan, now **Mrs Sheena Ledingham**

Before Elgin High School first opened its doors, it had been made very clear that Elgin, and in this case particularly New Elgin, had a long tradition of producing talented musicians and lots of music making. So the pressure was on for Elgin High School to maintain and hopefully, enhance that talent and tradition.

The first PT Music was Miss Sheena Cowan, who, at the tender age of 23 was deemed "too young" in some people's eyes to lead the Music Department. Bill Hope attended a social gathering shortly after her appointment and was told "you've gone too far this time!"

At the time of opening in August 1978, the Music Department was not quite finished, so music was put in a room on the top floor which would later become Mr Allan's Modern Studies room. This proved to be somewhat of a challenge as a piano had to be moved up from the ground floor. However, with the help of a local delivery firm, the piano was upended into the lift and soon reached the top floor- much to Miss Cowan's horror! It did not go back down the same way! The Music room was worth the wait and was greatly envied by some other schools in the area. Because of its remarkably high vaulted roof It was named "the Cathedral" by the contractors!

The first instrumental instructors were Inga Gibb—strings, Ella Taylor – 'cello, Pam Gillan—piano, Bill Armstrong - brass and Shona Gidney – woodwind. Isobel John soon joined as percussion instructor and Linda Emslie took over as woodwind instructor. These instructors were all very talented musicians and they produced many good players in the school. They also took instrumental groups who were involved in school concerts and Prize Givings.

Other musical groups were quickly established and rehearsals took place for the first concert which was to take place in December 1978. This concert featured two choirs, percussion group, recorder group, brass group as well as several soloists. Mr Gavin Currie, PT Music at Forres Academy, assisted as accompanist. As there was no school hall, difficulties had to be overcome to stage this in the community area. This remained a challenge for every production/concert.

At the end of that first year were performances of "Tom Sawyer" and "Pilgrim". These took place in New Elgin Primary. Many of the principal players went on to take major roles in subsequent productions.

As the school grew, bigger and more adventurous productions were possible. *Joseph and his Amazing Technicolor Dreamcoat* was performed in December 1979. Who can forget Richard Anderson's performance of Pharaoh (Elvis!). The brothers were, by and large, the boys choir (pictured, from PP19). Our first pantomime, *Babes in the Wood,* was performed in December 1980. This was followed in December 1981 with *The Wizard of Oz* and in 1982 by *Puss in Boots*. These productions all had large casts. *Cinderella* followed in  December 1983 where the musical director was Mr Peter McKay and it featured quite a number of staff. Details and photos for all of these productions can be seen in the relevant issue of *Pigeon Post*: see listings in previous pages and under "School Concerts" in Part Two of this book.

Over the years, other performance groups were established. The guitar group/folk group regularly entertained at care homes and hospitals accompanied on guitar by our talented Depute Head Alistair MacLachlan. A Gaelic choir was established to take part in the local Mod in Forres. Mr Donnie McLeod -Learning Support PT and native Gaelic speaker and singer- trained the choir in Gaelic language and stylistic detail. This choir won their class and brought a trophy back to school. They were also the only entrants in their class!

A string group also started rehearsing which was followed by a school orchestra. This featured instruments you wouldn't normally find in an orchestra but there was lots of enthusiasm. The woodwind group and madrigal group also played an important part in the extra-curricular life of the music department. All of these groups were up and running in the first four years of the school.

Ian Wallace's 1981 photo of the first school orchestra: Back (l-r) Shirlene Adam, Douglas Logan, Iain Still, Jennifer Young

Front: Anna Hamilton, Gillian Murray, Andrew Marshall, Lorraine Waterson.

Performers need a platform to perform and pupils were encouraged to do so at many events. There were three "Café Chantant"s – 1981, 1983 and 1984 (*below left*). In these informal concerts all groups took part, as well as soloists, duets etc. Our annual Burns Supper—*see next page*— provided a platform for solo singers and fiddlers as well as the opportunity for community singing and learning some Burns songs. The school was well represented at Moray Music Festival in 1980, 1982 and 1984 with some very good results. Groups and/or soloists always took part in the Prize Giving at the end of the school session.

As we a community school, groups regularly entertained outside school at hospitals, day centres, homes, clubs etc. Each Christmas, New Elgin's senior citizens (*below right*) were invited into the school for entertainment, tea, mince pies and a blether! Sometimes this was a concert and other times a show. These

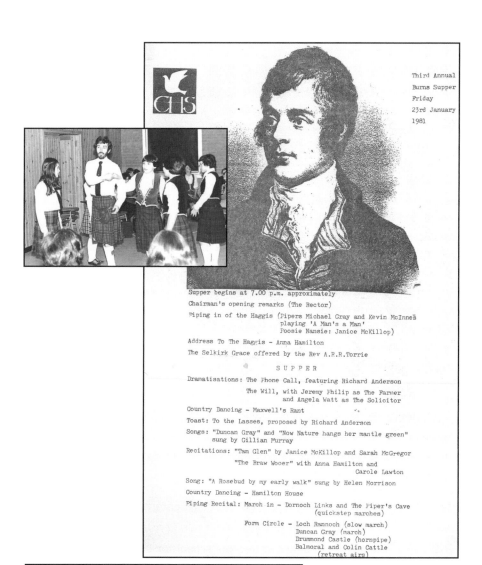

Third Annual
Burns Supper
Friday
23rd January
1981

Supper begins at 7.00 p.m. approximately

Chairman's opening remarks (The Rector)

Piping in of the Haggis (Pipers Michael Gray and Kevin McInnes
playing 'A Man's a Man'
Poosie Nansie: Janice McKillop)

Address To The Haggis - Anna Hamilton

The Selkirk Grace offered by the Rev A.R.R.Torrie

S U P P E R

Dramatisations: The Phone Call, featuring Richard Anderson

The Will, with Jeremy Philip as The Farmer
and Angela Watt as The Solicitor

Country Dancing - Maxwell's Rant

Toast: To the Lasses, proposed by Richard Anderson

Songs: "Duncan Gray" and "Now Nature hangs her mantle green"
sung by Gillian Murray

Recitations: "Tam Glen" by Janice McKillop and Sarah McGregor

"The Braw Wooer" with Anna Hamilton and
Carole Lawton

Song: "A Rosebud by my early walk" sung by Helen Morrison

Country Dancing - Hamilton House

Piping Recital: March in - Dornoch Links and The Piper's Cave
(quickstep marches)

Form Circle - Loch Rannoch (slow march)
Duncan Gray (march)
Drummond Castle (hornpipe)
Balmoral and Colin Cattle
(retreat airs)

Programme for 1981
Burns Supper dancers led
by Mr Carstairs and
singers Gillian Murray
(left) and Helen Morrison

148

were always very popular and well attended by the community.

Opportunities were available for pupils to go on theatre trips to Aberdeen, Inverness and Edinburgh to experience the thrill of live performances of musicals. Places were always in great demand.

Some of the earliest pupils went on to study music and became music teachers themselves. They are still teaching today. Others continued their interest in their chosen instrument and became members of bands, theatre groups, choirs etc. (See chapters on Former Pupils.) Some, have even taught their own children how to play!

Right a clipping from the *Evening Express* for February 1995 showing Anna Hamilton pictured as a junior pupil on a previous page, starring in the Aberdeen Operatic Society's production of *My Fair Lady*. Anna herself is now a Music teacher in Aberdeen. See PP: 103

■ **FAIR LADY:** Anna Hamilton as Eliza

Some Important Musical Events which took place after 1996

Scottish Opera Workshop

Members of the school choir took part in a joint venture with Milnes High and Scottish Opera. The choir learned various songs before a workshop which took place at Milnes High. On the day of the workshop, Scottish Opera personnel put both choirs through their paces to create a show called "Showtime". Moves and costumes were added, and, in the evening, the show was performed in the auditorium at Milnes High for parents and friends. The choir thoroughly enjoyed the experience of working with professionals.

Moray Music Festival Millennium Moravian Suite

Elgin High School choir joined the Moray Music Centre choir and Moray Music Centre orchestra to perform Moravian Suite 2000 at the final concert of Moray Music Festival 2000. This piece was specially commissioned by the Music Festival committee to celebrate the beginning of the new Millennium. It was written by Jim Letham and contained local references and tunes. The Music of the Spey was the basis for one of the movements. This was an amazing opportunity for the choir and they thoroughly enjoyed the experience.

Hightime

A concert was held in Elgin Town Hall which brought Elgin High together with its three associated Primary Schools. Each school provided musical items for the concert and the Grand Finale was a performance, by all performers, of the song "Hightime" which was written by guitar teacher Andy McIntosh. All the pupils enjoyed performing to a packed Town Hall, as illustrated from PP 157 below.

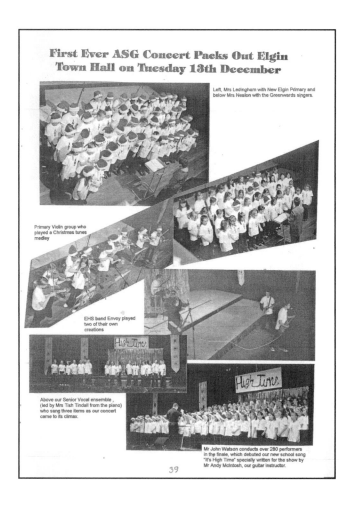

First Ever ASG Concert Packs Out Elgin Town Hall on Tuesday 13th December

Left, Mrs Ledingham with New Elgin Primary and below Mrs Nealon with the Greenwards singers.

Primary Violin group who played a Christmas tunes medley

EHS band Envoy played two of their own creations

Above our Senior Vocal ensemble, (led by Mrs Tish Tindall from the piano) who sang three items as our concert came to its climax.

Mr John Watson conducts over 280 performers in the finale, which debuted our new school song "It's High Time" specially written for the show by Mr Andy McIntosh, our guitar instructor.

39

A Dramatic Time

*Mrs **Anne Duncan** our first Head of Drama and later Depute Head writes about her experiences during her first spell working with Elgin High actors*

Leaving Forres Academy to join the staff at Elgin High was like stepping into a different world. The first a school with a long history and many traditions—the second brand new and good to go! As the PT Drama I also taught at all the associated primary schools which was an excellent way to get to know the locality, the community and the pupils who would ultimately join us at the High School. Elgin High was a vibrant and stimulating place to teach. Under the leadership of Bill Hope new ideas were explored and developed but never at the expense of the quality of the learning and teaching experienced in the classroom by the pupils. Pupils seemed to be aware that something new was on offer and they rose to the challenge. Extra-curricular clubs and societies thrived. Perhaps the lack of senior years in the school removed all the usual inhibitors from the younger age groups?

I have fond memories indeed of a large number of pupils. I can never hear the soulful music of Gerry Rafferty's 'Baker Street' without visualising the school dance group performing to it at the monthly disco. Our first large scale school production of 'Joseph and the Amazing Technicolor Dreamcoat' (*photo here and next page*) alerted me to the extent of community support: bribes were even offered to try to secure tickets which sold out at an amazing rate. Plays, pantomimes, those were the days when every department that could, supported the school show and the atmosphere leading up to each event was brilliant. The audience response on the night always compensated for that exhaustion which overcame the production team at show end.

As far as teaching my subject was concerned I relished the fact that Drama was a non-certificate subject in those days. Yes, pupils could actually spend an entire period with no pen nor pencil, no worksheet nor folder and certainly no homework! Ah how things have changed. Cross curricular work between departments was prevalent and a true eye opener for me. As a subject considered 'superfluous' in many other schools, collaborative work with the Business Studies, Geography, History and Music departments let the pupils (and me) experience the value of drama both within and out with its usual spheres. Truly exciting times.

There is a danger, in hindsight, of rose coloured spectacles. In trying to capture the essence of my first eighteen months as PT Drama at Elgin High I eventually realised the impact that short period had on the rest of my career. I had the privilege of conversations with teachers who were later to become leaders in national developments. In those early years the school didn't publish 'core values' or 'mission statements'. Nevertheless its staff had a genuine belief in creating a community that met the needs of those it served – its pupils. Elgin High celebrated the achievements of all every month and the publication day of *Pigeon Post* was eagerly anticipated by pupils, parents and friends. How fitting that as the pupils and staff settle Elgin High into its new building that a book celebrating its wonderful legacy is shared.

12   PIGEON POST

The Story behind the Stories*

My first experience of school journalism was as a pupil at Arbroath High School,

whose secondary department I attended from 1960-66. I recall each year in the Summer term such a buzz amongst some of the senior pupils who formed The Magazine Committee and a real sense of excitement when *The Magazine* arrived in bound piles from the local printer.

I was involved in my Fifth and Sixth years making small editorial contributions, but my keenest memories relate to the strong chemical smell of the newly opened magazines crisply printed on glossy paper – and of each pupil's rush to buy a copy and get as many people as possible to sign the front cover.

At Aberdeen University I enjoyed leafing through the student newspaper *Gaudie* but had no real interest in being part of the production team so when I was appointed to

Mr Dugdale is second from the right in this section of a photo of S5/6
Boys from the 1965 *AHS Magazine*

153

my first teaching post at Forfar Academy in 1971 I took only a passing interest in their school newspaper *Sirius* which was produced every now and then (when there was enough material for it) by one of the Art Department staff. The newspaper however was much more topical and lively than the solemn Arbroath High *Magazine* I recalled and I liked its brevity (6-10 sides), its topicality and the fact that you paid only a few pence for it and then discarded it or passed it on.

My extra-curricular interests in that first post lay in sport, organising inter-house competitions in rugby, football, debates, quizzes etc so it was not until I arrived as Assistant Principal Teacher in the English Department of Banff Academy in 1975 that I decided to become involved in school newspapering. I had a lot of encouragement in doing this from the Senior Management Team and within a few months I had produced the first issue of *Vivat* – so called because the school motto is the Latin tag "Vivat Academia" (Long live the School). The first edition comprising 12 A4 sides of white paper produced @ 4 pence went on sale on a Friday in March 1976 and we immediately sold out all 750 copies, which meant that every second pupil or so had bought one.

Vivat was thereafter produced monthly and I was editor for the first 23 issues until May 1978 when I left to become Head of English at Elgin High. In addition to the regular issues, produced in portrait format, each summer there was a much thicker edition printed in landscape and bound with tape over the stapled spine to make it look different - and a couple of specially themed issues for example about local fishing communities, traditions and practices.

So in coming to Elgin High, it was the most natural thing for me to want to continue to produce a school newspaper. Indeed the last issues of *Vivat* and the first of *Pigeon Post* are clearly out of the same stable, though the production values of EHS's first issues were not as high as those I'd been used to at Banff because at first we had much poorer equipment.   The first issues of *Pigeon Post* were produced using a Gestetner machine, which involved my typing – I've done most of the typing/word processing of *Pigeon Post* myself across the years – onto a long sheet or "skin" of specially prepared waxed paper.   Errors on this were very difficult to correct neatly.   This sheet was then strapped onto a cyclostyling machine which noisily and with considerable chemical smell churned out your sheets of paper, a very primitive form of our modern school digital printer, which in retrospect looks very crude.

In fact it was essentially because of the volume of printed material required for so many copies of *Pigeon Post* which was originally produced every month, that it was decided in 1980 to buy firstly a second-hand off-set litho machine, which because of its weight just about wrecked our lift in raising it to Z floor!. Later came along completely new off-set litho equipment which greatly enhanced *Pigeon Post's* appearance. If you look through back copies of *Pigeon Post* you can quite easily tell when these changes took place.

The first issues of *Pigeon Post were* printed by our A/V staff and collated and stapled by pupils and staff usually during a single English period. Each had 30 A4 sides and was supported by lots of local advertising and many contributions from our associated primaries. These not only made those schools feel part of our community in a real sense, preparing their pupils for coming up to the "big school" but also provided us with a bigger sales catchment area.   The contents of an early issue which you can see by flicking through the *Pigeon Post* archive on line at **pigeonpost.info** will give you an idea of how the newspaper has changed compared with the final issues produced ten years ago. *Pigeon Post* – under the banner "Elgin High's Monthly Newspaper" - continued to be produced eight times a year until late 1984 when there was a major break in production since an embargo on teachers getting involved in all extra-curricular activity had been

decreed by the teaching unions because of a long running major pay dispute. So edition #59 (December 1984) was followed by edition #60 in May 1987! By that time I had been appointed as an Assistant Rector but the newspaper still continued to be produced monthly until the start of 1988 when my work load meant it had to be reduced from eight issues a year to five and it continued with that regularity for the next twenty years.

Across the years a number of staff and pupils were very significant players in our newspaper production. My first colleague in the English department, Mrs Linda McPherson (above left, pictured in 1978 was most enthusiastic as was photographer Mr Nick Ledingham (PT Science and then PT Chemistry) and cartoonist Mr Maurice Jackson (PT Art & Design) above centre and right respectively

Latterly I had tremendous support from my English colleague Ms Donna Innes whose classes regularly contributed editorial content. Mr Mike Crossland our Technician produced his valuable column on Road Safety for over 20 years. In terms of production, Mrs Fay Watt and a series of colleagues like Mrs Jackie Hay were tireless in maintaining the high standard of printing. My wife Eve Archer, who has a tremendous flair for graphic design, produced some of the most striking covers during the last decade of the newspaper's production. You won't find it difficult to spot them.

From time to time particularly enthusiastic pupils emerged and were given lots of responsibility for helping with the editorial content as Pupil Editor or Senior Reporter, the first of these being Ian Wallace who retired as Chief Inspector of Police with Grampian half a dozen years ago. Since the Millennium such pupils as Gordon Lowe, Rachel King, Lauren Campbell, Sean Dawson and Callum Reid to name but a few have been stalwarts in these roles. A number of pupils who cut their reporting teeth on *Pigeon Post* went on to make journalism an important part of their life such as Gary Robertson (of BBC Radio and TV fame), Beth Dawson (*The Herald*) and my editor Andrew Cowie (*Clyde & Forth Press*).

Pigeon Post won awards from *The Scotsman* newspaper in the early 1980s and from *The Northern Scot* in the Noughties but the biggest reward for me was to see how each edition sold so well and how the paper was always looked for as production day loomed. Latterly we were producing 230 issues and those left after school sale were made available to the public at Adolfo's chip shop so that former pupils could keep up to date with news of the school.

Across my 30 years in the school I was asked many times by colleagues from other schools amazed at the newspaper's continued existence, "How do you manage to keep it going?" as they had tried to produce a similar newspaper and succeeded for a couple of issues before enthusiasm waned and effort dissipated. You might think that the answer is to have a small group of enthusiastic and committed pupils – an equivalent of The Magazine Committee from my days at Arbroath High – but this is not the answer for two reasons.

Firstly "committed pupils" is something of an oxymoron: there are too many other competing interests for young folk – and that is a good thing - for them to be faithful to *one* extra-curricular activity for very long, with some outstanding exceptions. And secondly, having a newspaper committee to rely on makes the production of the paper seem rather elitist or cliquey to those excluded who then are possibly demotivated from offering copy. My approach was always to seek for one or two keen bodies and work with them but to be prepared to approach any pupil or group of pupils to contribute to any edition: I can honestly say I very rarely rejected any freely volunteered contribution of writing because I realised the kudos pupils enjoyed in having their work published for their pals to read – and sometimes mock!

Pigeon Post lays a claim to being unique in Scottish school journalism history and possibly further afield – as over 171 editions it has covered every noteworthy story in the history of the school since it opened in 1978 till Summer 2009. More than that, an image and short profile - and in many cases much more - of over 99% of the pupils who attended the school in those years appeared in its pages!! This was because at first teaching class and then later registration class photos were used alongside pupil penned comments about themselves, in series such as "Classpot" and "Classified Information".

Below from The Northern Scot *of June 28, 2002 the Pigeon Post team who won The Best Newspaper Award: Back l-r reporters Rachel King and Lauren Campbell, printing technical assistants Mrs Lorna Adam and Mrs Fay Watt, Mr Dugdale and front, beside Rector Bill Hope, reporter Sean Dawson and cartoonist Euan Sinclair.*

I suppose the real answer to how *Pigeon Post* kept going for so long is that I always found it so much fun to do regardless of the hours of word-processing, photograph taking and page design - and the smiles from pupils on each issue day always spurred me onto the next edition.   Photo above reproduced from PP 169.

The Second Coming of *Pigeon Post.*

In mid-August 2017 I learned of the Facebook site, "Former Elgin High School Students" created by former pupil (FP) Gary McKinney eight years earlier. When my application to join was accepted the site had around 450 members and was ticking over without much being added to it, though legendary EHS Technician and FP Roy Young seemed to be adding photos to it regularly. I started contributing scanned pages to it from my collection of *Pigeon Posts* in my study at home and all of a sudden interest in being an EHS FP seemed to rekindle and flare up. I then began to add large parts of past *Pigeon Posts* daily and through the suggestion of FP Leon Lumsden complete issues were scanned and put on the cloud facility Dropbox - **pigeonpost.info**

Within a month of the start of *Pigeon Post* pages appearing on the FB site, many FPs were contributing their own pictures and souvenirs like old Yearbooks they had made in Sixth Year and membership of the site grew five-fold, standing at the time of writing at just over 2,600.   In order to contribute pages of *Pigeon Post* to the site or the cloud I had to scan thousands of pages but the positive reaction from site members was so encouraging this became a joy and not a chore. I was "doing *Pigeon Post* again" in a very real sense. If you wish you can see all 171 copies of *Pigeon Post* (minus the advert pages) and various subsets like registration Classes, Sports teams, Percy Pigeon cartoons etc on the cloud where they are preserved for posterity.

Writing on the FB former pupil site in October 2016, Lorna Alexander seemed to have summed up the value of the *Pigeon Post* archive with these comments, which were much "liked"...

"There will always be that narcissistic element to it, but there is also the reconnection with old friends and the desire to show our partners and children unseen aspects of our lives. Many of us will have moved about and unless mum and dad have old school books, pictures and such secreted in the attic we have lost school work and records of achievements. There is also the fact that especially in the early years photos were not as available as they now are, so these little snippets of ourselves are welcome reminders of our youth and the uncomplicated days of childhood to adult. For some the best days of their lives, for others a time of confusion, struggle and maybe even bullying, these insights reminding them of how far they have come".

---

* This section is an abridged and updated from an article on the history of *Pigeon Post* in issue #169 (May 2008)

Striking Front Covers Across the Years

Interlude No.2

Doos' News

Slightly amended from the author's Editorial to the first edition of *Pigeon Post* [1] in September 1978.....

"...Perhaps a word of explanation of our name is necessary? My first idea on learning that our school symbol was to be a dove (from Doo'cot Park behind B&Q in New Elgin) was to call the school newspaper by a rather fancy name – "Hi-fly" perhaps - and then the hilarious "Doos' News" found favour with colleagues at The Haugh, until we struck a middle course and chose our present name".

But I couldn't get "Doos' News" out of my mind and so each edition was to carry a page or more of brief and light-hearted tittle tattle or gossipy items - "stories from around the lofts" - sometimes referencing photos which had inspired or complemented the items on the opposite page called "Doos' News Views" (!!). Below I have gathered together (with minor editing) some of the best of these curios for your amusement. Naming the staff involved in most cases is fair game but where pupils are concerned unless it's absolutely necessary to make sense of the story the name of the pupil has been redacted out of professional respect. But, of course, by looking up that edition[1] referred to at the end of each item you can find out identities and further detail of what you don't know or simply can't remember....

BOGGED DOWN – **Mr Douglas Campbell**, Assistant Rector, found himself in dire straits on the morning of 22nd August (the day school opened for pupils). He realised he had locked himself into the staff toilet (opposite the Conference Room) which because of the school's incomplete state, had no handle. He escaped via the route of the proverbial three old ladies and was rescued by **Depute Alastair Maclachlan**, who reassured him that he had had a similar experience himself. (PP#1)

COWBOY HOPE – Amongst the thousand and one things **Rector William Hope** has turned his versatile hand to since arriving in the new buildings was a spot of cattle herding – in the school grounds. On the morning of 5th September three calves escaped from a nearby field and cantered about at the back of the school. A local farmer, assisted by our intrepid Rector quickly ushered the stray beasts back to their field. (PP#1)

SKLEF - **A pupil** whose hysterics at our visit to see "Joseph and his Amazing Technicolor Dreamcoat"" were almost as entertaining as the show itself caused some hilarity on Wednesday 4th October when, whilst discussing in an English lesson with Mrs Linda McPherson a splinter he had had in his finger, he informed her that Mr **David Cameron** (pictured) had seen it and had offered to take it out with "his biceps" - but he was having none of it! (PP#2).

FREUDIAN SLIP – We're all working hard here at Elgin High. No more so than Geography P.T. **Alister Hendrie.** However what do you make of an identification badge made up for him by our all-purpose lady Miss Karen Seiche, which read "Blister Hendrie" ? Surely he he's not all that hard-worked?? (PP#4)

MISUNDERSTANDING – Prefacing a lesson on a Sherlock Holmes story **Mr Jeff Dugdale** asked 2C about other fictional detectives and got the obvious names of Kojak, Columbo, Starsky and Hutch etc. "Now then," he asked, seeking to add historical dimension to the discussion "which of these would you say was the most dated?" **A pupil** bamboozled him by suggesting Starsky and Hutch. Why, young Lady? "Because they're the best looking, sir!" She certainly added hysterical dimension to the discussion. (PP#5)

PUTTING YOUR FOOT IN IT – Mr Jim Hamilton's First Year classes have recently been doing some research into people's surnames. They've learnt for example how some nobles' names like Bruce came from France (de Brus) whilst others, those of the common people, were sometimes related to their place of origin or their job e.g. Baxter (a baker), Cordiner (a shoemaker) and Webster (a weaver). Pupils were asked to do their own  research on similar names but **one pupil** could come up with only one – Maxwell. "Oh yes" said Mr H, "And what was Maxwell responsible for" – "Coffee, sir!" (PP#6)

PUTTING YOUR FOOT IN IT 2 - Suffering from soaking trousers in March '79 was **one pupil** in 1C, invited in the Art Dept to lower the blinds because of the strong sunlight. In order to do this he had to climb up over the sink, at which point another pupil went for a drink and absent-mindedly (so he says!) turned on the tap somewhat violently, ignoring the fact that there was already a leg in the sink. (PP#7)

STARTLED BY A FERRET An important visitor to the school in June 79 was an Inspector. Having just recovered from seeing Janitor George McKenzie rescue a Frisbee from the Games Hall roof via a precariously balanced ladder, our visitor on a tour of the school with Mr Hope just about jumped into his arms when he encountered **a certain pupil** walking his pet ferret. (PP#10)

SLEEPY HEAD As Mr Iain Hamilton arrived on Y floor on the morning of November 8th he noticed a notoriously talkative member of 2A crouched in a corner beside the lift. He said hello, as did some fellow pupils but our anonymous friend was really fast asleep. We pride ourselves on running a school where pupils feel relaxed but this is ridiculous. (PP#13)

HELLO HELLO HELLO!!! During a recent bicycle inspection by the Police guess whose bike was found to have a defect? Well, it belonged to well-known competitive cyclist Mr Iain Hamilton, of all people! The offence was not having a rear reflector but H says it will be sorted soon. (PP#21)

NO, REALLY! Pupil (to friend who has just been talking to a new member of staff in corridor) "Fa's that?"

Other pupil "I don't know her name but she's Mr Dugdale's wife".

Absolutely true! (PP#23)

GOOD POINT, NANCY With four staff ladies now expecting happy events, Mrs **Nancy Prentice** has posed the question, "Is Percy becoming a stork?" Indeed so popular is this condition becoming that a certain "innocent" member of staff is reported to have been confronted by some S3 girls bluntly asking, "Are you one of the pregnant ones?" (PP#24)

OOOPS ! During last week's prelims in Oral French which **Miss Ross** was supervising, there was an amusing occurrence when **Mrs Drysdale** popped into the Language Lab to see how things were. Being very harassed Miss Ross had forgotten to switch off her microphone so when Mrs D asked about progress she replied – to the whole class's amusement, "I'm just a nervous wreck!"

HOW'S YOUR VOICE, IAN? Failure of the official referee to turn up at Pinefield for the First XI football match with Elgin Academy caused team coach **Mr Ian Walker** to make a most unusual refereeing decision – he would ref the game himself, *without a whistle*. Thus he had to SHOUT for fouls, goal kicks, corners etc.

[1] see pigeonpost.info

13 THE SOUNDTOWN EXPERIENCE 2005-2006

Jeff Zycinski

Undoubtedly a major highlight in the history of the school the BBC SoundTown experience gave a significant number of pupils a unique work experience and brought media glamour to the campus for well over a year on a weekly basis.

BBC Scotland had always sought to have local as well as a national presence and in the first decade of the new century it ran its SoundTown scheme in a handful of secondaries across Scotland, for example in Dalmellington, Kelso and Grangemouth.

The chance to be the next SoundTown school attracted great interest in schools across the country after the first ones had shown the way as it offered unique media exposure placing that secondary's name in the consciousness of tens of thousands of listeners to BBC Radio Scotland "92 – 95 FM, digital and on line". It meant the construction of a fully functioning radio station in the school, the presentation of iconic radio programmes like *Good Morning Scotland* and *The Radio Café* from its campus and visits to the school of well known radio personalities such as Fred MacAulay, Ken McDonald, John Beattie, Vic Galloway and Clare English.

Clearly, being chosen was prestigious but BBC Scotland had to ensure geographical balance in their choices and in 2005 EHS pitched for the prize when it looked as if the radio station was looking for a rural/remotish school. The selection process involved auditions of the school as a whole. Our audition saw the arrival on 25th May of three production assistants who spoke to pupils in formal and informal situations across the school. Activities involved a small group of pupils rehearsing a short radio play, taking part in a mock press conference and a 60-1 quiz, won by Stephen Gauld on his knowledge of Bannockburn. (See photo of Stephen with his prize ex PP 155).

Additionally Hellen Fleming of the PE Dept., and Music teacher Gillian Anderson were very persuasive. Of course speaking to BBC Scotland personnel, Mr Andy Simpson did not omit to mention - just a few times - that one of BBC Radio Scotland's stars was EHS former pupil Gary Robertson, who had cut his journalist teeth on *Pigeon Post* in the early 1980's.

Mrs Fleming was without doubt the most excited person in the school about the project and enthusing about our virtues filled out the application for Mr Simpson to submit. That enthusiasm continued throughout the whole project.

On return from the Summer break staff and pupils found the Conference Room, next to Mr Cadenhead's Office completed transformed with loads of seemingly complicated broadcasting modules and wires replacing the group of desks used for various meetings. On the far wall were huge boards declaring "BBC Radio Scotland" and "SoundTown" which were later used for collecting celebrity autographs: see the cover of PP 156. Above the door was a dramatic red "On Air" light which would illuminate when a broadcast was live.

On Tuesday 20th September, a group of five school pipers welcomed scores of local guests and BBC Radio Scotland personnel to witness the opening ceremonies in the Tuck Shop Area, at which our Junior Choir sang *Ungaua*, a Swahili Welcoming Song and the Vogue Dance Group performed a Chair Dance. The first pupil to be interviewed was Ben Mortimer (S5) who spoke to reporter Craig Gordon.

Ben then discussed the potential of SoundTown in a three minute slot broadcast on *Reporting Scotland's* TV news that evening.

Mr Jeff Zycinski, Head of BBC Radio Scotland, officially cut the ribbon and declared the recording studio open and within half an hour as a Daily Dementor item in the *MacAulay & Co* two S5 pupils soundly thrashed two staff members on items of local knowledge. In the afternoon EHS former pupil Gary Robertson one of the best known voices on BBC Radio Scotland had some embarrassing details of his life as a schoolboy cruelly exposed by former teachers Mr Dugdale,

Mr Hamilton and Mrs Duncan. Gary then interviewed Mr Simpson and later senior pupils from EHS and the Academy including Josh, son of our Mrs Fiona Davidson, on his *Scotland Live* programme.

Within a week, BBC Scotland staff from the Glasgow HQ and from Inverness came to school on various occasions to induct and train members of two pupil Production Groups under the supervision of Mrs Fleming, Miss Anderson and Mrs Flett whilst Mr Dugdale led the Press Group who were to research and write copy.

Later in the term, our Head of Geography Mrs Highmore contributed to an item on *Macaulay & Co* on the usefulness to teaching of the Google Earth program and website. Some pupils began to contribute to *The People's War* project, encouraging their own relatives who had lived through World War Two about their memories, whilst others began preparing their contributions to *The Nation's Favourite Poem*.

Live on Hallowe'en night Clare English broadcast *The Radio Café* from school speaking to a couple of experts about associated customs and legends and later in the day Melissa Paterson interviewed Ms English for *Pigeon Post*. (As shown on the cover of PP 157, right).

A small group of the BBC Scottish Symphony Orchestra musicians broadcast live on 17th November (PP 157) having worked with Higher and Advanced Higher Music pupils and next day the schools Children in Need (CiN) fund raising efforts were featured live. Also in November two French chefs from the Glen Moriston Hotel, Inverness guested

in our Home Economics Dept for the *Scotland Licked* cookery programme.

At the end of November veteran journalist Ken MacDonald interviewed parents Mrs Wendy Toner (mother of Stacey) and Mr Kenny Ferguson (father of Struan) as part of *The Investigation* on the subject of exams. In late October TV journalist Iain McDonald talked to the Press Group on "How to interview a politician" – in advance of their welcoming MP Angus Robertson to school to answer questions on the controversial Elgin Super School – or not- issue.

Throughout the Christmas term pupils appeared regularly on shows presented by Gary Robertson and Fred MacAulay: full details in PP157. On Armistice Day (11.11.05) one of team of Chaplains, Rev Rolf Billes delivered the early morning BBC Scotland *Thought for the Day*.

On December 14th Jim Spence's *90 Minutes* football discussion show was broadcast from the Lecture Room with a panel comprising international players Joe Harper and Brian Irvine (soon after this Elgin City manager !!) - and Graham Tatters (Elgin

City President), BBC sports journalist Chick Young and MP Alex Salmond appearing before a live local audience. The BBC *Christmas Watchnight Service* led by Rev Julie Woods was pre-recorded at Elgin High Church with pupil contributions.

In the new term on January 30th Fred MacAulay with guests Scottish rugby international John Beattie (See photo ex cover of PP 158) and *River City* actor Paul Samson presented his programme live from our gymnasium and he was later interviewed by *PP* reporter Calum Reid with caricaturist John Arbuthnott drawing him as they spoke. Fred was not a little annoyed when Calum asked if he would ever like to become a celebrity!! John Beattie was astonished to be easily thrown over her shoulder by Sandra Pirie, half his weight, but a Scottish Schools judo champion: photo ex PP 158.

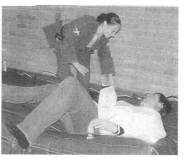

Jeff Zycinski and Andy Simpson swopped jobs for a day during January and wrote about it in *PP*. Regular appearances on *MacAulay and Co* continued throughout the month, as detailed in PP158.

Former pupil band Fickle Public played live on *The Vic Galloway Show* on March 3rd, Gary Robertson interviewed audience members live on the topic of Scotland's Energy Needs when presenting *Scotland Live* from the Lecture Room on the 10th March and at the end of the month Andrew Leil and Natalie Henderson co-hosted *The Tom Morton Show* live from the same venue.

Following the death of local MSP Margaret Ewing a Scottish Parliament by-election was held in Moray, shadowed by a Mock election conducted by Elgin High's Modern Studies Dept., on the same day, Thursday 27th April. For the real election all five candidates descended on the school to be interviewed by various print and media journalists two days before polling day. The mock election was conducted during period 5 on polling day (April 27th) with the result – a win for SNP candidate Jodie Clayton - broadcast only after the real polls had closed at 10 pm that night. The real election produced an SNP winner in Richard Lochhead.

The next day the Moray Council's final decision that the Super School for Elgin idea was being ditched and that there would continue to be two schools was relayed immediately the news broke and two local Councillors including Alasdair Urquhart, formerly Elgin High's first Head of Technical were interviewed. With local reaction to Richard Lochhead's election and a hot story of Youth Unrest in Elgin being broadcast later in the day the end of term had been an amazing two days SoundTown-wise.

But it was not all one way traffic and early in the Summer term, a group of SoundTown team members met *Reporting Scotland's* Bob Wylie and Jackie Bird at Broadcasting House, Glasgow where they also renewed their acquaintances with Gary Robertson who was presenting his mid-morning show. On 8th May a small group of pupils travelled through to Inverness Caley Thistle ground to meet and interview Radio 1 disc jockey pairing Colin and Edith.

PIGEON POST

SoundTown Team Members meet Reporting Scotland's Bob Wylie and Jackie Bird at Broadcasting House, Glasgow on 6th April

Andrew Leil and Natalie Henderson co-host The Tom Morton Show Live on March 29th

Issue No 159

May 2006

Gary Robertson Interviews local celebrities on the 10th March edition of Scotland Live on "Scotland's Energy Needs"

EHS **Glowing With Radio Activity !**

Pupils and staff continued to feature regularly on a variety of radio programmes as the session drew to a close. On 16th May, Vic Galloway encouraged local youth panels to *Mouth Off!* (a youthful version of Any Questions) with pupils from Elgin High, Lossie High, Nairn Academy, Forres Academy and Milburn Academy, Inverness, recording two shows in one day On June 20th Elgin High folk joined Frieda Morrison in , again broadcast from the Lecture Room.

And at our 27th June Prize Giving Gary Robertson presented pupils with their prizes having previously become the first of our celebrated former pupils to do so, in July 2001. He commented later that it was very odd that he had attended our Prize

Givings twice as a guest - but never as a pupil!! (The photo in PP 161 shows Gary giving his address).

The final SoundTown related event came from Elgin High Street on July 29th when *The Janice Forsyth Show* with musical items compered by Mark Stephen entertained passers-by from a small marquee on the Plain Stones. (See item cropped from PP 161 below).

Janice introduces *Soulmates* with our own Debbie Macdonald 6E centre stage. (Behind Janice with guitar is Mark, son of Mr Mike Stewart). Moray Concert Brass play later in the programme with Struan Ferguson 6O shown on left of photo

Before the end of the year Mrs Hellen Fleming wrote an article for *The Times Education Supplement (Scotland)* about our wonderful experiences over three terms. The money earned from that went to fund The SoundTown Trophy which is still awarded annually for "Service to the Community", one sign that the legacy and memory of SoundTown continues.

The SoundTown studio gradually disappeared from the Conference Room over the Summer weeks with BBC Radio Scotland generously donating equipment to permit in-school broadcasting. In the first *Pigeon Post* of the new session (PP 161) three senior pupil participants, Struan Ferguson, Claire Munro, Shelley McDonald who had been invited down to Queen Margaret Drive to the BBC HQ building in early Summer, wrote articles under the heading "What SoundTown Did for Us". Shelley seemed to sum up what many pupils had thought about the year...

Although SoundTown gave the pupils of Elgin High many valuable individual experiences, I feel that the whole school was given a unique learning opportunity....The communication and cooperation skills developed in pupils were widespread and affected nearly everyone.

The feeling the school was wonderful...I hope that the ethos and eagerness SoundTown brought to the school will last for many years to come.

Footnote: Our stats show – and you can see them in detail in PP161 for October 2006 – that Elgin High voices were heard on *MacAulay and Co* twenty-six times across the year, half a dozen teachers spoke live on at least five different occasions, with another twenty at least once. Ten pupils spoke live on at least three separate occasions, with Jon Arbuthnott, heard on twelve different occasions being the most profilic. In all close to ninety of our pupils were featured at least once on live or recorded programmes.

A RadioActive school for a year – You bet!

(See **pigeonpost.info** for hundreds of photographs)

A page from PP 162 showing how one pupil made the most of the SoundTown experience.

Above and below Jon Arbuthnott's caricatures of Fred MacAulay and Gary Robertson, published in editions during our run as SoundTown school

Postscript : The SoundTown Project continued with schools in Dundee, Baldragon Academy and Alva Academy – curiously a school in the town (Alloa) where Mr Hope had begun his career as a teacher - selected later in the decade.

14 Former Pupils
Updates on Some You May Have Known & What Elgin High Did For Me

Schools with longer histories and more prestigious backgrounds than ours would possibly use such a section to write about "Celebrated Alumni", but that seems pretentious for a school less than forty years old.

Nevertheless, when I planned the outline of this book in the Autumn of 2017 I did indeed intend to have a section on "Well Known" pupils, of whom I would write at some length. However, when in late November I asked on the Facebook website "Former Elgin High School Students" for comments on this idea, listing around 14 pupils I intended to feature at length, responses were such that this was not such a good idea! It was clear the chapter had to be democratised.

So instead, this feature will have three parts to it.

1. Brief to short accounts of the careers of a substantially larger number of Former Pupils **including many suggested by FB fp members**—in alphabetical order without much indication of vintage. You can use the pupil index in Section 2 to identify most of them if you need to.

2. A series of articles by former pupils entitled **What Elgin High Did For Me**, in which individuals provide a retrospect of their time with us and how it affected their lives. Former pupils were invited to contribute to this via the FB fp site.

3. (In Section 2) Very brief accounts of a large number of pupils who comprised **our first S1** in 1978-79, researched by Janice and Hamish Hyndman and Angela Matchett.

There are very strong threads of sport and the arts across these mini-bio's and as you will see a few came in too late to be properly sequenced.

This was always going to be a controversial chapter e.g. your thoughts of "Why am I not in it?" I have tried to democratise it as much as possible by repeatedly inviting contributions via the FB fp group pages as well as approaching folk directly, but this is the N.E. of Scotland and a some folk don't want to be thought of as boasting about what they've done, believing "It is enough to do it". I have therefore had to cajole information out of some of you or go back to old PP reports and rewrite them. You should know however that a number of pupils I approached did not reply or declined out of modesty or a desire for privacy.

1. Some Former Pupils—Pen Portraits

Dr Andrew Alexander Dr Andrew Alexander is currently Reader in Chemical Physics at the University of Edinburgh. After leaving EHS in (cough) 1990, he studied for a BSc degree at the University of Edinburgh, and then a DPhil at Magdalen College, University of Oxford. He worked as a research associate at the Chemistry Department of Stanford University, California, before returning to Scotland as a Royal Society University Research Fellow and Lecturer. Andrew teaches subjects at the boundary  between chemistry and physics. His research interests include dynamics of chemical reactions and nucleation. Highlights of his research include invention of a method for inducing growth of crystals with pulses of laser light. His research group has recently been working with GlaxoSmithKline to develop techniques for crystallisation of pharmaceutical compounds in micron-sized droplets. Dr Alexander was guest of honour at our Prize Giving in 2002.

Michael Alexander wasn't sporty or athletic when he was at EHS. However, he took up target archery in late 2007 simply as something different to do, and with no thoughts of being competitive. He was persuaded to enter the county indoor championships and managed to win his class, the competitive bug took hold, and by 2011 he was selected to represent Scotland at the "Euronations" – the European Commonwealth Championships. Since then he has added a further nine caps to his total, as well as reach the level of Grand Master Bowman which represents the top 1% of archers in the UK. 2015 has been his most successful so far; 2nd overall in the UK Masters, then helping Team Scotland to their first ever win at the Euronations in Edinburgh (with a 3rd place individually). He followed up with becoming Scottish Champion, and finally winning Gold at the European Masters Games in Nice. Rounding off the year he was nominated for and won the Sport Moray Sports Person of the Year. Mr Carstairs would never have believed it possible! (Andrew and Michael are brothers).

Ross Allan With help from the brilliant Drama department at EHS  Ross was lucky enough to attend a year long course at Telford College in Edinburgh. From there he won a place on the BA Acting Course at Queen Margaret University and studied acting for three years. Since graduating in 2004 he feels he has been extremely fortunate to be making a living as an actor, working in theatre, television and radio. In theatre, he has toured extensively throughout the UK and abroad and worked with many established theatres and theatre companies including the National Theatre of Scotland—for example *Empty* by Cathy Forde and *The Miracle Man* by Douglas Maxwell both in 2010, *Truant* (devised and written by the company) in 2011 and *Thieves and Boy* by Hao Jingfang in 2013. For Eden Court Theatre Ross has done five pantos in a row since 2013. In TV and radio, he has had the privilege of working with companies including the BBC and STV. He says he is indebted to EHS for helping him on the road to pursuing his acting career.

Tino Allan Martin Allan featured on the music scene in his final years  at school, mainly as a pianist. After completing a genetics degree at Aberdeen University Martin took some years to identify a suitable a career path until a volunteer work placement at Aberdeen City Archives and an interest in family history suggested a possible way forward. Completion of a PG qualification in archives was followed by posts at Highland Council in Inverness and Dundee City Council where he now works as City Archivist. One of his favourite memories of EHS is being asked to provide piano accompaniment for the 1993 "Bi-ennial Revue" after being recommended to John Aitken as being 'good at playing crap stuff'. He continues to pursue music as a hobby, one of the highlights of which was playing keyboards for an Aberdeen based band which landed a support slot for Jamie Cullum at Crathes Castle in 2005.

Richard Anderson On arriving as part of our first S2 in 1978  Richard quickly established himself as a performer, playing principal roles in our Easter one act plays and Jacob *and* Pharaoh in *Joseph* in December 1980. His main interest, however, was the bagpipes, being one of a small group of talented lads who were tutored by piper extraordinaire Mr James Hamilton our first PT History and performing at many school events like Burns Suppers and Prize Givings. Richard credits Mr Hamilton in particular and the school in general for influencing his life beyond measure. "I would have been a bit of a delinquent had it not been for Mr Hamilton and the pipes" he blushed. Mr

Hamilton, in turn, applauded Richard calling him "my best ever pupil". When he left school Richard continued to play the pipes and is very well known as a local pipe major, much called for at Highland shows around the North East—and beyond. He has travelled abroad on piping duty on many occasions. He was in the armed forces for a period and served for four months in the Gulf War when called up as an RAF reservist in 2003. In PP 146 (October 2003) Richard recalled with pride and some amusement playing the pipes in the Iraqi city of Basra to keep up the spirits of the British troops. His professional career has been as a civil servant with The Moray Council and he now serves as Head of Housing and Property.

Jon Arbuthnott At school, Jon's passion was art - you may well  recall his caricatures in *Pigeon Post,* particularly during our SoundTown year, 2005-6—and when he left he completed an HND in Graphic Design. However his graphics career always overlapped with another of his passions: music. He now designs posters and artwork for various bands in Glasgow, whom he has met through playing in bands himself.

Graphics has taken a backseat in recent years to his music career, as his band, Pinact, are signed to an American label and they write, record and tour extensively. Jon plays bass in the band, and they play slacker fuzz-filled rock. In the past year, they have made numerous trips to Canada and US to play gigs. It's been so incredible to tour in places he might never have seen otherwise like Montreal, a city he instantly fell for. This year they hope to have the opportunity to play on the West Coast of the US and more cities in mainland Europe.

Isla Graham Benzie is the first woman to become a director of  Elgin City F.C. After leaving Elgin High, the school her dad (Martin Graham) helped design, Isla moved to Aberdeen for Robert Gordon University. After graduating she returned to Elgin to commence her career with the Halifax Building Society before heading back to the Granite City in 1997. She is now a Regional Manager with Bank of Scotland, covering everything North of the Forth Bridge. Having supported Elgin City since her teenage years, throughout this time she regularly returned to follow Elgin City and travelled to away games as a loyal supporter. In December 2016 she made her own mark on City history when she was invited to become the first ever female of the board and officially started as a Director in January 2017.   In this she was warmly welcomed particularly by directors Cecil Jack (a lifelong friend) and Ian Clark and Chairman Graham Tatters who very much looked forward to the injection of fresh blood and diversity. With her experience in finance, HR and management Isla supports the management of the day-to-day running of the club and also looks after match day hospitality at home games.

Dr Robert Blyth Robert left Elgin High in 1989 and immediately  returned as a stand-in science technician before beginning a history degree at Aberdeen University. This was followed by a Ph.D. on the history of British Indian external policy in the western Indian Ocean and a period of teaching at the university. In 2000, he left Aberdeen for new role as a curator at the National Maritime Museum in Greenwich, where he worked on new gallery displays, acquisitions and a book based on his Ph.D. thesis. Missing teaching, he moved to Queen's University Belfast in 2006 and taught history there for two years before being lured back to Greenwich. He is now a Senior Curator and continues to curate galleries and major temporary exhibitions like the one on Samuel Pepys in 2016.

Fraser Bremner was our first Under 18 Schoolboy football cap,  playing in a victorious Scotland side v England in April 2003 at Banff and a further two times for his country. A product of various Elgin City Youth sides, Fraser made his senior debut start v Queen's Park at Borough Briggs in April 2002, whilst he was in S5; he wrote at length about the thrill of these two first occasions in PP 142 and PP 143. Fraser then became a football columnist for *The Northern Scot*. In all Fraser played over 125 times for Elgin City in The Scottish Third Division then moved to Highland League side Deveronvale for two seasons before joining Forres Mechanics for six seasons. During his spell at Mosset Park he was lucky enough to play in sides which won the League Cup, the North Cup and The Highland League. Aged 27 he became player/manager of Dufftown FC where he was for two and half seasons, after gaining promotion to the super league. He then spent 18 months as manager of Rothes FC and is now manager of Forres Thistle in the North Junior League.

Alasdair Brown comes from a musical family and was learning piano  from the age of 8, entering the Moray Music Festival under the tutelage of Blair Cargill two years later and winning many awards whilst at school. Whilst at Elgin High he developed a catholic taste in music and began to learn the French horn with Alasdair Grant as tutor. After graduating BMus (Hons) from Aberdeen University he has made a career out of his hobby and most recently was Musical Director of the 2017 pantomime *Aladdin* at HMTheatre, Aberdeen.   Having studied Musical Production at the Mountview Academy of Performing Arts in Peckham Alasdair has directed full scale productions of musicals like *Cats* and *Grease* on a number of huge passenger liners, most recently with the Royal Caribbean International Line.

Laura Chalmers Athletics champion many times over – see Sports Day records in Part Two, - on leaving EHS in 2004 Laura studied at RGU qualifying in sports and exercise science is now a primary school teacher in Lincolnshire where she lives with her husband and young son.

Laura started athletics while still at primary school as a runner and jumper. She was one time North District age group High Jump Champion and Hurdles champion. The coaching team at Elgin Amateur Athletic Club spotted potential in her as a thrower and she had immediate success as an under 13 (U13) at shot and discus. Laura then began to specialise in discus and latterly hammer.   She had success at North District, North Schools, Scottish and Scottish schools throughout her U13 and U15 age group years.

As an U17 athlete in 2002 Laura went through the whole season undefeated in any hammer competition. Her haul of Gold medals included North District, North Schools, Scottish Champs, Scottish Schools, British Schools and The British (AAA) Championship. She also added the Celtic Games and French Schools titles to the tally and completed the year by winning the Scottish Hammer Grand Prix title. This success earned her a first U20 International cap at only 16 years old. The same year Laura was also Scottish Schools and Scottish champion at Discus.

The combined efforts of 2002 and 2003 saw Laura selected by Scotland for the 2004 Junior Commonwealth Games in Bedigo, Australia. The experience of a lifetime in December 2004 led to her winning a Bronze medal and an invite to a Gala reception at Edinburgh Castle on return. The Australian success led to her being nominated in the Moray Sports Person of the year awards in 2005 which she was grateful to win.

With commitments to University work and continuing back problems Laura continued to compete but not as regularly as she would have liked. Ultimately due to injury she stopped competing in 2009.

Laura loved her time at EHS and still appreciates the support the school afforded her when she was there. Laura wishes everyone good luck and a happy future in the new EHS.

Peter Chalmers On leaving EHS Peter began an apprenticeship with Tullochs of Cummingston as a Joiner.   Peter followed his older sister into athletics while still at primary school as a runnerand jumper. It did not take him long to realise that he was never destined to be a runner. Like his sister, Laura, Pete liked to throw things.

The coaching team at Elgin Amateur Athletic Club spotted his potential as a thrower and he took to it with varied success to begin with. Being a "leftie" did not go without its coaching problems. He began competing as an under 13 throwing shot and discus winning Silver medals in both at the North District Championships. In 2002 he began to concentrate on throwing the hammer and with his move up to U15 was eligible to throw hammer in competition. In his novice year he won the North District Champs. and the Scottish u15 Championship. He was also ranked No1 in Scotland for age. As a bonus he also won the Scottish Schools discus title.

2003 saw Peter retain his Scottish u15 Hammer title and add the Scottish Schools Hammer title to his achievements. These titles helped him maintain his No1 ranking. 2004 saw a move up to U17 where he finished 3rd in Hammer at the Scottish Champs. Behind his team mate Mark Dry who went on to be an Olympian in Rio. In this year Peter also diversified and had a go at the "Highland Games". He took the "Young Heavy" title at the last Elgin Highland Games. After 2005 where he won Bronze at the Scottish Champs and Silver at the Scottish Schools Champs and finishing 3rd in the rankings behind 2 current Commonwealth athletes Peter was forced to give up athletics due to a combination of injury and work commitments.

During his athletics career Pete was selected for both Scottish Schools and Scotland and was a regular competitor and age group winner at the Scottish Hammer Grand Prix Festivals.

(Laura and Peter are siblings)

Robert Clark - Bob as he is now known—left Elgin High in 1984 with no qualifications having been offered a joinery apprenticeship, which he was allowed to begin early on the condition he returned to take his exams. Bob is the first to admit he wasn't the most academic but he did enjoy practical subjects and was a good athlete and rugby player. He served his apprenticeship and joined Gordon Forbes after a few years. He  then started fitting kitchens for their Kitchen Studio and after doing that for almost 10 years he and one of the team from the Kitchen Studio decided to leave and start their own Kitchen business. They found premises in the Tyock Industrial Estate and created a showroom with the kitchens they would be selling. He had at least two fitters he knew join him to do the fitting. Over the next 18 years they have built up their business and now employ around 20 staff and have an impressive showroom at the old Oakwood Motel along with a cooking school which invites different chefs every month or so to teach cooking of different countries and cuisines. He may not have paper qualifications but he's a great example of someone who has worked hard and achieved great things professionally and is a well liked Elgin lad.

Rob Collie grew up playing football for his local SFL side Elgin City F.C before progressing on to play rugby for Moray R.F.C. A change of employment in 2010 led to him quitting Rugby, at which point training in the gym took over and he never looked back as he discovered he was truly "Born to the Iron" and developed a love of strength training. In 2015 he made his amateur debut in the IFBA Highlands and Islands Classic in Inverness and took third place in the First Timers category. It was at this time his passion for natural competitive bodybuilding was born.

Since 2015 he has had the privilege to appear on stage seven times taking two Firsts, two Seconds, two Thirds and one Overall. 2017 marked the best season of his career to date, taking a first place at the UKBFF Scottish Grand Prix, being named the 2017 Classic Champion. He thereafter went to compete at the British Finals in Nottingham taking a top ten finish and had the privilege of competing at the Arnold Schwarzenegger Classic 2017 in Barcelona. This marked a metronomic rise from a first time show held in a nightclub in Inverness, Scotland to one of the biggest amateur shows in the world with over 1,500 bodybuilders competing and over 50,000 spectators attending over the course of the weekend and all in the space of three years. Rob says Schwarzenegger has been his hero from the moment he was old enough to know who he was. Rob also visits schools to give motivational talks. (From https://www.sunsupp.co.uk/rob-collie adapted and expanded)

Garry Collins   Very well known in Scottish acting circles, Garry played a number of lead roles in school productions, notably Seymour Krelborn in *Little Shop of Horrors* (1996) and Cap'n Tempest in *Return to the Forbidden Planet* (1997). He was also part of Gaz n Jazz who won our 1996 Talent show. Garry was already well known for taking on principal parts with The Moray Youth Theatre and St Giles Theatre Group.

Immediately after playing the later role Garry then went on to a three week placement with the National Youth Theatre in London. Garry then spent a year studying theatre arts at the Northern College, Dundee Campus before beginning in 2000 to study at the R.S.A.M.D. in Glasgow supported by the award of a £3000 Behrens Bursary.

Garry has a very impressive acting pedigree. His theatre credits include: *The Artist Man and The Mother Woman* and *My Romantic History* with Borderline Theatre, *Of Mice and Men* and *Romeo and Juliet*, (Royal Lyceum Edinburgh), *Handful of Dust* and *Venice Preserved*, (Citizens Theatre). *Houghmagandie Pack,* and *Decky Does a Bronco* (Grid Iron). *Macbeth* and *Swan Song* (Open Book). *Cyrano* and *John Muir* (Oran Mor). *Mr Placebo* and *East Coast*

Chicken Supper (Traverse). *Dr Korzack's Example* (TAG), *Cave Dwellers* (7:84), *The Doll Tower* (Unity Liverpool), *Cleansed* (Oxford Stage/Arcola), *Coriolanus* and *Under the Flag* (Shakespeare's Globe Theatre). Filmwork: *Dear Frankie* (Pathe Films) and *I'm Away From Here*. Radio work : *Side Effects* (BBC Radio 4), *A Man's World* (BBC Radio 3). Closer to home he has worked with The Red Shoes Theatre and the Out of The Darkness Theatre Company in Elgin. Garry was Guest of Honour at our 2009 Prize Giving.

Mark Conti who was big on the Elgin High music scene left school in
1988 to pursue a career in the Army with whom he did a two year tour of
Northern Ireland in 1994. Music played a big part in his life even during his
army days as with every posting he formed a new band. He returned to
College to study computing and became self-employed in 1999 In 1997
Mark formed the local band *Crannog* which released 2 EP's. They
extensively toured the UK as far afield as Truro sharing the stage that night
with Danni Minogue. *Crannog* won the T Break battle of the bands in 1999 which gave them
a slot at the T in the Park festival. *Crannog* went on to tour France, Florida and their
favourite place Ireland. Mark left the band in 2002 due to family commitments but went on
to play with various local cover bands like *Snap Dragon* and *Crunch*. However he always had
a passion for song writing and in 2013 Mark formed *Edgar Road* along with Mike Byiers,
Simon Watterson, Allan Hall (all ex Elgin High) and Magda Wellenger. *Edgar Road* have been
working hard at their sound and promoting themselves. They have recorded 3 EPs at the
Chairworks where the likes of Kaiser Chiefs and the Beautiful South record alongside their
producer David Watts. The band have had great feedback and support from their fan base
and have been playing festivals like xponorth, Belladrum and frequently in Glasgow and
Edinburgh. Recently a sold out event at Elgin Town Hall led to much delight followed the
next day in the Scottish Sun newspaper with an article by Jim Gellatly (holder of the John
Peel award). Mark hopes to push the music further in 2018 with a publishing deal and to do
some touring in Europe. Mark is an enthusiastic supporter of the Lantern of the North
Community Group. See https://www.facebook.com/edgarroadband/

Andrew Cowie Son of our late school Chaplain, Rev Gordon Cowie,
Andrew became Pupil Editor of *Pigeon Post* in session 1990-91. With
guidance from legendary *Press and Journal* reporter Alistair Bissett, and
after taking a degree in journalism at Edinburgh's Napier University, he
embarked on a career as a newspaper man becoming first a reporter and
then editor of various titles within the Clyde & Forth Press Group for
some 12 years. However, at that time the local newspaper industry was
shrinking and Andrew decided to find pastures new, developing a growing interest in

psychology, the benefits of mindfulness-based meditation and the untapped potential of the human mind. He is now a freelance hypnotherapist and life coach with a particular interest in working with addiction and helping motivate young people to achieve their goals. He also dabbles in the fun side of hypnosis, including magic and mentalism, is a keen snooker and pool player and has edited a number of books, making him the obvious choice for this one, given his continuing strong family connections to the area. He has been an invaluable guide and support to Mr Dugdale in the forming of this book.

Kevin Cruickshank After leaving Elgin High Kevin gained an Honours degree in Business Studies and worked for eighteen months in the USA for a car rental company in Oregon. He then spent a few years with both Elgin City and Montrose as a general factotum - in charge of all administration, a mind boggling task. Being selected from a short leet of eight people, Kevin joined Premiership side Blackburn Rovers in 2008 as  Scouting Coordinator and he can hardly believe he's now spent ten years working in the Premier League, the last five as Chief Scout of Stoke City. He travels the world getting paid to watch football. This is not always as glamorous as it sounds but certainly a job he loves to do and he is lucky that every day he looks forward to going to work. He has worked under some interesting managers namely Sam Allardyce, Mark Hughes and Harry Redknapp and been heavily involved in the signing of players such as Arnautovic, Shaqiri and Bojan but he takes most pleasure from spotting young players who go on to make the grade even if he can't always persuade the clubs he has worked for to make the investment.

Stuart Cruickshank After negotiating 6th year and escaping with a few Highers, not English though: "Mr Downie lost my work!" Stuart sat down with his results in High Spirits (no he wasn't happy, he means the pub) contemplating what his next step should be, eventually choosing the local College to study Hospitality Management. One year later he was the proud owner of a HNC, but unfortunately, also a bad back when he  suffered spine damage whilst playing the extreme sport known as lawn bowls. The injury resulted in a change of career path, to the less physical world of Accountancy. Two years later he successfully gained the HND and was offered a job in the Finance department at the College. You may be wondering by now, what ever happened to the bowls! Well, after a few months off, Stuart went against doctor's advice and started playing again. The rest must have worked well as he soon become the Scottish and British Champion, eventually amassing five Scottish and two British titles over the years. The pain in his lower back never disappeared but he never let it affect his performance, blocking the pain to focus on pushing himself to put a shift in, which is why he has 3 amazing children, Owen, Cora and Elsie. Stuart has now been at the College 15 years, been promoted four times, moved from Finance to Administration, gained a Degree in Business Management and now manages a great bunch within the Administration Service Centre. (Kevin and Stuart are brothers).

Sarah Darnley A large number of Elgin folk reacted with shock and dismay on learning that one of Elgin High's most vivacious former pupils had been killed when the Super Puma carrying her and 17 others from the Borgsten Dolphin oil rig crashed into the sea on its approach to Sumburgh on 23rd August 2013. Sarah had been working for caterers Sodexo UK a well-known general services provider to many industries and was about to holiday in Spain.   Tragically she thus became the first woman killed in a UK offshore accident.

Sarah arrived in Elgin High School in 1980 and quickly established herself as a fun-loving character, who was a joy to have in the classroom. Writing about herself as a member of 1C in PP 22 she confessed to loving the pop groups Madness and Bad Manners, enjoying gymnastics, going to discos, looking after her horse and supporting Celtic. Throughout her years in Elgin High she was regarded by staff as a real "loud" personality who was a fun loving free spirit.   Her entry also reveals her mischievous side as she threatened to set a challenging former pupil upon her Modern Language teacher Mrs Gillian Dugdale , who was one of her favourite teachers!

On leaving school Sarah first worked in ASDA but hankered for a career providing services to the oil industry because it would allow her to see rare parts of the world. And this came true as she worked on rigs off the Falkland Islands, in the Congo and in Turkey as well of course as well routinely in the North Sea. In her final posting she was doing long-time relief work.

Sean Dawson was senior *Pigeon Post* reporter whilst in his final years with us: he was a member of a very good Sixth Year in 2005-6 (our BBC SoundTown year).   He was a very faithful, reliable and hard-working contributor of Pupil Profiles, Teacher Features and other reports to each edition. At the same he was making a name for himself as a competitive swimmer and he has written about his swimming exploits at school and since in the "What Elgin High School Did For Me" section later in this book.

Sean studied further at Aberdeen University, graduating MA (Hons) in Geography & International Relations and then MSc (Environmental Science) in 2010 and he is now a

Regional Development Manager for the Grampian & Tayside Region at Scottish Swimming, (The Scottish Amateur Swimming Association) the national governing body for swimming in Scotland, representing clubs, swim schools and aquatic disciplines.

The Dean Sisters were actively involved in the life of the school but were best known for their sporting accomplishments. In the photo below : (l-r) Sandra, Karen and Susan.

Dr Susan Dean experienced most success in hockey. She was part of league and

tournament winning school teams. She also represented Highland Schoolgirls at under-16 and under-18 level both indoors and out. Along with fellow EHS pupil, Nicky Gravener, Susan was part of the Highland under-18 team who won the Scottish inter-district tournament in 1991. This as a notable feat for a small region like Highland. Nicky had the honour of scoring the winning goal in a narrow 1-0 win. In 1991, Susan was selected to represent Scotland under 16s at a 6 nations tournament in Dusseldorf, Germany. The pinnacle of this was a comprehensive 6-0 victory over France and a Player of the Match award in a 3-0 defeat to England. In 1993, Susan joined the Scotland under-18 squad for tournaments in Maastricht, The Netherlands and Dublin, Ireland. Susan made 13 appearances in total for Scotland squads.

Susan also formed part of a successful 5-a-side football team who won various tournaments. Coached by Alan Sturrock, the girls won Grampian Police 5 a-sides on two occasions. Undefeated by any girls or ladies side, they were also British Youth Club champions. On leaving school, Susan continued to play club hockey. She is now Depute Head Teacher at New Elgin Primary having worked as an Educational Psychologist for 13 years. In 2014, achieved a Doctorate in Educational Psychology from the University of Newcastle.

Sandra Dean was also involved in

the very successful school hockey teams and represented the school in football and badminton teams playing alongside her sisters on many occasions. She played hockey for Highland Under18s. At the age of 10 Sandra took up the sport of bowls and has now been playing for

(l-r) Sandra, Karen and Susan Dean

around thirty years. Since leaving school she has amassed many titles at club, district and national level. Alongside many other club competition wins, Sandra has won the Moray Bowling Club ladies championship 12 times and been runner up in the mixed championship three times. She has been District Singles Champion 6 times and District Triples Champion twice. Her best performance at the Scottish Championships was last year when she reached the quarter finals. In the last 32 she beat World silver Medallist, Lesley Doig.

Arguably 2016 was her best year when she won her club championship, the district triples, City of Aberdeen Singles and the Super Series Singles. The Super Series Singles was a National Competition with Sandra beating favourite and Commonwealth Gold medallist, Lorna Smith in the last 16. Sandra also beat other international players *en-route* to the title picking up £3000 in prize money. This led to Sandra winning SportMoray Althlete of the Year. Sandra is hoping to make the Scotland team herself. Sandra still lives in Elgin and has been teaching over 17 years. She has taught at Lhanbryde Primary School for 15 years and is now Depute Head there.

Karen Dean is the youngest of the trio Karen participated in Hockey and Football at school, winning a number of tournaments along with sister Sandra. She was in the Highland training squad for hockey but had to make a choice between that and her chosen sport Judo, as major tournaments fell on the same weekend.   Karen was selected for the Scotland Junior Cadet squad and travelled to France, Wales and London representing Scotland. In the Junior national tournaments she won five Scottish silver and a bronze medal. She continued her Judo into senior level where she became the female black belt 1st Dan at Elgin Judo Club and was North of Scotland Open and Closed champion.   Due to her job as a Chemist offshore at the time, she has found it difficult to continue with the sport alongside her chosen career path.

Graeme Donaldson Whilst still at school Graeme, a member of Elgin Bowling Club and son of our canteen supervisor Cath, became a very successful lawn bowls champion. For example in 1992 he won the Junior Singles (and with a partner from Tain) the Junior Doubles at the prestigious City of Aberdeen Tournament. Two years later, aged 18, Graeme won the Scottish Junior Singles at Dalkeith and in April the Scottish National  Bowling Trophy (for under 25s). Graeme was capped by Scotland several times and in Autumn 2003, aged 27, defeated the World Indoors Champion (and his former international captain) Alex Marshall at a tourney in Nairn. Graeme has many other hobbies including golf and football but has continued to play some bowls and has won Scottish fours championships twice in 2009 at Dundee and 2014 at Prestwick also the triples in 2015 with club mates from Elgin. Graeme won through qualifying at Falkirk to compete in the televised stages of the world singles championships in which he lost out in the last 16 to holder Darren Burnett. In 2017 Graeme was fortunate to be the first ever Scottish Masters champion defeating Darren Weir from Prestwick in a televised final in Perth. This year he will be back playing for Scotland again for the first time in a good few years.

Dr Rebecca Dumbell left EHS in 2004, and despite aiming for a  career in music for much of her time there, instead decided to study Zoology at the University of Aberdeen. It was here Rebecca's interest in physiology developed. Rebecca gained her PhD in 2014, and works as a research scientist on how the body regulates appetite and stores / expends energy and how these factors interact, particularly with respect to biological rhythms. This is important to understand obesity, exercise response and metabolic diseases like diabetes. Rebecca has worked in labs in Aberdeen, Glasgow, Hannover and Lübeck in Germany and now works for the Medical Research Council in Oxfordshire, investigating the genetics of diabetes. Rebecca regularly publishes peer reviewed research articles, contributing to scientific understanding, and travels all over the world for work. Does Rebecca regret not following a career in music? Certainly not. After all, it's much more difficult to do science as a hobby!

Isla   Dunbar-Yiannoullou began swimming at an early age  and started synchronised swimming at around age 6 with Duncan McRae who started the club in Elgin in 1984. By the age of 8, she was selected for the Scottish Elite Squad and became Junior Scottish Champion three times in a row and senior championship twice during her career. Aged 17 she represented Scotland in her first international competition in Bratislava in Slovakia and made the finals. Following this she was invited to train in Southern California, was lucky enough to be supported by Elgin Rotary Club and various businesses and spent a couple of months receiving expert coaching. At 19 she returned from competition in Germany with a bronze in both the solo section and duet competition. A year later she was off to Sweden, returning with a bronze in solo and silver in the duet. Following these successes she was chosen to represent Scotland at the 1998 Commonwealth Games in Kuala Lumpur. Unfortunately two weeks before the team was due to leave, Scottish Swimming decided not to send a synchronised swimming team. This sent her life off in a different direction and she travelled widely before returning to train as a nurse. She now lives in Australia working as a Diabetes Nurse Educator across two busy public hospitals. She still loves getting in the pool and who knows may return to competition one day.

Ricky Foster   Currently playing professional football for St Johnstone in the Scottish Premier League, Ricky is the highest male achiever of the many talented football players

who have pulled on an Elgin High school strip. As soon as he arrived in
school it was obvious that he was going to be an athlete of some
description. As the listings in our "Inter-House Athletics / Sports Day"
section show in Section 2, Ricky (a Falcon) was Junior Champion in
1998, Intermediate Champion in 1999 and 2000, and Senior Champion
in 2001. The School's Sports Day records (see in the same chapter) show Ricky still as the
reigning Champion in a handful of events such as 400m, 800m and High Jump at S4 Boys
level and the 400m as Senior Boy.   In 2004 he returned to present some of the prizes at the
end of Sports day. Ricky has previously played professionally for Aberdeen, Rangers, Bristol
City, and Ross County.

Colin Grant One of the original pupils who joined our First Year in
1978, Colin made a name for himself whilst at school as a champion
badminton player—his first non-family coach being Mr Nick Ledingham.
He featured in many team photographs in *Pigeon Post*, the sport being a
strong one in his family. He joined us as groundsman in October 1991
having previously trained as a painter/decorator with Alexander Beattie in
New Elgin. Since 1992 He has been a member of the janitorial team in school working with
senior janitors Hamish Simpson, Neil Munro and now Paul Wilcox   Colin is married to…..

Karen Grant Depute Head at Elgin Academy since 2007, Karen joined
our Third Year in 1980 and immensely enjoyed her time at Elgin High as a
pupil particularly liking Modern Studies. After taking her BSc degree at
Robert Gordon's Institute in Aberdeen she trained as a teacher and went
to her first post as an Home Economics teacher at Brae School in Shetland
in August 1988. She was promoted to Inverness High in 1993 and joined
us to replace our original head of Home Economics Miss Sylvia Campbell in January of 1996.
During her time with as a PT Karen was involved in many innovative aspects of curriculum
development, became Acting DHT for a spell and her promotion to the Academy was richly
deserved.

Nichola Grant Nicky Grant returned to her roots at Elgin High School in November 2016
to join the Senior Leadership Team as Depute Headteacher. Nicky received almost 100 caps
for her country; and was the first ever female footballer to amass 75 caps in an international
footballing career that spanned 14 years, from 1993—2006 and cut short due to a serious
knee injury. Nicky was captain of her country on the day that she scored the winning goal
against Switzerland in the game which secured Scotland A category status.

Nicky developed her footballing skills while still at New Elgin Primary School and further honed this talent at Elgin High, coached by her dad initially to take part in school and community 5-a-side events before embarking on a winning run with Elgin High School teams as well as Aberdeen Ladies, She went on to win a number of Scottish and English league championships, league cups, Scottish Cups and other awards  during her time playing for Cove Rangers Ladies, Celtic, Hamilton Academicals, Arsenal, Doncaster Rovers Belles and Forfar Farmington as well as a variety of periods in Iceland, Germany with champion league winning side FFC Frankfurt and Sweden; many of these in a professional capacity. Her former Arsenal Ladies manager, Vik Akers –opined that she was the best midfielder of her generation.

References to Nicky's sporting prowess and athleticism appeared regularly in *Pigeon Post*. In #76 Nicky's trial for the U21 International Ladies football team in an article by Paul Grant, whose father Dr Ron Grant is a well-known football historian, relates that Nicky's interest in football had begun at New Elgin Primary. In #79 her first international game for her country. In #91 her astonishing keepie-up performance: 1,898 times in a 25 minute spell. In #97 her international cap v Italy whilst #104 pictures her with the Scottish Cup won by Cove Rangers Ladies whom she captained. Finally in #159 her cap v Switzerland and the fact that Nicky, then a PE teacher at Bathgate Academy, had been the Guest of Honour at our Prize Giving in June 2003.

As well as a clear talent and success in football, Nicky was a keen and successful North of Scotland Badminton champion and Scottish schools hockey internationalist as well as the Intermediate Girls Athletics Champion in 1989 and Senior Girls Athletics Champion in 1991, 1992 and 1993.

Mark Gravener's biggest sporting achievement since leaving school lies in his success playing pool. Both he and **Mike Clark** (in the same year) regularly represented Scotland between approximately 2000 and 2014 (for Mark) and till now for Mike at the Home Internationals, World and European Championships, travelling all over Europe to compete. The photo shows the winning Scotland team at the 2004 Home Internationals. Mark is front row far right and Mike is in the middle of the back row. Mike has won multiple national titles and is the current Scottish Singles champion. Mark won the Scottish Open back in 2001, his only national singles title. They were also part of the current national 5 man team champions.

The lads both started playing for bars in Elgin while only 13 years old, firstly at the Kingsmills Bar, then Mark moved to play for the Cottar Hoose and Mike played for the Springfield Bar.   After school and university they then started playing for teams in Aberdeen,   joined the Scottish Pool Tour, qualified for the Scotland squad and finally progressed to being in the Men's team.   See further photo in PP 143 (2003).

Alan Gray On leaving EHS Alan studied HNC and HND in Acting and Performance at UHI Millennium Institute before being awarded a professional acting contract with Eden Court Theatre. This in turn led to him becoming a Theatre Arts Worker in Nairn, Badenoch and Strathspey. After two years in the role he moved on to Study BA (Hons) in Acting at the Birmingham Conservatoire; appearing as a professional actor mostly

in children's theatre.   Alan was also involved in Youth Football as a coach with Clachnacuddin FC Youth Development, touring Holland, Denmark and the USA with youth teams. He then made the decision to work for a Soccer Club in Orlando Florida, FC America (now GPS Orlando) which at the time was aligned with Italian side Roma; he worked there for just over a year and a half. During his time in the States he realised his true passion was working with young people - in Football or Theatre or whatever didn't matter - but he wanted to help give young people opportunities they might not otherwise have. On his return to the UK he moved to Lochaber to once again work for Eden Court Theatre and currently works in schools, nurseries, old folk's homes and community groups. He also gives talks at local schools regarding careers, bullying and social issues, compéres events and champions community involvement. In his spare time Alan runs a local Saturday Amateur Side, South Lochaber Thistle which he started with a friend in 2015.   See a piece penned by Alan later on in this section.

Michael Gray M.B.E. Michael, then a Warrant Officer 2 with the 1st Battalion the Highlanders was made M.B.E. in the Queen's Birthday Honours list of 2003 and presented with the honour by Prince Charles for whom shortly before he had played at a dinner held for His Royal Highness. Michael joined the Army on leaving Elgin High aged 16 and piping has taken him all over the world. He has played with the Pipes and Drums of his regiment in the Far East, in Africa and all over Europe and the USA. In 2002 Michael was the lone piper picked out by floodlights to play the lament each night at the end of that year's Edinburgh Military Tattoo. He was the Senior Pipe Major warrant officer class 1 (WO1) in the British Army in 2007 when tationed at the Army School of Bagpipe Music and Highland Drumming in Edinburgh. At Hogmanay 2007 he again featured as a lone piper on the Edinburgh Castle battlements in the BBC Scotland TV show *Bring in the Bells.* Michael credits Elgin High for interesting him in the pipes and referenced Mr James Hamilton as being so influential in this role. Michael left the Army in 2007 and now teaches bagpipes at the prestigious Edinburgh Academy.

Tom Griffith left Elgin High School, where he was well known for his swimming achievements, in 1990 but missed it so much he decided to go back and re-sit some Highers he didn't get first time around. He then went on to the University of Strathclyde to study Sports Management. Whilst there he broke the Scottish Record for the 50m freestyle and then took a year off to train and swim for Scotland at the Commonwealth Games in Kuala Lumpur in 1998. After that he then went on to work in sports and event sponsorship before moving on to help launch a new advertising medium on metro systems around the world. He is married with two boys, living in the Cotswolds, and is now working as Executive Vice President & General Manager for a company that helps Pharmaceutical companies analyse the results of clinical trials.

Anna Hamilton left Elgin High in 1984 for Aberdeen University graduating in 1988 with a BMus (Hons) degree before teacher training. She worked at Fraserburgh Academy for 16 years before moving into Aberdeen City to promote singing in schools. Now she sees over a thousand children a week: they sing, play games, form choirs etc. She is on the Aberdeen and N.E.S. Music Festival Committee where children are given the chance to perform. At school Anna sang in choirs, took part in Burns Suppers, school plays and theatrical performances. At university she joined the Gilbert and Sullivan Society then with Aberdeen Operatic Society she did a lot of G&S. and some musicals singing Eliza in *My Fair Lady* to a packed HMT in 1995, Ado Annie in *Oklahoma*, Carrie in *Carousel*, Chava in *Fiddler on the Roof* and of course, Yum-Yum in *The Mikado*, Mabel in *Pirates* and Phyllis in a Scottish Parliament themed version of *Iolanthe*. She still sings with AOC, enjoys G&S as much as ever and sings with her pupils at school every day. When she joined AOC she sang the small part of Kate in *Yeomen.* Lately she sang the part of Dame

Carruthers—her elderly aunt. Alas, age catches up with us all.

Barry Jarvis   well known for his forthright expressions of opinion in class
debates as a senior pupil at school, Barry was the first and one of only two
former pupils to be elected as a Moray Councillor—when in May 2007
he began to serve as Labour Councillor for Elgin North at the age of only 22.
Barry whose dad Graham is a former chair of the EHS School Board did a
B.A. degree in politics at Stirling University and then began working for TMC's Community
Care department. He gave serious consideration to becoming a Modern Studies teacher but
decided in the end that that was not for him and today he now works for the Langstane
Housing Association. He has also switched political allegiances and now is a prominent
branch member of the local SNP. Barry is an enthusiastic supporter of the Lantern of the
North Community Group.

Andrew Lyle left in 1998 and five years later graduated from Edinburgh
University   with a masters degree in mechanical engineering with
management. His career has been in the renewable energy industry,
starting as a consultant developing wind farms, solar, hydropower and a
wide range of other renewable energy projects across the UK. In 2009 he
set up a company called Locogen to develop, own and operate renewable energy projects.
The company has grown over the years and he now has a group of companies, including
offices in France and investments in Africa. Andrew has really enjoyed being involved in
such a wide range of interesting projects during his career. He was married in 2017 and with
family life in mind he hopes to hand over running the company to someone else and focus
on something new.

Lee McBride, at the age of 8 started amateur boxing at Elgin Amateur
Boxing Club where his father was the boxing coach. After learning the basis
of the sport for about a year, his father and other members of the
coaching team decided that he was ready for his first competition, which
took place in the small venue of Lhanbryde village hall in front of a crowd
including friends and family members. Lee won his first competition and was hooked on The
Noble Art.

Lee continued amateur competitive boxing up to the age of 26 winning numerous North of
Scotland district championships which resulted in selection to compete at national
championships. When in primary 7 at Greenwards Primary he won his First School boys
championship of Scotland, beating all competitors at his age and weight in the country. This

meant that he was then eligible to represent Scotland and enter the English regional championships where he competed and got to the last 16 for his age and weight in the UK. A year later when at Elgin High School, Lee again won the Scottish national school boy championship and progressed to the last 8 in the English (UK) championships. These results contributed to his selection to represent Scotland at International level and he represented Scotland schoolboys against England schoolboys at the age of 12, in the first of many encounters with the Auld Enemy.

Although after this year the Scottish title evaded him, he was in the finals of every national competition that he entered and continued this momentum in the Seniors (over 17 years of age). Again winning the North of Scotland district championships at senior level meant selection to the Scottish Senior championships, where all boxers over the age of 17 and in the same weight category competed to be the best in Scotland. Lee was never out of the top 8 reaching the semi-finals on 4 occasions and the Scottish final on 1. Throughout his senior amateur career Lee represented Scotland at international level on several occasions traveling to various foreign lands. The first of these was the prestigious world championships which were held in Ottawa Canada in 1992. This was followed by selection to the Commonwealth Games Squad in 1994, but unfortunately an injury at work as a joiner resulted in him being overlooked for this top rate event. His last international—and also one of his last amateur contests—was against Norway 1996.

On the 13th February 1998, after a year of training with professional boxers and trainers Lee entered the paid ranks and had his first and only professional contest that was televised by Sky. After losing because of a nasty cut Lee realised that the professional game was not going to be as lucrative as first thought and decided to try and be reinstated into the amateur ranks. The ruling being that boxers could have up to 3 professional contests and return to the amateur rank if they wished. Lee was unfortunate as this ruling had changed in the months previous and amateur status was denied.

Lee continued to be involved in boxing as a coach in Moray Amateur Boxing Club, a club that he founded in 2002 up until 2015 when due to family commitments he could no longer give the young boxers he was coaching the time they needed to progress in the sport. He still enjoys watching the big fights and also the top class boxers at amateur level and would recommend the sport as a great character and confidence builder to any young boy or girl interested.

Shelley McDonald is synonymous with Music in Elgin High. A participant of many productions as a pupil, early in 2018 she was appointed to the full-time post of Principal

Teacher of Music, having been job sharing with Mr John Watson for two  years. From the age of two, Shelley was keen on dancing and participated in a number of dance shows as a student of June Roy School of Dance. She has taken part in many drama productions - in school and with local societies. Shelley was to the forefront of activities in our BBC Soundtown year (2005/6) and wrote in *Pigeon Post* of her enthusiasm for meeting and interacting with BBC personalities. In session 2006/7, Shelley was fortunate to be nominated by Mrs Norma Watson for a People to People Future Leaders Summit for Theatre and the Arts in New York, which confirmed her desire to pursue a career connected to the performing arts. In her final year at school, Shelley played Scaramouche in Elgin High's production of *We Will Rock You.* She then went on to study Music Education at Aberdeen University, and spent the first three years of her career teaching at St Machar Academy in Aberdeen, before returning to Moray to take up posts in both Elgin High School and Elgin Academy. A singer and pianist, she has performed as part of a busy wedding and function band for a number of years, and is actively involved in the local performing arts scene in Moray.

Craig MacDonald An accomplished musician at school—pianist  Craig won the Talent Contest with singer sister Debbie in 2003—he studied for a BMus (Hons) at the RSAMD in Glasgow winning a Leverhulme arts scholarship to study for a masters degree at the Guildhall School of Music and Drama. He left in 2009 and since then has gone on to have a successful performing and teaching career. As an orchestral musician Craig has performed with the Royal Philharmonic Orchestra, BBC National Orchestra of Wales, Royal Scottish National Orchestra, Scottish Chamber Orchestra, Welsh National Opera, among others. He has also performed with artists including Alfie Boe, Katherine Jenkins, Russell Watson, Tony Hadley, Cockney Rebel and Rufus Wainwright Craig has performed at various venues throughout the UK and abroad including the Royal Albert Hall, the Royal Opera House, London Palladium, Concertgebouw Hall and Berlin Konzerthaus. Craig has also performed on a number of soundtracks including Dr Who and Louis Theroux's Scientology Movie and on a number of touring shows including *West Side Story, Mary Poppins, Sunset Boulevard* and *La La Land* Live UK tour.

Fraser McGillivray whilst at school was a stalwart of our talent shows, Burns Suppers and musicals. He was widely regarded as an extrovert, charming entertainer with an "I'll do anything attitude" and show business in his blood. Whilst only in S2 Fraser won the 2004 Talent contest singing "Baby, When You're Gone" (PP 152) and featured in all the following ones, sometimes as compere. In 2007 having come Third in the talent contest Fraser took on the role of Kashoggi, the Killer Queen's right hand man in our musical "We Will Rock You". Fraser continues the story in his own words: "It was at Elgin High I really got the performing bug. Drama and music were my favourite subjects and I really got to know the two subjects under the fantastic teaching and guidance of Mr and Mrs Watson. Since then I have gone on to become an entertainer in holiday parks and most recently I have moved to Cyprus to perform where I do various local gigs and shows. In between performing, restaurant management and coffee shop work have helped me pay the bills".

Emma McIntosh spent great times at Elgin High doing a lot of community work and organising events, trips to London and extra curricular activities in dance and theatre which stood her in good stead for the future. On leaving school Emma studied dance at college and went on to gain a teaching certificate for ballet teaching from the Royal Academy of Dance. Then she packed her bags and lived a life in London, performing with Pineapple's Performing Arts Industry group and found the right agent. She also was cast in a political drama for the Old Vic Theatre while Kevin Spacey was the resident artistic director. It was then time to pack again, and she headed back home to pursue her ultimate dream of having her own dance, theatre and production school and company. Now, in their 4th year they have over 200 pupils in Elgin over two days of classes, and perform continuously throughout the year. They put on shows, local community and charity events; exams and professional college acceptances and castings increase in number each year. Emma is very proud of S.E Productions (www.facebook.com/seproductionselgin/) and its current link to Elgin High School, having delivered the first Higher Dance in Elgin with the school's support, and now working on the school show "School of Rock" (Summer 2018) involving EHS and associated primary pupils within the cast.

Rory MacKay Arguably the most talented cartoonist who attended EHS, Rory is now a twice-published fantasy author, his first novel *Eladria* being published in 2013, followed by *The Key of Alanar* in 2015. Rory's first Percy Pigeon cartoon appeared in PP 101 (October 1994) and each edition thereafter until he left in May 1997 with PP 114 carried one or two pages of  his intricately drawn satirical cartoon strips in addition to *ad hoc* drawings at various times including front covers. One of Rory's complete tales—*Winter Weirdoland*— appears in the "Talented Cartoonists" section of this book and Rory's artwork made a welcome return as the final page of the last scheduled issue of *Pigeon Post* # 170. Rory has been doodling and drawing from his earliest days at primary school and has studied fine art and social science at college. He now works out of his home in Cullen as a full time writer and professional blogger. His website is dreamlight-fugitive.co.uk.

Julie McKenzie attended Elgin High from 1985 – 1991 and was the first of our students to achieve the Bronze, Silver and Gold Duke of Edinburgh award at the school. This encouraged her to take responsibility, take on additional roles and challenge herself for which she is grateful.

After school Julie attended Moray College for a year doing the pre- nursing course then started her nursing career as a student on the new Project 2000 nursing diploma course at Lothian College of Health Studies in Edinburgh run by Queen Margaret University. She then Worked in Maua Africa for two months at the end of her training. This certainly added to her life experience for sure and she has an absolute desire to go back and work in the underdeveloped countries again.

In 1996 she started working in Dr Gray's Elgin in the general medical ward leading in later years to working in the high dependency unit (HDU). Over the years she has worked her way up in her nursing career from staff nurse to senior staff nurse and now is the Senior Charge Nurse / Sister, in the HDU. This job holds a great deal of responsibility as the role is demanding and she is challenged on a daily basis.

She has travelled extensively all over the world and this is her main passions in life. She also enjoys hobby cake making for her family, going to the gym and being an active part in the life of her amazing nephew Finlay and niece Vaila

Louise Mair Taekwondo (TKD) has played a major part in Louise's  life and led to her becoming Moray Sportsperson of the Year in 2007. Her career started in 2000 when she was 11 and she began competing a year later. During Sixth Year at Elgin High she became a first Dan Black Belt, under the instruction of Mark Russell (Spike) of Focus Martial Arts and Fitness Centre. By the time she'd left school in 2006 she had won the Scottish Cup three times, gained a Gold in the British championships and had begun training with the British Olympic Squad at Loughborough University, where she had the thrilling experience of working alongside members of the Chinese national team. In her last year at school she competed at the Trelleborg Open in Sweden and won Gold in the under 51kg Advanced Senior Female Division.   Later that year she competed against world class opposition in Belgium, Germany, Holland and the Far East. However her ambition to represent Team GB at the Beijing Olympics Games was foiled with only a fourth place in the

European Olympic qualifying event held in Turkey in 2008. In all Louise won the British championships 8 times, between 2005 to 2012 and within those years she also won the Dutch open and many other European A class tournaments. The best experience of all her travels was training in China and Korea where she went five times.

Dr Melanie Marshall   Currently working at the University of Cork,
Melanie is a musicologist with research and teaching interests in gender, sexuality and eroticism in music, and music of early modern Italy. She holds a BMus from the University of Edinburgh and an MA and PhD from the University of Southampton. Since joining UCC in 2005, Melanie has taught at undergraduate and postgraduate levels within the Music Department and on interdisciplinary programmes within the College of Arts, Celtic Studies and Social Sciences. From 2011-2014, Melanie held a Marie Curie International Outgoing Fellowship to conduct research into music and eroticism in early modern Rome. During the fellowship, Melanie spent six months as a Visiting Scholar at UCLA Department of Musicology and eighteen months as a Visiting Scholar at NYU Department of Music. From Sept. 2015, Melanie will also be a Visiting Research Fellow at the Centre for the Study of Music, Gender and Identity at the University of Huddersfield.

Lee Millar played professional rugby with London Scottish who play in
the RFU Championship for three seasons starting in 2013-14, having previously played with Gala in the Borders. The following is taken from the LSR website: "Scottish fly-half Lee Millar joined London Scottish from Gala in the summer of 2013. The youngster kicked over 300 points in the RBS Premier One competition in Scotland during the 2012-13 season and he starred in Gala's victory over Scottish at Netherdale in the British and Irish Cup in October 2012. A product of Moray RFC in Elgin, he spent three years developing his game at Gala and was a key figure in helping the club return to the top flight in Scotland. He has also represented the Scotland Club international XV. The stand-off vies for selection with Welshman Dan Newton in the most hotly contested position at the Club. He scored 110 points in 21 appearances in season 2013-14 which earned him a new two-year deal".

Kevin Morrison left in Fifth Year and spent a year at Moray College before going to university in Dundee to take a degree in Business Studies. After graduating, he moved to Berkshire where he has remained ever since. He qualified as an accountant with Marley plc and held several finance director roles in companies backed by private equity firms including 3i. Later he started a business with a colleague and the business having grown grew rapidly they sold it after five years by which time the turnover was in excess of £90m. Having had some time off Kevin moved from industry to practice and joined a firm of accountants before moving back to industry where he now works for Midwich plc a specialist European distributor of audio visual products. This year he and his wife Claire will celebrate their Silver Wedding anniversary; they have two daughters, one at university in

Manchester and one at Edinburgh. He occupies himself trying to keep fit and playing the saxophone.

Julie Munro-Flanighan was with us from 1986 – 1991. On leaving she worked locally in Grigor and Young then as a nanny before going in Germany for a few years. Having returned to Moray briefly, she moved to Cornwall and qualified as a Psychiatric Nurse after study at the University of Plymouth. With the encouragement of husband Adie and two daughters Daniella and Aimi (19 and 7) Julie wanted to start running and control her

lifelong asthma condition and in time she worked towards a half marathon. She ran the London marathon in 2017 raising awareness and money for the British Legion and Combat Stress, having lost her brother to PTSD. She was part of a team that raised over £200k for The British Legion, gaining recognition for being one of the top fundraisers that year. She had always had a yearning to write a children's book and so last year she put pen to paper and her two children's books, 'Two Socks' and 'Cute a Doodle Do' will be on the shelves this spring. She now plans to do The Great North Run this year, London marathon again next year and there's another book or two in her yet......

Dr Megan Palmer-Abbs At Elgin High Megan was well known as an athlete: she was Intermediate Sports Champion in 1984; she represented Scotland (Scottish Juniors) at the UK Schools Cross Country Championships; she was North District (Scotland) Cross Country Champion for multiple years and was 3rd in Scotland for both Cross Country and 1500m (Junior Girls).

Since leaving school she has held numerous roles. She has predominantly been involved in development as an education officer, she then undertook a Sustainable Development and History of Urban Technology degree, establishing a Sustainable Construction Consultancy. Working across the UK on large public construction projects, delivering some of Scotland and the UK's, most sustainable residential and education buildings, she then turned her focus to digital technology and development.   Now with a Doctorate in rural digital communication and development, she remains engaged with sustainable development and technology.

In this time she has lived in many places across the UK from London, to Bath returning to Moray while her children grew up. Whilst living in Moray she has been an advocate of education, its role in offering opportunities, sitting on the Board of Management of Moray College (for eight years) and latterly the Community Planning Partnership (for three years). In this time she has continued to run but also enjoys the wilderness of Scotland and further afield, hillwalking, mountain biking and cross terrain running, enjoying the Cairngorm Adventure Triathlon and Nairnshire event but ultimately, a love of the outdoors.

Morna Pearson Despite showing a quiet enthusiasm rather than a particular talent for drama while at EHS, the school - crucially - never discouraged Morna from following a theatrical path. She went on to study drama at Queen Margaret University and has been a professional writer now for almost 15 years, with her work taking me to Sweden, Australia and Canada. Her writing draws huge influence from the place,  people and sense of humour of Moray. Here is where her imagination grew up and continues to explore. To date she has mostly written plays, with productions at theatres such as Traverse Theatre, Lung Ha, Catherine Wheels, National Theatre of Scotland, National Theatre Connections. She has recently begun to write for the screen, with her short screenplay *I Was Here*, which was filmed in Moray, produced by the STFN's Scottish Shorts scheme and she is currently developing a sitcom with BBC Studios.

Sandra Pirie Sneddon Looking back over 20 years of experience in Judo Sandra could not have known at the age of 8, where the sport would eventually take her. She started competing soon after beginning training and became Scottish National Champion in 2001 as well as British Schools Champion twice and represented Scotland at the Fife Olympiad in 2003 gaining two silvers. Whilst at EHS, she challenged herself to take up  refereeing and progressed to a National Referee rank and also attained her black belt in 2005.

After High School, she continued in the sport. Whilst training at Inverness Judo Club, she achieved Fifth place at the Commonwealth Judo Championships and a Silver at the National Team Championships. One of her highlights was volunteering at the London Paralympics 2012 and Glasgow 2014 Commonwealth Games. Now living in New Zealand with her Husband, Jamie - who also does Judo - she continues to train and compete and pass on her knowledge and gained her first national Silver Medal at the end of 2017. She knows without the support and dedication of people - like her Mother, Audrey - too many coaches to mention and countless others, all of her achievements would not have been possible.

Kirsty Reid (Johnstone) who joined 1K1 reg class in 1995 felt extremely privileged to be elected as a Moray councillor for Elgin North following the 2014 Independence Referendum, the first woman fp to be elected and only the second altogether. She had been asked by the local SNP branch if she would stand as a candidate following her involvement with the YES campaign. In that she'd spoken to lots of different people - a task she thoroughly enjoyed: as a few of her teachers might remember she did like to chat!

This was a very unexpected chapter in her life. She was then bringing up three young children and working from home in order to be with her kids as much as she could. However she decided that she couldn't just shout from the side lines having been offered the opportunity to play an active role. The by-election through which she became a Councillor had been triggered by the resignation of another fp—Barry Jarvis (then a Labour member) and she felt had some big boots to fill. Kirsty felt it was a shame because she believed Barry and she would have worked well together. Maybe they will one day. Being a local councillor is a tough job. It is impossible to do or be all the things that all the people expect. It was extremely eye opening and hugely challenging but she would highly recommend anyone putting themselves forward to do it. She was elected in Dec 2014 mid term and stood down in May 2017. In that short space of time she learned an immense amount about public service, politics, procedure - and herself. Everyone has something to give and nobody has the answers to everything. Listening is a far greater skill than talking.

As a side note she would say her greatest achievement to date is meeting her husband Douglas Reid (another former pupil) having three wonderful children and keeping them all safe, well and smiling.....to date!.

Stephanie Reynolds Our first reference to Steph comes in PP 123 (Feb 1999) where the 12 year old is featured in the local press for writing and producing her own poetry book, "Friends". However, most references are to her as a runner for example in PP 139 where Steph now in S4 has been capped by Scotland in cross country running. In the next issue her success at the Scottish Schools Athletics championships is noted and in PP143 there is a full Pupil Profile feature on Steph's running achievements. On Sports Day 2003 then in S6 Stephanie broke four long standing school records, for the 100m (established in 1984), 200m (1989), 400m (2001) and 800m (1990). After leaving EHS as "The Runner", Steph was blessed to train with Bill Parker of City of Glasgow AC and won many sporting accolades. Today running helps her mostly now when she late but she has won a few races between 800m - half marathons in the last few years, and run some marathons, ultra marathons and a few 100km races. Steph studied Immunology at University of Glasgow, retrained as a counsellor and now runs a private counselling clinic in London and a worldwide online therapy website with a team in the US. She currently commutes from Malta, where she is studying and volunteering at the local hospital in the hope of applying for medical school this year See a little of her own story in "What Elgin High Did For Me" later in this section.

Dr Neil Rhind Neil was a well-known personality and thespian during his time in Elgin High. He was the continuity compere during our *Fallen Angels* review of Summer 1995, soon after which he presented his one man *Ebolia* Revue in outrageous costume . (See PP 106). He then featured in our 1996 musical *Little Shop of Horrors* playing Mr Mushnik, the flower shop owner and Dr Prospero in the following year's *Return to the Forbidden*  *Planet*. There is a full scale feature on Neil in PP 115 by Robert Cown. After leaving school, Neil didn't get any further than Edinburgh University, where he took a degree in Scottish Literature, and then a doctorate on Alasdair Gray. When Aileen Marshall (EHS librarian) suggested he might like to do his RPR on Gray's "Lanark," she probably didn't think he'd still be studying him fifteen years later. He now works for a bank specialising in financial crime in Edinburgh, but still contributes pieces on Gray to journals, and is kept too busy as one of the organisers/drummers/acrobats of the city's Beltane Fire Festival every May.

Nina Roberts A passion for fashion design took Nina Roberts to Heriot-Watt University where she studied a Clothing Design & Manufacture BSHons degree, graduating in 2007. Whilst studying Nina was commissioned to design an exclusive collection for an alternative clothing brand, some of these designs were later published in a fashion book (Goth; Vamps and Dandies, 2010). In January 2009 Nina moved to  London to join fashion designer Ashley Isham as studio assistant, working at London fashion week and hand finishing pieces for London, Paris and Singapore fashion shows. After working in High Fashion, Nina moved to the Costume industry working at Angels Costumiers (the world leaders) handling costumes for hundreds of productions and for films such as *The King's Speech* and *Harry Potter and Pirates of the Caribbean*. Nina has now worked in Clothes Design for over 10 years, in various roles across Scotland and London, including High Fashion, Bridal-wear, Knitwear, and Film/TV/Music Video Costumes. In 2011 Nina returned to Elgin to create NinaHQ, a design/make/teach studio. NinaHQ has continued growing with private commissions, fashion events and many sewing and craft courses on offer.

Gary Robertson BBC Radio and TV broadcaster and presenter, Gary was a most enthusiastic member of our second S1 in August 1979. He served in the Pupil Council, took part in many dramatic roles, e.g. playing Ernie in *Ernies' Incredible Illucinations* in 1980 and wrote regularly for *Pigeon Post,* his first piece appearing in PP13 (12.79). He was a member of the first ever school Trip to London's West End attractions in late 1982. On leaving school he worked in the local *P&J* office, then for Moray Firth Radio as roving reporter before joining the BBC, working in Dumfries, then London before settling into producer roles at the BBC Glasgow HQ. He featured strongly during Elgin High year as BBC Soundtown and has twice presented the prizes at our prize giving. Today he regularly presents *Good Morning Scotland* and Political Programmes on BBC TV.

Graeme Roger After completing a BA (Hons) in Fine Art / Sculpture, MSC Electronic Imaging at Duncan of Jordanstone College of Art & Design, Graeme has pursued a creative career. His work includes sculpture, film, performance, photography, installations, theatre and residency projects, often collaborating with other artists and musicians, forming part of ROGER & REID and GANGHUT. His projects include residencies at Culloden Battlefield & Aden Country Park. He is also recipient of the Royal Scottish Academy Morton Award for lens based art as part of ROGER & REID. He has experience as a video designer for theatre including the National Theatre of Scotland, Mull Theatre, Theatre Hebrides, Eden Court / Open Book Productions and The Big Fat Electric Ceilidh. Graeme leads the digi team and 'Cashback for Creativity' programme at Eden Court Theatre in Inverness, is Associate Artist at Grampian Hospital Arts Trust and Moving Image tutor for 'Understanding Cinema' for the Filmhouse, Edinburgh. (See also wildbird.org.uk)

Mark Ross Golf was always Mark's passion so much so that he works as a Green Keeper at Elgin Golf Course. Since leaving Elgin High School he has been successful at different levels of competition. His current handicap is Scratch but three years ago it was as low as +3. In 2005 whilst playing in a local Open at Elgin Golf Club sponsored by a very well-known business, Mark shot a score of 62 which broke the course record of 6 under par by one shot. This record still stands today and he is extremely proud of it.

Mark has played in a number of amateur events and has won the North District Championship once, the Moray County Championship twice and holds the title of "Moray Golfer of the Year". As a member of Elgin Golf Club his biggest achievement is winning the

Club Scratch Championship (played over four days) on nine occasions, the most recent being 2017. He has also won the Elgin Golf Club 5 day Open event on three occasions. This annual July event attracts amateur golfers from all over Britain and even as far as America.

At the moment Mark is currently volunteering at the club to promote and encourage Junior Golf, supporting budding golfers in their quest to enjoy the game. So if anyone knows children of any age and ability who would be interested in taking up the great game they can contact the Manager at the club for more information. Had Mark himself not had the support from volunteers during his time as a junior then it would all be very different for him and he is always very appreciative of that.

Georgia Boyd Russell is a Scottish artist who slashes, cuts and dissects
printed matter. In a Brit art scene monopolised by aggressive statement pieces and shock factor, Georgia Russell seems almost controversial. Her subtle, beautiful and laboriously constructed works focus on text, old books, maps and stamps and are gloriously lacking in bizarre elements favoured by some. The daughter of an architect, Georgia grew up just outside Elgin and studied fine art at Aberdeen, before taking a Masters at the RCA. In her first summer holiday, she went to Paris on a residency and became intrigued by text. She trawled the bookstalls along the Seine for material, and became obsessed by old books which formed the basis of her degree show and most of her subsequent work, which has been bought by several major banks, Catherine Deneuve and Brighton's new library. Georgia, our presenter of Prizes in 2005, now lives and works in Germany. Ms Russell was guest of honour at our Prize Giving in 2005. (Most of this taken from an internet article by Polly Vernon in 2005)

Bruce Shepherd Highland Games heavy athlete. Late in 1993, *Pigeon*
Post quoting an article in *The Northern Scot* reported that Bruce (then 26) had won all of the sport's seven major tournaments that year and was "in danger of becoming the greatest amateur Highland Games athlete the North has seen"…"He has consistently thrown, heaved and tossed various objects further, higher and straighter than anyone else on the circuit". That year he broke a ten year old Nairn Games record for the 16 lb Scots hammer.

Bruce explained how much he had enjoyed sport at school and how he had joined Elgin AAC and praised his mentor Mr Alex Valentine, a former technician at Milne's High. With his encouragement Bruce started on the circuit when he was 15. In 1997 Bruce became only the third person ever to be awarded honorary life membership of the Elgin club.

Bruce then worked as a systems analyst in Aberdeen. He had a 17 year career in the oil industry then retrained and is currently a Maths teacher in an Aberdeen school.

Hannah Smith

Twenty six year-old from Aberdeen had booked a holiday to the party town to celebrate being cancer-free, after falling ill with a rare malignant peripheral nerve sheath tumour at the age of just 24. The rare illness, which saw Hannah undergo painful treatment for a year, left her with difficulties walking. But she and her pals were astonished when they arrived at Heathrow's Terminal 5 to find they had been upgraded to 'First' with all the perks that come with it, including free Champagne, flat bed suites and access to plush lounges.

After a luxurious First class flight, Hannah and her friends were whisked off to Las Vegas' most iconic resort – Caesars Palace – where they were upgraded from their standard rooms to the Nobu Hotel's glamorous Hakone Suite. The stunning suite in the luxurious boutique hotel within a hotel included a living area, its very own bar, two separate bedrooms fit for celebrities, and a sweeping panoramic view of Las Vegas Boulevard. Hannah, said: "Being ill makes you realise that life is for living - and Las Vegas is certainly a place to feel alive! Our trip turned from a holiday in to a something out of a Hollywood film, with limos, helicopters, a glamorous hotel suite, even a private breakfast for us with a local celebrity chef overlooking the Grand Canyon. It was more than I could ever have dreamed of, I'll never forget it." (Edited from a *British Airways* publication of 27.1.17. Thanks to Donald Squair for drawing our attention to it).

James Smith

A strong case can be made to award to the late James Smith the accolade of the Most Remarkable of All Former Pupils of Elgin High—ever. As such he deserves special treatment, which we have given in a feature at the end of this section

James joined our S1 reg class 1F1 in August 1998 and immediately stood out from the crowd, because he went about school in a wheel-chair, on account of his suffering from brittle-bone disease. But to say James was "wheel-chair bound" could not be more wrong and he rose to become one of the top wheel chair athletes in the country. However, James knew that he had a limited life expectancy and he died very suddenly having gone with friends to the Rock Ness Festival in June 2009, aged 22. He succumbed to an asthma attack and passed away in Raigmore Hospital, Inverness, amid much grief from his mates. His mother Susan Farley paid tribute to him, saying "James never moaned or grumbled about his condition. There was nothing he couldn't do and he had a wicked sense of humour."

Mark Smith Now using his birth and professional name Mark Cameron, Mark is well known nationally as a dancer, dance teacher and choreographer, currently working for the MGA Academy of Performing Arts, in Edinburgh. He has also established Mark Cameron Dance/Corporate building on years of international experience as dancer and director, for example working for Disney in Paris and Tokyo with the Scottish Youth Theatre and on P&O cruise liners as singer and versatile dancer. From Primary school days Mark was  interested in acting and performing and memorably spent the whole of Summers 1997 and 1998 with the Scottish Youth Theatre. Mark cut his teeth locally in school productions and working with Elgin Amateur Dram Soc. and the St Giles Theatre Group.

Tracey Devine Smith Cyprus based Tracey who trained at Clancy's hair salon in Elgin in the 1980's is a major force in the international hair industry, her success reinforced by back-to-back victories as Scottish Hairdresser of the Year (2006, 2007, 2008 and 2009). In September 2007, Tracey was crowned Fellow with Honours by the Fellowship of British Hairdressing in recognition of her achievements as both innovator and  educator. She is regarded as an inspirational figure in teaching. As a Master, she is a regular on stage at major events including Salon International. In the same month, she also secured Most Wanted Photographic award. In 2012/13, Tracey added to her accolades by winning the title of British Men's Hairdresser of the Year. In 2013/2014 Tracey was the British Fellowship Hairdresser of the Year, a title she is immensely proud of then British Image of the year winner in 2015/16 for the Fellowship for British hairdressing. 2017 saw her win *Hair Now* magazine's image of the year. She has also established a reputation as a photographer.

Christopher Starkie loved being at Elgin High and clearly has a sense of humour about it. He recalls that you could fit inside the pigeon holes in the canteen - butt first; the thrill of crossing the forbidden threshold on Y floor and hearing Mr Cadenhead bellowing after you. Every day was a laugh and there was never a dull moment. His favourite place was the music practice room, in which he felt like a rock star. After school he studied  drama at college, then worked on a cruise ship as an entertainer and went to London to study acting at The Central School of Speech and Drama. He worked as an actor for eight years after graduating. He enjoyed spells stints at the BBC, Shakespeare's Globe Theatre and around the world with the Gregory Burke 'Black Watch' drama. He travelled a lot and worked with some very talented people. He also married his beautiful wife Lisa (also an EHS fp as Lisa Douglas) in Chicago whilst on tour. Somewhere along the way he lost his hair. After having a family his priorities changed. He needed to try something completely different, so in 2016 joined the Police. Last year he won a Bravery award and managed to make 1204 cups of tea, allegedly.

Barry Stephen first began stockcar racing in 1990, aged 11  years old, when he raced in a Junior Class called Ministox and did so till he was 16 after which he progressed to his first adult class. There were a few Classes he could have chosen from but the one he wanted to be in was Brisca Formula 2/ Superstox. In an autobiography he wrote whilst at Elgin High School, he set as his ambition in life becoming World Champion in this Class of Stock Car racing. In 2017, at the age of 39 he fulfilled this childhood ambition and became Brisca Formula 2/ Superstox Champion of the World! A dream come true for him and a great moment in his life. It has taken many years of hard work and effort not only from Barry but by his team to secure this title. He and his team are looking forward to racing in 2018 as the World Champions and defending this title later on this year in Northern Ireland.

Dr Janet Stewart is currently Professor and Head of School in the  School of Modern Languages and Cultures at Durham University. Previously, she was Senior Lecturer in German and Film & Visual Culture at the University of Aberdeen, having received her PhD in German and Sociology from the University of Glasgow in 1998. In 1995, she was a Junior Fellow at the International Research Centre for Cultural Sciences in Vienna. Her main research interests lie in visual culture: she has published widely on Austrian and German literature and visual culture, cultural sociology and urban history. Dr Stewart was guest of honour at our Prize Giving in 2007.

Martin Lee Thomson started playing euphonium aged 8 having initially wanted to play trombone but ended up falling into euphonium, being taught by Alasdair Grant and George Simpson. Through Moray music competition, he heard about St Mary's Music School from Francis Cummings, the ex head of Music at St Mary's who was at the festival and encouraged him to audition. From then on, he badgered his mum to let him audition, finally getting the chance to go down two years later, with the help from his teachers Alasdair and George, and was awarded a place. However, with no way of purchasing an instrument it was looking unlikely for him to accept the place. Through the help of Elgin High School, Elgin City Band, Moray Swing Band, Moray Concert Brass, St Giles Church, local businesses, and anonymous benefactors, he was able to overcome this socioeconomic disadvantage and accept a place at St Mary's. During his time at Elgin High School he made many life-long friends, and was particularly inspired by art teacher, Mr John Brady, along with his main brass teacher, both of whom encouraged him to take the path that led him to where he is today. Martin has many memories of having spent breaks and lunch times in the practice rooms often making music with friends.

Some of his happiest times are rehearsing and performing with Moray Concert Brass, Moray Wind Orchestra, Elgin City Band. More recently, he was asked to be a featured soloist at the Moray Concert Brass 25[th]anniversary concert, which was one of the most memorable and special concerts he's ever played. Now a student at Trinity Laban Conservatoire, London Martin plays euphonium, trombone, tuba, sousaphone, accordion, piano, and sings. He is hoping to soon get into synths, such as: Organelle and Korg. He has a wide range of music tastes and plans to pursue his dream to perform internationally as a soloist and alongside friends in groups such as Aeris Brass, Dopey Monkey, the Old Fountain Jazz Orchestra, and the Old Jelly Rollers. He hopes to further these groups to an even more professional level, as well as making his personal creative ideas a reality. Finally, he hopes to get a dog, and name it Nanook, hopefully in the very near future.

Kevin Walker Along with David Gray (see above) Kevin was a stalwart of  the first Elgin High football teams—serving as Captain of our first Under 14 side—and making football a major part of his life ever since. Kevin was the first of our pupils to become Player of the Year. He played for Burghead Thistle juniors when he was in our senior school and after he left and was Player of the Year there in his first season. He signed for Highland League side Forres Mechanics in 1984, was part of their title winning side in 1985/6, and played over 600 games for them in his 16 years with the club. He missed only one game through injury and was also Captain for a spell. Kevin gained a testimonial from the Club in a game at Mosset Park v Heart of Midlothian in 1994. Teams he played in won the League Championship, North of Scotland Cup and Inverness Cup. He then became player/manager of junior side Forres Thistle for 12 years, winning the North Regional Junior League. Kevin had a season as manager of Lossiemouth Highland League side and latterly was manager of Burghead Thistle, whom he left in 2017.

Malcolm (Mac) Walker An accomplished public speaker at school—where his other interests included cello, piano, crime drama and chess—Malcolm won the accolade of Deloitte & Touche/CIBS Young Banker of the Year in 2002. After taking a B.Sc in Organic Chemistry at the University of Edinburgh he joined the Royal Bank of Scotland's Corporate &

Commercial Division. Between 2004 and the great crash of 2007, Mac (as he is known to colleagues) moved to work on strategy development for the bank and worked in Hong Kong, Singapore and Boston whilst several large banks were integrated into RBS. Following the crisis banking went into contraction, and whilst he made it through the cuts (to date!) in workforce, it spurred him into starting his own businesses. On top of his day job he also operates his own vacation rental business, *Hebridean*
Home, and is the founder and proprietor of a web and business design and advice business called *Another Angle*. Both these have provided key insights on what its like to run your own show. Mac is still with RBS today, however, and is part of the Innovation team, driving a strategy which is bringing to life the way RBS customers tell the organisation how they want to bank in today's digital world. Malcolm was Guest of Honour at our 2004 prize giving.

Ian Wallace was the first pupil editor of *Pigeon Post* and contributed words and photographs to many of the first forty issues. Ian became a Police Cadet in 1982 and went on to write about his early police experiences in PP 41. Ian served with Grampian Police for 31 years at various stations in Aberdeen and Aberdeenshire, retiring in 2013 at the
rank of Chief Inspector. Since then, he has worked in several local authority roles and was the Guest of Honour at the 2008 Prize Giving.

Roy Young No person better personifies the school than Roy who having entered it in 1978 as a Second Year pupil, has spent only one year away from the campus—as a Costings Clerk for Robertson's— and now works day and night in the school, as technician and handyman/ caretaker.

At school Roy was a member of the Pupil Council, captain of the combined S1/2 rugby squad. He was also Eagles House Captain two years running. He holds a trio of extant sports records e.g. in discus, long jump and the 100m (11.9 secs) created during his rivalry with Neil Proven and others on Sports Days. He was Intermediate Boy and then Senior Boy Champion in 1980 and 1981 respectively. He and Neil jointly presented the Sports Trophies in 2009. He returned to work in school in 1983 as the Technical Department Technician. He has always exuded a macho image— playing rugby for Moray College and then Moray RFC—and during Red Nose Day fund raising events willing to endure pain as in getting his legs waxed.

Poignantly, as one of the first pupils of the school, Roy kept a daily photographic record of the building's last days as it suffered demolition in the early part of 2018: see Chapter 5 for some of his photographs.

Lyndzie Jeffrey   After school, Lyndzie took an HNC Child Care & Education course then worked as a nursery nurse before undertaking Nursing training in Paediatrics and she has been a qualified paediatric nurse, working RACH theatres since 2006.

Her main sporting interest is Taekwondo in which became a black belt in 1999, 2nd Degree black belt in 2001, 3rd Degree black belt in 2004, 4th Degree black belt in 2008, 5th Degree black belt on 2013, and sat her 6th Degree black in 2018.

As Master Lyndzie she is the head instructor at her own very successful school, teaching Olympic style World TKD - Granite City Taekwondo, - which she has run as a non-profit making club for 16 years. She has won numerous competitions for both sparring and patterns. She was selected for the Scottish poomsae (patterns) team in August 2010; she attended the Commonwealth Taekwondo Championships representing Scotland in January 2011 in Chennai India returning as a Bronze medallist. At the British Championships in February 2011 in Sheffield she won a Gold medal and so became British Champion. This led to selection for the British Taekwondo Poomsae squad with whom she has trained regularly and she was selected to compete in the European Championships in Italy May 2011, and the World Taekwondo Championships in Vladivostok, Russia July 2011. She achieved Great Britain's best ever results – coming in 8th at the Europeans and 11th at the Worlds in the 2nd Senior individual female category. Following this she was selected for the European Championships in Alicante April 2013, and proved herself worthy of another selection for Commonwealth Championships in Scotland 2014, at which she achieved Gold. She was selected for the World Championships 2016 in Serbia and won Gold in the master Games in Nice in France in 2016 She was selected for the Europeans at Rhodes in 2017.

Donna Burns Class of (1992 - 1997) is an inspiration to many of us. The charity work she has undertaken is admirable, especially when you take into account her ill health and debilitating medical conditions. The following few snippets indicate what an amazing wee gem she is: In 2001 Donna and Lyndzie Jeffrey raised money and awareness for the National Deaf Children's Society by skydiving. A terrifying experience for Donna as the harness dislodged and caught around her neck, but she survived to tell the tale and of course have a wee joke about it. In 2005 only months after breaking her hip, she completed a wing walk on a 1940's bi-plane facing wind speeds of 100mph in aid of the Anthony Nolan Bone Marrow Trust. With a sense of humour that puts most of us to shame, Donna even saw the bright side of a suspected fractured spine after a little too much...er dancing at Speyfest. She has fire-walked, learnt to fly a plane, travelled widely and abseiled off the Forth Railway Bridge. That abseil was for a charity that means a lot to her, The Chest, Heart and Lung Foundation. Alongside Kerry Henderson and Sue Rodwell Donna abseiled around 145  feet from the bridge. As well as being a wonderful mother figure, Donna has become a Chernobyl host and has hosted children from deprived and underprivileged backgrounds, welcoming them into her family and showing them love and wonderful experiences of Scotland. She has an absolute heart of gold!

Namaste. (From Jane Ross)

Kevin Isaac Most of the time Kevin was at school the teachers weren't doing extra activities because of industrial action so he missed out on school plays, sports teams etc. Therefore EHS wasn't the best years of his life : don't tell his kids, though. When he left he had 11 jobs in 13 months after two years at college. His main earnings came from playing in a band at weekends but he wanted more. Having never been abroad he moved to  Spain aged 21 and found it was exciting—hard work with long hours and low pay as holiday rep. But the socializing, the adventure and the Spanish way of life he loved. He worked at first for Thomson Holidays and used that as a platform to success as an entertainer in a hotel then to work as a compere in a bar. He practised most days and had a few sidelines so saved money and enjoyed a good quality of life. But he always wanted to be better and entertain more people by going on the Cabaret circuit as comedy tribute to Elvis. Through experience watching others and practice he began as a comedian and now has been 20 years in Tenerife south presenting a popular show, working in 4-star hotels and British cabaret bars. He has featured on numerous TV shows but his biggest achievement is his three girls.

Contact comedyelvis@hotmail.com facebook COMEDY ELVIS SHOW

The page reprinted on p 210 from PP60 (May 1987) suggests that Kevin was always a cheeky lad.

PUPIL PROFILE

KEVIN STUART ISAAC (Sixth Year) born 10th February 1970 in Aberdeen, lived in Burghead until he was five then moved to the bright city lights of Birnie. He has three brothers, Ian, Duncan and Gary and many other admirers like his mother Isobel and father Kenny.

If you know Kevin well - Congratulations ! - you'll know he enjoys a laugh and dislikes being serious. He is 6ft tall and his weight is two, too heavy; he has blue eyes, blonde hair and a large physique.

School for Kevin has been a long hard fight but now its time to make an exit. He has some happy memories of school especially when it's closed. His favourite teachers in Primary School were Mrs Thom and Mr Farquhar whom he had a good laugh with. He remembers the Xmas concerts most in primary because he always had a big part. Does anybody remember the time when Kevin burst out laughing on stage ? Or the year he shouted out to Mr F., "That's my mam's knickers !!"

He has tried to get the best out of school even though he is not exceptionally brainy, but has tried to enjoy his school years. Secondary school led to Kevin meeting many more friends through football/rugby teams and other activities. Football has always been important to Kevin: he supports Aberdeen F.C. and has always been a loyal faithful supporter of Elgin City. But whatever team anybody supports he would chatter all day long (probably ending up arguing.) He is very active when it comes to sports, has helped to set up the Youth Club in Birnie and likes being involved in organising events.

Music is what he spends most of the time on if he is not out in the garden. He can play the trumpet, a little on the bass, rhythm guitar, harmonica and he tries to sing. His formation of the band The Ballboys has been a break through in his life and he hopes to hit the big time. He likes a wide range of music from Country n Western to Heavy Metal but generally enjoys good singable, lively popular music.

Pictures of Kevin when he was a nice little lad.

Television is another pastime of his, favourite programmes including Grange Hill, The Saint and Greavesie, Tutti Frutti, Spitting Image, Coronation Street, Eastenders etc. His other likes include motorbiking on his mod mean machine, his Sunday paper job, gardening, being a Managing Director, and good shin-digs.

Kevin's future at the moment looks bleak but dreams of becoming a musician/comedian/actor professionally may come true one day. But it looks as if he will just go to Moray F.E. College to become even more brainy.

(Extracts from "Life's a Laugh" by Kevin S. Isaac)

3

210

Paula Marion Aldin-Scott

23rd January 1966 – 3rd October 2017

One of the first pupils of Elgin High when it opened in 1978, Paula sadly died in 2017 from secondary cancer, but it's worth remembering that for Paula cancer was never a battle to win or lose, but an experience to navigate with courage and dignity. As she'd done all her life, Paula did and saw as much as possible, and appreciated every moment she had with friends and family, as the following account contributed by brother Gordon and sister Beverly demonstrates.

Paula was born in the border town of Selkirk. At Elgin High School she was a sporty, popular girl, with a warm winning smile. She participated in many aspects of school life, particularly

enjoying basketball and drama. The photo left shows her seated left in the one act play *The Bloaters* in 1980.

With an eagerness to learn, Paula studied for a HND in Business Administration at Telford College, followed by an honours degree in Social and Management Science from Napier University, and a post graduate diploma in Information Systems from Napier in 2000.

Paula had a strong work ethic from the outset. Her first job was cleaning the toilets in a solid concrete block at the Bay Caravan Park in New Elgin, upon which she started in January 1977, so one can only imagine how chilly that must have been!

She worked for incoming tour operator MacKenzie River Travel, then as a Customer Service Manager for Eurocontrol in Brussels. In 2000 Paula took on a Communications and Strategy role for the Edinburgh Youth Social inclusion Partnership, a role she felt particularly passionate about, always believing that young people had so much more to offer.

From 2004 there was a stint in London working for The National Council for Palliative Care as a Support and Development Manager. Then in 2006 she returned to Edinburgh to work in Policy and Outreach for Edinburgh's Voluntary Organisations' Council. She also joined the Management group of the Citadel Youth Centre, a voluntary role that was very close to her heart.

She also worked for COMAS, the social innovation charity which uses community

Paula at a 2005 reunion of some of the first pupils : front left...Michael MacRae, Kenny Green, Geoff Lee, Elaine (Hutchison) Ford, David Hector, Paula, Shirlene (Abbott) Halbert, Martine (Fletcher) Baillie. Back row from the left Kevin Morrison, Gregor Milne, Ian McDonald, Angela (Watt) Matchett,

development to help people find the solutions they need. From 2013 to 2016 Paula worked for the National Neurological Advisory Group, and latterly as a Project Manager for the Health and Social Care Alliance, until her health made that impossible.

Paula's commitment to the community of people who had a neurological condition was unswerving. Irene Oldfather, Director of The Health and Social Care Alliance Scotland said that Paula was meticulous in the production of work plans, and one of the most organised people she'd come across. She was the epitome of everything they believe in as an organisation - the person with the long term condition in the driving seat, testing, challenging, researching and fighting.

It is so typical of Paula that when she spent time in the hospice with Islay her dog, she was part of a trial to see how pets could fit into that environment.

In her role as the Chairperson of TCAT 'Transforming Care After Treatment' and through her involvement with the Cancer Experience Panel, Paula made an impact expertly managing the activities of the panel and serving on the project board where she was never shy of expressing her point of view.

From her upbringing in Selkirk, Galashiels, Elgin, and Edinburgh, to living in Glasgow, Saint-Tropez, Tubingen in Germany, Chicago in the States, St. Ettienne in France, Brussels, London, Cumbernauld, and latterly back in Edinburgh, Paula showed could make anywhere home, and made lasting friendships wherever she went.

She is dearly missed by all who knew and loved her.

A graduate guy

Wheelchair bowling champ James Smith has reason to be cheerful after gaining his latest accolade – this time not in the world of bowling, but rewarding academic success.

The former pupil of Elgin High School, has graduated from Moray College with a BSc in computing. James, of 14 Newfield Road, Elgin, had to wait a year for his graduation day, as he was part of the Scottish team competing in the Indoor Bowls for the Disabled World Bowling Championships in Sydney, Australia, when last year's ceremony took place.

James is busy job hunting, and while he waits for the right break, he's spending his spare time getting in plenty of bowling practise.

From *The Times* November 2nd, 2002

From the Autumn 2009 (#95)

Newsletter of the Brittle Bone Society

Reproduced with permission

JAMES SMITH

We were all very sad to learn of the death of James Smith from Elgin. James was only 22 years old but was already a very accomplished international bowler and was an inspiration to everyone who knew him.

James was introduced to bowling at Stoke Mandeville when he was 13 years old. He was soon playing in the junior section of Elgin Bowling Club on Wednesdays, after school and got a specialised wheelchair for the bowling greens.

By the age of 16 he was competing in the South Pacific Invitational in Sydney and the WIBC-U 25 Singles in Belfast. A year later he partnered Ivan Prior to the British Isles Wheelchair Pairs title and went on to help Scotland win the Home Counties International series in 2004, 2006 and 2007.

James really enjoyed playing in Australia partly because he really enjoyed bowling in hot conditions on fast greens and he returned there in 2007 when he finished fourth in the World Wheelchair Singles and in the same year he won the Scottish Wheelchair Outdoor Singles.

He said that he would never forget the people he had met and the experiences he had had because of bowls and he remained a very positive person despite all his health problems. He enjoyed life to the full and was at a rock festival with his friends when he took ill.

213

Great Scot - James Smith

As BWBA Chairman I have many of what I call 'good news' phone calls. Hearing from James Smith's step-dad Peter that he had died suddenly was a 'bad news' call, an extremely 'bad news' call.

James died in June from a suspected asthma attack after becoming ill during the RockNess music festival in Inverness; he was just 22-years-old.

Born with Osteogenesis Imperfecta, known more commonly as brittle bone disease, James didn't let the condition prevent him from becoming one of the UK's most talented and successful bowlers.

He first came onto the BWBA radar at a National Junior Wheelchair Games in Stoke Mandeville when, to the best of my knowledge, he was 13-years-old.

The BWBA coaches were raving about how talented he was - and they weren't wrong.

His frail frame and, at the time, small stature belied the bowling talent held within. Even at that age he was good.

He was a real bowling talent who happened to be in a wheelchair.

James was invited by Brian Davies, secretary of the World Indoor Bowls Council, to play in the WIBC Under-25 Singles Championship in Belfast in 2002, at the age of 16. Indeed, he beat Safuan Said, who had won medals at that year's Commonwealth Games - and who went on to win the world outdoor singles title in Christchurch.

Also that year, James competed in the South Pacific Invitational event in Sydney, and, a year later, partnered Scottish fellow wheelchair bowler Ivan Prior to the UK National Wheelchair Pairs Title.

As a longstanding member of the Scottish wheelchair bowls team, James helped Scotland win the Home Countries' International Series in 2004, 2006 and 2007 and had been earmarked as an important part of the Scottish team for the Glasgow Commonwealth Games in 2014

Since discovering bowls at Stoke Mandeville, James had travelled all over the world, and was always delighted to meet new and interesting people along the way. He also gained a degree in computing at Moray College earlier this year.

James' funeral was held at St Columba's Church in Elgin his hometown. The Rev George Rollo told mourners it was only the second time in 23 years that he had seen the church so full.

Universally liked for his open, friendly and laid-back demeanour - along with a very dry sense of humour, everyone has good memories of James and some great stories too, some of which cannot be printed but have been shared in bars in the past and will be shared in bars in the future.

He died a young man who was on his way to maturing into a fine man, what a shame we will not see that. I miss him and I know many others do too. My heartfelt condolences to mum Susan, step dad Peter, sister Lauren and to dad Andrew.

From issue 15 of *Nationwide Bowler* magazine

By Ian Blackmore

BWBA Chairman

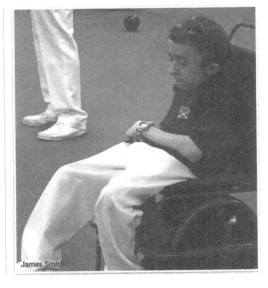

James Smith

And some who "got away".....

A listing of some of the fps suggested as candidates for inclusion within the previous pages by their peers on the Facebook site, but whom we couldn't persuade to be featured (with a hint of what you might have learned about them).

We'll leave it to you to link the pix to the captions......

Dr Dominic Boyter — NHS Grampian

Claire Cameron — social worker /music wellbeing sessions

Johnnie Edmonston — Engineer, British Antarctic Survey

David Dick Gray — Mainstay of early EHS football teams.

Gregg Leppard — Musician

John McCallum — Musician

Dr Barry McKenzie — Operations Manager at BWSC.

Jenny Milne — Champion golfer

Alan Robertson — Acclaimed chef

Jane Stuart — Model and actress

2. What Elgin High Did For Me

Former Pupils were invited via the Facebook FP website Former Elgin High School Students to contribute some thoughts about how their schooling had influenced their future careers, what pleasures, inspirations and challenges they found as pupils.   Here are some of their responses……

Fraser Cluness, currently Head Janitor, Braehead High School, Brae Shetland

Elgin High? How can I drag my memories out of their 30 year old bank?

I remember my first day well. I arrived with my mum and was handed over to Mr Hope who took me into the room next to his office where I met Lenny Peel and his two brothers who were also new that day. We remained friends our entire schooling there.

I was quite shy but I can also be a bit gobby so I was well in there as I had moved from Elgin Academy and knew a few people from there who had also come to Elgin High..

I seemed to get on ok; most subject teachers were fine, although I can only remember a few of their names now. I wasn't the brightest kid in the box but it took until I was 28 to find out my writing problems were down to dyslexia and I was not "just thick" as my bullies often taunted.

I found all of the teachers very supportive and they never let on that I was ever below any academic level to me, raising my personal academic self esteem to as high a level as it could go at the time. I learned how to cope with it and that there was more than one way to skin a cat. And they gave me the tools to get there too.

During the first December (1978) I realised For the first time I was going to be in a school play and I just loved drama.   Unknown to me it would stay with me all my life, as after I left school I joined a drama group's lighting team where I live. This one element of my life to this day I will always be grateful for as I rose to become the chief lighting engineer in our local theatre and whenever I'm near theatres (e.g. when I go to London) I go and see as many shows as I can, and my total is now in the hundreds.

I also started producing plays for the school I worked in and adult groups for the local drama festival and it's good to think that my name is on a few cups now all because of Mrs. Duncan in drama, and Mr Ross who directed me in Foiled Again! (See cropped photo from PP 10, right).

A year later I was in "Joseph" (PP 15) and a few of the smaller plays, but this stopped dead when my main bully joined in the Christmas show drama productions too.   I was so sad then, but remained in the smaller productions to keep my hand in!

Yes I left school with poor grades but I left also with a power of self worth which has lasted 40 years. I have worked nearly 30 years with children here where I live and always tell them to work hard, always try their best, and always think if you want to do something, you can! Some get an easy road and some have to go a longer harder road but their paths do all meet at the same place. I got all this from Elgin High, though I later returned to college at 28 and got those academic qualifications in business and a few years later again in childcare.

I was taught at Elgin High if I wanted to do something there was always a way to get there. So as the school headed for its 10th anniversary, I found myself working and with a bit of money behind me.   I always remembered what the school had done for me and I took a notion to thank the school in one way. I wondered if I could donate a prize? I asked Mr Hope what he thought too. I got a massive "Yes" from him but for what subject would I give it? I had two in mind, Drama being the first, but Mr Hope said that would be harder to give out every year and Service to the School, would always be given out, so service to the school it was.

I thought in the past I would never receive a prize at the school prize giving, I never even registered it was ever on! I accepted from my bullies that I was 'too thick', not built for sport, or talented musically as we could never afford the lessons or instruments anyway. I hated everything about PE. Then to my utter amazement in my last (Fourth) year at EHS I got the Service to the School Prize, the one where you don't have to be sporty or exceptionally brainy! This one was just for people who showed commitment and worked hard for the school. I think I have always done that everywhere I have worked.

So that's how **The Fraser Cluness Service to the School** trophy came about, (even although the school often spells my last name wrongly!) It is available annually, to be given to the person/s who don't have to be sporty or top academically, it's to get that pat on the back for those who try their best and work hard for the school or at their work, a thing all employers look for now too.

Even although the bullies were there and I stopped going to things at the school because of them I always remembered that I was better than them inside. Yes I became shyer and built a mistrust in people, which I still feel today sometimes. But hopefully one day those bullies met their match. I often wonder if I had kept in the Christmas shows at school if I would have a hobby of being on stage rather than in the lighting box or taking tickets at the door (both paid jobs I've had in theatre) but I've managed to make a good path anyway so they never won in the end.

Some things I will remember most from days at EHS is in my last month Mr Dugdale saying to me a piece of work I did was worth an A if you discounted the spelling. (Yes, I had to give him that!) Mrs. Duncan and support in the drama department, which became a part time job. Mrs. McPherson and Mr. Anderson running the Elgin Crusaders and SU where I then became a youth leader part time then later a classroom assistant and Play worker full time for 15 years. I look back and all the bricks in my life wall and they definitely created the biggest foundations which as an adult I was able to rely on— so a big thank you to them.

I was sad to hear EHS1 is leaving us. We remember our school days for the good and the bad memories. Hopefully its more good. But one thing that bonds us around 200 of us is we went to Elgin High when it started.

Carole Miller (née Lawton) currently musician, arts promoter and educator.

Having been asked what Elgin High School did for me, I've had a good long think about my school days. I had been off sick on the P7 induction day so, not having been in the school building at all, on the first day of S1 I was quite apprehensive about what to expect but I

needn't have worried. Over the many years since leaving school, I have come to realise that our time there was really quite special.

It's said that the staff are what makes a school along with a firm hand at the helm. It's true that you never remember how you were taught and the teaching methods used but you remember the adults who went above and beyond. Here we are 40 years later and my contemporaries and I can name all our teachers and other staff within EHS during our time there. This stands testament to the opportunities the staff provided for us to learn and to excel within and out with the academic curriculum! The strongest memories I have are of the extra-curricular activities. There were shows every year, one act plays, pantomimes, debating, Burns Suppers, musical evenings and anyone could take part if they wanted to. I wasn't sporty

Carole as the Good Fairy Tranquilheart in "Puss in Boots" (1982)

at all so it gave me a chance to shine in other ways but you were always encouraged whether you excelled or not!

So what did EHS do for me? Well it's for sure that I would not have the confidence to speak to audiences when I perform if it hadn't been for all the performing opportunities given

including getting taken to Burns Suppers by Mr Hope in return for a plate of Haggis, Neeps and Tatties. So thank you staff of 78-83 for everything you did for us. We might not have appreciated it at the time, but I, for one, am extremely grateful.

Carole *left* with fellow originals Kate Yeo, Angela Matchett and Janice Hyndman in 2017 during a visit to the old school

Kate (Teenie) Cottam...(now Kate Yeo) currently based in London, working as a road safety auditor for a large American engineering company.

In the early days of the Elgin High School, the Hillwalking Club introduced me to the joys of climbing big hills, and started me on a route which enabled me to fulfil my late husband's dream to the best of my abilities.

The hillwalking club was run by Mr Birnie, my biology teacher. Once a month on a weekend, the club members would meet at eight in the morning in the school car park and travel by bus into the Cairngorms for a day's walking. It cost £2 a trip per person, and we had to bring our own lunch.

I didn't have any proper gear, but Mr Birnie kept a stock of boots in the cupboard for pupils to borrow, and I was lucky enough to be able to make use of a pair. Having access to those boots made it possible for me to take part.

I loved our days out despite the aching legs and always being at the back. I have happy memories of deep snow, steep climbs, and being sustained by pot noodles prepared using hot water carried in a thermos flask. Best of all was the feeling of satisfaction at the end of it, and of being able to see for miles when we were up high. My view of the world expanded, literally, and I became hooked both on travel, and on hillwalking.

Suffice to say I've climbed a fair few hills since then – mostly in the UK, but some farther afield.

When my husband (also a keen walker) was alive, his dream was always to climb Mount Everest. Sadly, he died in 2007 before realising his dream, so I decided to take some of his ashes to Nepal, and to get him as close as I could. I'm not a technical climber so Everest was always going to be beyond my abilities, but a chance to climb Mera Peak came up that same year- 6,476m of trekking peak with a close-up view of Mount Everest from the summit—and I jumped at the opportunity. It was a three week

Kate with Everest in the distance

trip; two weeks to approach and climb the peak, and a further week to descend back down to Lukla. The mountain was higher than I'd ever been before; there was a glacier field to traverse and an ice bridge to cross to get to the summit, so it was a very serious undertaking for me.   But I just kept on keeping on (always my motto), and our small team eventually summited on a clear sunny morning with enough wind to carry my late husband's ashes into the air and hopefully across to nearby Mount Everest. I felt I'd done my best for him.

Without my early introduction to hillwalking at Elgin High School, I may never have built up the experience to be able even to attempt such a climb, let alone achieve it, and for that I'm eternally grateful to both Mr Birnie, and the Hillwalking Club.

Stephanie Reynolds, now a Counsellor and part time runner

I have such fond memories of EHS and feel really indebted to all the teachers; you struck this perfect balance between getting the curriculum into us and the flexibility to develop as individuals. I remember being allowed to go training out the back of the school on my free periods!

Continuing after leaving EHS as "Steph the Runner", I was blessed to train with Bill Parker of City of Glasgow AC and won the Scottish University Championships Silver, Scottish Outdoor Championships Silver, Scottish District Outdoor and Indoor Championships Gold and Scottish Indoor Championships Gold in 2004; ranking 5th in the UK for the 800m. I was capped and won bronze for Scotland and shortlisted to be mentored by Dame Kelly Holmes, although sadly became injured and couldn't compete in the selection race.

Running helps me mostly now when I'm behind my work schedule but I've won a few races between 800m - half marathons in the last few years, and run some marathons, ultra marathons and a few 100km races; a highlight being a 24 hour race dressed in double denim alongside my (very loyal) sister Bernie Reynolds Walker: see photo of us together in which I am getting a piggyback.

221

I studied Immunology at University of Glasgow, retrained as a counsellor and run a private counselling clinic in London and a worldwide online therapy website with a team in the US. I currently commute from Malta, where I'm studying and volunteering at the local hospital in the hope of applying for medical school this year. A huge heartfelt thank you to all at EHS for everything you do.

G. J. (Gordon) Thow (1999-2005)

My Experience Helping At Kestrel House

During my six years at Elgin High School. I helped out at Kestrel House when it was lunch time, most of the time. Kestrel House was a special needs unit where children who either needed extra help or who had severe difficulties were taught and looked after. Some of the activities I was involved with included helping the pupils with their work, some chores like washing the dishes, taking the trolley to the school canteen and doing games with the pupils. I enjoyed my experience there, as not only did this give me something to do at lunchtime and some free periods as well. I learnt some lessons and skills about how to work with and communicate with children and making some new friends along the way and even dressed up as Santa twice for Kestrel House Christmas Services. I also did part of my Duke of Edinburgh there. At the 2005 EHS School Awards I was given an award for my contributions to Kestrel House for the past 5 years. After I left school sometimes made a visit and even had spells at helping out. Overall it was a great place to have helped out at Kestrel House and I am glad I am did and gave some good memories along with other good memories I had at Elgin High School. (Gordon is currently working with Friendly Access which involves raising more awareness and understanding of hidden disabilities and mental health conditions. He previously worked in the Moray Council doing Autism Presentations in front of people from different professions such as Teachers, Carers, etc).

222

Moira Turner (nee Farquhar) Technical Assistant, Wells Oil & Gas Services

Being a 'forty-something' now, having journeyed on life's path and being a bit wiser (allegedly), I'm in a position to look back and reflect on some milestone moments. I think it is the milestone experiences that mould you into who you are and where you are going. For me, my time at Elgin High School looks like a painter's palate – full of colour; some bright, some grey, experimental and vibrant. My primary education was at a small country school, Mosstowie, so having to forgo my bike and get a bus to school with some 300-odd pupils and many staff was a BIG change. I remember when the bell rang for changing class, the sight of X, Y or Z floor corridor packed with people, bags and noise was fearsome. Gradually I got used to the mass and bustle and enjoyed being part of the corridor tide. My confidence grew and making new friends became easy.

I think of the many people staff and friends, I was lucky enough to have crossed paths with; great characters who helped me grow. The late Mr McDonald and Mr Stewart come to mind; Mr McDonald's passion for history was palpable, such a great, great teacher. I always had difficulty with Arithmetic and Mathematics, to the point that I had lost interest in the subject entirely and was frightened by it. Mr Stewart changed that completely. With Mr Stewart and my trusty Maths partner Wendy Greaves (nee Jamieson) who was also no fan of Maths (our motto was 'Let's Fail Maths Together'), I learned from them that by just giving things a go and keeping an open mind, much could be achieved. Mr Stewart had the patience of a saint; I cannot imagine how it must feel to try to teach someone who had no enthusiasm for a subject and convinced themselves that it was impossible. His gift was to see through that and focus on the possible, hence I now have no issues with numeracy.

I am so grateful to the many staff who gave up their own personal time for the various activities that were on offer post the teacher strikes in the early 90s. Mr Carstairs spent many Saturdays with us hockey players attending various fixtures, Bucht Park in Inverness, Speyside Academy spring to mind. With the Duke of Edinburgh Award scheme, Miss Haddow (Now Mrs Highmore), Mr Davidson and Mr Downie spent weekends away with us hiking in the hills. The expeditions were my favourite thing. Such good fun and truly character building; what I didn't appreciate at the time was the amount of effort they must have put in behind the scenes to ensure that it all came together. I went along to a Reunion of my Year five years ago. I was a bit apprehensive of going as sometimes such events can be 'one upman-ship', but I was so wrong. If anything, it was life-affirming, back in touch with friends starting again where it was left off previously. I loved learning how everyone

223

was getting on and equally how they had just extended from the person they were at school.

Elgin High School had a great community feel. You were encouraged to develop whatever your passion was, whether it be sports, academic, arts, music and to be the best that you could be. The support network was phenomenal from teachers and friends; I truly felt that I could achieve anything that I wanted to and I still do. I think a lot of this was down to the leadership and ethos of Elgin High which undoubtedly came from Mr Hope – his surname is very apt when you think about it.

Nowadays I work in the Wells Department of an oil company number crunching all day long with spreadsheets, performing data analyses of live and historic operations. If you told 12 year old me what I'd be doing for a living now, I would have burst out laughing!

I feel lucky and honoured to have had the opportunities that I did whilst at Elgin High and the grounding it has given me throughout my life – it's been nae bad!

Victoria Higgins (Tori McIntosh)

Sports Development Executive at Aberdeen Sports Village.

EHS helped me discover my thirst for travelling and develop my love of sport. I was part of the first group to go to Zambia in 2008 for the Connecting Classrooms Project and was also the junior, intermediate and senior girls' sports champion for consecutive years. I then went on to get my BSc in Sports Studies at Aberdeen University and landed my dream job as a Sports Development Executive at Aberdeen Sports Village. During my time at EHS and University I played premiership football and have since run two marathons including London. I was in 1F2, 1D and little did I know the man I would marry was in my 1D class too—that's Dean Higgins! We didn't speak to each other much until 6th year - from then we both moved to Aberdeen for university, bought our first home, got our first puppy, got married and who knows what next!

Angela Matchett (née Watt) Jill of many trades

So, what did Elgin High school do for me?

It made me the person I was destined to be.

Learning , performing and just being free

Such a fab school, being young and being me.

I've only great memories of my time at the school.

I loved all the teachers and thought it was cool.

I've gained so much more than a higher or o grade.

It gave me my confidence (my personality made)

I'm still shy at times, but won't let others see.

Because Elgin high school made a confident me!!

I've had many jobs, retail management, waitress, banking advisor and owner/ landlady of a pub/restaurant to name a few! I'm now working part time in a call centre and trying to sell my arts/crafts at QuirkyCoop!!! I've also been a contestant on Channel 4's "Come Dine With Me!!! " TV show. I'm an aspiring writer of poetry and children's books. I have been published in two poetry anthologies but unsuccessful with the kids books (so far).

David Kelly Director at DGK Consulting

In 1991, whilst in Fifth Year at Elgin High I was inspired to join the first Scottish Venture Scouts' expedition to The Gambia in West Africa. These six weeks (which were referred to in a Pupil Profile article in PP 85) would change my outlook on life and lead to a wanderlust that would bring me to another nine countries on the African continent.

Following on from Elgin High School I completed a BSc (Hons) in Brewing and Distilling Science from Heriot-Watt University, initially hoping to move back to the area and work in one of Moray's many distilleries. I instead found myself in Hereford making cider for a few years. A quick foray into grain whisky and vodka making in the South West of Scotland was then followed by working in the Roseisle Maltings for

Diageo. This career with Diageo was to last for over a decade and found me moving to Ireland in 2004, initially as a raw materials expert for the business and then as an assurance auditor.

Travel became an added benefit of the job and gave me the opportunity to visit Africa, Asia, Australia, North America and a good portion of Europe. In between travelling for work I found time to take a trip to South America and Antarctica to complete a personal goal of visiting all seven continents. In 2014 I decided to leave Diageo and set up in business with my wife, Helen, whereby we offer management consultancy in Ireland to organisations that are looking to implement quality, environmental and health and safety standards. We also offer a mixture of teaching and auditing in the standards and last year I had the privilege to give a lunchtime lecture in University College Dublin. Thinking back, when looking at the maps in school library I could not have imagined that over the twenty-six years since leaving Elgin High school I would end up travelling enough to circumnavigate the world over eleven times.

Sean Dawson British Swimming referee

I started swimming from a young age but only competitively from about 11 years old. I progressed from competing at local club events to District and regional events quite quickly. By the age of 13, I was regularly competing at Scottish level. From there I progressed to medalling at National level and progressing on to competing at British and International levels. I was very lucky to get the opportunity to compete in major events in Britain and across Europe for a number of years. I was selected onto several National camps and teams and was frequently away on training camps abroad. I was very lucky that both Elgin High and The University of Aberdeen—where I studied ....._  *were very flexible and supportive of my sporting activities, which made it easier to juggle everything.*

I became involved in officiating when I retired from being a competitive athlete. I rose quite quickly through the various qualifications and I'm now a British Swimming referee. I have had the opportunity to officiate at events such as the 2014 Commonwealth Games, 2015 World Para-swimming Championships and the LEN 2016 European Masters Championships, with more events to come in the next few years. Being involved in sport has taught me so much and the swimming world has and still continues to give me so many great experiences and opportunities.

Alan Gray chef, actor, football coach, youth worker

Coming from Mosstowie Primary School, I found the move to Elgin High School a big step with masses of people, most of whom I didn't know. I struggled for the first three years, being a bit soft and had my fair share of being bullied.

In 1st and 2nd year I took part in the 'Get set to cook' competition coming runner up in first year and along with Shaun Dean winner in the second year. We headed to the final at Baxters in Fochabers and came out as winners there too with plenty of photos in the paper and a day working at Baxters as a prize. It was clear from then that I wanted to become a chef like my dad and went on to work at numerous, cafes, restaurants and even an army barracks in my teenage years and adult life.

Alan with Gus

The school looked after me, in particular Falcons Guidance Teacher Mr Walker and tried to keep me going on my studies; I enjoyed PE, Music, HE and Drama in particular. It was towards the end of 3rd year when we had a new drama teacher called Miss Chesterton that EHS really started to work for me.

Having seen me struggling to fit in at the school she suggested I join the St Giles Theatre Group. So that's just what I did and with her help I grew to love theatre and the arts. Unfortunately Miss Chesterton was only at the school a short while but I continued my learning in the field with Mrs Watson supporting me in understanding the industry and what I would need to secure work within it. My love of acting was fuelled at the end of my 6th year with the trip to the Edinburgh Festival organised by Mr Downie, a fitting end to a varied six years at EHS.

Throughout my senior years at EHS I was involved in hosting the Talent Contest, being on MFR on behalf of the school, doing comedy sketches at assemblies and helping with the

227

younger years' Drama classes. I was also a member of the Pupil Council and sat as a student member of the School Board.

I remember sitting with the Careers advisor in 6th year and casually telling them that I was going to study acting instead of professional cookery, though I had already been accepted unconditionally for the Glasgow College of Food Technology. Needless to say she wasn't impressed but my mind was made and off to Inverness College I went on to study Acting and Performance doing my HNC and then my HND.

This began a varied journey taking me to where I am now. I graduated from the Birmingham Conservatoire with a BA (Hons) in Acting, worked as a professional actor, a soccer coach for GPS Florida in the United States and more recently a Theatre Arts Worker – working with young people in schools and community groups alongside doing talks to pupils about the acting industry and social issues. On top of that I have toured extensively with youth football giving young people the opportunities that I was unable to have.

Elgin High helped me to realise that the journey through working life doesn't have to stay the same but can change and take you to amazing places. Who knows what the next 30+ years have in store. Thank you EHS and all the teachers who helped me get to where I am today.

Barry Jarvis, former Moray Councillor, now working with Langstane Housing Association*

When considering the role of Elgin High in my development as an individual it is important to consider the role of Elgin High within Elgin itself. Built at a time when the reputation of Elgin Academy was at a premium for many it has always sat in the shadow of its more illustrious, more grandiose, comrade in the north. For many it was considered (quite wrongly) as the 'technical' school to the Academy's 'grammar'. There was no strict uniform(during my time, with the notable, and ruthlessly enforced, exception of no denim), no school motto and certainly no imposed rigid social structure of

prefects and head pupils. Even its size, and location in the Freestate of New Elgin in itself was enough cause for some to cock their snoot.

But to those of us who attend this theory and outside impression would be seen as the worst kind of canard. Led by Bill Hope the eclectic, but completely dedicated, staff team mostly set about their roles as educators with alacrity and enthusiasm, support staff worked industriously to ensure that the wider functions of the school building and operations, functioned and pupils for the most part, played their part. Each doing their own towards the wider collective outcome of providing educated, enlightened citizens to fulfil the work places of tomorrow. Honest graft and endeavour permeated through the work ethic of many and the relatable human nature of many teaching staff in particular left happy memories, even for those whom school was not a particularly happy time.

It is this that left an indelible mark on me as a person. Elgin High served as a reminder that it does not matter what people think of you, or how the outside world sees you. If you stay honest to what you believe in and focus on your cause then success is always possible. I like to believe that throughout my life I have stayed true to what I believe in and stayed true to the example that was set for me by Elgin High.

*(Langstane Housing Association's aim is to provide quality housing which promotes social inclusion and generates sustainable communities).

Hannah Benson full time mummy "best job in the world"

I started EHS in the early 80's, a week later than my peers due to a food poisoning episode (unrelated to the school). I wasn't always an easy child to get along with—neither fashion savvy, socially adept nor sporty. I struggled with numbers and my co-ordination wasn't brilliant as P.E. teacher Miss Abel then found out. Despite these things I felt that EHS had an ethos of acknowledging differences between pupils whilst still fostering a sense of belonging.

This didn't really became apparent to me until after I left the area for a year and returned to the school. Having then experienced the English private education system I can say that the level of education in EHS was far superior. Although, like everywhere, there were flaws. For example in recent years there has been a shift towards being more open and supportive regarding those with specific learning or health issues. I feel that the 80's in general was a time that allowed more people to fall through the net. That said, EHS was foward thinking enough to provide a trained hypnotherapist to assist me with my residue negativity from various troublesome life events.
On a lighter note, I can say that I managed to excuse myself from any prearranged scraps round the back of the bike shed, having to catch

the school bus home every afternoon!
I have also taken away with me a lot of positive things from my time at EHS.

I feel that my love of reading and writing was nurtured. First, I had Mr Burns laying down the foundations of English for me. Then I found Mr Dugdale to be a very supportive and encouraging teacher. We were taught to not just read but question and observe, whilst having the confidence to put our opinions across in a practical and authentic way. These tools have been useful in life and I enjoy encouraging others as they grow in confidence with their reading skills also.

Abiy Orr, Full Time Carer

Not even the clever kids always find school easy. I was considered "bright" but I found secondary very hard. It wasn't the work: apart from Maths beyond arithmetic and the misery of PE I could keep up fine, and even excel in some areas. It wasn't the staff, who treated me with the grave respect teachers give to pupils who never cause any trouble and genuinely want to learn. It was the rest of you who scared me to death, you milling throng of normal, healthy teenagers. I just couldn't understand you, with your enthusiasms and your hatreds, your hormones, your mischief and your moodiness, your loudness, your humour, your ever-changing focus. I could never fit in.

So I kept my head down and worked hard. Schools are for learning. I understood that all right. Give me a piece of paper and a biro and I was my own boss. But give me a group discussion and I melted out of sight. Ask me for a solo talk and watch me almost expire from sheer horror!

You weren't unkind. I was never bullied at secondary, a real relief after primary, in spite of my utter weirdness (not to mention the embarrassment of being "the mannie Taylor's dochter"), and I attribute that largely to the sterling leadership of Mr Hope. At the very first rumour of bullying in his school he would explode from his office, red faced, pop eyed and spluttering with fury, to deal with the culprit instantaneously and effectively. He was backed up in this zero tolerance attitude by all the staff, so I felt safe at school and able to learn. Besides, some of you were genuinely kind to me and none were actively hostile, for which I thank you!

So I drifted through school, academically able but otherwise inept and as near to invisible as I could make myself, and so I would have left, had it not been for one teacher. Yes, I mean you, Mr Downie!

English Higher class, 1986-7. We were studying the first of T S Eliot's "Preludes", which talks of winter dusk, cooking smells lingering and the lamps being lit. Mr Downie told us not to look ahead to the other poems in the sequence, and being a good girl (and weird) I didn't. The descriptions in the poem seemed appealing to me and I was baffled and silenced as one pupil after another commented on its negativity. Of course they had looked ahead and seen how the images become sleazy and sad!

He stopped me as the class was leaving. "You didn't agree, did you?"

Mortally embarrassed, as I always was back then when anyone paid any attention to me, I agreed that I didn't agree.

"Why not?"

So I told him. I told him that I thought "The winter evening settles down . . ." was a beautiful personification, speaking of rest and comfort; that the "smell of steaks" sounded rich and luxurious, steak not being something we ever ate in our house; and that I loved "the lighting of the lamps". Winter was a time for gathering together and battening down the hatches, and to me that was a positive thing.

Then he said to me, "Never be afraid to share your opinion. If you have the evidence to back it up, you can't be wrong, no matter what anyone else may say."

Who would have thought that that tiny conversation would change my life? Not immediately, of course, but it planted an idea which grew into me. As I grew older I grew less afraid of you all, you confident, bustling, laughing, raging mainstream people. I know I'm never likely to appear on a list of Elgin High's most successful pupils, but I count myself as one anyway.

You see, a few years ago now I was diagnosed as autistic. This answered a lot of questions and helped me come to terms with always feeling like an alien life form. Hardly anyone had ever heard of autism when I was at school, so I can't blame anyone for not spotting it, even if

I wanted to, which I don't. My two sons and my husband are also diagnosed autistic. My husband is also dyslexic, so when there are issues to be sorted out or agencies to be reasoned with, it's me who has to throw on the cape and fly to the rescue. At work, too, I've often found myself becoming the challenger of ignorance and the defender of the baffled and bemused. I even taught English myself for ten years, and often found myself echoing Mr Downie's sound advice to other roomfuls of teenagers! The fact that, in spite of my own difficulties, I have been able to cope with these challenges daily for around a quarter of a century so far, is at least partly down to the good grounding I received at Elgin High, and particularly to Mr Downie, who gave me permission - nay, ordered me - to stop faffing around and get on with the business of being myself.

Euan Ogilvie IT support for Vodafone in London, since 2001

Back in Autumn 1984 I was about a month into Fifth Year at Elgin High. I was not very happy about being there as I had missed out on a job/traineeship with an oil company in the summer holidays and the last place I wanted to be was at school, especially as most of my

mates had left at the end of Fourth year. I was in my metalwork class and Mr Ken Duncan was teaching David Fraser and I, the only two Higher Metalwork pupils! One day he asked if we would be interested in taking part in a competition/project about road safety with the winning team getting a trip to the Volkswagen factory in Germany.

I was reluctant as my spirit was down but Mr Duncan talked me round and asked if we knew two others who might be interested in joining the team. Peter Moffatt and Mark Bruce were suggested and asked and the team was complete. At the time I believe all secondary schools in Moray were being asked as it was being run

Euan with his Hawco Award trophy

by Hawco, the local VW dealers. Industrial action by teaching unions then cut the number schools in the competition to two, ourselves and Elgin Academy and what seemed like a tough battle became much less daunting. We could beat the Caddy we thought. Mr Duncan had an idea of what we would do - a video on road safety - and every week we would have a get together and discuss progress.

THE PRESS AND JOURNAL MONDAY MARCH 18 1985

Fifth-formers take safe way to trophy

Ex P & J

18.2.85

We were also

JOINT managing director of the Elgin garage firm of Hawco and Sons, Mr John Hawco (centre right) presents the Hawco Road Safety Award — an inscribed Caithness Glass bowl — to Elgin High School technical teacher Mr Kenneth Duncan after a team of pupils from the school had been judged winners of the safety project.

Team members (from left to right) David Fraser, Euan Ogilvie, Mark Bruce and Peter Moffatt — all fifth-year pupils — each received an inscribed goblet. They have also won a two-day trip to Germany at the beginning of April to visit the Audi/Volkswagen car factory at Wolfsburg.

They were narrow victors over a team from Elgin Academy with their video-based road safety presentation project, and Mr Hawco said the standard of presentation had been so impressive that it was his company's intention to extend the scope of the competition in future to encourage more secondary schools in the area to participate.

He felt the scheme was of particular importance to young people in helping to make them more aware of road safety matters.

Around 300 people turned up for Saturday's road safety demonstration in the grounds of Elgin High School. The highlight was a simulated road accident which involved full-scale emergency procedures being carried out by police, ambulance anf fire crews.

Members of the public also had the opportunity to take part in a driving-skills course supervised by police traffic officers, while youngsters were able to take part in a similar event for BMX bikes.

going to interview teachers on what factors they consider when buying a car. The day that most of this took place I was off sick but the rest of the team managed to interview quite a number of the teachers with some quite funny answers - and safety didn't feature all that high on the list. Mrs MacLachlan mentioned colour and I think Mr Stewart brought safety into his list. He did like cars. Not sure if the video is somewhere in the archives of EHS: it would be interesting to see it back again.

Along with Mr Duncan the four of us went through to Aberdeen one day to edit the video into the high quality production that won the competition. We had a great day travelling through on the train and spending the day having a laugh at some of the teachers' answers. A real team bonding session.

As I had missed out on the video interviewing I was given the job of standing in front of the judges and the other team to read a piece on how important car safety now was. To me this was my worst nightmare—standing in front of people and talking for what seemed like a lifetime but was only five to ten minutes. Mr Duncan and the team gave me the confidence to get through it with plenty of encouragement that I would be fine. But I was relieved when it was over. We then had some demonstrations by the Fire Brigade and emergency services outside while the judges made their decision. When we went back inside and were told we had won.   It was a great moment as I hadn't been in any teams that won anything before. We then got our photo in the papers. I remember my mum being very proud and cut out the pictures and stuck them on cardboard then covering them with clear plastic. It's thanks to her that they appear alongside these words.

I think I asked her why and her saying it was a good thing to keep and show at any job interviews at which I probably scoffed. Little did I know she was spot-on. I had an interview with Shell UK in April 1985 and was asked to bring any examples of achievements that would show I was worthy of a place on their training programme. I took the two photos she had carefully cut out and protected and also a metalwork exercise that showed off all the things we had to do for our Metalwork prelim. The two men interviewing me were very impressed with the Hawco Award and asked loads of questions on what we had done. It was then I realised how right my mum was and knew what would impress them, but they also liked my metalwork.

Not being in any of the sports teams at school it also made me realise how great it was to be part of a team and working together to achieve the same goal.

About a week before we were due to fly to Germany for our tour of the VW factory Mr Hope got our team together and reminded us that we were representing the school and he didn't want us bringing any shame on it. Mark Bruce seemed to be Mr Hope's main target as he asked him not to be photographed in his Botan Blazer about which we had a chuckle. We were wondering if he was going to send us off to get measured for matching Blazers to look the part but instead gave us all an EHS navy sweatshirt. We never did wear them and thankfully were not questioned by Mr Hope on why we hadn't been pictured in them.

It was near the end of March 1985 when we travelled to Aberdeen Airport and flew to London and then to Hannover from where we travelled by coach to Volfsburg to stay in a hotel and go to VW factory the next day. We had a meal the evening we arrived with all our team and someone from the police, Ambulance and Fire Brigade along with Kevin Hawco and a number of people from VW marketing. I think Alistair Bissett of The P & J was also with us to take photos.

I don't remember too much of the tour of the factory but do remember seeing panels being formed using massive pressing machines then seeing the cars being put together at different stages. On one of the cars every panel was a different colour. We had our lunch in the factory restaurant and I kept as a souvenir a tea spoon with the VW logo on the back of it *into my pocket and still have it. The last part of the tour was in the wind tunnel where they tested the aerodynamics of the cars. We had our picture taken in there and it was on the front page of the P & J later that week but it wasn't very clear in black and white.*

I remember bumping into Sarah Darnley that night and her jokingly asking me for my autograph after seeing me on the front page. Just one memory of many I have of Sarah! My mum kept the crystal goblet I won on her wall unit which was probably a good thing as it would no doubt been broken or lost in my travels since leaving school. I have it now on shelves in my house in Shepherds Bush and visitors often ask what it was for. I now proudly tell anyone who will listen about how we won it. And after my mum passed away I found the pictures she cut out of the paper and mounted on cardboard and covered with plastic, still as fresh as when she cut them out.

So in the end I was quite glad I stayed on for that Fifth Year.

Donald Squair Board member at Lantern of the North Events*

Donald *left* with friends

Elgin High School Music Department did nothing for me. There, I said it. Well to be fair I have no musical talent whatsoever, no rhythm, no singing voice and no patience to learn an instrument. So where does my love of music and live performance come from and which has lead me to try promote and help local artists today? Well that started squarely at Elgin High.

I spent many hours watching the various school bands rehearse or play their lunch time gigs, be it the School Metal Band or the Wayne Chisholm/John McCallum band playing their crowd pleasers of Summer of '69 or Wonderful Tonight and, if asked nicely, a Rush cover that they really didn't know but would play anyway.

I look back to those times and think maybe because I couldn't play, hanging around the bands was maybe the next best thing. This love of being around bands progressed into maybe there was something I could do—and that was promote.

Since leaving school I have found a real passion for helping the local bands out any way I can, be it putting on shows for them, promoting their releases, giving advice and on the odd occasion driving them round the country on tours.

Whoever booked the tour for Small Enclosed Area, a group made up of Elgin High pupils, that went Inverness, Elgin, Glasgow, Elgin, Edinburgh, Elgin then London in the space of a week deserves to be shot! An excellent experience but very tiring.

For the last ten years I have been bringing bands up to Elgin or Aberdeen from as far afield as the Czech Republic in the East and America in the West, mainly in the Metal/Punk genre but since forming Lantern of the North with a group of like-minded souls, all previous members of Elgin High, we have been more focused on local acts of all styles and trying to show what great talented artists we have in the local area.
*https://www.facebook.com/lanternnorth/

Jamie McCudden writes about his life after school

After leaving Elgin High school in 1990 just starting into my Fifth Year my only real interests at that time were computing and physics. My inspirations were mostly from Mr. Ledingham and Mrs Gravener who inspired me to become more than I thought I could be. After leaving

school I had to get a job to find out what I really wanted to do with my life, and eventually I decided to go back into education in 1997 to study Mechanical Engineering. After gaining my HND in Mechanical Engineering from Moray College in 2001 I was successful in getting a job within the electronics manufacturing industry at Scotland Electronics in Forres. It was whilst working there that I gained experience in many different sectors such as Aerospace, Defence, Oil & Gas and Computing. My most memorable contracts were working with CERN the European Council for Nuclear Research.

We had several contracts with them including manufacturing of over 700 CCUM detector printed circuit boards (PCBs) which were used in the Large Hadron Collider particle accelerator. The LHC eventually found the Higgs Boson particle (The God Particle) on the 4th of July 2012 and it was found by detector PCB's that we had manufactured in Forres, something I am immensely proud of. Aside from circuit boards we also manufactured several server cluster farms for the European Space Agency and CERN. On the previous page is a picture of our 64 node cluster as installed in the European Space Agency in Frascati just outside of Rome Italy.

Wendy Toner, Youth Worker— another of the Originals and still there

Walking out of the doors of EHS in 1983 after four years of fun and laughter I had absolutely no clue of what the future held. I didn't know what I wanted to do with my life or where I wanted to be.

I had successfully gained a place at Moray College to study social care, but patience was never my strong point. I looked for a job in the summer interim and landed a job as a pharmacy assistant in a local chemist. Six years later I was still there.

I married in 1987 and by chance was asked by a friend to come down to EHS to check out the youth club they ran in the building in the evenings. I was smitten. It was full of life, full of fun and just where I knew I wanted to be.

I supported the junior and senior youth clubs every week. I loved the different activities we had on offer and gained many a skill myself whilst learning with the young people. I felt youth work ran through my veins. I knew it was what I wanted to do with the rest of my life.

In 1994 I decided to put those skills to further use. I applied to work in a residential childcare unit called Andrew Thomson house situated in Elgin. I worked there for over five years whilst still doing my youth clubs in the evenings.

I received a phone call one day from my old rector, Mr William Hope. He was looking for a youth worker to work one to one with a pupil returning to education on a fresh start and wondered if I was available. Full time back in EHS...of course I was available. Easiest interview I ever had!

I have never looked back...I have been the youth worker attached to EHS for over 30 years. I have run Participate courses, Princes Trust courses and Accredited awards like the John Muir Award and Youth Achievement Awards. I have been the listening ear and counseling service to many a pupil. (And staff).

Over the years I have built gardens and youth shelters, and run some amazing residential experiences for young people. Each and every one teaches me something new. I was a street youth worker for 17 years of those 30 years and some of the most challenging pieces of work were born on the streets of Elgin.

I have worked with young people from both secondary schools, colleges and residential homes. I have done two youth exchange programs to Greece and Sweden. I have run youth forums, DJ Workshops, dance workshops, issue based groups and supported other youth led services within the Moray area.

Today my work concentrates on targeted provision. I still support classes in the schools but I also run groups for 16 plus young people, I work in New Elgin Primary running awards and within supported accommodations in Elgin who support some of our most vulnerable young people. I have worked with addictions, crime and health services on activity early intervention programs.

Youth Work has changed a huge amount since I started in 1987 but maintains its core values of empowerment and affecting positive change.

Life in 2018 is very different to life in 1987 when I first started on this road. Family dynamics have changed and the introduction of social media has taken me into new and unchartered waters for our young people to deal with. However youth workers remain a constant for many.

I am so proud of all the young people I have worked with over the years and the things we have achieved together. I would never have enjoyed this work if it had not been for them allowing me into their lives to share their secrets, their friendships and relationships, their humour and their fun.

My family gave me love, morals and respect. My school gave me relationships and friendships that last to this day. My youth worker gave me compassion and acceptance. I am proud of the work I do and so lucky to be able share it with the young people of Elgin.

Nikki Darling International DJ, LGBT and youth support worker

It was always about the music. Ever since the end of primary school music played a huge part in my life. I would spend hours in my room, listening to the radio and taking note of any bands or artists that caught my attention. By the time I began Elgin High School music had become a full blown obsession!

I started high school in 1998 and things were a lot different back then. You couldn't stream or download tunes, nor could you jump on Youtube and Spotify and search for new artists based on your current tastes or browsing history. Instead I was taping songs off the radio and saving up the change from my lunch money to buy CD singles, or if I was lucky take my pocket money and buy an album. I would spend hours browsing through music magazines and flicking through the albums in Sound and Vision, trying to find something new or obscure. Everything from the standard pop that I got into, along with all my friends in first year, right through to the punk and metal that dominated my latter days as a pupil. Whilst all my friends were off buying clothes and makeup, I was adding to my massive pile of CD's and if I ever did opt to buy clothes with my pocket money it was normally a band hoodie or t-shirt. Music was everything to me.

When I was about 13 I put this obsession of mine to good use and began presenting my own show on Keith Community Radio, a local branch of Moray Firth radio (MFR). My Dad had spoken about me to his workmate who was heavily involved with the radio station and they seemed pretty impressed that a 13 year old was just as interested in Neil Young and The Sex Pistols as she was the local pop starlet of the day. I went along for an audition, with the promise of a monthly slot if it went well. I being naturally shy, it took some skills that I had honed in my favourite class, drama, to come across as competent and natural (rather than the bundle of nerves that I actually was.) My 30 minute slot passed in the blink of an eye and before I knew it I had a permanent slot on the KCR rota. I became more confident as time went on, and as my music tastes evolved with age so did my show. It wasn't long before I started integrating some death metal and drum n' bass into my timeslot, ensuring that I stood out like a sore thumb in between the Scottish fiddle music and combine harvester sale ads that are a staple of the local station. Elgin High was ever supportive of my ventures into radio and before I knew it, I was operating a lunch time "radio" show over the tanoy, although I promised that I would keep my death metal records at home.

I left school at the end of fifth year. I would have loved to have stayed on and done a sixth year but health reasons meant that was an unlikely option. I had gained enough grades for uni though and so spent a year building up my strength again before heading to Queen Margaret University in Edinburgh to study Film & Media. I remember my 18th birthday well. I was still living in Elgin at this point but was in Edinburgh with friends. We were going to a club called Velvet, which at the time was the biggest lesbian club in Europe. Little did I know as I danced the night away that by the time my 19th birthday rolled around I would not only be DJing at this club but I would hold residency there.

Club DJing and radio DJing are completely different. DJing in a club requires you to "work the room" and adapt your set to what people are responding to. Every night can be different as every crowd is different. My first taste of DJing at a venue was when I began putting on punk nights at my student union. These were popular and led to other genre nights, which helped me to practice skills like beat matching and scratch mixing etc.

The Velvet team were well known in Edinburgh's gay scene. Their promoter and agent for most of the DJ's Jean was seen out advertising most weekends. I remember one night I walked up and asked if Velvet were looking for any DJ's. (Velvet was not the sort of club that would ever look for DJ's. Most established DJ's in Edinburgh at that time would chew their own arm off for a slot at Velvet!) Jean told me to hand a CD in. I know now that she must have been asked a million times by budding DJ's if there were any slots available and her answer would always have been the same "hand in a CD." I took this as a challenge though. In my head I had a shot, and in the cut throat world of DJing, you take every shot you are given. I worked on my mix CD for about a week, perfecting mixes, listening out for any new remixes that were climbing the dance charts, looking out for new tunes about to drop etc. then mixing them all together in my wee pot until my CD was ready. "Here's my CD" I said, handing it over to Jean one night as I entered yet another full to capacity night at Velvet. "Thanks" she said, pocketing the disc before being dragged in the opposite direction by one of the crew. I'd put my mobile number and e-mail address on a torn up piece of paper and slipped it in with the disc. I never really expected to hear back from her but at least I had tried.

"Come and do an hour before our DJ in residence takes over. Let's give you a shot." My mouth went dry and I nearly dropped the phone as Jean called me a week after I had given her my disc. "Thank you" my voice croaked as my heart sped up. I couldn't quite believe it. I phoned everyone I knew to tell them that I had an hour at Velvet and my friends and family were just as shocked and delighted as I was. All my mates came out to support me that night as I set up behind the decks. I only had an hour to impress and the crowd was looking tricky. The dance floor was pretty empty as the queues to the various bars snaked their way around the venue. "Good luck" said the DJ who had gone on before me as she handed me the cans (headphones.) Right it's now or never I thought to myself as I loaded up the first tune, relieved that my first choice had the same BPM (beats per minute) as hers making it easier to match the beat smoothly. My first song kicked in, the new Madonna track at the time but with a slightly mixed up bass. The floor started to fill, people started to dance, my mates cheered me on and my confidence grew as I got the thumbs up from Jean. The hour passed by in a heartbeat but by the end of it the entire floor was full of people dancing. The applause I got at the traditional volume dip before the next act goes on is something that will stay with me for the rest of my life. Jean came up to me and putting an arm around my shoulder said "you did it kid. You just tore Velvet a new a*sehole. The job's yours if you want it." Want it? Of course I wanted it!! We shook hands and agreed details like pay and timeslots etc. & I went home the happiest girl in all of Edinburgh.

Things just went up and up from there. Feedback from the crowd was that they wanted me headlining and so I was offered residency as the previous headliner went on to pastures new. Other clubs started scouting me and I was offered prestigious gigs such as Hogmanay and The Edinburgh Festival. I featured in the gay press frequently and began to take gigs in other cities and eventually other countries. I would never have done any of this though had it not been for my drama classes at Elgin High. I was far too shy and I would never have had the guts to hand in the CD, let alone DJ to a few thousand people had I not learned to overcome some of my shyness through acting. Even the part of being "Blaze" (my DJ name which I thankfully changed from my original DJ Random moniker) was an act in itself. Stylists and a rigorous fitness routine helped me look the part but I also had to act the part too and thankfully the skills I had learned in drama meant that I wasn't a gibbering wreck, crippled with shyness when it came to performing behind the decks and meeting the fans (particularly the hot ones hahaha.)

By the time I had finished uni my DJing style had changed quite dramatically. I had grown tired of the constant chart music of the gay scene and had begun to make inroads in the dance scene. A huge industrial music fan at the time, I began to find a niche in the fetish scene and started playing fetish clubs and parties around the country. I also got into various types of bass music and started playing at raves and warehouse parties. The crowds were smaller perhaps but I was loving the gritty, almost seedy underbelly of the cities I played in as well as the culture surrounding the music. I had started travelling a lot by this point too, fulfilling a lifelong dream by working a crowd on Sunset Boulevard in LA. San Francisco, Toronto, Stockholm, Oslo, Brussels etc, I was cramming in a lot of the World but I was still based in the UK. After five years in Edinburgh it was time for me to move on.

Australia - that was where I decided to move to. I had a couple of friends out there who would house me until I got sorted out with work. As heartbreaking as it was at the time I sold the vast majority of my CD's to fund my move. Over 10 000 CD's were sold in the first two months of saving. My home became like a factory for Amazon. I was sad to see rare *collector's items go, as well as CD's that had gotten me through things like my first broken heart or my first gig etc. Everything was moving towards digital though. There was no point in me keeping a hold of stuff when I could make memories instead.*

The summer of 2009 I moved away, but I ensured that I had plenty of stopovers first. Malaysia, Cambodia, Vietnam, Singapore and Indonesia were all taken in before I landed in Sydney. I worked my way up the East coast until I landed in the small town of Lismore near Byron Bay, where I stayed with my lovely friends Lana and Andie for a couple of months before moving back down to Sydney for work. Again I found my music tastes welcome in the dark underworld of the BDSM/fetish scene. It was a much bigger scene in Sydney though and as the "foreign DJ with the accent" I began to get noticed outside of the niche market I was then working in.

I had heard rumblings of this "new genre called dubstep" around the end of 2008 and by 2009 I had begun dropping dubstep tracks into my sets, harder mixes but still with that squelchy bass rumble. People started to take notice and a couple of promoters, aware that the genre was about to explode, nabbed me for a couple of festivals and events. Boom!! By 2010 dubstep was everywhere. Acts like Skrillex, Caspa and Rusko had become household names and every genre from pop to metal was adding in dubstep production techniques. I showed up at festivals and outdoor raves or "bush doofs" as they're called down under expecting to have a handful of people come to my sets, only to see the fields full of people all dancing to my own sets, at times my own songs. I still kept a foot in the gay scene though and worked the odd club night here and there. On one occasion I DJ'd a celebrity boat party for gay celebs that weren't out. And no, before you ask, I'm not telling you who was there. The non-disclosure form I signed ensured I will get into quite a bit of bother if I did that. It was a fun night though and one I won't ever forget.

My visa for Australia was 2 years and then I had to come back home. I kind of knew that 2011 would be the turning point for me and that I was going to start moving away from DJing and step into the real world. I had taken it as far as I could. I had caught a few lucky breaks and did things I never dreamt possible but I knew it couldn't last forever. I started volunteering with young people as well as at a centre for sex workers with drug and alcohol issues. I knew then that I wanted to work with people, to help them. I came back to Elgin in 2011 and I secured two jobs that I love. One is working as a homeless support worker in Elgin and the other is as a youth worker with LGBT Youth Scotland in Inverness. Work is the only reason I have stayed back here so long. I'm still a city girl at heart. I'm getting itchy feet and know that a move will happen sooner rather than later. I'm also writing a book based on my experiences in the fetish scene. If successful, I'm hoping that writing may become a more permanent vocation. Who knows? Only time will tell. I do know that it has been quite the adventure that has led me to this point, an adventure that would not have happened had I not had my roots firmly planted at Elgin High School.

Richard Anderson, Pipe major and civil servant

In 1978, I moved from Elgin Academy to Elgin High School. It was the best decision of my life. The High School gave me a solid grounding that would shape so much of my life to date. The one thing that stood out was the Headmaster and all the teaching staff. They cared about you and encouraged you to fulfil your potential. I have much to thank them all for that. It was here that I met Mr James Hamilton (History Teacher) and began attending his piping classes. This gave me a future I could not have imagined at the time. I kept in touch with Mr Hamilton and have enjoyed a personal friendship with him that has endured for over 30 years. In terms of employment, I have been a civil servant, a serviceman and council worker. Thank you Elgin High for everything you did for me.

Janice (McKillop) Hyndman, original pupil and now Careers Adviser at EHS

Being part of a brand-new school and only having S1 and S2s at the very start was such a unique way to start secondary education. From day one the character of EHS started to develop. We had a young head teacher in Mr Hope, and a gang of enthusiastic and energetic teachers to start our next stage of learning. We grew with the school, as it got busier each year with the new intake of S1s and we got to meet new teachers recruited for the increasing roll.

We were so privileged getting a new building with new equipment in all departments. The community area kitted out with comfy chairs, pool tables, juke box, table tennis tables and tuck shop kept us busy at break and dinner times.

We were encouraged to not only do our best in our subjects but also to try new things – plays, shows, sport, helping with Pigeon Post, debating club, inter house activities, dance groups….there was something for everyone…Friday night film club, Christmas dances, Burns suppers and the much-anticipated school discos!

My time at EHS gave me a great experience of secondary school and I got the chance to make lots of happy memories and lifelong friendships. Although we didn't get together at school, I also met my husband Hamish on day one of EHS. It built my confidence in lots of ways and I learned a lot about myself and what I enjoyed and was good at, despite the usual teenage awkwardness!

EHS has always had a special community feel and gives pupils a sense of belonging. That spirit and culture still exists in the new building, even thought it's been hard watching the old school getting knocked down. I now spend most days back in EHS working with the current pupils: I haven't travelled very far in one sense, but it's still a welcoming and warm place to be.

Counterpoint

Nostalgia leads usually to rose-tinted memories of school but that's not always the case, of course as some of you will readily recognise. Already in this section a handful of former pupils have spoken about their unhappiness, being the subject of bullying and not feeling they fitted in all that well.

However, we finish this section with some heart-breaking personal testimony which has been heavily redacted to protect the writer's identity.

I enjoyed school but never loved it. I was never an outstanding student so I just kept my head below the parapet and tried to stay out of trouble.

Things at home were extremely difficult and I had a series of quite appalling and bewildering family experiences. The senior management of the school did not believe my accounts of what had happened and gave me a bad time for being absent so many times but that was all down to what was happening at home.

To be truthful I've found it hard writing this without coming over as bitter but I have to say there weren't too many good memories, or perhaps it's that the bad ones stick in my mind more.

This is supposed to be about what Elgin High School did for me but I have had to write this so you understand why my feelings about school are so mixed. Several teachers were supportive: drama gave me a sense of purpose and I enjoyed English. I suppose it was the escapism of a good book or story a hobby I still enjoy very much and well art although I wasn't very good at it was always therapeutic. As for music and singing I could dream and be a different person by involving myself in activities and events through these.

Elgin High School taught me to never give up, it taught me that I'd have to be strong and stand on my own two feet, but it also taught me to use my imagination and it gave me a passion for drama and singing

I learned to treat people as you expect to be treated and to not let the bullies win. One of the most important things it taught me was to apologise when you're wrong and to never make a child or another human being feel worthless, so you see I don't hate my old school but I don't miss it.

I have many friends from my days there and even those who were bullies back then now speak to me. My past has made me the person I am today and I hope with all my heart that the new pupils of the new Elgin High enjoy their years there and can speak up against bullies should they experience them.

I remember fondly many of my teachers because they taught us respect and encouraged us. Unfortunately I remember some staff for all the wrong reasons and because of this I have avoided school reunions and the possibility of bumping in to them.

Since leaving school I have had a successful career and met many wonderful people, including celebrities, through the opportunities I have had.

Elgin High gave me a huge love of singing and I have been so lucky to perform with various groups. None of this would have been possible without believing that I could, a belief that was instilled in me by some of my teachers at EHS.

So even if you don't excel at school, you will learn things that you will take with you forever. One day you will look back and realise that school days may not have been the best days of your life but they taught you a lot of important lessons that will see you through life and help you be a better person.

First Year Team: Shirlene Abbott (Captain), Aileen McIntosh, Wendy MacGillivray, Kim Spence, Sharon Duroe, Dawn Cooper, Janne Commons.
Front: Brenda Tyson, Julie Turnidge, Elaine Hutcheson, Wendy Murray, Angela Tyson.

Second Year Team: Patricia Ogilvie, Wendy Scott, Angela Davidson, Lynne Kelly, Alison Farquhar, Marion MacKinnon.
Front: Jane Ralph, Jacqueline Wardlaw, Lynne Craib, Mandy Leppard (Captain), Lesley Still, Lynne Beaton.

15　Champion Teams

The two sports which proved most popular in the early days of the school, largely thanks to the enthusiasm of staff, were Girls field hockey and Boys football and before long our young sides were making a mark in local leagues.

Early success in hockey came from the encouragement of natural talent by hockey aficionados David Carstairs, head of PE and Rector Bill Hope, coach and qualified umpire, supported by Isobel Wasilenska the second member of the PE department when we opened.

David Carstairs—see Teacher Feature (TF) in PP 11— had played hockey and football whilst at Harris Academy, Dundee and his teams at his first post Linlathen High in Dundee met with some success. He also played hockey for Harris Academy FPs. Isobel Wasilenska (TF in PP 6) had enjoyed playing football with the boys at Tomintoul Primary and other sports whilst at Keith Grammar, hockey, ski-ing and gymnastics in particular. Bill Hope, as explained elsewhere in these pages (but see also TF in PP 10), first got into Hockey in a big way at his first teaching post at Alloa Academy and went on to hold a number of important posts in Scottish Schools hockey organisations, becoming an international selector and umpire at senior men's hockey level across Scotland.

All the posed photographs of sports teams which have appeared in *Pigeon Post* can now be seen at **pigeonpost.info** where they are grouped by session—and given the importance of girls hockey to the school it's appropriate that the first two photos to appear (in PP 2, reprised in PP 10) were of hockey teams. For historical accuracy you can find these photographs (with patronising comment) there but higher resolution prints by Mr Nick Ledingham are printed opposite.

However the names of the girls in the captions feature regularly in Hockey reports (e.g. in PP 19 for June 1980 below) and many of them continued to play hockey after they left school.

Our Senior Hockey Team with Mr. David Carstairs, sporting one of the new EHS sweat shirts in light blue with dark blue dove motif.

Back (l-r): Jacqueline Wardlaw, Mandy Leppard, Lynne Craib, Michelle Scott, Patricia Jane Ralph, Marion MacKinnon, Mr. Carstairs (Team Coach).

Front: Lynne Kelly, Diane Craib, Lynne Beaton, Lesley Still, Alison Farquhar.

Our first Champion side (the Under 15s) is pictured below in PP 34 (March 1982) - with new coach Willie Finnie (PT Geography) winning their league for the second time running and champion sides regularly are recorded in our pages thereafter, for example in PP 51 (January 1984 on the next page).

Just Champions! Back (l-r); Fiona McGrath, Shirlene Adam, Elizabeth Wheeler, Sara Edwards, Elaine Hutcheson, Jeanette Brown, Mr Willie Finnie (Coach.)
Front: Fiona Morrison, Julie Campbell, Sharon Duroe, Susan Sutherland, Julie Turnidge, Avril Milne. Absent: Jill Ellwand.

Our League Champion Under [...]
Hockey Squad:

Back(l-r):Wendy Fraser, [...]
Jones, Karen McEwan, Dor[...]
Wheeler, Sandra Young, an[...]
David Carstairs (Coach)
Front: Fiona Donaldson, [...]
Edwards, Janet Stewart, [...]
Fraser, Lorna Tait, Trac[...]
Shiach, Paula Campbell.

Two champion

sides from PP 51

(1.84)

Our League Champion Senior
Hockey Squad.

(Back l-r) Fiona McGrath, [...]
Garvie, Elizabeth Wheeler,
Rosemary Scott, Pamela Mil[...]
Laura Goodwin.
(Front) June Cruickshank, [...]
Easterling, Elaine Hutche[...]
Susan Sutherland, Jill El[...]
Elizabeth McCallum, Avril [...]

Not in photo: Jeanette Bro[...]
Sara Edwards.

As in most Scottish schools football was the most popular sport for boys right from the start. With the help of members of staff and parents, Bill Hope and later Alan Sturrock who along with hockey enthusiast Debbie Abel (later McDonald) joined our PE department at the start of session 1983-84 (see TFs in PP 53) the school regularly fielded four football teams—at Under 13, Under 14, Under 15 and Senior level. Two of the earliest teams are featured in PP 10 (Summer Special) extracts from which appear on the next page.

As with the hockey players but not quite so often (!) our football teams became local champions from time to time. Three of the finest teams we produced are shown on following pages: from PP 80 (Summer 1990) - 1989-90 Under 14 League Champions, from PP 89 the 1991-2 Senior XI who won the Central League, and Cup and from PP 149 our Under 13 team who were North of Scotland champions in May 2004.

Our 1978-79 Under 14 Squad and below Under 13s (l-r)

Steven Davies, Michael Gray, James Bennett, Kevin Reid, John Gair, Michael Hills, Stephen O'Hare.

Colin Petrie, David Calder, Darrin Cameron, Kevin Walker (Capt.), Brian Ross, Graham Johnstone,
Angus Whyte, Steven Campbell.

John Rollo, Angus MacKinnon, Steven Richardson, John Williamson, Anthony Marchi, Alan Logan,
Ian MacDonald, Robert McDonald, John McQueen.

Colin Grant, David Hector, James McLellan, Gregor Milne (Capt.), David Bremner, Robert Anderson,
Andrew Mellis.

Our 1989-90 Under 14 League Champions

Back (l-r): Mr Alan Sturrock, Johnathan O'Brien, Steven Ross, Mark McPherson, Barry Stewart, Paul Watters, David Willets. Front: Michael Duncan, Darren Cameron, Paul Menzies, Scott Mullen (Captain,) Craig McAndie, Graeme Wright

Our 1991-92 Senior XI who won the Central League, and Cup

Elgin High School's senior football team with the new strip, presented to them by Elgin Refrigeration. Captain Alan Cormie (rear, fourth from right) accepts the kit from Mr Gordon Shanks, managing director of Elgin Refrigeration. The group also includes the school's rector, Mr Bill Hope (extreme left), assistant coach Hamish Simpson (second left) and coach Alan Sturrock (extreme right).   NS Photo

Our first football teams, as with hockey contain the names of many boys who later enjoyed football at amateur, juvenile, junior and in a few cases senior level. For the 2008 booklet celebrating *30 Years of Elgin High School* Willie Finnie created a whole team of fps

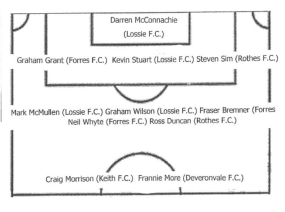

who could have made up a Highland League side (*shown above*). Exchanges on the Former Pupils' Facebook site in late 2017 suggested that this exercise could be repeated with different players several times during the life of the school.

However, the early successes of our hockey, football and other sports teams were to come to a sudden halt which had nothing to do with a shortage of talent…..

As explained in PP 59 (For December 1984) a teachers' dispute with the Westminster government over pay was about to bring all extra-curricular activity to an end….. as it turned out, until the Spring of 1987.

To dedicated teachers of my generation and many before us, getting involved in the broader life of the school (unpaid, and beyond contract), putting on school shows, dances and discos, running debating and chess teams and helping to run sports teams etc. was not only evidence of commitment to the school we were serving in but also a very enjoyable part of the job, permitting different kinds of rapport with pupils away from the formality of the classroom. However not doing any of that for around thirty months changed the mind-set of many teachers across Scotland, who were not only annoyed and irritated with the attitude of the government re pay but who were beginning to find quite different and more enjoyable ways of spending that freed-up time in their family and private lives.

This major hiatus in extra-curricular activity proved to be a watershed in modern Scottish educational history and to use a cliché phrase, "things were never the same again". When the dispute was over—with the publication of the Main Report after an independent pay review which resulted in a very significant improvement in salaries—extra-curricular activities recovered very slowly and what sports there were, were managed by many fewer staff and many more willing parents. Parental involvement had always been an element in extra-curricular activities but it had been limited largely to accompanying and supporting teachers and now required Criminal Record Checking and insurance to be put in place so it was problematical but a way forward in new circumstances.

The slow restart is reflected in the dearth of team photos in *Pigeon Post* over the next few years after it resumed publication in May 1987.

See PP 74 (June 1989) and PP 97 (December 1993) for the related articles

Former Pupil Nicky Grant, now training to become a P.E. teacher sports the international cap she won playing football for the Scottish Ladies side v Italy earlier this year.

It was not only the boys who achieved success in football. Lots of girls wanted to play and one group in particular became national champions, more than once. From within this group emerged one star player in the form of Nichola Grant who played professional women's football across Britain and Europe and was capped by Scotland 99 times. See photos overleaf from PP 74 (June 1989) and PP 97 (December 1993)

In addition to staff, parents and friends of the school who were willing to help run teams, a small group of referees from SFA Referees (Moray & Banff) were keen to support school football. These included from the staff Ken Simpson, James Farquhar, Jeff Dugdale, shown right with David Macdonald and Callum Jenkins (in light coloured top), and from the neighbourhood Eddie Coutts, and Sandy Smith.

These referees would often do a middle in the morning at a school game and then go off to run a line at a Highland League game.

An additional factor in the strength of football in the Elgin area was the existence of Elgin Boys' Club to which many of our pupils also belonged. During the industrial action, pupils were not short of football because of the existence of this organisation.

Back (l-r) Charles Farmer, Michael Allan, David Campbell, Neil Munro, Michael Johnstone, Jeremy Philip, Michael Pirie. Middle: Brian Stewart, Steven McIntosh, Brian Shortreed, Kevin McInnes, Gary Isaac, Gordon Duthie, Raymond Shiach. Front: Neil McDonald, Brian Kelman, Neil Shiach, Roy Young (Capt.,) James Ralph, Nigel Squair, Brian Fraser.

Rugby sides came and went depending on the arrival of interested staff, like John Aitken and Stephen Wilkinson. Our first rugby side, as coached by Mr Alister Hendrie is pictured in the PP 10 Summer Special (above).

One pupil who was very keen on rugby was the captain of the combined S1/2 side, Roy Young, of whom much more elsewhere in these pages.

Also well supported under the guidance of Miss Isobel

Back (l-r) Miss Wasilenska (coach), Dawn Cooper, Wendy MacGillivray, Paula Aldin, Lynne Kelly, Lynne Craib, Karen Mutch, Marion Mackinnon. Middle: Mandy Leppard, Julia Hogg, Michelle Booth, Alison Farquhar, Lesley Still. Front: Julie Turnidge, Jane Ralph, Elaine Hutcheson, Julie Campbell, Shirlene Abbott.

Wasilenska was our girls basketball side shown here from PP 10.

With arrival of new staff in August 1979 we were also able to compete successfully in in table tennis and gymnastics : see pictures on next page ex PP 19.

254

Other Champion Teams

Our 2003-04 Under 13 North of Scotland Champions (ex PP 147)

Back (l-r) : Adam Dunbar, Grant Duguid, David Craig, Craig Sutherland, Callum Reid, Dean Higgins
Middle: Lee Millar, Andrew Jackson, Danny Edwards, Gary Denoon, Stuart Wilson,
Front: Matthew Johnston, Fraser Wilson, Daniel Pearson, Brian Cameron, Rhys Wotherspoon, Craig Hay

See also in PP 165 The 2006/07 League Cup Winning football squad, in PP155 The Under 14 side who were League Champions and more photos of the victorious Under 13 North of Scotland Cup side (above) in PP149 on match day.

LEAGUE CUP WINNERS 2006/07

Back row L to R: Christopher Duncan, Michael Taylor, Grant Duguid, Darrin Cameron, Andy Jackson
Front Row L to R: Adam Dunbar, Dean McPherson, Craig Hay, Cameron Dixon, David Wilson, Ross Arif,
Andrew Anderson, Duncan McPhee, Graham Robinson

Some of our gymnasts:

Back (l-r) Darrin Camerom, Ian Peel, Mark O'Shane

Centre: Carol Johnstone, Shirlene Abbott, Michelle, McLaren.

Front: Patricia Oglvie, Lynne Kelly, Alison Farquhar.

(Shirlene, Patricia, Lynne and Alison won the local Intermediate Team championship in March)

Ex PP 19 (June 1980)

Table Tennis

Stephen Bremner, Mr David Allan of our PE Dept., and Gregor Milne who won the Division B title in 1979-80

Ex PP 19 (June 1980)

Published photos of all teams can be found on the Dropbox site **pigeonpost.info.** See also our Sports Day and Swimming Gala data in Part 2 and individual articles in the sections on Former Pupils about athletes with exceptional talent such as Laura Chalmers, Stephanie Reynolds, Roy Young , Ricky Foster and many others.

16   Inspections

"We're Having An Inspection"...........news to bring anxiety to any school.

Inspections have taken many forms in the past. Typically a school would have a "full inspection" which meant, given roughly a month's notice, all aspects of the school's delivery of education would be observed, commented on verbally and a draft report written and later published with amendments.

Such an inspection would see every department visited by a subject specialist H.M.I. (His Majesty's Inspector) formerly a teacher or education official but sometimes a lay person and the teaching of most staff in that department wouod be observed for say half a lesson.   Other aspects like the school's delivery of Guidance, Careers Advice, Social Education, communication with parents and its General Management would also be scrutinised. A sample of promoted staff, unpromoted staff, pupils and parents would be interviewed in a kind of Focus Group. The lead players in the Inspectorate team would also sit down with the Head and some of the Senior Management Team to discuss policies or implementation of new government led initiatives, of which there has never been any shortage in the past fifty years.   When the inspection period was over, the lead Inspector would give immediate verbal feedback to the Head and indicate the kind of comments that would appear in his/her report and then a draft of that report would be sent to the school for comment before being published in a pamphlet for those interested and filed for public reference.

But sometimes Inspections would be much more limited, concentrating for just a few days on a suite of related subjects like Sciences, or the Creative Arts or an education theme, for example Differentiation or Learning Support. In the lifetime of Elgin High School the traditional arrival of a mini-bus of "men in suits" as the Inspection team were called were long gone and there was typically a cordial atmosphere throughout the event. The intention of the Inspection was never punitive or designed to embarrass any school found to be underperforming in some area but to offer the advice of a critical friend to promote improvement, to be looked at again after a reasonable period time had passed.

"Inspections" were carried out by HMII but regularly the equivalent would be undertaken by officers of the local authority, The Moray Council, who would visit schools in rota to examine how they were coping and what major issues were. The purpose of these visits would be to report to Councillors (and hence the public) about how such and such a school were performing. These events would be more low key than HMII visits but the other side of that coin was that those carrying them out were on your doorstep and would remain there after the formal visit was over, unlike the HMII team which would move onto another part of the country for its next work.

Schools could be expect to be inspected every five years and since Elgin High opened late in 1978, the Quinquennial Inspection duly took place in the Spring of 1984 and was reported on in PP 54, where it is covered in some detail on cover, page 2 and page 4, The Rector's Headlines column.

The front page article notes that the eighteen page published report was adjudged by *The Northern Scot* to be "glowing" giving the school "top marks" and a series of prominent education officials had said the report was "first class".

We learn in paragraph two that the "jewel in crown" was the school's suite of imaginative courses for the Junior School, though it found the Middle School courses more restricted in freedom, with too much emphasis on the national exams. The Senior School curriculum was also praised, but was the school challenging its brightest pupils enough?

The Report, extracts of which are given on page 2 of the issue, found that school generally "bounded with curricular initiatives" (Point 4.1) and that the staff and pupils had achieved a remarkable amount in its short life to date.

Bill Hope commented in his own column that the Inspection experience had been "less traumatic than expected", that he was "well pleased" with their Report and found it "a compliment to the staff, pupils and New Elgin community". He had been delighted with comments from many, many sources and thought the Report set the school up well for next five years.

"How Good Is Our School?"

A revolution in how Inspections were conducted came twenty years ago with the HGIOS documentation which provided "Quality indicators" (later "Performance indicators") providing statements at four (later six) levels of what schools could be found to be delivering across a vast range of aspects of school life. This gave HMIE detailed criteria to work from in awarding schools scores for performance and at the time by inference an indication of what the school needed to do to gain advancement to the next level. The current government website on this topic states

"Since 1996, How good is our school? (HGIOS) has become a nationally and internationally recognised brand, which underpins effective self-evaluation as the starting point for school improvement.

It is a key aspect of the Scottish approach to school improvement. The framework is designed to be used to support self-evaluation and reflection by practitioners at all levels".

HGIOS is now in its Fourth Edition.

The first major Inspection of Elgin High using these new criteria took place during April 2004 and is referenced in in PP 149.

As the front page headline suggest, one of the Key Strengths the HMIE team found was the way pupils behaved, which was commented by on all members of the Inspection team.

Other positives were noted in how well staff knew and cared for and about their pupils, the plethora of opportunities offered by out of classroom learning for example in school trips and extra-curricular activities.

However the report also suggested that there was need for improvement in exam performance relative to that by pupils from similar schools.

(Continued on Page 4)

The report to the Moray Council Education Committee can be found at

http://www.moray.gov.uk/minutes/archive/EL20041006/
hmieschoolinspectionpublishedreport.PDF

Where the main points for action are summarised as follows:

• raise attainment at all stages particularly in English and Mathematics;

• review senior management remits to ensure greater rigour and effectiveness in self-evaluation,and in improving learning, teaching and pupils' attainment;

• make more effective use of attainment information in order to set individual targets with pupils and parents and raise expectations;

• ensure the progressive development of pupils' learning in the personal, social and health education programme and enable staff to measure its success;

• improve arrangements for religious observance; and

• address the health and safety issues identified in this report.

Elgin High was last inspected at the start of session 2011-12 and the HMIE report is dated 29.11.2011: https://education.gov.scot/inspection-reports/moray/5210038

Interlude No.3
That's a Belter

I posted the following comment on the Facebook FP website in late November 2017 and was amused to see flow in reactions to and memoires of corporal punishment, abolished in Scotland's comprehensive schools in 1986. Some were quite amusing.

Ya belter! One pupil has just contacted me through Messenger (he is on this site under a pseuodnym/avatar) to remind me that we made history together in EHS in August 1978.

I was at first alarmed and then dismayed to recall that he was the first pupil I belted in the school. I won't reveal his name for professional reasons but some others of you may recall it happened. Please think carefully before writing about this.

How shameful that the belt ever existed. "It never did me any harm!!" Well, maybe, but those were not good times.

One of the earliest pupils of EHS claimed...

Well I'm pleased to say I never experienced the belt --- on a Saturday/Sunday (lol) I am sure there was a sweepstake in the staff room every morning for me and the winner got first dibs. I remember once got I the belt from Mr C for offending Mrs G and just after he gave me the tash Mr T came out and wanted to give me another six. Fortunately I managed to grab the tash, leg it and exchange a few "pleasantries". As he was in his clogs he couldn't catch me but even if he'd been wearing trainers and had had a head start he still wouldn't have. I returned the following day with the old man and Mr T was reluctant to meet my dad!!!!! so thus begun two weeks exclusion for my "outrageous behaviour".

Another commented (not about EHS however):

When we were at (a local Primary) School the Headmaster took the belt to 4 classes of pupils because a pupil had broken a window with an ice snowball. The irony is it turned out to be the daughter of one of the other teachers and no one would tell. There were only five or six pupils in each class but everyone of us received the strap as we called it. (It hurt too!) I was in P5 at the time : long time ago but still remembered. P4 to P7 all punished for the actions of someone else: I think was really harsh but we all survived it.

A handful of Others – re EHS experiences...

I remember getting the belt from Mr F because someone threw a rubber. No one admitted it so I was picked at random to be punished. I still don't know who threw it to this day.

I got it once from Mr C for talking when playing table tennis. All I said was "You're next to play" to a fellow pupil. Terrible.

Next time was by Mr Hope. I was in English class and the guy behind me (can't remember his name) was hitting me on the head with a jotter and being generally abusive. After about the 20th hit I got up, turned round and punched him. Just at that moment Mr Hope passed the door!! What timing! We both got it and the other guy cried loads. English teacher was very sympathetic to me.

Miss Campbell our sewing teacher gave it to me for laughing but Mr Hope's delivery was the worst experience. I did pull my hand away ....trust me I think my hand was red for a week when as a result three times that leather strap went across my hand. Yes I did deserve it for using someone's coat to clean the black board.....sorry JM You know who you are.

Oddly..I can thank you The Board of Studies, that I didn't have the actual tash before it got phased out..somehow. I used a lot of agricultural language)but somehow,went from standin stock still to attention in offices,to writing essays instead..mr hopes/ mr cadenheads sort of(i know now  *why,direct that energy into usefulness instead)included library,finding certain tomes(history usually)and setting x amount of required paperwork,for the essay..oddly,youd start to get into it..(ofcourse the usual bin bag,big stick duty as well) and yours being the bookshelf in yfloor mid room,(with computers one side) and then essay set to book youd choose(which of course required be taken home and read fully to understand which too,did not mind at all..the only teacher that nearly gave me the belt was mr sturrock,who had three of us lined up for overheated tempers and tried to hit one with a climbing ropes end(dont ask)and pupil dodged hand at last minute,which so did we when tried..he got furious,roared at us to see mr hope,who wasnt in and we stood in shorts/tee shirts for about hour and half..lunch bell then rang,and mr cadenhead came out office,asked us what we were doing,we tried to say we had been sent to see mr hope but,sensing long winded explainations, versus his lunch awaiting, he waived us off with" its a bonny day out boys go on, out and play, away wi you".......ah yes..the belt at ehs*

Got it from Mr Hope for breaking the lift. There were four of us Mr Hope was waving his arms about like a wind turbine he was so mad. But who knew that pressing two buttons at the same time could break it .

Mr Fyfe always warned you if you were bad... with the immortal words 'You will get a tap wi the strap if you don't stop the comedy capers"

im one of the luckyist pupils in ehs..stupid,i know-but attempted the "record"(unofficial) for trying to skateboard from top z floor by back stairs over techie dept,through y floor(you bumped down stairs if fast enough goin slightly sideways,shortest route and got "grabbed"(literally off board)by mr cadenhead (second time hed done this,first outside his home as caught similar using his garden wall that summer and asked,if im returning to school..see you in autumn season then)and this sent board flying down past the (we thought vacant,wasnt)teachers lounge and stopped by the doors to stairs.detention by cleaning teachers lounge(see,thats how we got that punishment-see earlier confession on previous post)but this was luckily under mr donalds supervision(yaaah,fisherman friends 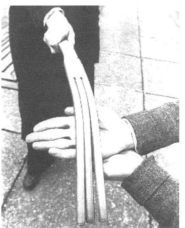 *and he'd leave you too it,cough. not advisable)and after the strap had been repealled legally..a lot of kids did push teachers straight after it,in a kinda,ach yer cannae do nothin now,but some of us were just too energetic and thought up brilliant things(only to us though,sheer chaos to normal.people i suppose)and egged each other on..and yes,i got my skateboard put in the infamy room for a bit,next to my studded wristbands,bullet belt,a horrific teeshirt,that err,full hand to elbow leather mosher thing full of nine inch nails that mr buchan didnt realise quite,what i was making at time and various other things that even me mam thought,yes,best took off him really..ah,the folly of youth.cough.*

Two FPs combined to give this account

Mr L. used to stand in front of a stroboscope waving his strap around. As the light slowed down the motion of his arm it looked like he was moving very slowly. It didn't take long to work out that when he asked you to come and stand in front of him the answer was no.

He used to stand on his upturned waste paper bin for extra leverage. He even did this when he gave me the belt in first year, and I was the shortest boy in the school.

Editor's Note: I did consider editing the stream of consciousness item starting at the top of p263 but it defeated me and I decided to leave it as I received it!!

17   Talented Cartoonists

The first years of the school's newspaper were blessed with a sizeable number of very talented pupil cartoonists whose work greatly enlivened our pages.   The covers of the first twenty or so editions of our newspaper were designed by Maurice Jackson, our Head of Art & Design who created Percy Pigeon, the naughtiest schoolboy in Elgin High, but that cheeky bird was later drawn by some three dozen different pupils. Almost every front cover of the first 100 editions (and some later ones) contained a cartoon of Percy and some of his adventures also appeared in strip form.

Through the life of the newspaper new cartoonists / caricaturists presented themselves regularly and had their work widely appreciated.

This next section celebrates some of the best work—I regret that more of it cannot be shown here for reasons of space—but you can see much more of it in a special section of the Dropbox at **pigeonpost.info.**

Three of our most prolific cartoonists were **Robbie Linton** (profiled in PP 20) who sadly died in a climbing accident when he was in his twenties, **Scott Johnston** and **Lindsay Hutchison** both of whom were profiled in PP 27 The two boys' styles were very oddball whilst Lindsay produced a series of charming cartoons about Percy. It would be remiss not to mention the cartoon work of artists such as **Gillian Morton, Jacqueline Morton, Gary Watt, Louise** and **Victoria Whittaker** and **Fionna Shearer**

Over the next six pages the work of the first three named artists is exemplified.....

From PP 29 and 30 (Sept and Oct 1981) Two parts of Robbie's *Annie*

From PP 23 (December 1980) Scott's *A Christmas Tail*

From PP 21 (October 1980) Lindsay's tale about *Percy's dinner ticket.*

Robbie's work appeared in the newspaper from PP 5 when he began illustrating his own story *The Rowdy Class*, (PP 6 illustration is shown right) right through to PP 41 where he illustrated a German language version of *Snow White* written by the senior German class. He was responsible for the design of four front cover pages.

Scott Johnstone created a series of weird characters such as Herman, Dynamic Duck and Pac-Men. If Robbie's style was sharp and cutting, then Scott's was certainly more rounded as this example from PP 28 shows.

Lindsay's work appears in our editions from PP 20 to PP 55 and this example from the cover of PP 48 (with Lindsay now in S5) suggesting future careers for Percy illustrates her versatility and charming style.

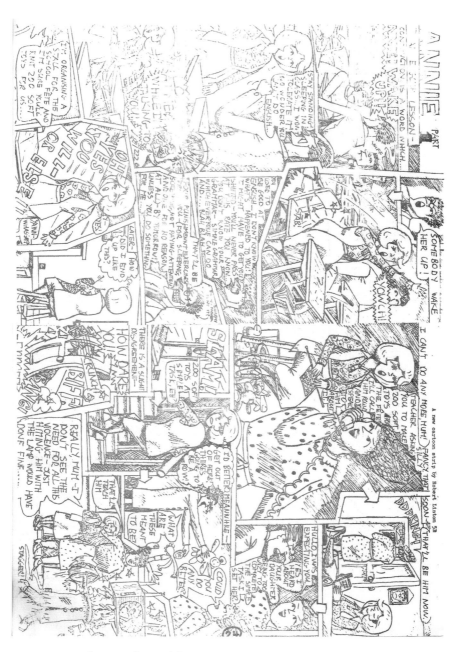

Part One of *Annie* by Robbie Linton

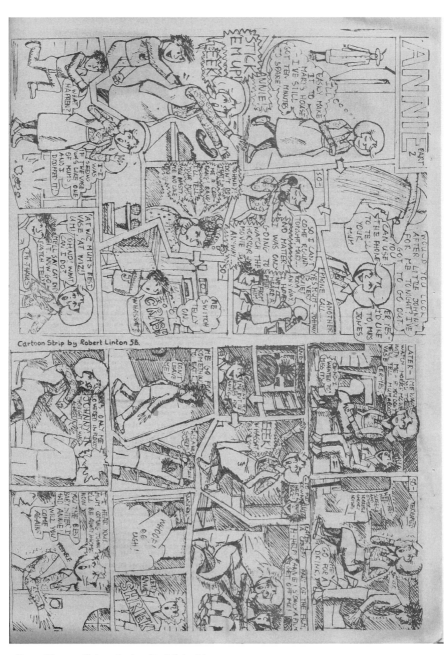

Part Two of *Annie* by Robbie Linton

272

Robbie, Scott and Lindsay were all either in S1 or S2 when they began producing cartoons for *Pigeon Post* and continued to do so until they left school with many of Lindsay's smaller cartoons appearing on the cover, Robbie contributing material inside and Scott's work often on the back pages.

However by now others are chipping in with portrayals of Percy for example **Louise and Victoria Whittaker** (PP 40 and PP 41 covers). Robbie Linton's illustrations for the story of Snow White written in German by a senior German class in PP40 and pp 41 is remarkable. **Fionna Shearer** who went on to become an Art teacher is also now featuring (cover of PP 42) as are a whole series of new artists whose work appears on the covers of issues in the mid-1980's

Lindsay Hutchison's last cartoon appears on the cover of PP 55 in June 1984 (right).

The last issue before the two and half year break in production PP 59 shows Percy drawn by **Fionna Shearer** and the first once we had recommenced in May 1987 is by **Dawn Rose**, inspired by one of Lindsay's original drawings.

A huge variety of artists created Percy cartouches relative to the main news story

or theme for the front cover from issues PP 20 to PP 73 when a new style of cover emerged. Amongst those who produced more than one cover were **Gillian Morton, Janette Pilling, Louise Whittaker, Fionna Shearer, Jacqueline Morton, Dawn Rose** and **Darrell Richardson** whilst **Michael Johnston** began to contribute some cartoon strips

With the 100th edition (in June 1990) a major new talent emerged in the form of **Rory MacKay,** a very self-effacing but multi-talented pupil, now a published fantasy author. Rory loved to draw caricatures of staff as that cover suggest but it was his strip cartoons that were of a near professional standard as the two page story from PP 112 demonstrates,

Rory's satirical, complicated and caricature laden cartoon strip, showing his
fascination with Mother Theresa and Bill Hope from PP 112 (Dec 1996)

You can see all Rory's cartoons and other work at **pigeonpost.info** (Dropbox)

After Rory, Percy's adventures were drawn in strip cartoon form by **Donna Logan**—see for example PP 128—133 and **Euan Sinclair** created his own cartoon heroes in Fuzz Buzz and Tripe in PP 138 to PP 144.

The final artist to be noted in these pages is caricaturist **Jon Arbuthnott** whose work came to the fore during our SoundTown Year 2005-06—see Chapter 13 for some examples.

Jon's work appears in editions from PP 142 to PP 160 with a couple of

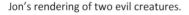
Jon's rendering of two evil creatures.

18   Uniforms

When Elgin High opened, there was a real possibility it would come to be regarded as a junior partner to Elgin Academy, so it was important for the school to show to observers that it aimed to set the same standards in presentation. Therefore when New Elgin parents had a choice of which school to send their children, Elgin High's having a smart traditional uniform like the Academy was one important factor.

The first uniform was a traditional one of black blazer with a badge showing a dove in flight over the "EHS" initials. The dove, of course, was a symbol of love, peace and communication but also referenced the Doo'cot or dovecot in the eponymous main recreation park of New Elgin (*as pictured*). The badge (and the navy blue tie with similar dove) had been designed  by the Head of Art & Design at Bill Hope's previous school, (Lochaber High) there being no time to invite the new appointee to Elgin High's Art Dept to do it and have items manufactured in time.

This was to be complemented by white or pale blue shirt or blouse with the school tie bearing the same motif—and navy blue, black or dark grey trousers or skirt.

Photo by Nick Ledingham of Miss Sheena Cowan's Boys Choir for the 1980 Moray
Music Festival. See more such photos in PP 19, where this one is captioned

Unpublished photo by Nick Ledingham of one of his first year Science classes in 1978-79

Formal photographs of pupils of course show that they largely turned up wearing this uniform on the first day or for special occasions but if you compare that with an informal class photograph, as opposite taken by Nick Ledingham, the respect for uniform seems, shall we say, more patchy.

Pupils, of course, recall reacting differently to the first uniform, some being delighted to wear it because of the sense of identity and pride any uniform provides whilst others wore it because their parents said so and couldn't wait to get out of it. Wearing uniform also meant pupils were under no peer pressure to flaunt the latest fashion fad in clothing—to school. In the early 1980s girls were permitted to wear trousers for the first time as part of the uniform—in the Winter term only to begin with—and corduroy in black or navy was stipulated. Pupils representing the school as sporting teams were asked to wear uniform when they travelled by bus to other schools and their trooping off the bus in it always cut a dash.

There was also heartfelt negative comment from girls about what they had to wear for P.E. lessons and how it put so many of them off the subject, a perennial issue for schools over the decades and going back to the 1940s or earlier, mainly re girls' body image.

One item which received lots of approval though was the school tie, which being navy blue with a crisp small white dove logo looked quite distinct from typical school ties of the time. These either had stripes of one colour over another or had a quite a fussy school badge which didn't look good when reduced in size. Pupils in the 1980's also recall being told off if ties were worn showing the dove too near the knot or off centre!

They particularly remember Mr Hope's Rules about "NO DENIM" and "NO FOOTBALL SCARVES", the former presumably because it was too casual and the latter in order to reduce potential strife between rival groups of supporters (e.g. between fans of Aberdeen and The Old Firm).

However, after only five years, you can see that blazers are becoming less popular and the trend in late Summer at least is a sleeveless pullover: see photo of 1K1 from PP 59 (December 1984), where only one person wears one. Five years later there has been no recovery: see 1F1 from PP 85 (April 1991) where uniform has

Reg Class 1K1 Ex PP 59 (December 1984) - see captions in pigeonpost.info

Reg Class 11 Ex PP 85 (April 1992) - see captions in pigeonpost.info

been interpreted in many different ways, though the tie is worn faithfully.

So from time to time attempts were made to promote the wearing of full uniform with registration class teachers asked to make reports about persistent non-compliance and points off in House competitions for the classes with the best uniform turn out.

Then in October 1994 as shown on the cover of PP 101 (the first for session 1994-95) something new is tried. In this we learn of a revolutionary casual approach to our uniform challenges.

Several things are clear from the article in this edition article: the new approach has been inspired by some of our own pupils being impressed by the Elgin Academy uniform and wanting something like that themselves, lots of consultation has gone on before the new casual choices emerged, the new garments bear a new *EHS* logo and—the fact that wearing uniform is not at this point, compulsory.

So has this new approached worked? Well judge from yourself from the first day photo of 1O1 from December 1996 printed in PP 112:

A year after Andy Simpson had arrived as Headteacher in late 2003 a further approach to relaunching uniform was tried and the article inside suggests great success.....

85% wearing new uniform

From a survey of around a third of the school (220+ pupils), conducted across 14 registration classes and one S6 English class in mid-September, returns indicate an enormous success story around the launch of our new uniform. The Pupil Representative Council deserve full credit for coming up with a logo designs and doing the research on colour and garments that pupils would be willing to wear. For any school to go from almost 0% uniform to 85% over the Summer is quite something !

"What item of school uniform are you wearing today ?"

	hooded sweat shirt	sweatshirt	micro fleece	none
S1	35	9	8	3
S2	32	8	8	6
S3	22	8	8	1
S4	17	5	4	5
S5	7	7	5	7
S6	3	3	1	10

"How happy are you about wearing it ?"

	Very happy	happy	not happy
S1	24	25	3
S2	4	38	10
S3	5	27	8
S4	2	16	13
S5	5	16	4
S6		8	7

"What is your estimate of the number of pupils who are wearing uniform ?"

	100%	90+%	80+%	50+%
S1	6	28	18	3
S2		35	16	2
S3		23	11	3
S4		5	20	4
S5		10	10	5
S6		2	9	6

"Do you think the school image has been improved by the wearing of uniform ?"

	Yes, very much	Yes, a bit	No, not at all
S1	21	23	7
S2	9	39	4
S3	11	22	7
S4	3	23	5
S5	7	15	3
S6		16	1

What other "EHS" items would you like to be made available for later sale ?

	Baseball Cap	beanie hat	sports shirt	T-shirt
S1	16	3	17	23
S2	14	11	18	9
S3	6	19	5	10
S4	7	5	2	6
S5	5	5	1	15
S6	1	4		8

Make Your Views Known

If you would like to see new items in the range made available, as above or indeed other ideas of your own do please let people know—for example members of the Pupil Representative Council. *Pigeon Post* understands that senior pupils might like to have a distinct colour for their garments to mark them out.

What do you think about the idea of having the horizontal line through the EHS logo which is white or silver—in your house colour—yellow for Eagles, blue for Falcons and green for Ospreys ?

Hopefully with the Spring and Summer terms in mind there will be new styles and colours for you to consider.

Staff Sport "EHS" logo

Staff are also beginning to wear garments with the new logo, for example Mr Finnie sports a blue short sleeved shirt, Mrs Duncan a black waistcoat and Mrs Hyde a fleece. Orders for other garments are on order.

Further Views Sought

This page shows the results of a sample of pupils quizzed by *Pigeon Post* about their views at the start of the new session. Later in the year the school intends to ask parents more formally for their views on the launch of the uniform. At this point questions of quality, fading, bubbling of material and related price which have been raised in this survey will be addressed.

Thanks to all who have contributed to the composing and analysis of these questionnaires

Order Forms Still Available

Please contact the school office for details.

29

From PP 151 for September 2004

Non-Uniform Occasions

The history of uniform across the first three decades of the school's life is that, in a nutshell, it was school policy that it should be worn and generally it was but certainly not by nearly everyone. Yet despite trends and relaunches it survived and at times flourished.

However, any pupil was delighted not to have wear uniform if there was an excuse not to—like on charity supporting Dress as You Like Days for Red Nose Day, or Children in Need, on Activities Days or on the last day of any term—and controversially during the SQA exam diet.   *Pigeon Post* issues are full of photographs relating to the joy experienced by pupils and staff in dressing up for a bit of fun in order to raise money for charity for example from 2000 below.

Elgin High School's Effort for Comic Relief

Top left: Sixth Year girls as St Trinians with school nurse: from left Jillian Geddes, Dionne Rodgers, Lynn Davidson, and Caroline Cleiff

Top right Marc Cascarino and Shanine Smith vamping it up !

Above in the staffroom : Mrs Lorna Allan, Mrs Fay Watt and Mrs Aileen Marshall

Above right: 2A girls are cool in blue – Donna Logan, Brenda Stronach, Leanne Mair and Amy Sutherland

Right: Pupil Council organisers, counting out the funds raised, supervised by Granny Darling (extreme left)

19 School Clubs & Societies

Today the period structure across Moray's eight secondary schools is standardised: when the bell rings at 8.55 (after Registration) to start Period One in Forres Academy it also does in Speyside High and when school closes at 3.20pm in Keith Grammar, pupils are also streaming out of Lossiemouth High at 3.21.

This was not always the case and the pages of *Pigeon Post* show two major changes, both using the same headline on the front page, "Big Changes Coming For You in New Timetable" - in PP 98 (February 1994) and PP 133 (February 2001). In the first change we moved from six periods to eight and in the second we moved from eight periods to—six!

When the school opened, Bill Hope designed the school day so that pupils had a long break of 1 hour 15 minutes for lunch, in order to go home, if they lived with easy walking distance or to relax and recreate themselves in various ways for a substantial period of time—and to encourage clubs and activities to run at lunchtime, as well as at the end of the day.

The school that opened its doors in August 1978 was full of young staff who didn't think twice about having a quick lunch and then offering an activity at least once or twice a week to interested pupils, who long before the days of mobile phones, tablets etc. installed with computer games, might otherwise have been kicking their heels. Some of these activities were the obvious ones involving physical exercise of running and skill-training—football, rugby, hockey, etc.—and weren't really clubs at all whilst others offering more sedentary entertainment had a more formal structure. The longer lunchtime even allowed pupils involved in physical exercise time enough for a shower before the first period of the afternoon, to which many arrived panting and with dripping hair.

Many of the clubs that formed were ephemeral, depending on the interest of the teacher who ran them and then ceasing when that teacher (and his/her expertise) departed but others existed for most of the life of *Pigeon Post* and regularly reported in its pages in order to encourage others to join. Here is a reminder of some of those lunchtime and after school activities that were open to pupils.

The Scripture Union / TEAR Fund

Led by Mrs McPherson, Mr Cameron and Mr Macleod the S.U. is first mentioned in PP 4 where a residential weekend involving Christian fellowship with pupils from Lossie, Buckie and Banff at Kilravock Castle, Nairn is described. Later in the edition the international Christian and charitable activities of The Alliance Evangelical Relief Fund (T.E.A.R.) are described and pupils encouraged to become "TEARaways" in order to raise funds locally to support those works in poorer countries. There are reports throughout editions of *PP* for the first four of five years: see also for example PP 21 where a Club Spy features details pupil activity such as quizzes, games and watching short films mostly with a Christian slant.

Biology Club

PP 11 introduced the Club Spy column with a feature on the club which "indulges in a fascinating variety of activities every Friday lunchtime in Mr Polson's room". Watching films about nature is the staple diet but pupils are allowed to observe at close hand a number of small creatures in their department tanks and "by arrangement" bring in their own pets. Birdwatching opportunities are described and a trip to the Kincraig Wildlife Park organised. A mainstay of the club is Douglas Scott who regularly writes a Nature column for PP.

The Highlights etc

Elgin High's new six-girl dance troupe, coached by PT Drama Mrs Anne Duncan were introduced in PP 12: Photo by Mr Ledingham. Jackie, Susan, Karen, Donna,

Paddy and Lynne are all profiled and we learn how they love putting on exhibition dancing routines at our regular discos. Mrs Duncan also ran another group comprising Sarah, Lyne, Shirley, Paula, Doreen, Angela and Janice also shown above right from the captioned photo in PP 19. Initially this group were nameless.

STEP (Schools Traffic Education Programme)

This was an after school course run by Technical Teacher Mr Alec McKenzie (shown here with the group from PP 12: photo Mr Ledingham) over many evenings over two school sessions for pupils beginning in S3. They were introduced to vehicle (moped) control skills, then went on to learn something about the mechanical principles of motor vehicles and how accidents can happen. The moped had been most generously gifted to the school by Doug Gordon of Burghead.

Bagpiping Group

In PP 13 Club Spy visited this small group (four of the most dedicated being pictured) tutored by experienced teacher Mr James Hamilton our PT History. From l-r the group comprised Michael Gray, Kevin McInnes, Richard Anderson and Jeremy Philip. The group met every lunchtime in Mr Hamilton's top floor classroom, mainly practising on chanters only.

Moray Music Festival Choirs

This was another option for pupils at lunchtime and after school with two girls and one boys choir being formed to first participate in the March 1980 festival under the direction of Miss Cowan, whose success was reported in PP 17 with pictures and captions in PP 19: photo Mr Ledingham. Shown above the Junior Girls Choir who won a Second place.

Aeromodelling Club

One club which lasted longer than most, under the guidance of Technical and later Guidance teacher Mr Ian Walker was reported on in PP 29 (Sept 1981). The club offered a variety of activity from building simple chuck gliders, rubber powered aircraft, right up to control line models and model boats. The club had two sections for novice and older pupils.

EHS Majorettes

This was another group started by Miss Cowan who were very popular and called upon to perform their routines in a number of public arenas. They first appear on the cover of PP 10, having just displayed their baton twirling skills at our Summer fête. These unpublished photos show them preparing to go off to a display at the

1979 Keith Show. See also PP 38 (June 1982) at Elgin Round Table derby day.

What's on at Lunchtime?

A news item in PP 42 (January 1983) gives a snapshot of the impressive variety of activity available to pupils:

Computer Club

This met most lunchtimes with a different type of activity on each day. For example, Mondays were for Games "freaks" with Space Invaders, Exterminators, Pac Man Eaters available, whilst at other times Mr Philp Penrose was interested in teaching BASIC

Club/Activity	Venue	Times	Charge ?	Person in Charge
Aeromodelling	Tech Dept.	Mon -Thurs 1.15	-	Mr Walker
Drama	Drama Rm.	Wed 1.15	-	Mr McMillan
Golf	School & Course	Summer Term 4.pm	Nominal charge for tuition	Mr Urquhart
Motor Cycle Training	Tech Dept	Summer - lunch times	-	Mr Urquhart
Ski-ing	Cairngorms	Sunday Jan-March	Cost Varies	Mr McWhirr
Football (senior)	Fields & Games Hall	Tues 1.10 Fri 3.50	20p per match	Mr Hamilton
Christmas Show	Music/drama		-	Mrs Ledingham Mr McMillan
Orchestra	Music 1	Mon 1.15	-	Mrs Ledingham
Choir	Music 1	Thurs 1.20	-	Mrs Ledingham
Madrigal Group	Music 1	Wed 1.15	-	Mrs Ledingham
Guitar	Music 2	Wed 1.15	-	Mr McKay
Recorders	Music 1		-	Mrs Ledingham
Field Club	Rm 28	Mon and Thurs lunchtimes Mon after school	only on trips	Mr Finnie
S1 Hockey	Games H.	Mon 3.50	-	Mrs Grant
Country Dancing	Gym	Thurs 1.10	-	Mrs Grant
Badminton	Games H.	Wed 1.00 (Team training) Thurs 4-6 (Club)	-	Mr Davidson assisted on Thurs by Mr Grant
Running	Gym/ X country	Wed 3.50	-	Mr Morrison and Mr Thorburn
Basketball	Games H.	Mon/Fri luncht.	-	Mr Thorburn
Circuit Training and Running	Gym	Daily 12.45 running Tues/Thur circuits	-	Mr Carstairs, Mr Birnie, Mr McNeil
Friday Club	Lect.Rm	Friday Night approx once monthly	60p memb.	Miss Gordon
Hillwalking		Last Sunday in month	£1 for bus and small charge for equipm. hire	Mr Birnie
Football U13		Sat and mid-week training	20p bus charge	Mr McDonald
Debating	Y13	Thurs 1.20	-	Mrs Wilson
Stamp Club	Library	Every other Tues 3.50 - 5.00	-	Mr Croseland
Rugby U13	Tech Dept Games H	Monday 4.00 training Sat. matches	20p for bus -	Mr Spence
Scripture Union	Z10	Friday 1.20	-	Mr Anderson Mr McLeod Mr Cadenhead.
Table Tennis	Gym	Mon 3.50 Wed 1.15	Membership	
Computer Club	Computer Rm	Mon and Thurs S1/6 Tues S1/2 Wed S3 Fri S4/6 Lunch.	-	Mr Penrose

using "three of the school's five Apple II computers" and a few black and white ZX81s. The club also met two days a week after school in which time senior pupils were attempting to build a robot.

Dungeons and Dragons

A feature in PP 59 alerts us to the fact that there is an active group in school who play this very complicated fantasy adventure role playing game in an English classroom most lunchtime, but you are warned that it is expensive. The main drivers are Allan Dean (S4) and Scott Hadden (S2).

NEDS

An amusing acronym for New Elgin Drama Society, run by drama teacher Mr Phil McMillan and English teacher Mrs Jane Ross. The report in PP 47 (Sept 1983) refers to a sketch show the group has just put on for an invited audience and other drama associated skills related to make-up, improvisation and stage fighting are described. Dedication was the one thing required, it seems.

Guitar Club

New English teacher Mr David Sangster reports on this. The school is building on many Primary age pupils coming up with skills and senior pupil Anna Hamilton is also helping out at the club. Mr Peter McKay of the Music department teaches in both sectors and is a valuable link. The school has already formed two bands of pupils using electric guitars and a number of staff who play like Miss Diane Gordon and Mr Ian Walker also attend to assist from time to time.

Rock Bands

Formation and regeneration of these bands was a regular feature of life in Elgin High. In PP 62 and 64 there are features about the band called Sweet Success, originally comprising, Mark Conti, Jan Ettles, Martin Graham, Wayne Chisholm, Colin Milton and Ruaridh Hutchison, some of whom would go on to form other bands later in their school career. These groups were now meeting on their own in Music rooms at lunchtimes and playing gigs at school discos as well as doing a turn at the forthcoming Christmas 1987 concert. They were so enthusiastic that they met *at morning intervals* and lunchtimes.

The High Notes

One of the longest and most successful groups which are first featured in PP 77 and regularly thereafter in items about concerts: see table in Section Two.

Head music teacher at Elgin High School, Mr John Watson (centre) surrounded by pupils who performed in the school's New Year Concert.

New Year Concert Wed 17th January

The New Year CONCERT

PROGRAMME

ENTRY MUSIC: PIPER FIONA DAVIDSON
Medley of four Scottish Marches

PART 1

THE BAND	'Come Follow the Band' 'Carillon'
JUNIOR VOCAL GROUP	'Just Another Star'
ANN SIMMERS (VOCAL)	'Starlight Express'
WOODWIND GROUP	Spiritual: 'Joshua' 'Morning Prayer' by Tchaikovsky
IAN WALKER AND DAVE SANGSTER (GUITAR DUET)	'La Roossimo' by Jane Pickering 2 Dances by Pelter Van Der Staak
DAWN BACHELOR (FLUTE)	Allegro from sonata in F by G F Handel
MARK BRAMLEY (FLUGEL HORN)	'My Little Suade Shoes'
THE BAND	'Chariots of Fire'
SENIOR VOCAL GROUP	'Raindrops Keep Falling on My...'

PART 2

JUNIOR CLASS GROUP	'Jamaica Farewell'
FRENCH VOCAL GROUP	Selection
STANDARD GRADE CLASS	'Christmas Colours'
MELANIE MARSHALL	'Invocation'
FOLK GROUP	'Celtic Field'
JAN MARSHALL (VOCAL)	'Only Me'
ROCK GROUP	'Knockin on Heaven's Door'
	'Leave a Light On'
ALL	'When a Child is Born'

Wed 17th Jan.

Mark Bramley (S5) with Flugel Horn

Flautist Dawn Bachelor (S3)

Jan Marshall (S6) vocalist

P & J 26/1/90

School concert launches new club

A CONCERT by Elgin pupils proved a real tonic for the head music teacher.

Elgin High School's annual Christmas concert had to be cancelled because Mr John Watson had flu.

Rehearsals could not be held because he was off work for a week.

With Mr Watson fully recovered, the event went ahead under its new title, the New Year Concert.

Around 160 parents and friends saw 120 pupils perform a variety of music, from rock to classical.

The concert also marked the launch of the school's new music club, the High Notes.

"There is a fairly healthy interest in music in the school," said Mr Watson.

Club members will present lunchtime and classroom concerts, end-of-term concerts and entertain outside the school as a concert party.

They will also go to Aberdeen and Inverness for theatre shows.

"We have pupils who learn music in school, pupils who teach themselves and others who play in pipe bands and accordion groups," said Mr Watson.

"The club will bring all the music-makers together."

291

The Duke of Edinburgh Award Scheme

This was mainly promoted by Miss Karen Haddow PT Geography for many years and produced our first Gold Award winner in Julia McKenzie: see report below from PP 87 (October 1991):

Golden girl reaps reward

The first winner of a Duke of Edinburgh Award Gold Medal at Elgin High School, Julie McKenzie (centre left), receives her award from Mrs Janis Thomson, the scheme's development officer in Moray District, at a ceremony in the school. Also pictured with bronze medalists are (left) Miss Karen Haddow, who organises the scheme at the school, and (fourth left) Moira Farquhar who gained a silver award.

NS Photo

ELGIN High School's first gold award winner in the Duke Of Edinburgh Award Scheme received her medal at a presentation on Wedneday.

Along with other winners in the Bronze and Silver sections, Julie McKenzie, of 2 Brinuth Place, New Elgin, was presented with her award by Mrs Janis Thomson, the Duke of Edinburgh Award Scheme Development Officer for Moray District.

Julie, who will be receiving a certificate from the Duke of Edinburgh at Holyrood Palace on Monday, gained her success by undertaking various ventures, including a 50 mile expedition in the Cairngorms after training on the West Highland Way.

She will be accompanied to Edinburgh next week by her parents, and teachers Miss Karen Haddow, who organise the scheme at the school, and Mr Les Davidson, who runs the expedition training.

Other award winners at the school were: Silver — Moira Farquhar; bronze — Michelle Anderson, Tracey Kennedy, Deborah McLeod, Sarah Noble, Marianne Young, Fiona Jappy, Victoria Kirkwood, Karen Milne, Kay Wink and Sharon Bremner.

ex N. Scot 28.6.91

Duke of Edinburgh Gold Residential

report by Sarah Scott 60

It was one of the hottest weeks in July and I was off to do the residential section of my gold Duke of Edinburgh Award Scheme. From the 23rd of July to the 29th I was to be staying in Findhorn Residential Centre looking after 8-12 years olds on Camp Caledonia organised by the Recreation Department of the Council. The Camps were three days long and on the first day it was a case of getting to know everyone and as it was I knew most of the young people so it wasn't as bad as I thought.

Once all the young people had arrived they were split into groups (all named after boats.) I was in charge of The Catamarans and we went on a treasure hunt around Findhorn. Once dinner time had come everyone was beginning to get to know each other. Even I was getting to know the other leaders, especially Miranda who was also doing her Gold residential.

In the afternoon we played games and one of adultleaders (Fiona Robertshaw) played a trick on Miranda and I but I won't go into that ! After tea we had a leisurely evening playing games and some groups went to the beach. What I didn't know was that I wasn't going to get to my bed until three in the morning.

The following morning the activities included sailing and canoeing which was an advantage for me as I did a canoeing course in February so I enjoyed that. During the afternoon we got ready for our evening in the cave where we were to spend the next night and day.

The cave that we stayed in was at Primrose Bay. I slept in the cave better than I thought so I was quite surprised. The following day was eventful as we started off with rock climbing and then abseiling. I had a go at the rocks and had the war-wounds to prove it but I chickened out of the abseiling, having a good excuse — I had to supervise the young people, hadn't I ?!

Julie McKenzie being presented with her Gold Award at Holyrood Palace by snooker mega-star Mr Stephen Hendry on 1st July

3

Other Clubs

Many other clubs/groupings came and went depending on staff and pupil enthusiasms, for example, Chess Club, Stamp Club, Young Enterprise (e.g. PP 77) , Highland Dancing, not forgetting one of Mr Hope's favourite activities, which made the front page of PP 94...

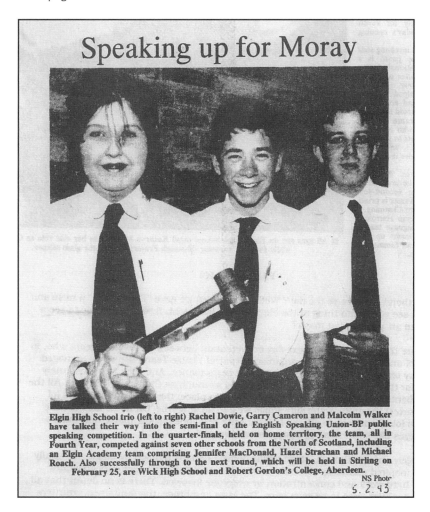

Speaking up for Moray

Elgin High School trio (left to right) Rachel Dowie, Garry Cameron and Malcolm Walker have talked their way into the semi-final of the English Speaking Union-BP public speaking competition. In the quarter-finals, held on home territory, the team, all in Fourth Year, competed against seven other schools from the North of Scotland, including an Elgin Academy team comprising Jennifer MacDonald, Hazel Strachan and Michael Roach. Also successfully through to the next round, which will be held in Stirling on February 25, are Wick High School and Robert Gordon's College, Aberdeen.

NS Photo
5. 2. 93

The Library

Mrs Aileen Marshall our first and long serving librarian writes about how this vital school service developed from books on shelves to a whole school resource facility over decades.

It seemed like a good idea at the time! Youngest just off to Greenwards, new High School just a few minutes' walk from home, a term-time school hours job as a Library Assistant – why would you not apply! Stamping a few books, tidying a shelf or two – I can do that!

It was just that nobody told me I'd be on my own, that I'd have to choose the books and run a budget and speak to classes. AND I got missed off the first day staff photos!!! So it was all a bit of a culture shock for the first few years. I was a Youth and Community Worker by training so some of that came in handy and I met up with Library Assistants and increasingly with professional librarians from other schools. Gradually I got a handle on what I was actually supposed to be doing. In retrospect I can only apologise to those that were pupils in the first few years!

And the library itself? Loads of shelves, not so many books, some filmstrips and slides (google if you have no idea what they are). And tapes, audio and video, some of them even the old reel-to-reel type. They were replaced by audio and video cassettes – both of them fiddly and prone to sticking and breaking. Seem to remember a pencil coming in handy for moving the tape manually! In turn they were happily replaced by CDs and DVDs, much easier to use and look after. We also had a primitive sound loop (you might remember the big white headsets) though it never seemed to work quite properly.

Over time the book stock grew and we added graphic novels, a much greater variety of fiction and we chose non-fiction to support the projects in the classrooms. The library became a real resource for the school with materials to suit everyone from those who weren't too keen on reading, right through to CSYS (6th

Year Studies) and staff. We could borrow in from other libraries UK wide and had a special arrangement with Aberdeen University Library. There was a Paper Cuttings section to help with current issues and local information. Our wall and book displays often fitted in with what was going on in school such as mock elections, or other current events.

As time went on a Careers Section was added and I had to do talks on using it. Remember being startled by one pupil who in mid S2 told me he wanted to work in the Post Office "because they have great Pensions"! Eventually Mr Finnie organised the building of an erection in the corner to create a Careers Office. And we acquired a TV which I seem to remember could also have the sound heard through headsets (or was that just for sharing audio tapes?).

By the late 1980s/early 1990s the computers arrived in school. Along with them came email, and software like Word and Excel and school networks and a whole new language. I remember my first time on a computer in Mr Penrose's office along with Mrs Margaret Goodlet and Mrs Fay Watt, holding onto this mouse thing like grim death, arm as stiff as a poker. But I loved them from the start and they were to revolutionise the library and everyone's lives. So much easier to find information, so much easier to write documents (goodbye Tippex!). We tried the first online systems based on BBC Teletext, exciting but broke down all the time, as the computers tended to do too. Then, hugely exciting, we were allowed to get on to searchable newspaper databases. I remember being told about the World Wide Web and struggled to understand the concept of it – and the first search engines came along (whatever happened to AltaVista?). All so new and unexplored! Nowadays we take it so much for granted and can do more with our phones than I could do with the whole library.

But there was a downside – who thought it was great fun to turn the screen display upside down then! There was endless scope for footering and being diverted from the task in hand, and that was just the staff. Solitaire anyone?

Finally the old borrowing system via the yellow cards (you all had one) was

replaced by the *Heritage* computerised library system that created a nice searchable database of all the library stock as well as dealing with the borrowing. I learned so much being left to create it all on my own. The pupil librarians loved it. I really would like to thank all of the wonderful pupil librarians for the time and effort they put in to running the library. Lunchtimes could be "challenging" and I couldn't have coped without them.

We were able to arrange author visits, often sharing expenses with other schools. Although many of the authors were wonderful at sharing their work with pupils, my own most memorable one was Ian Rankin, who came just before he got really famous.

As the library changed so did I. By the end of the 1980s I was working full-time and was able finally to qualify as a Chartered Librarian in 1991. At last I felt I could do the job!

And now looking back I realise how very fortunate I was to work in such a great school community. The people, pupils and staff, were what made the job for me. Sure there were dreaded study periods and awful lunchtimes, but there were

Smartie Charts (for proper use of study periods) and happy library visits from Kestrel House, and Spiderman on the wall, and the pleasure of seeing wee kids arriving in S1 becoming young adults leaving in S4/5/6.

I was fortunate to meet my successor Alison Bache (now Harding) before I left so it was a contented librarian, last shelf tidied, last book returned, who retired in summer 2006. It was a joy to keep in touch with Mrs Harding and later Mrs McLean. In appearance the old library changed remarkably little right up to the move to the new school, but how it worked was light years away from 1978. We didn't realise it of course, but we had lived through a revolution.

Above one of Mrs Marshall's last group of library helpers and right our second Librarian Miss Alison Bache at the Grampian Children's Book Award

Glossary, Notes and Index to Part One

Glossary

Board of Studies. Traditional term for the small group of school managers now referred to as the "Senior management Team" or "Senior Leadership Team"

Cohort. Educational jargon for all the pupils entering a school in any one particular year. In Elgin High School the First Year intake or cohort was typically around 110 pupils and that number rarely varied as that cohort progressed through to S4.

Comprehensive School— a state secondary school which does not select its intake on the basis of academic achievement or aptitude, in contrast to the selective school system, where admission is restricted on the basis of selection criteria

Cyclostyling Machine—The Cyclostyle duplicating process invented late in the 19th century by David Gestetner, is a form of stencil copying. A stencil is cut on wax or glazed paper by using a pen-like object with a small rowel on its tip. A large number of small short lines are cut out in the glazed paper, removing the glaze with the spur-wheel, then ink is applied. (Wiki)

Eleven Plus—a series of tests intended to differentiate between pupils and make judgments about future potential. But see "Qualifying Exam" below.

Formative Assessment (verbal or written) provides feedback to the pupil regarding a piece of work and may not always be accompanied by a mark or grade. The best formative assessment will start with an account of positive features of the work and then go on to making suggestions about improvements in future tasks.

Grampian Regional Council (GRC) a local government region of Scotland from 1975 to 1996. Elgin High School was the first rural school built under its aegis and the last extended.

Linear Learning. Some subjects require pupils to have mastered or achieved well in certain areas before more challenging aspects are tackled. Essentially such learning requires A to be well known before B can be tackled and so on.

A **mansard** or **mansard roof** (also called a *French roof* or *curb roof*) is a four-sided gambrel-style hip roof characterized by two slopes on each of its sides with the lower slope, punctured by dormer windows, at a steeper angle than the upper level. (wiki)

Microfiche. Spool containing microphotographs of the pages of a newspaper, etc.

Mixed Ability Teaching. An antidote to "setting and streaming"—see below.

Per capita. Local Councils allocated monies to schools based on the number of pupils in each cohort at a certain date (usually in February of the session before). The "capita" term relates to the Latin word for a head.

PPP—Public Private Partnership—a cooperative arrangement between two or more public and private sectors, typically of a long term nature (Wiki) Somewhat now discredited as a method of financing public building.

Qualifying Exam "Eleven Plus" and "Secondary Modern" were properly terms used exclusively in England. The exam used in Scotland was officially and correctly known as the "Qualifying Exam", (or unofficially "Qually"). Depending on performance in that pupils were allocated to either a "Senior Secondary" or a "Junior Secondary".

Setting. Following testing in primary schools and early secondary years, traditional secondary schools would identify a group of pupils who would be taught together for *different* subjects, respecting the idea that one might be good at maths but not a Geography for example.

Stake holders—modern jargon phrase for those with a committed interest in a project

Streaming. Following testing in primary schools and early secondary years, schools would identify a group of pupils who would be taught together *for all subjects* irrespective of any one pupil's performance in any one .

TVEI

The **Technical and Vocational Education Initiative** was an initiative in the 1980s. TVEI was announced in 1982 and a pilot scheme started in 1983. TVEI was extended nationally in 1987, and was thereafter often known as TVEI extension, sometimes abbreviated TVEE. It ended in 1997.

It was the first major intervention by central Government in curriculum development and was organised on a local authority basis, with each local authority able to develop and implement plans relevant to their area. Computers were revolutionising the workplace and providing new opportunities for employment as well as requiring new skills and attitudes in the workforce and in society. The BBC and the UK Government developed the BBC micro computer for the schools sector and TVEI supported the channelling of funds and training into the schools sector to enable computer rooms, equipped by BBCs to be set up in schools. Prior to this, typically, the mathematics department might have had access to one computer at a remote location.

The strategy for the implementation of TVEI provides an example of positive change management in an education system with government engaging with educators and industry to support innovation and development in uncertain times. It can be argued that this investment which led to pupils having access to the latest technology, a supported creative curriculum and an encouragement with experimentation, had a seminal role in providing the foundations for the successful UK animation industry.

The history of this period is recorded in publications by several UK organisations - the Association for IT in Teacher Education (Hammond et al 2011), the Mirandanet initiative. The ITTE Voices project provides a record of educators experiences in this period. (Edited Ex Wikipedia)

"Bilbohall"

Though the meaning is obscure, the first syllables of the name could be derived from the name of one individual historical person or may be related to the Irish and Scottish Gaelic "baile" meaning "home" or "homestead" as in Baldragon, Balfron, Ballachulish etc. Again it could come from the Gaelic "bealach" meaning a pass or valley. The "bo" element could be related to a Gaelic term for cattle and the "hall" element a reduction of the Scots "haugh" meaning a plain.

This in turn *could* relate to the old system of the Scottish *fermtoun*, a hamlet populated by a large extended family or groups of extended families working together: See Chapter 6 of *Deskford, a lower Banffshire Parish* by John Aitken (2016).

Bilbohall Farm, marked by the oval shape in the centre of this map extract provided on the internet by Historic Environment Scotland* was located 200 metres south of the Aberdeen Inverness railway line. Wide at its northern extremity adjacent to The

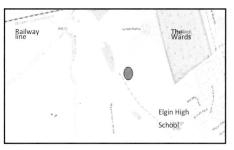

Wards it tapered south towards what is now Hardhillock housing estate.

*https://scotlandsplaces.gov.uk/record/hes/88766/bilbohall-farm/rcahms

The Bilbohall Farm area is now (30.10.17 newspaper report) the site of a proposed major housing development :

see https://www.pressandjournal.co.uk/fp/news/moray/elgin/1349637/first-look-at-vision-for-elgin-housing-development-that-could-lead-to-370-homes/

Bilbohall Hospital

Extracts from https://historic-hospitals.com/gazetteer/moray/

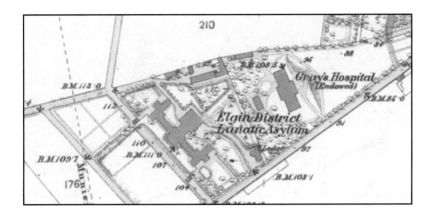

The *Buildings of Scotland* volume covering Moray published in 2015 is a some-what dismissive of Moray's hospitals…..Only one section remains of Elgin's 'colossal' lunatic asylum, 'now subsumed within Gray's Hospital'.

Extract from the 1st edition OS map surveyed in 1868. Reproduced by permission of the National Library of Scotland.

BILBOHALL HOSPITAL   Elgin Pauper Lunatic Asylum was founded by the manag-ers of Grays Hospital *c.*1835 and was the earliest asylum built specifically for paupers in Scotland and indeed, the only pauper lunatic asylum built in Scotland before the Lunacy Act of 1857. This makes it particularly unfortunate that it is now almost impossible to see the original extent of the buildings, designed by Archibald Simpson. In the 1860s extensions by A. & W. Reid began to obscure Simpson's asylum but now the whole has become lost amongst piece-meal mod-ern additions, none of which has been sympathetic to the older blocks. A & W. Reid's extensions comprised a north and south wing each of two storeys and an extension of three storeys to the rear at the centre of the building. This last con-tained a new dining-hall and kitchen.

Index to Part One

Where references appear on consecutive pages in a chapter only the first is noted

V

W

Y

Part Two
Compendium
Lists
Index
Records

Synopses of *Pigeon Post* Contents

Abbreviations used: TF—Teacher Feature, WX—Work Experience, WBD—World Book Day WWWDWT—What would we do without them (non-teaching staff) Regular features e.g. Headlines, Health Matters, Doos' News etc not referenced.

#1 (September 1978)

Introducing the Staff, (P2 was blank), Mr Dugdale's Editorial, Rector's Headlines, Letters to Editor, Brief History of Elgin, First Impressions, Primary Creative Writing, Quizzes/Crosswords, Anne Advises, Programme for The Centre Elgin High (your local Community Centre) Doos' News gossip, Subjectively Speaking - GUIDANCE by Mr Doug Campbell, Sports reports.

#2 (October 1978)

Community Area opens, TF Mrs McPherson, Mr Ledingham, Mr J. Hamilton's History of Elgin cont., Jokes & Quizzes, EHS & Primary Creative Writing, Anne Advises, Letters to the Editor, Historic Elgin : The Cathedral, Subjectively Speaking: GEOGRAPHY, Sports results, Scripture Union Report, S1 & S2 hockey teams—pix.

#3 (November 1978)

Introduction of CSEm3, Spotlight on School Kitchen, TF Miss Cowan & Mr McKay, Short Stories: The Lucky Find by Teenie Cottam, The Silly Schoolmistress by Douglas Logan and The Mystery of Elrum Low by Ethel Brown & Agnes Smith, Xmas Carol Concert, Inter-House Competition begins Letters to the Editor, 2B poetry, Primary Creative Writing, Subjectively Speaking: MODERN LANGUAGES, Football report and U14 Team pic, Rugby pic. (NB Sports team pix are faint but were all reproduced crisply in issue #10, The Summer Special)

#4 (December 1978)

Festive Fare, TF Mr MacLachlan, Miss Campbell, Staff v Parents Quiz, Historic Elgin cont., Quiz/Crossword page, Subjectively Speaking :TECHNICAL, Your Letters, AHT joins GTC, TEAR Fund activities, EHS and Primary pupil Creative Writing, Doos' News, Career adviser Isobel Wilox, Elrum Low (part 2), Anne Advises, Inter-House Competition, Our cleaning staff - formal pic, Legscion Quiz, Catchphrase competition.

#5 (January 1979)

"Foiled Again" brings the house down at The Town Hall: review
TF Mr Ingram and Mr A. Farquhar, "Foiled Again" review, Historic Elgin,
Your Letters, Rowdy Class by Robbie Linton Pt 1, Elrum Low Pt3, Primary
Writing, Short stories by Lynne Beaton, and Lesley Still, Spotlight on
Office staff, Subjectively Speaking: MATHS, Looking After Your Teeth,
Anne's Advice.

#6 (February 1979)

That legendary Burns supper - report and pix!!
TF Miss Wasilenska, Mr Hendrie, Elgin High and Primary writing, The
Rowdy Class Pt 2, Elrum Low, Pt 4, Your Letters (and complaints !) Brown
ladies WWWDWT, Subjectively Speaking : HOME ECONOMICS, Anne
Advises, Angus McKinnon's adventure, Basketball team pix, Inter-House
competition, Superstars & Souperstars.

#7 (March 1979)

Tyson Twins Trouble, TF Miss C. Mitchell, Mr Phimister, TEAR Fund and
Gymnastics reports, Looking at Animals, History of Elgin, Sir Patrick Spens
parody, Thoughtshapes, Primary Writing, Mrs McQuillan WWWDWT,
Subjectively Speaking: MUSIC, The Rowdy Class (Pt 3), Ambitions Survey,
Elrum Low (Pt 5) InterHouse competitions.

#8 (Spring 1979)

Easter comedies - "The Pie in the Oven" and "The Centre Forward" on
stage, Valkenburg ditties and photo album, TF Mr Urquhart, Mrs Clark,
Anne's Advice, Historic Elgin - Andrew Anderson's Free School, Your
Letters, Primary and Elgin High Creative Writing, George McKenzie,
Janitor WWWDWT, Subjectively Speaking: MODERN STUDIES, 1A's
Nicknames - Teenie Cottam and Geoff Blogg report, French Fun, Staff
Hockey Team pic.

#9 (June 1979)

Fete previewed, Valkenburg Diary, Mr John Cruickshanks, Div Ed Off.,
Subjectively Speaking: SCIENCE, Pastime Page, Anne Advises / Your
Letters, Primary Creative Writing + controversial reaction to it !!,
Canadian evangelist visits, Robbie Linton serial (part 4)

#10 (July 1979)

"Summer Special" at 60pp (inc ads) would prove to be the biggest issue ever..

EHS Majorettes, Pigeon Post success story to date, TF Bill Hope, Tom Sawyer play, EHS Fete postscript, All sports team in hi-quality pix with landscape captions, Primary Creative Writing and All sports teams, Groundsman Eric Duncan, Your Letters, One Act Play actors and Tam o Shanter dramatised in Burns Supper, Rector's Summary of the school's first year, "The Rowdy Class" serial by Bobby Linton (Part 5) Douglas Logan short story, History of Elgin - Pluscarden, Sports Day data , Alan Rodger schoolboy golf champ, EHS T-shirts, Autograph pages, with some pre-signed by celebs!!

#11 (September 1979)

Sizeable group of new staff arrive. InterHouse competitions Primary writing. Four staff weddings. Your letters. The cell next door – short story by Susie Webster. Anne's Advice. TF Mr Jackson, Mr Carstairs, Subjectively speaking: DRAMA. Club Spy: Biology Club

#12 (October 1979)

We are "The Highlights", Sponsored Walk, TF Mr Campbell, Mrs Drysdale, "Wreckommended" reading, Primary and EHS Writing, STEP up to cycling success, Mrs McGonigal WWWDWT, The Crusaders are coming, First Impressions, Your Letters, Anne's Advice, First Impressions, Interest in Paris at Easter 1980, Club Spy: Gymnastics Club. Subjectively Speaking: PE. Football reports

#13 (November 1979)

Our Pupils' Council—Profiles, TF Mr Cameron, Mr MacLeod, Primary and EHS Writing, Buying a calculator – advice from Mr McKay, Your Letters, Mod Lang Assistants arrive, Staff Engagement, Gary Robertson's first contribution to printed media?, That's My Business : Moray Model Shop, Staff Superstars, Anne's Advice, Spot the handwriting competition, InterHouse Competitions, Club Spy: Bagpiping, U12 Football and Gymnasts pix, Sports reports

#14 (December 1979)

Christmas Special. TF Mr Hamilton, Mr Polson, Historic Elgin cont., Primary and EHS writing, SU Chaco Challenge, Spot the Santa, Farewell to Leslie! CSE Progress report from around the school, Pupils' Council Profile and report, Anne's Advice, What Christmas Means to Me, Christmas Childhood memories, Basketball Team photos, Staff v Parents Quiz teams.

#15 (January 1980)

"Joseph" at Christmas. TF Mr Leslie, Mrs Duncan, CSE Computer Studies, The Runaway sh story, Percy cartoon, Spotlight on teaching class 1A, Anne's Advice, Visit to Mayne farm, Childhood Games, Primary & Elgin High Writing, Avril McKnockiter – our first "age" leaver, Club Spy: Table tennis, Country Dancers, Sports reports, Boys v Girls at Sport.

#16 (February 1980)

Another Elgin High (USA style), Uproar at Burns supper, TF Mr I.Hamilton, Mr Dugdale, Jokes, Primary Creative Writing, Teaching Class 1B, Mrs Easton WWWDWT, Pastime Page, Are disco's cattle marts ? One Act Plays reviewed, Percy Strip Cartoon, Doos' News x 3 pages, InterHouse Competitions, Subjectively Speaking: RE.

#17 (March 1980)

Cairngorm Skiers, Moray Estates Visit, TF Miss Blease, Mr Watt, Primary and EHS Creative Writing, German Assistant Appraises Schottland, Pupil Council Report, Robbie Allen reports from Culloden, Dougie Sinclair's Shoppie, Your Letters, Anne Advises, Moray Music Festival results, Table Tennis Triumph, Victorious Gymnasts, Sports reports, U14 Football team pic.

#18 (May 1980)

Percy in Paris, TF Mr Anderson, Mrs Hall, Primary Writing, Easter plays pix: Bloaters and Ernie, Kevins go to Allarburn, Pix of our Moray Music Festival Choirs - S1 Girls, S2/3 Girls, Boys and of our Pipers and Sen Hockey XI, Anne's Advice, New Dance Group need a name, Teachers' Pay Dispute: Extra-curricular activity to be banned, Inter-house competitions, Swimming Gala, Outward bound reports, Percy cartoon strip

#19 (Summer Special June 1980)

Eight pages of good quality team and group photos with captions, Quiz of the Year, Rev Torrie our first chaplain, EHS Writing My Career Ambitions and short stories, Spotlight on Teaching classes 1C, 1D & 1E. Our prize winners. Primary writing. Gary Watt cartoon strip, InterHouse competition Sports Day results. Anne Advises
+ pages from the Special reprint edition e.g.- TF Mrs Meisner explanation, & additional news.

#20 (September 1980)

A dozen+ new staff for our third session, Profiles of PP stalwarts - Robbie Linton, Ian Wallace, Wendy Scott, Primary & EHS writing - short stories by Anna H and Jeremy P. Staff wedding photos, Yet another Elgin, InterHouse Activities, STEP programme running, Thinking Careers - Mr Campbell, Sports reports, TF Mr McKenzie, Mr Allan (PE) Percy Cartoon Strip

#21 (October 1980)

Robbie Linton's Percy cover, TF Miss Hughes, Mr Allan, Wendy's World, Primary and EHS writing, Roy Young and Gillian Murray, Eagles Captains, Beautiful Babies, Ms Wood AV Technician WWWDWT, Miss de Beaux's Letter from Canada, Club Spy: Scripture Union, Anne Advises, Earthquake devastation illustrations, Sport reports, Two Page Percy Pigeon cartoon strip from Lindsay Hutchison.

#22 (November 1980)

Percy cover by Lindsay Hutchinson, TF Mr Walker, Mrs Scott, Creative Writing from half a dozen pupils, Spotlight on 1A, Shirley Moir & Janice McKillop profiles, Letters, Audrey Morrison Asst Librarian WWWDWT, Pupils in "The Mikado", Findhorn Field Trip, WX reports, Percy Cartoon by Julie Jamieson and Gillian Morton

#23 (December 1980)

TF Mr Fyfe, Mrs Reid, Primary Writing, Percy Cartoon, Scott J Cartoon, Ian Morrison WWWDWY, Prelims Ahead - how to prepare, "Babes" Panto Review, CSE extra-mural visits, Sports news, 1B Spotlight, Model Making Club, Living in Cyprus, Anna Hamilton sh story. Profiles Michael Gray and Lynne Craib

#24 (January 1981)

Extension plans revealed. Ian Morrison weds. Lesley Still and David Gray profiled. TF Mrs Dugdale, Mrs Hamilton, Class 1C spotlight, Panto pix, Scott Johnston cartoon, Primary and Elgin High writing, Hockey and Rugby Sports teams and S2 Choir pix, Sports reports

#25 (March 1981)

Percy Goes Chinese: Profile of Ki and Fan Wu, TF Miss Duncan, Miss Smith, Burns Night photos, Primary and EHS writing, Miss de Beaux's letter from Canada (no 2), Our hobbies, Spotlight on 1D, Percy cartoon by Robbie Linton, Pix of Gymnastics, 1st XI Football and S1 Dancers, Sports reports

#26 (April 1981)

Robbie Linton Percy cover, Miss Campbell explains the role of the SCE, TF Mr McNeil, Miss Stanley, Mr Finnie arrives, Pupil Opinion essays, Primary Writing and News, 1E Spotlight, Cafe Chantant and extension pix, Staff goodbyes, S1 Rugby, Highlites and U14 football team pix, Josh McAuley short story by Anna Hamilton, Yeadon's bookshop, Our champion Hockey girls.

#27 (May 1981)

Primaries in the news pix, Scott Johnston and Lindsay Hutchinson profiled, TF Mrs Stewart, Mrs Kirk, 4A, 4B spotlight, primary writing, Easter plays reviewed, Football, badminton and Hockey team pix, Leysin Alpine trip reports, Scott Johnston cartoon, O-grade review.

#28 (June 1981 Summer Special)

Lots of team and group pix, Prize List, TF Mrs Swain, Mr Finnie, Osprey Captains—Jackie Wardlaw & David Grey Quiz of the Year, Staff photo 1981, Sundance band, Outward Bound at Locheil report, Sports day results, Primary Creative Writing and team pix, 4C and 4D Spotlight, Staff Goodbyes, Swiss Trip report, Dental experiences, Autograph page, Scott Johnston cartoon strip.

#29 (September 1981)

Percy is 3! Pupil Council Elections, A host of new staff, two more staff weddings, Four staff babies (in Doos News), Primary and Elgin High writing, Kestrel Captains, Steven Davies and Carole Lawton, Eddie Laing table tennis star, Classpot 4A, TF Mrs Gibb and Mr Davidson, An Audience with The King (Willie Grant), Club Spy Aeromodellers, Elgin High folk in the news, S1 review of the year past, Sports reports, Robbie Linton Cartoon Strip

#30 (October 1981)

Twins x 2 TF Mr Spence, Mr Cadenhead, Cartoon strips by Robbie Linton, Scott Johnston and Lindsay Hutchison, Primary and EHS Creative Writing, Teaching Class 4B profiles (i.e. our first S1 as S4) Jackie & Sandra WWWDWT, Police Interview, DofE Scheme introduced

#31 (November 1981)

Percy invites you to meet the Wizard, Twins x 3, TF Mr Penrose, Miss Wood, Primary and EHS writing, cartoon strips by Robbie Linton, Scott Johnston and Lindsay Hutchinson, Classpot on 4C (S1-S4), Foreign Language Assistants arrive, GirlTalk column debuts, Elgin High folk in the News, Interview with Class 1 Referee Sandy Roy, Computer Education at EHS

#32 (December 1981)

Hallowe'en disco pix, Wizard of Oz principals, WX reports, 4D Spotlight (S1 as S4), Our Cleaners, Primary Writing and News, Pupils and Staff in the news, Mr Bert Laurenson DEO interviewed, Girl Talk/Anne Advises, Your local MACE mart.

#33 (February 1982)

Our new extension cover and progress photos by Ian Wallace, Girl Talk, Anne Advises, Primary and Elgin High Writing, Classpot 1A, Our YOPpers WWWDWT, That's My Business : Torr House Hotel, Goodbye Mrs McGonigal, Table Tennis, Basketball and Badminton team pix, "Wizard of Oz" review and pix

#34 (March 1982)

Cabarfeidh FC, Focus on our Canteen, Hockey Champion Team, Kevin Walker & Julie Campbell profiled, TF Mr Jim McDonald, Primary Creative Writing, Classpot 1B, Extension - internal pix, Lesley Still interviews Sister Noble, Best Kept School Award, Pupil Council pic.

#35 (March/April 1982)

Interview with Consumer Protection agency, Holland Trip Previewed, Confessions of an Examiner, Our first Queen's Guide Sarah McGregor, and Richard Anderson to pipe in USA, TF Mrs Grant, Mr Thorburn, Primary and Elgin High Writing, Classpot 1C, Anne Advises, That's My Business: Alex Beattie and G.S.Lee, Elgin High folk in the news, Annette Roy WWWDWT, U13, U14, U15 Football team and S1, S2 and Senior Hockey team pix with captions on nearby page.

#36 (May 1982)

SCE Review, Holland Trip Diary, 3 x Twins profiled, TF Mr McWhirr, Mrs MacLachlan, Easter Plays: Billy Liar, Rory Aforesaid, Primary Writing, 1D Classpot, "Trapped" and "Computer Dating" short stories, Swim Gala report and pix, Interview with Regional Councillor E.P. Harrison, Staff v Pupils football, Scott J's Cartoon strip.

#37 (June 1982)

New Guidance System introduced, Our Prize List, Wheelchair pupils profiled, 3 TFs, Primary Creative Writing & Sports teams pix, Interview with Bobby Clark Aberdeen FC goalkeeper, Classpot 1E, Abernethy Outdoor & Holland Trips pix, Sports and Fun Sports pix & results, Staff Goodbyes, Quiz of the Year, EHS gymnasts, Robbie Linton Cartoon Strip.

38 (September 1982)

EHS Pilots S-g SocVoc, Percy is 4!, Introducing new staff, TF Teenie Cottam, Karen Hawkins, Miss Wood marries, Police concern over Cyclists behaviour, Primary and Elgin High Writing, Classpot 4K1 & 4F2, Anne Advises, Elgin High folk in the News, Summer events including majorettes at Elgin Round Table derby day, Mike Crossland WWWDWT, Sports reports, Scott J's cartoon strip

#39 (October 1982)

Subject Reports on the Way for S1&2, Local MP visits, Pupil Council Elections, TF Mrs Wilson, Mrs Ross, Eagles Captains, Anthony Marchi, Elaine Hutcheson, London Drama trip, Primary and Elgin High writing, Classpot 4O1, 4E2, Anne Advises, Elgin High folk in the news, HE Teachers launch catering firm, Heather Amos, Frances Martin, Lorna MacLachlan, Billy Kelly WWWDWT, Scott J cartoon strip, Sports reports

#40 (November 1982)

"Puss in Boots" panto sell out, Kestrel House Captains, TF Miss Gordon & Mrs Offill, Primary Creative Writing, Classpot 4K2 & 4F1, Local business feature, Interview with Cllr Roma Hossack, Two serial stories, Pupils in the News, Foreign Language Assistants, Winter Games, Snow White in German,

#41 (December 1982)

Mr MacLachlan promoted to Forres as Rector, Mr Cameron promoted to Lossie as Depute, Mr Cadenhead arrives as Depute, "Puss in Boots" cast profiles and review, Pupils and FPs in the News, Skills Group ask staff about interests, Primary Creative Writing, TFs Dr Kerr and Mr Edwards, WX reports, A German fairy tale rewritten in German with original illustrations by Miss Ross's senior class.

#42 (January 1983)

Prelims rescheduled, Puss in Boots panto pix, TF Mr Gibson, Mr Morrison, Primary Writing, Reg Groups 4E1 & 4O2, SocVocToc, Solitaire sh story by Agnes Gault, Club Spy - what's on lunchtime and after school, Sports reports, Scott J's cartoon strip.

#43 (Feb/Mar 1983)

Extension to Technical dept., Focus on Tech Dept staff with caricatures by Lindsay Hutchinson, Pupils in the News, Primary Creative Writing, Reg Groups 1O1 & 1F1, SocVocToc, Agnes Gault serial (Pt 1), Burns Supper, Archive of Sports pix from 1980, Badminton, Hockey & Rugby teams, Scott Johnston cartoon strip.

9

#44 (Spring 1983)

Easter Holidays in Europe for 100+, Falcons House captains, TF Ms Warham, Primary and EHS writing, Computer Club, Reg Groups 1E1 & 1K2, What's Good about Rock? Social Studies reports, Archive material ex June 1980, Primary Sports teams, Our Sports teams and Highland dancers pix, Scott J's cartoon strip

#45 (May 1983)

including O-Grade and H review, Easter in Europe: Italy and Germany trips, TF Mr Ken Simpson, Primary Creative Writing, Reg Groups 1F2 & 1E2, SocVocToc, Pupils and Staff in the News, Mrs Goodlet AV Tech, Mr McKay promoted to Advisor in Fife, Cafe Chantant pix, Swimming Gala, Gymnastic competition, Archive material from 1980: Mosstowie football team, our Pipers and Gymnasts, Scott J's cartoon strip

#46 (June 1983)

New Courses and staff, Our Prize List, FP News, Primary Creative Writing, Team photos from Primaries, Classpot 1K1 & 1O2, Quiz of the Year, Staff Goodbyes, Gary Robertson's WX at N.Scot, All Elgin High Sports Teams - good quality pix, SocVocToc, Sports Day Results and Current Record tables, Scott J's strip cartoon.

#47 (September 1983)

Staff Marathon runners, Percy is 5!, biggest ever school with 762 pupils, New Staff arrive, Alan Rodger champion golfer, Paula Campbell gymkhana girl, Visit to the US, Primary and Elgin High writing, Classpot 4E1 & 4E2, SocVocToc, Club Spy: NEDS (drama club!) Prize winners group pic, Sports reports, Elgin High folk in the News, Staff wedding, Scott J cartoon.

#48 (October 1983)

In-school Careers Convention attracts 60 employer stalls, New PRC elected, Eagles House Captains, Marina Jones sh story, Primary writers, TF Mr Burns, Reg Groups 4O1 & 4O2, SocVocToc - Enterprise Project, Aeromodelling Club, Host of new staff - pix, New Mod Lang assistants arrive, Famous authors including Roald Dahl & Joan Lingard visit Elgin, Scott J's strip cartoon.

#49 (November 1983)

Cinderella panto, Best Kept Award, Games we used to Play, Primary Creative Writing, Reg Groups 4F1 & 4F2, TF Mrs McKenzie, Mr K. Duncan, SocVocToc, Interview with Mr Graham Wiseman, Pupils and Fps in the News, S1 Breakfast survey, Champion Hockey squads.

#50 (December1983)

Cinderella panto review and Behind the Greasepaint profiles, Our First staff in 1978 - where are they now? Primary Creative Writing, Reg Groups 4K1 & 4K2, Work Experience reports, Soc Voc Toc, Winter Sports Pix, Archives - the best of the gossipy stories from issues #1-25 Scott Johnston's Crazy Xmas cartoon strip

#51 (January 1984)

ISIS closes school, Pupil Council Officers, Italian Ski Trip, Several good quality sports team pix, TF Mr Sangster, Mr F. Allan, Mr Sturrock, Miss Abel, Cinderella panto pix inc staff "superheroes", Primary writing, Reg Groups 1K1 & 1K2, Donnie sings goodbye, Interview with Mr Drew Todd, Substantial Teenie report on Uni life

#52 (March 1984)

Three more PTs depart, Two international schoolgirl trialists, Mr Sangster on The Guitar Club, Burns Supper - pictures all lost!! A perfect essay wins 10/10 for Nicola Campbell, Primary Writing, Reg Groups 1O1 & 1O2, TF Mr Prentice, Mrs Hyde, La Plange ski trip report and pix, Mr Douglas Campbell, President of SSTA, appointed Head of Bell-Baxter High, the largest school in Scotland, Interview with John Grant, Secretary of Highland League, Rangers Quiz, Rugby, Football and Hockey team pix

#53 (April 1984)

NZ guest pupil likes Scotland, Golf & Table tennis medallists, Cafe Chantant, Primary Writing, 1E1 & 1E2 Reg Groups, TF Mr Sturrock, Miss Abel, Interview with Mike Seton Elgin Heritage Librarian, Ist XI Hockey Tour report, Basketball, Badminton & Rugby team pix, Best Things writing, Sports reports, Scott J cartoon.

#54 (May 1984)

Inspectors praise school on first visit, Champion girl athletes, Austrian Tyrol Trip, Primary Writing, 1F1 & 1F2 Reg Groups TF Mr Frost, Miss Carnegie, Fine Fare manager interviewed, Former AHT now i/c prestigious Fife school, Staff v pupils football pix, Recorder Ensemble at MMFestival, One Act Plays review, Mr Sturrock gains Scottish water polo caps, Sport teams pix - football and volleyball.

#55 (June 1984)

Introduction of 1st S-Grades, Soccer starlets USA-bound, Auction/Treasure Hunt, Primary Creative Writing and sports teams pix, TF Mr Donald & Mr Grant, Roy Young WWWDWT? Quiz of the Year, Staff Goodbyes, Sigi's Spence's Tribute to Adrian Dunbar, Our Prize List, O-g & H Review, Hockey Champion teams - pix, Sports day results.

#56 (September 1984)

Duran Duran mania, New staff arrive, TV debut for young singer, TF Mrs Hookey, Primary Writing, Reg Groups 4E1 & 4E2. Synch & swim!, Scott J cartoon, EHS folk in the News, US Soccer tour for Elgin Boys Club

#57 (October 1984)

Kent Maths Scheme welcomed, House Captains, TF Mr Taylor, Mr Buchan, Office Ladies WWWDWT, Primary Creative Writing, Reg Groups 4O1 & 4O2, New Staff arrive.
WARNING RE IMPENDING STAFF INDUSTRIAL ACTION

#58 (November 1984)

New Computing Studies dept Created, Eagles and Ospreys Girl Captains, Welcome Foreign Lang assistants, Primary and EHS writing, 4F1, 4F2, 4K1 & 4K2 Reg Groups, TF Miss Farquhar, Miss Laing, Elgin High folk in the News, Dress the model winners.

#59 (December 1984)

Dress as you like day, Falcons and Eagles Boy Captains, WX reports, Dungeons and Dragons club, Primary and Elgin High Writing, 1K1 & 1K2 TF Mr Archibald, Mrs Munro.

THE LAST ISSUE BEFORE THE BIG HIATUS.

60 (May 1987)

Another historic issue - the first for 2½ years.

One page summary of events since PP59, Profiles of Kevin Isaac who's "not brainy" and Jacqueline Taylor who was, Mock Election candidates, Primary Creative Writing, School in the News, Staff Goodbyes and Hellos since 1985, 1C & 1D groups, TF Mr Watson & Mr Vaughan, Young Enterprise Group, SocVocToc, Elgin City Starlets, 5-a-side Champs, O-g & H Review, Handwriting and Colouring Competitions.

#61 (June 1987)

TVEI begins, Talented Tara Stuart, Tom Griffiths and Lee McBride, Staff Goodbyes, TF Mr Duncan, Miss Haddow, Primary News and Creative Writing (TF Miss Hutcheon) Teaching Classes 1A & 1B, FPs news, SocVocToc, Percy Strip cartoon, Sports reports, Non-teaching staff WWWDWT Teachers' name rebus quiz, Mock Election - Question Time, SNP landslide win, Diary and Post Script, Amanda McLean's winning design.

#62 (October 1987)

Secondary School Careers Convention, New Staff, TF Mrs Grant, Mrs Gravener, TVEI in Elgin High, A bonnie pair of dancers, S1 roof art, First Impressions, a Day at Gordonstoun, Sweet Success rock band, Elgin High folk in the News, Scottish Football Quiz from Dr Ron Grant, (dad of Paul 3k2), SocVocToc, Youth Club Staff, Mrs Galbraith, Mrs Alexander WWWDWT.

#63 (November 1987)

School and House Council system revived, Pupils in the News, TVEI in Elgin High, Ist XI & U14 football pix Biology Field Trip, 2E and 2F (as e.g. English teaching sets, i.e. not Reg Groups) Percy strip cartoon by Cheryl & Lisa, SocVocToc, Martin's Army WX, Martina Hickey Community Ed Officer, Scottish Football Quiz (Part 2) from Dr Ron Grant, (dad of Paul 3k2)

#64 (December 1987)

Hallelujah - The return of Music at Xmas, House Council elections, Brave Mark Gregor, TF Miss Taylor, Mr Dey, TVEI in Elgin High, Primary writing, 1E1 & 1E2 Reg Groups, Sweet Success rock band, Table Tennis team, Andrew Kelly attends World Scout Jamboree, Third Elgin BBs, SocVocToc Visits, U13, U15, Sen Football squad pix, Sports reports, Christmas in USA and in Germany

#65 (February 1988)

Local Firm Donates printing machine, Pupil Council, TF Mr Hope, Mr Cadenhead, TVEI in Elgin High, Teenscope, Greenwards Creative Writing, Geography Field Trip to Aviemore, Reg Groups 1F1 & 1F2 Pupils in the News, Table Tennis teams, Christmas Concert pix, Red Nose day, SocVocToc, Festive Fotos, U13 Football Squad.

#66 (March 1988)

School's first foreign trip (France) for 4 yrs, Swim Gala to be revived, Reg Groups 1K1 & 1K2, Red Nose Day pix, House Councils pix, Pupils in the News, TF Mrs Claypole, Mrs Collins, Aeromodelling Club, SocVocToc, US exchange teacher (Mrs Wold) on US schools, World Scout Jamboree - Andrew Kelly reports, The Invention of Football - Darrel Richardson's competition winning fantasy story, Geog Field to Mayne Farm, Sports reports

#67 (June 1988)

Ten Years of EHS celebrated, Mayne Farm Visit, TVEI residential to Belmont, TF Mr Frost, Mr Cruickshanks, French Trip at Easter report, DofE Award notes, 1O1 & 1O2 Reg Groups, EHS interest in Moray RFC, Falcons House Council, Elgin High Folk in the news, SocVocToc, Mr McDonald reports from San Francisco, Swimming Gala, Moray Music Festival Successes, Girls Football

#68 (July 1988)

Goodbye Mrs Wold and Mr Fyfe, Eagles House Council, TF Mr Finnie, Mr Dugdale, Our Prize List, Twin Troubles, H Geography Field Trips, Elgin High folk in the News, Mr McLuckie – Careers Officer, SocVocToc, Language festival, Quiz of the year, S2 visit Aberdeen Discovery Dome, Indoor football champs, Sports day pix and results

#69 (October 1988)

House Council elections, New staff arrive, Ann Simmers at Eton, TF Mrs Lambert, Miss Moss, Bottle turns up in Norway!, Community Studies report, First Impressions, Elgin Crusaders, S5 Trio in MYT Smike! Staff v Pupils Ladies football pix, Mr Fyfe's farewell do, S3 biology Trip to Hopeman beach, DofE Notes, Activities week Holiday to French Alps, Elgin Boys US Tour, SocVocToc, Sport Aid 88 events, New canteen menus.

#70 (November 1988)

SCAMP MIS in our Office, House Councils elected, New Community Area facilities, TF Mr and Mrs Reid, TVEI report, Jacqueline Taylor reports from Aberdeen uni, Frau Macrae and Eric Trude interviews, Rev Gordon Cowie, Reg Group 102 & 1K1, Keran's Gateway to success, Skateboarders push for facilities, Welcome Mrs Davidson, Elgin High Folk in the news, SocVocToc, Rural Studies visit Mayne Farm, Scottish Boxing championships, Girls into Computing, Sports reports, Michael Johnston cartoon strip.

#71 (December1988)

Pupil Council pic and profiles, TF Miss Ross, Miss Campbell, TVEI in Elgin High SocVocToc, Dress As You Like day, 1E1 & 1F2 Reg Groups, Greenwards' Mr Stitchbury and Mr Ellwand, Aeromodelling Club competition, Christmas in Germany and France, Fifth Annual Swimming Gala - School swimming gala records,   Michael Johnston Cartoon strip – Caveman

#72 (February 1989)

Cleaning Service taken over by DSO, Senior School House Council members, TF Mr Carstairs, Mr Iain Wilson, Visit to Murrayfield, Festive Fotos, Reg Groups 1F1 & 1E2 , Euroweek, Elgin High folk in the News, Kestrels win School Quiz, SocVocToc design model bedrooms, Michael Johnston cartoon, Moray RFC visit Twickenham, Senior and U15 Hockey Squad pix, DoE report

#73 (March 1989)

Ready for Holland again, Red Nose Day pix, Euroweek in school, Sheila Rowand budding journo, TF Mrs Marriott, Reg Groups 1O1 & 1K2, Mother and son in classroom together, Stephen Duke wins Colours, Techno Studies robots, Selfless pupils raise money for charity, SocVocToc visits, Michael Johnston cartoon, Hockey team champions, Staff v Pupils six-a-side Rugby, Fisher in deep water, Miss Abel top of staff snooker ladder.

74 (June 1989)

Janitor George retires, TVEI Parents Evening, TF Mr I.Hamilton, Mr Douglas, Valkenburg and France Cookery Trips, TVEI: "Oil Strike" Extravaganza, Music Club Formed, Anonymous rock band, George Paterson - heavy metal fan, Summer Sounds Concert, SocVocToc, DofE report, Football reports, 5-a-side Girls Scots Champions, Girls Hockey XI Champs again, Sports Day pix and results.

#75 (October 1989)

New Staff arrive, Pupil Councils elected, TF Mrs Davidson, Mr Nicol Summer Trip to France report, Model Club lay down tracks, German Pilots in Primaries, BBC TV records *Antique Roadshow* in Games Hall, Prize Giving 89 pic, Summer Concert, End of term events pix, Janitor George retires, First Impressions, Centre Elgin High, New S-grade Technological Studies, SocVocToc, Sports News, Sports day pix (WITH SHOCKING TOPLESS PHOTO), Football mad Nicki, Greenies Pre-teenies cooking!

#76 (November 1989)

Oliver! Cast and Preview, Dress as You Like Day pix, TF Mr Walker, Miss Duncan, Sheila's look into the future, Aeromodellers, 1E1 & 1K1 Reg Groups, Elgin High folk in the News, Mayne Farm Visit, SocVocToc, First PT Geog Appointed Rector in Edinburgh, Cupid Stunts our new band, Lake District Geog Field Trip, Come Along to the Centre Elgin High!

#77 (February 1990)

Oliver! Young Enterprise Group, Community Studies Visits, Reg Groups 1F1 & 1O2, SocVocToc, TF Mr Ferguson, Mrs Wright, Staff in the News, New Year's Concert, Swimming Gala, Scottish Football Quiz (Pt 1) Champion Hockey Girls!

#78 (March 1990)

School Board formed, TFs on Mr McDonald, Mr Allan, Community Studies Visits, Reg Groups 1F2 & 1K2 Spotlight on our non-teaching staff, Young Enterprise, High Notes News, DoosNewsViews, SocVocToc, Spot the Teacher from baby pix, Mr Finnie sails to Russia, Scottish Football Quiz (Pt 2), SocVocHockey U13 lose in Cup Final

#79 (June 1990)

Girls gain Scottish caps, Michael Munro - a very special pal, Primary Summer Fayres, Easter Dramatic productions, Reg Groups 1E2 & 1O1, New Y2 IT facility, DofE report, Aviemore Field Trip, SocVocToc Soccer, Girls football thrives in EHS

#80 (Summer 1990)

U14 Footballers League Champions, Pupils in the News, TFs on Mr Aitken, Mr Penrose, School Board Profiles, Prize List, Mr Finnie's Russian Adventure, Reg Classes 1E1 & 1E2 as they were in 1987 and now as 4E1 & 4E2, Centre Elgin High activities, DoE Scheme reports, 5-a-side Girls Football SAYC Champions again, Sports day results, Staff v Pupil Football team pix

#81 (October 1990)

Andrew wins £1K for school, Loadsa new staff, S3 History field trip, New House Council, Staffroom & Office refurb plans, 1F1-4F1 & 1F2-4F2 then and now class profiles, New Pupil Editor Andrew Cowie, Staff & Pupils in News, First impressions 1F1, France Trip July 90 report, Mrs Marshall WWWDWT, S5 Initiative Challenge, Sports News 1990 staff photo with captions.

#82 (November1990)

Robinson Crusoe panto, Soccer & Hockey trialists, TF but who is it?, Starhenge by Christopher Dewfall, MP grilled by S4s. Fay n Kay WWWDWT, Martina's letter from America, Two's Company, 1K1-4K1 & 1K2-4K2 then and now profiles, Gav D's poetry, Mod Studies welcome Sen Citizens, Pupils in the News, New Careers Adviser, Community Placement Reports, Sponsorship means new strips for U13 and U15 football teams, DoE reports

#83 (December 1990)

Hockey Champs again, Robinson Crusoe panto review, TF Mrs Maclachlan, Christmas in France, Germany and USA - guest staff write, WX pix, Pupils and Staff in the news, Gavz Poemz and profile, 1O1 as 4O1, 1O2 as 4O2 then and now profiles, Mr Bob Stewart, MC's Director of Physical Planning, Hamish the Jannie - WWWDWT, St Giles complex grows, Quiz Champs, Starhenge Pt 2, Drama residential, Swimming Gala, Hockey Teams pix.

#84 (February 1991)

Robinson Crusoe panto pix, TFs on Learning Support Dept., Starhenge Pt 3, Martina's Letter from America, St Giles Centre investigation, Reg Groups 1E1 & 1E2, EO conference, Book and film reviews, Staff & Pupils Indoor Soccer, Custard Pie Challenge, Xmas dances, Pupils in the News.

#85 (April 1991)

Red Nose Day - costumes & events, TF Miss McLennan, Miss Neish, Easter in Germany, Susan- Dean's hockey cap, Venture Scouts in The Gambia, Reg Group 1F1 & 1F2, Andy McPhee iconoclast, Keren's Prize winning Gate designs, The Fall of Darvon VI (sci-fi sh st), School Board profiles, Mrs Goodlet WWWDWT, Gavz Poemz, Sports reports. Football season retrospect - Mr Sturrock.

#86 (June 1991)

Grease - our first summer show for a decade - pix and review, Our Prize List, TF Miss Abel, Mr Sturrock, Reg Groups 1K1, 1K2 & 1O1, Mrs Robertson WWWDWT, S3 TVEI Residentials - reports, EHS Compared with Gordonstoun, S3 Geography Field Trip, Badminton Success, Sports Day results.

#87 (October 1991)

New non-teaching staff, Julie McKenzie winds our 1st DofE Gold!, "Grease" production pix, S5 Initiative challenges met bigtime, School Council Report, Prize Giving pic, End of term events pix, Fete Accompli, First Impressions, English Dept - dramatic reports, George Nicol WWWDWT, Sports news.

#88 (November 1991)

Christmas Crackers revue, Pupil Council officers, TF Miss Farquhar, Mrs Haddow, WX evaluations, S-g History Investigation, Promoting Healthy Hearts, Gavz Poemz, 1E1, 1E2 & 1F1, Sarah Scott pupil editor, Public Speaking Success, Euroscola report, Community Involvement Placements, Fringe trip and theatre reviews, Football & Hockey reports.

#89 (March 1992)

First Activities week details, Success for Public Speakers, Best Kept School for 7th time, Pupils in the News, Report from the Gambia, Plumbers Paradise Pigout, Reg Groups 1K1, 1K2, 1O1, & 1O2, Village Shop drama filmed, Healthy Eating enterprise, Pudsey and Taggart arrive by helicopter, InterHouse quiz, Xmas Crackers review, Xmas Fête, Festive Fotos, Gav Mc D poems, Swimming Gala, Hockey and Football team pix.

#90 (June 1992)

All 14 pages of a Special Activities Week themed edition, printed in Man City blue giving lavish coverage to the school's first such event.

#91 (June 1992)

Thumbs up for our First Ever Activities Week, S5 Initiative Challenge, Greenwards Rubbish! Industrial Awareness Day, GTV Screen test for Quiz, Our Prize List, Nikki keeps it up 1,868 times, Pupils' cartoon strips, Staff News, Staff Football and Golf "stars" Sports day results

#92 (October 1992)

Reunion for Class of '78,1E1, 1E2 & 1K1 pix, New Staff arrive, First Impressions, Teenage Bowls Champs, FPs and Pupils in the News, Build a Buggy Comp, Mark Ross - Golf Champ, Local newspaper Presents Prizes, Girl Footballers - national champs, Sports Day pix.

#93 (November 1992)

Cinderella Cast, Pupils in the News, Reg Groups 1O1, 1O2, 1F1 & 1F2, Twin Trouble x 6, Artist in Residence, Class of '78 Reunion pix, Our Auxiliary Staff, Mr Stewart 10-ten Champ, Football reports, David Shewan cartoon strip.

#94 (February 1993)

Public Speaking Team, Cinderella Panto, School Fête Fotos, Pupils and Staff in the News, Christmas events, Reg Classes 1E1, 1E2 & 1K1, InterHouse Quiz, Artist in Residence, Foreign Language Assistants, Changes to School Day mooted, Swimming Gala.

#95 (June 1993)

Activities Week #2 rained on but not ruined, Josephine Ho (Pianist), Industrial Awareness Day, Red Nose Day, Prize Lists, Mr Finnie stuck in lift, Staff & S6 say goodbyes, Pupils & Staff in the News, Wilderness Drama for DoE Expedition members, Artist in residence exhibits, Jordanhill College film S-grade English introduction, Sports Day.

#96 (October 1993)

New staff, Heavy FPs, "Rector Expects Too Much", Activities Week, Changes to School Day, Reg Groups 1E1, 1F1, 1K1, & 1O1, MIS introduced, Pupils and Staff in the News, Handwriting Quiz, Staff Golf, Bowls Champ, Sports Day— with Holly Louise Spence and 10 others.

#97 (December 1993)

Rector Comments on League Tables, Swimming Gala, DofE Award Scheme, InterHouse Quiz, Mature Students, Reg Groups 1E2, 1F2, 1K2, 1O2. Nikki Grant's first international cap.

#98 (February 1994)

Period Length Change, Mr Crossland retires, Festive Fotos, Revue Review, Mock "Hello Mag" style pix of belles and beaux at Senior Christmas Dance, Spotlight on Canteen ladies, Anne Advises

#99 (May 1994)

Pupil Council, Talent Contest, features on Mr Burns, Mrs Marshall, & our cleaning staff, Gary Robertson working at BBC, Sports teams, Mr Dugdale retires from Highland League football.

#100 (June 1994)

Classic front and back anniversary covers, Activities Week—pictures and reports, Landmark issues of *Pigeon Post* since 1978 + how an edition is born, Our Prize List, Ultramarine Pt 3, Staff Goodbyes, Industrial Awareness Day, Aviation Society, U13 Football Central League Champions, Sports Day Results

#101 (October 1994)

New uniform image, New Staff arrive, Mrs Scott retires, AW - Lido di Jesolo trip and other reports, Anne's advice, Staff golf pix, First Impressions, 100 issues of PP, Witkowski Bros, Fringe Trip report, DoE Silver report, Prize winners and graduands, FP heads to Oxford to do doctorate, S5 Initiative Challenge, Percy Cartoon, EHS folk in News, Mr and Mrs Cameron - African chiefs, Media celebs in Aberdeen, The 40 min period - your views, Sports reports and pix: U13 soccer's great season, Try Snowboarding, Sports day pix, MDC in EHS

#102 (December 1994)

High Notes Concert, No AW in 1995!, International synchro star, TF Mrs Hyde, New Mod Lang assistants, Pupil marries and returns to classroom, 1E & 1F Reg groups, Meeting stars at Pittodrie, WX @ GTV, Sporting Players of the Year, Christmas Customs Abroad, cartoonist wins strip for football team, Hamilton Drive Links expand as they prepare for move to our campus, Percy cartoon, Anne's advice, Fancy an exchange?, Swimming gala, Volleyball Club, Army Mobile Assault course in Games hall, Headlines meets Noble Thoughts.

#103 (February 1995)

School to gain new Wing by August 1996, Two Talented Cartoonists TF Mr Schlomkowitz who directed the Body Parts Review, War Gaming club, FP Anna Hamilton in Musical lead, FPs in the news, TF Miss McIlraith,, Christmas events, Rory's Percy cartoon, Swimming Gala, Junior Rugby Squad Photos

#104 (May 1995)

Champion Football Teams, New Pupil Council, Stacey waits for that phone call, Miss Neish's Letter from America, Talent Contest, Reg Groups 1K1, 1K2 &1O1, Easter trip to Spain, Percy Cartoon strip, Girls go to work with parents, Grounds for Complaint essay, Champion Former Pupils

#105 (June 1995)

Staff goodbyes, New S5 Induction experience praised, Summer show review, Our Prize List, Mr Schlomkowitz's retrospect, Extension Takes Shape, S3 IADay, Sheila Duncan new C.E.W., Percy Pigeon cartoon strip, Mr Crossland's trousers, Rory Morrison cycling enthusiast, Sports Day

#106 (September 1995)

Extension proceeds, New Staff & Goodbyes, Lauren Kelly disco champ, First Impressions, Mayne Farm Visit, FPs in the news, IADay, S6 Prom, Comedy sketch shows, U14/U15 football medals, Percy Pigeon cartoon strip, Girls rugby, Staff Golf, Sports Day

#107 (December 1995)

Rector's Tribute to Miss Zena Mitchell, Former Staff member promoted to Depute Director of Ed, Miss Campbell retires, to be replaced by FP, Emma Noble's unusual WX, Reg Groups 1E1, 1F1, 1K1 & 1O1, MIS students hoodwinked, FP news, St Andrews Day, Extension progress, Percy Pigeon cartoon strip, Army in school, Talent Contest review, Sen and U14 Soccer Teams, InterHouse games, Mrs Kelman "Queen of Puddings" retires.

#108 (February 1996)

Kestrel House Extension Nears Completion, Adult pupil in S3, TF Mrs Liz Turner, Mrs Janet Kelman (Asst Cook) retires, Sixth Year Show - pix and review, Reg Classes 1F1 & 1O2, FPs in the News, Talent Show, Percy Pigeon cartoon strip, Festive Fotos, Swimming Champions.

#109 (May 96)

Kestrel House extension opens, TF on Ms Karen Gordon, Stacey Knight's Transplant, "Little Shop of Horrors" preview, Technician Norrie Jamieson, Concert & Musicians in the News, Football and Rugby Reports, Chess Club, Cinderella, Anne Advises.

#110 (June 1996)

Activities Week pix galore, The Hamilton Drive Story, "Little Shop" review, Our Prize List, EO Day, Our First Ever Leavers ceremony, S5 Induction, Construction across the school, Girls in the News, S1 Mock Election, S6 Prom, Percy Strip cartoon, Sports day results

#111 (October 1996)

Goodbye Mr Sturrock, New Staff, Pupil Council, Mr Hope's WX, Reg Groups 1E1 & 1F1, Education Roadshow, S1 Visit Mayne Farm, FPs graduate and Sporting success, "Little Shop of Horrors" pix, Percy Pigeon strip cartoon, Sports Day, Under 13 soccer team. — with Lauren Wright and Martin Simpson.

#112 (December 1996)

Hamilton Drive comes to EHS, Mr Douglas retires/Mr Sturrock leaves, Dress as You Like Day, Reg Groups 1K1 & 1O1, Pupils & FPs in the news, St Andrews Day marked, Music Concert, Percy cartoon strip, InterHouse competition : Swim Gala and Winter Games.

#113 (Feb 1997)

Fund Raising fete, Glasgow visit by LS group, Mosstowie PS's new headteacher, EHS 107 car in film, London Drama Trip review, Reg Groups 1E2 & 1K2, Mr Farquhar ambushed, FP nurses, Pupils & FPs in the news, Festive Fotos, S4 cooks do Xmas lunch, John Sinclair's short story, Percy cartoon, Ice Hockey Report, Pupils meet Soccer Celebs, Mr Sturrock Surprised.

#114 (May 1997)

"Return to Forbidden Planet", Summer Fete raises £1.3K, Talent Contest pix, CiN Dress as You Like day. Pupils and fps in the news, Mosstowie News, TF Mr Duncan, March Theatre visits, Changes to Y & Z floor accommodation, Anne's Advice, Winter Games, School wins Prestigious Sports Mark Award and £1.5K, The last ever Percy two-page cartoon strip from Rory MacKay

#115 (June 1997)

Activities Week - loadsa pix and reports, Our Prize List, Bibleworld 2 visits, S3 IADay, S2EODay, Helloes and Goodbyes, Neil Rhind Thespian, TF Mrs Ledingham, "Return to Forbidden Planet" pix & review, S5 Induction Week/ Initiative Challenge, Sports Day and School Sports records for all events at June 97.

#116 (October 1997)

AW reports e.g. Paris-Disney, New PRC profiled, TF Mrs Marriott, School Security Improvements, Kelly Slater is bus-ted! MIS Conference in school, Reg Groups 1E1 & 1F1, First Impressions, WISEbus visits, Garry Collins profile, Lauren C's new regular pop column, Prize Giving moves to capacious location, FP graduands, Art corridor murals, FLOODED!!, Edinburgh Festival visit, Sports Day pix

#117 (December 1997)

How to write an essay - Kelly S, Mates Move to Music, TF Miss McLennan, Mrs Hamilton, S5 Skills for Life, Hallowe'en Disco, Reg Groups 1O1 & 1O2, S3 Biology Trip to Hopeman, Staff & Pupils in the News, Imagine Homelessness, Get Set to Cook, Vampire Villa drama, Lauren Campbell enthuses over TKD, Swimming Gala & InterHouse Quiz

#118 (Feb 1998)

Festive Foto Gallery, Keith's Grand Design, TF Mrs Wanless, Mrs Thomson, Staff Changes, Reg Groups 1E2 & 1F2 Paul Fyvie - smiling starlet, Pupils in the News, Mock Election, Volleyball Club, Swimming Gala.

#119 (June 1998)

New Janitor arrives, Hollie McBride Talent contest winner, Foiled Again! (again), Hobby Talks in Drama, Moray Music Festival results, 1O3 Reg Class, S3 EODay reviewed, Staff Changes, X2 Refurb, Twins, by Twins, Driving Advice, Ms McLennan's international cap, Pocket Money Questionnaire, Ryan Witkowski signs for St Johnstone, Winter games pix, High Homes Graph Comm comp, School fete.

120 (June 1998)

Our Prize List, S5 Induction Activities, S6 Prom, DoE Practice expedition, C'mon Scotland, IADay, 3pp Pop News, Activities Week pix and reports galore, Name & Age Staff Babies, Sports Day - Records Blasted.

#121 (October 1998)

20th Anniversary - 20 years of Achievement

Sound Investment for Robert, TF Mrs Rhind, Understanding Industry Course, 1978 staff - where are they now? Celebrated FPs - list, Buggy Build Comp, S6 Saunter South, 3rd Academic Year Calendar, Spain Trip, Pupils in the News, Prize Giving pix, FPs graduate, First Impressions, West Park Court Visit, Mr K Simpson hangs up his whistle, U12 & U13 Football team photos

#122 (December 1998)

New Pupil Council, Reg Groups 1E2 & 1F1, Gary Robertson and other FPs in the news, Profiles on Rikki Foster, Lauren Kelly, Lucy Hyland, Jacqueline Anderson and Lauren Campbell,

If the staff did "Cinderella" cartoons, Archive material from 1979, CIN dress up day, U15 Hockey team — with Nicola Gates and 9 others.

#123 (Feb 1999)

Makeover for school, A fine pair of Scotts, TFs on Mr Farquhar & Mr Mainstone, Reg Groups 1O2 & 1F2 Archive 1979-80 Actors & S1 Hockey Girls, FP in modelling comp, Best Kept Award won, School involvement in EOS "The Gondoliers", Festive Fun Foto Feature, Christmas Concert, Swimming gala, Healthy Cooking, Close shave for Roy, Senior Football XI, FP Jenny is golf champ, Goodbye Mr Leslie & Mr Burns.

#124 (May 1999)

Activities week, Pupil Profiles on S6 Actors Michael Duncan & Mark Smith, & on James Smith 1F1 and Leigh-Anne Duncan S6. London Theatre Trip, Reg Groups 1E1 & 1O1. Archive from 1980-81 featuring Roy Young, Fund raising Lunchtime Concert, Disco and Red Nose Day, S2 EO Day, S1 Mod Studies Mock Elections, Talent Contest, Winter Games, U14 Football team are double champs.

#125 (June 1999)

Activities Week - pix & reports, Our Prize winners, Tribute to and Obituary of Mr Alistair MacLachlan, Archive material from 1981-2 : wheelchair pupils and extension, Behind the door of Z1A!!, Pupils in the News, Archaeolink Visit, IADay, School's 21st Birthday, Sports day. (+ Pamphlet from Mr MacLachlan's funeral service)

#126 (October 1999)

Welcome to New staff, CCTV and new ICL computer network installed, S1 Impressions at length, Prize Giving pix, Pupils at opening of Scottish Parliament, S5 Induction, FPs graduate, Police Liaison Officer and Police Theatre Company visit, Pupils in the News, Paris/Italy trip, S3 Biology Beach Trip, Sports Day pix. Rachel King's short story

#127 (December 1999)

New Pupil Council, FP's career as journalist, First (Year) Impressions, Reg Groups 1E3 & 1F2, Dublin Postscript, Pupils and FPs in the news, TF Mr Munro, Skating starlet, Larch Court Visit, Major Woad Ahead, Youth Cafe Cash, Percy cartoon strip by Donna Logan, Talent Contest, Swimming Gala

#128 (February 2000)

New Office boss, Pupil Council Achievements and Charity Donation, London Drama trip, Christmas presents (cd/video) review, Reg Group 1E1 & 1F1, Argumentative essays on handguns and on fox-hunting, FPs news: graduations and other, Ross Allan thespian, Boyzone crush, Percy cartoon, Festive Fotos.

#129 (May 2000)

Library refurb, First Ever School's Charity Week, Natasha in Jamaica, Website reviews, Reg Groups 1E2, 1O1 & 1O2, Mr Aitken promoted to Rector, Louise Grant TKD enthusiast, Elgin High folk in the News, Moray Music festival results, Youth Cafe Roadshow in EHS, ModStuds Mock Election, S2 ModStuds "What if?" essays, H.E. Refurbs, Elgin City U18 side with EHS interest, InterHouse Quiz pix, Percy cartoon.

#130 (July 2000)

Mr Aitken becomes KGS Rector, Our Prize List, S3 IADay, S2 EODay, Pupils FPs in the news, Miss Frascone au revoir, S5 Induction "Titanic" Activities, Tracey Sievewright's retrospect, Jun Choir pic, Percy's holiday - Donna L., U14 Soccer pic, Elgin CC interest, Activities Week : 10 pages of pix, Super Sports day.

#131 (October 2000)

First Academic Year Pupil Art calendar, New Staff arrive, 1A's first Impressions, 1O1 pic, Bursary for young acting star, Prize Giving pix, PP editor remarries!, The Young Dependables, Profile Lauren Campbell, FPs graduate, Cross England ride, Percy cartoon strip by Donna L, First Sponsored Walk, Sports Stars in the News, Super Sports Day, Thoughts on Elgin South plans, Technical Department Alterations over summer.

#132 (December 2000)

Elgin Scenes cards sell well, Originals donated to local places, Hollie regains Talent trophy, Gary Collins plays Romeo in Royal Lyceum, Edinburgh, Letters of complaint, Best Kept Award won again, Reg Groups 1E1 & 1F1, Activities week postscript, School raises £5K for charities, Former pupils' successes, Music Dept Christmas Concert, Elgin City – in Scottish League – good idea or not? : essays, Football report by The Rector, Gala no more.

#133 (February 2001)

55 minute period returns (in an echo of February 1994, Like Mother Like Daughter, TF Mr Stubbs, Leanne's Indian Adventure, Reg Group 1O1 & 1E2, London Theatre Trip, New staff arrive, Farewell Bob Donald, Graphic short story, Planet MMMBop, Percy cartoon strip, Festive Fotos, Archive, Mr Dugdale's 1C class from 1980/1, Elgin High folk in the news.

#134 (May 2001)

School in Tiers of Floods, "Grand" Red Nose Day, TF Mrs Fleming, 1F2, 1O2 and 1F3 Reg Groups, Alan Gray's biographical retrospect, Small Enclosed Area, International Ice Hockey player, Bridge Building comp, Mock Election pix and reports The Pros & Cons of - Plastic Surgery, the Internet, The Old Firm in English Premiership. U12, U13 Football Team pix.

#135 (July 2001)

Our Prize winners, S6 Prom, Rachel's King retrospect re EHS, Activities Week 2001, Elgin's New Music Centre in Francis Place, S2 EO Day, S3 IA Day, Sporting success for senior pupils James Smith and Nicky Cramb, Sports Day

#136 (October 2001)

Our "Possie" scheme is launched, New Academic year calendar goes on sale, SYTheatre in school, Street Jam Fundraiser, Gary Robertson—Prize Presenter, FPs graduate, Ed Festival report, Miss Hanton Gigs on the Green, Elgin High folk in the news, AW post script, First Impressions, American football in Elgin, Sports day results and pix

#137 (December 2001)

First PPB ceremonies, Best ever S-grade results analysis, TF Mrs Flett, Street Jam Fundraiser, 2002 Calendar for sale, Reg Groups 1E1 & 1F1, Louise Grant wins Talent Show, A Surprise for Craig, CiN Dress as You Like day, Mr Finnie Sails to Victory, FPs graduate, Goodbye Mr Vaughan, Sci-Fun Roadshow in school, Elgin Eagles feature.

#138 (February 2002)

Major school refurb, Seeking African penpals, Sandra P, Alisdair B - judo and piano fans, TF Mrs Adamson, Farquhar's Flight of Fancy, Reg Groups 1F1 & 1O1, Nikki - Darling of the Airwaves, Fuzz, Buzz & Tripe cartoon - Euan Sinclair, Elgin Eagles EHS interest in US football, Festive Fotos.

#139 (May 2002)

Activities Week Foreign Trips for 100, PPB evaluations, TF Dr Wilkinson, Work Permit Needed! Andrew Flynn profile, Reg Groups 1F2 & 1E2, CITB pix, Bridge Building Competition at Moray College, Dress-as-you-Like Day, Threes lads not brassed off, African pen pal? Laura Chalmers - international athlete, "Life After Death" Rachel King sh story, Sporting Starlets - Fraser, Steph and James, Army Familiarization Day - Terry Christie

#140 (July 2002)

Activities Week reports and pix, Our Prize winners, Prizes for FPs including Banker of the Year, and *Pigeon Post*, S3 Geography Field Trip, S2 EO day, S3 Enterprise Day, S6 Prom, S6 Goodbye! says Rachel King, Yacht Modeller competition

#141 (October 2002)

Possie Scheme Changes, New Staff arrive, Louise Grant's Got Talent, Edinburgh Fest report, SYT Roadshow in town. First (Year) Impressions, Prize Giving pix, TF Ruth Christie, Calendar on sale, Goodbye Mr Stubbs, Nikki's First Crash! FPs graduate and make news, Local business feature, PP wins a prize, U15 Soccer squad, Girl Sports Champions, Final Day Frolix, Sponsored Walk, School Crew on crest of a wave.

#142 (December 2002)

Spotlight on Fraser Bremner and on Mod Lang Dept., Miss Saigon trip, Reg Groups 1E1 & 1F2, our Library Assistants, Pupils and FPs in the News, Sponsored walk raises £3K. EHS - rest centre for dramatic flooding: pupil report, Talent Contest, New Careers Advisor—Mrs Thatcher, Local Hair Stylists, Football squads, Pupils at Moray Music Centre, Nikki's Crash Xmas Special, EHS folk gain Moray sports awards, Pupil biker's bad break, John A's caricatures.

#143 (March 2003)

Red Nose Day, Steph Reynolds - International Schoolgirl Athlete, London Theatre Trip report, Reg Groups 1O1 & 1E2, Claire Cameron - Talent Contest Winner, Pupils and FPs in the News, Festive Fotos inc Xmas Assemblies, Fraser Bremner capped, Mr Farquhar's Model Behaviour, FPs' sporting success, FP band Small Enclosed Area, FPs capped at Pool, Graffiti Wall in Mod languages.

#144 (May 2003)

New Head Visits, Red Nose Day pix, Library Survey, Sixth year reflections, Jobs Fair, Reg Groups 1O2, 1F1 & 1E3, Pupils and fps in the news, Spotlight on Craig McDonald & Scottish cap Fraser Bremner, Mrs Elsie Smethurst retires, Jubilee Bible Group Visit, Euan Sinclair & Jon Arbuthnott cartoons, FP Gordon Lowe reports from around the world.

#145 (June 2003)

THE END OF AN ERA (aka Get your hankies out time)....
Goodbye Bill: Farewell Fotos, Appreciations, His first ever Headlines from PP#1, Staff Farewell Dinner
Other Goodbyes, S2 EO, S3 IA and S5 Induction days, Activities Week, 2003 Sports Day.

#146 (October 2003)

25 years celebrated*, Mr Simpson arrives, FP graduands, pipers and achievements, PP across the years, S1 Impressions, Mr Hope's last days, Prize Giving, Sports Day, Sponsored Walk
*The cover shows pupils from 2003 whose mums/dads were pupils at EHS in 1978.

#147 (December 2003)

Impressive Pupil Charity support, Reg Groups 1E1 & 1F1, TF on Miss Natalie Hargraves, Young Male Sporting Stars, Archive material showing first pupils of EHS in 1978/9, Talent Contest, Douglas Cameron on Drugs, Mr Farquhar & The Wright Bros, Youth Bank, Under 13 and Under 14 Soccer Squads

#148 (February 2004)

Pupils in the News, London Theatre Trip, "Dracula Spectacula" preview, Reg Groups 1O1 & 1E2, Freya Bathes in Beanz, Artists of 2004 calendar, Talented Musical pupils, Archive photo from 1979 : U14 Football team and S1 Hockey & Drama productions, Festive Fotos, "You Taught my granda, sir!" Ski-ing in Moray, Senior and U15 Footballers, Jon's "precious" caricature.

#149 (May 2004)

Inspectors Praise Pupil Conduct, Success at Moray Music Festival, Reg Groups 1F3 & 1O2, New PRC, Pupils in the News, Dress as You Like Day, Archive item : U13 Football, S2 Girls Hockey (from 1979) and actors (from 1982), Dracula Spectacula feature, New Quad seats, Janet Paisley Visits, U13 win North Cup

#150 (June 2004)

Goodbye Mr Cadenhead: tributes Prize Winners, Archive: Staff Football team 1981, Reg Group 1O3, Staff & S6 Goodbyes, S2 EODay, Activities Week, Dracula Spectacula pix, Artist in Residence, Sports Day, S6 Prom

#151 (September 2004)

New staff, 85% take-up of new uniform, Sean - National Swim Champ, FPs graduate, First Impressions, Goodbye Mr Cadenhead and Mrs Marriott, Pigeon Post wins a prize, RYLA report, Prize Giving and Sports Day retrospect, 1B Archaeology, Sponsored Walk

152 (December 2004)

Staff as festive characters - Who does these amazing covers?, Fraser McGillivray - extrovert, TF our new Depute, Dance for Lunch, Reg Groups 1E1 & 1F1, Pupil charity efforts, Dress to Stress, Archive: 1980 Pupil Council, Dance groups, Girls and Boys Basketball, U13 Football, Skateboard Park Sought, Skill City, Talent Show, Kirsty Thomson -Skating Starlet, Female staff and pupil athletes, Emma McIntosh - choreographer

#153 (Feb 2005)

Festive Fotos, Dance Academy, John Arbuthnott caricaturist, TF Mr Moonan, Miss Anderson, FP News—Georgia Russell exhibits in London, 1O2 and 1E3 Reg classes, Active Schools Coordinator, MP visits Mod Studies Dept., Pupils name local streets, FPs graduate, Archive - pix of 1981 extension, Mr Farquhar tilts at windmills, Focus on Girls in Sport, London Theatre Trip

#154* (May 2005)

PPB Awards summary, TF Miss Ollivier, Easter Concert pix, Dance Academy photos, World Book Day welcome for local author, Red Nose Day pix, Reg Groups 1F2 and 1O1, Eerie Tales from Olde Elgin, Goodbye Lillian, one of the original cooks, Top Actor prize for Emma, The McIntosh sisters!, TKD & Football Stars Profile each other, Sandra wins Judo Gold,U15 and Senior Boys Football teams   *(the wrongly numbered one!)

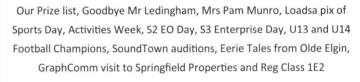

#155 (June 2005)

Our Prize list, Goodbye Mr Ledingham, Mrs Pam Munro, Loadsa pix of Sports Day, Activities Week, S2 EO Day, S3 Enterprise Day, U13 and U14 Football Champions, SoundTown auditions, Eerie Tales from Olde Elgin, GraphComm visit to Springfield Properties and Reg Class 1E2

#156 (October 2005)

Many New Staff arrive, our first SoundTown experiences—the Opening Ceremonies—we go live on air-A Gotcha for Gary– Radio Teams training Days , Ed Festival report, Chris Beard Community Warden, Mr Simpson on Solution Oriented Approaches, Staffrooms Reunited, Prize winners, FPs graduate, AAA Amy Sutherland!, Summer Concert pix, Scott Stables champion golfer, Elgin High to close within 5 years? Sponsored Walk, Aviemore Fieldtrip, Sports Day retrospect

#157 (December 2005)

SoundTown Activities: Clare English interview, French chefs in school—EHS folk on Gary Robertson & Fred MacAulay shows, Christmas Service recorded, Struan Ferguson and Debbie Macdonald profiled, Reg Groups 1E1 and 1F2, Emma McDonald wins Talent Contest, TF Mr James Farquhar, Miss Brown, FPs in the news, Staff wedding, Children in Need Day, St Andrews Day, High Time and ASG Concerts, Sean @ Aigas

#158 (February 2006)

SoundTown events: Fred MacAulay interview & caricature, Mr Simpson i/c Radio Scotland for a day, *MacAulay & Co* with John Beattie live from our gym, Fickle Public band return to play in school
A fine pair of pipers, XL Club launch, 1O1 & 1E2 Reg Groups, TF Miss Little, Miss Tierney, FPs graduate, Christmas Dances & Assemblies, Senior Football squad pic, Martial arts Champions Louise & Sandra

#159 (May 2006)

SoundTown events galore, Celeb interviews, Gary Robertson and Stuart McBride, Political and media personalities visit, Two visits from Vic Galloway, Colin and Edith, *Newsdrive* and *The Tom Morton Show* live from school, Visit to BBC Glasgow HQ. Badaguish Challenge, Reg Groups 1F1 & 1O2, TF Mrs Bews, Sponsored walk, NE Street Elite, Three Authors visit for WBD, S2 English field trips, Kieran Cameron profile, FPs gaining international football caps.

#160 (June 2006)

SoundTown events: More appearances on Gary and Fred shows, Vic Galloway encourages pupils to *Mouth Off!*, *The Beechgrove Potting Shed* from school. Our Prize Winners, Farewell Mrs Marshall, Reg Group 1O3, Sci-Fun Roadshow, Big Milestone for Mr S., TF Mrs Currie, The Adams Family Pipers, NASA astronaut & MSP visit, Healthy eating focus, Activities Week and Sports Day—loadsa pix.

#161 (October 2006)

Lots of new staff arrive, First (Year) Impressions, Staff Farewells, Our Prize Giving, Edinburgh Fringe Trip report, Final events of SoundTown experience - Janice Forsyth show from Plain Stones, SoundTown stats, UN Peace Day Assemblies, FPs graduate, Musical Maestros, Film Reviews, Staff Texas Scramble, S6 Day at Roseisle, Possie champs get a rewarding day out.

#162 (December 2006)

Cashless Catering arrives, Calum Reid , Shelley McDonald and Matthew Gardiner profiled, Possie Award summaries, TF Mr Ord, Mr French, Reg Groups 1E1 & 1F1, Staff arrive and depart, Staff Weddings, Bill's Last Supper, Talent Contest, St Andrew's Day Celebrations, Musical Maestros, FPs in the news, Sponsored Walk, Elgin High at Murrayfield

#163 (February 2007)

Possie Assemblies, TF Mrs McIver, Mr McGrath, Spotlight on non-teaching staff, Reg Groups 1O1 and 1F2, U14, U15 and Senior Football squad pix, Goodbye Norman, Staff wedding, Elgin High folk in the News, Christmas theme dress up day, Christmas dances and concert, Spotlight on chaplains—Rev Billies, Rev McQuaid, Undead—a short story, Musical Maestros. Pupil enjoy Moray College tasters.

#164 (May 2007)

Red Nose Day, Possie Awards, Rebecca Campbell MSYP, TF on Mr McCulloch, Mrs Lawson, 1E2 & 1O2 Reg Groups, Book Fair and World Book Day, Pupil Council Pic, Stuart & Shelley to bite the Big Apple, Mr Mainstone's shaven head, WBD pix, Staff v Pupils Football, School Chaplains– Rev Swanson, Rev Morison, Instrumental Tutors, End of term Concert, Melissa's Dramatic Success.

#165 (July 2007)

Our Prize Winners, Umoja—Ethiopia trip for Mr S, TF Mrs M Watson, Mr Strain, Reg Group 1F3, Activities Week, Pupils in the news, FP elected to Moray Council, Enterprise Day, Grampian Children's Book Award, School Chaplains—Rev Strange, Rev Woods, Sports Day—our Champions, Goodbyes, Pupils in Macbeth production, Helloes and Goodbyes, Football: League Cup Winners.

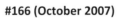

#166 (October 2007)

New Staff arrive, The Africa Connection—"Umoja", First (year) Impressions, EHS Staff Got Talent, Prize Giving, Shelley on the Big Apple, SoundTown PostScript, Peace Day Assemblies, From Latvia with Love, FPs Graduate, whilst some work in EHS and others have sporting success, Pupils in the News, SkillForce members gain awards, Mrs Grant leaves us for Elgin Ac, Hair Raising experiences for staff, Drenched at Dreich Roseisle, Football teams Seniors and U13s, Our very first football team 1978, and Street Football arrives on campus.

#167 (December 2007)

New staff arrive, Pupils in the News, TF Mrs Morrison, Mr Mann, Sponsored Walk Raises £4.5K, Reg Groups 1F1 & 1O2, New Behaviour Support Measures, Bullying Issues, "Wonderful" EHS - 2 sides ! EHS 30 events, Staff Novelists, Landshut Visit, Trixie Goes to India, Mr Allan to retire, Special Guests at Possie Assemblies, CIN Dress up Day, Musical Maestros, St Andrew's Day

#168 (March 2008)

FPs and current pupils in the news, Reg Group 1E1 & 1E2, Hope for Sports Centre on campus, Science Stories, Mukonchi High pupils profiled, Author Keith Charteris visits, Community Area makeover, International Classroom at Elgin High, School pupils raise money for charity, The History of Percy Pigeon, TF Mr Coll, School Chaplain Rev Cowie, Festive Fotos, School personalities stand for Council, Focus on our Library.

#169 (May 2008)

Possie Assemblies & summaries, Stephanie Cuthbert on Army Officer career training, TF Mr Hinchliffe, Mr Norrie, Reg Group 1F2 & 1O1, Awards for young volunteers, Retrospect from two foreign exchange students, Elgin High folk in the news, *Pigeon Post*—the story behind the stories, WBD Day Assemblies & recommendations, Three decades of School shows, New Uniforms on display, Talent Show, Kestrel House Open morning, Staff v Pupils football challenge match, Badaguish Report, FP signs for English Premiership side. "We Will Rock You" cast profiles. Sample pages from "30 Years of EHS" booklet.

#170 (June 2008)

Our Prize Winners, TF Mrs Mackenzie, Famous Authors visit, Goodbye Mr Dugdale, Mr Downie, Mr Duncan, Mrs Reid, Mr Spence and S6, "Jurassic Park" comes to Elgin High, Staff wedding and Elgin High folk in the News, "We Will Rock You" review. S6 Prom pix, *Pigeon Post* covers across the Years, Skill Force Residential, Activities Week reports and pix, Getting a whole car into the Games Hall for WWRY! Grampian Children's Book Award, His last post (see over)

And one final unexpected flourish!
Mr Dugdale (retired, but by then teaching English around Moray schools) returned
on supply in the last two months of the session and offered to do an issue as a
retrospect of the whole year….

#171 (June 2009)

Review of the Year: Our Prize Winners, Goodbye Miss Ross, Mr Penrose*, Mr Walker and their replacements, Obituaries Mr McDonald, Mr Stewart. A Passage to Zambia, Prize Giving 2008 (sic) pix, Activities Week 2009, TF Miss Fisher, Mr Watt, Mr Cumming, Miss Picozzi, Miss Gilruth, Miss Crossman, Miss Bell, FPs in the news, Transform Moray NYT event, Badaguish 2009 report, Adirondack Chairs, WBD 2009, Library Activities and events, Sports Day 2008 pix, Football report from Mr James Farquhar, S2 Pizza Enterprise day, Mr John Farquhar sends a postcard from Plockton.

* Since retiring Mr Penrose has completed a PhD and is now Dr Penrose.

The last page of what should have been the last *Pigeon Post* (#170) specially created by fp Rory MacKay

Alphabetical Index of Pupils Featured in
Pigeon Post

99% +

As explained earlier, most editions of *Pigeon Post* contained group photos of pupils in S1 and/or in S4 Registration Classes as they began/continued in Elgin High each session. These photos in the "Classpot" and "CLASSified InFORMation" etc series were typically complemented with around 40 self written words. Therefore we can state with absolute certainty that over 99% of the school's pupils between 1978 and 2008 have had *something* written about them in our pages.

Many of course merited fulsome features - in the "Pupil Profile" series on account of their achievements in school life or out of school. *Pigeon Post* also reproduced press reports of their activities as former pupils, particularly if considerable detail was given, not just a caption.

On the following pages all such pupils are listed with reference to the edition(s) they appeared in.

NB : This does not allude to occasional creative writing or regular contributed features by these individuals.

All these features are available for reference at the Dropbox site **Pigeonpost.info** Apologies for any omissions: I wasn't picking on you.

A

Ex PP146 : Richard Anderson leads the pipers at Bill Hope's farewell

B

C

D

Ex PP136 : Nikki Darling playing an old lady in SYT's *Equilibrium*

E

F

G

Ex PP97 : Nicky Grant wins the first of her 99 international caps

H

M

Ex PP163 : Shelley McDonald off to The Big Apple with Struan Ferguson

O

Ogg, Kevin & Julie	31
Ogg, Sadie	72

P

Palmer, Megan	54
Paterson, George	74
Paterson, Meilssa	164
Pearson, Beth	127
Phillips, Aileen	166
Pirie, Sandra	138, 146, 152, 154, 158
Porter, Alan	76, 82
Pullar, Adrian & George	31

R

Ramstorf, Anne	169
Reid, Alan	142
Reid, Callum	162
Reid, Daniel	166
Reid, Katherine	56
Reid, Lynn	32
Reynolds, Stephanie	123,139,143
Rhind, Neil	106, 115
Ritchie, Claire	113
Robertson, Crawford	53
Robertson, Fiona	133
Robertson, Gary	99, 122, 132, 136, 157, 160
Robertson, Laura Jane	63

Ex PP152 : Sandra Pirie wins Scottish Judo cap

Robertson, Leigh-Anne	72
Rodger, Alan	47
Ross, Stephen	73
Rowand, Sheila	73
Rowlands, Susan	102
Rourke, Lynn	92
Russell, Georgia	117,153,155

S

Saracevic, Sanela	97
Scott, Alex & Kevin	93
Scott, Gary	55
Scott, Sarah	88
Scott, Wendy	20
Shanks, Neil	143
Shepherd, Bruce	96, 116
Shewan, David	103
Shiach, Neil	44
Silava, Sanita	166
Sim, David	73

Ex PP146 : James Smith, Scottish bowls cap

W

T

Y

Alphabetical Index of Staff Featured in
Pigeon Post

The listings on the following pages cover such regular series of substantial articles (not just snippet allusions) as "Teacher Feature" (including associated Primary colleagues, youth and community workers, careers advisers etc), "What Would We Do Without Them", "Spotlight on—" e.g. Music Tutors, Chaplain and *ad hoc* items reprinted from local newspapers.

Staff with an * against their names were foreign language assistants, when such roles were common.

Re female staff who married and changed their surname during their time with us the listing appears e.g.: "**Smith** (Brown), Jane"

On the following pages all in these categories are listed with reference *to the edition(s) they appeared in*.

NB This does not allude to occasional articles or regular contributed columns written by these individuals about other topics.

All these are available for reference at the Dropbox site **pigeonpost.info**. Apologies for any omissions : it wasn't personal!

A

B

Mr Bob Burns

C

K

Mr Jim McDonald

L

Mc/Mac

Mr Alastair MacLachlan

The First Senior Staff of EHS and Their Current Status

All still living in Moray unless otherwise stated

Bill Hope, Rector	Retired 2003
Alistair MacLachlan, Depute	Died June 1999 as Rector of Forres Acad
Douglas Campbell, Assistant Rector	Retired as Rector of Bell Baxter High, Cupar in 2007, now lives in Edinburgh
Maurice Jackson, Art	Retired 2004 As SQA exams Officer, lives near Edinburgh (cf thestainedglassstudio.co.uk)
Nick Ledingham, Chemistry	Retired 2005
Derek Ross, Drama	Retired 2016, now a Moray Councillor
Jeff Dugdale, English	Retired as DHT 2008, did supply till 2016

This photo taken by Nick Ledingham in June 2003 shows a gathering of most of the original staff (some with spouses) to mark Mr Hope's retirement. Who can you spot? (Details given on the bottom of the next page)

Alister Hendrie, Geography	Retired in 2012 having been Rector at three schools, latterly Beath High. Now lives in Fife
David Cameron, Guidance	Retired in 2009 as Head of Senior School at Sekolah Pelita Harapan, Jakarta. Now lives in Cheshire
Jim Hamilton, History	Retired as PT History Kincorth Academy. Now lives in Aberdeen
Sylvia Campbell, Home Econs	Retired 1996, now lives in Kirkcaldy
Alex McKay, Mathematics	Retired 2001 as Director of Education, Fife. Now lives in Perthshire
Judy Ross, Mod Languages	Retired 2009
Sheena Ledingham, Music	Retired 2014
David Carstairs, P.E.	Retired from Forres Ac 2005. Now lives near Inverness
Alisdair Urquhart, Technical	Retired as Education Convener, Moray Council.

Who's in the photo?

Names of *original staff* given only:

Back (l-r) Jeff Dugdale, David Cameron, Donnie Macleod, then by right window -, Linda McPherson, Alister Hendrie, Alex McKay

Middle: Doug Campbell, then in centre Alasdair Uquhart, Constance Angus, Aileen Marshall, Maurice Jackson, Avril Clark.

Front: Sheena Cowan Ledingham, Sylvia Campbell, Bill Hope, David Carstairs, Derek Ross, Ann Drysdale, Judy Ross.

One of the original members of staff who made it to the top in his chosen career Mr Alex McKay, our first Head of Mathematics, summarises what happened to him after he left Elgin High

From Elgin High following secondment to a national project, Mr McKay moved to Fife, initially in the Advisory Service of the Education Department. He worked in Fife for the remainder of his career, although there were a number of job changes. His final post, from the last reorganization of local government, was Head of Education for Fife Council. He retired in 2003, and now lives in Scone.

Photo: Nick Ledingham 1978

He still has family and friends in the north-east and is often in the area. In addition, a significant activity since retiring has been a return to archaeology. He and his wife Jennifer were keen diggers for a number of years at the excavations at Birnie and Clarkly Hill in the Elgin area with Fraser Hunter of the National Museum of Scotland. Further digging took place in Perthshire, with Glasgow University as part of the SERF Project, and elsewhere in Scotland.

Archaeology was an interest from his own school days at Banff Academy and it has been complemented in retirement with involvement in a range of history-themed activities. As well as membership of a number of local and national societies, time was devoted to assisting with historical research on the site at Cullykhan, near Troup Head on the coast between Banff and Fraserburgh, where his archaeological 'career' began many years ago. This research contributed to the final archaeological report on the castle on the site. He wrote a book on Cullykhan published in June 2017 by the Banffshire Field Club.

Elgin High – or more precisely people associated with Elgin High – provides many, mostly good, memories. From day 1, there seemed to be a particular camaraderie amongst staff and pupils which was very positive.

It gives pause to realize the length of time that has flown by since then.

Some of the first First Years at a Reunion event in 2016

Back (l-r) Audrey (Young) Robertson, Brian Ross, Julie (Campbell) Moxham, Stuart Chambers, Paula Aldin-Scott, Yvonne (Mitchell) Tyson, Shirley (Moir) McWilliam, David Hector, Shirlene (Abbott) Halbert, Douglas Scott

Front: Hamish Hyndman, Alan Logan, Janice Hyndman, Gregor Milne, Angela Matchett, Michelle Mutch, Sandra (Murray) Ralph, Julie Robertson, Elaine Ford and Martine Baillie

And from a picture taken of a similar event in 2017

From left—Julie Robertson, Janice Hyndman, Kate Yeo, David Gardner, Shirley (Moir) McWilliam, Alan Logan, Gregor Milne, Yvonne (Mitchell) Tyson, Wendy Toner

The First First Year (1978-79)

Classified

By Janice Hyndman, assisted by Hamish Hyndman and Angela Matchett.

A selection of updates from some of the S1s who were there on the very first day of Elgin High School, 15 August 1978. There is a little nod to the long running feature in the *Pigeon Post* where we all learned more about our classmates.

Lorna Alexander

Lorna left in 1982 and began working in retail, initially with RS McColl's and then Fine Fare. She got engaged in 1983 and had her daughter before moving to Lossiemouth. Lorna worked at the Skerry Brae Hotel, progressing to manager and completing an HND in Hospitality Management. Lorna has worked in hotels across the west of Scotland before returning to retail as a manager at the Co-op. Lorna loves singing and is a member of Kinloss Military Wives Choir. Lorna got to spend her 50th birthday on stage with the choir singing with Lulu. The choir have recorded a Christmas album which was number 2 in the classical music chart and number 3 in an independent chart. Lorna has performed at the Usher Hall and the choir are due to release another album soon. She loves walking her two rescue dogs, reading and drawing. She still lives in Lossiemouth with her daughter and pets.

Rodney Badenoch

Rod joined the RAF when he first left school then moved to working in the Offshore industry in UK, Middle East, Kazakhstan and latterly Angola. Since the downturn in the offshore sector, Rod is working in the local whisky industry - he is keen to return to oil and gas soon. Rod met his wife Sarah, a primary school teacher, in Qatar and they live in Elgin with their two sons. Outwith work Rod enjoys music, cooking, foreign travel and hill walking when he gets the opportunity.

Martine (Fletcher) Baillie

After Martine left EHS in 1983 she began working for BT. After getting married in 1986 to David, who was in the RAF, she worked in the NAAFI at RAF Wildenrath in Germany. When they returned to Elgin in 1989, Martine worked at the Moray Playhouse for 10 years before starting college in 2002. She gained an NQ Administration and Information Skills and an HNC Accounting. She then worked for Baillie Brothers as an account manager for 14 years before recently starting a new job with Tennant's, Elgin. Martine has two daughters, Melanie born in 1989, Gemma born in 1994 and has a wonderful little grandson Oliver, born in 2016.

Angela (Davidson) Bruce

Angie has been married to John for 30 years and they have three children, one sadly deceased. She is also a Granny to two grandsons. Angie has had a career in retail and was the manager of Semi Chem until recently moving to Superdrug, also as manager.

Michelle (McLaren) Cook

Michelle left Elgin High School and married her husband Kevin, who was in the RAF which meant that they travelled a fair bit, including to Germany and various parts of England before returning to Kinloss in 1993. Michelle has three children, a daughter and two sons and now lives close to Alves. Michelle currently works in Tesco in Elgin as a manager in the non-food department. Michelle loves to travel, often to Boston USA where her oldest son lives. Still keen on sport, as she was at EHS, Michelle tends to watch now rather than play. She has however recently taken up archery which she finds a very relaxing pastime.

Gordon Duthie

Gordon worked as an electrician for 7 years after leaving in 1983 before working offshore, also as an electrician till 1996. During this time Gordon also achieved a BSc in Electrics and Electronics. A spell of working abroad followed before moving into IT. Gordon is currently a contract software engineer. In 1999 he met his wife Nicola and they have been married for 12 years. He has a daughter Iona (13) and two stepchildren, Kayla (22) and Daryn (21). Gordon is also a grandad to Alfie (4) and newly born Leigh-Roy. Training and running take up some of Gordon's spare time and he has run twice in the London Marathon and once in the Loch Ness event. He also enjoys Taekwondo and has gained his 2nd Dan Black Belt. Gordon also has a Labrador called Roxy.

David Gardener

After leaving Elgin High School David travelled a bit before settling in Newcastle. He says he drive trucks for a living and eats Yorkies! David has one grown up daughter and primary age twins, a boy and a girl.

Corrina Gray

Corrina has lived in Glasgow for the last 22 years. She has two daughters, one 24 who works in engineering after being at university. Corrina's younger daughter is 17 and currently at college studying art and design. Last summer Corrina's older daughter made her a proud Granny to a beautiful granddaughter. For the last 10 years Corrina has been working at the customer service desk at Silverburn shopping centre, a job she loves.

Elaine (Hutchison) Ford

When she left in 1984 Elaine went on to study at PE college in Edinburgh for four years. Elaine then moved to England where she stayed for 18 years carrying out various roles in education. These included Head of PE, Head of Year and Assistant Head Teacher. Elaine returned to Elgin in 2007 to be closer to her Mum. Elaine is married to Alan and has two children, Callum and Alice. Since coming back to live in Elgin Elaine has been a PT Guidance at Buckie High School.

Wendy (Fines) Fraser

Wendy has been working in Johnston's of Elgin for the last 26 years as a darner. Still living in Elgin, she has been married to Michael for 31 years and has two daughters, Leonie and Jade. Wendy also has two grandsons, Fraser and Finlay. Travelling is something Wendy loves to do and she also enjoys listening to music and watching sport, especially football, rugby and motor racing.

Colin Grant

When he first left school Colin worked for A G Beattie as a painter and decorator. In 1991, he became the groundsman at EHS and a few years later took up the role as janitor, a job he still does. Colin married his wife Karen in 2005 and they have two daughters, Beth (16) and Niamh (13). As a pupil at EHS, Colin began playing badminton and he continued to play competitively at regional level into his early 30s when he had to stop due to an injury.

Anna Hamilton

Anna left in 1984 to study a music degree at Aberdeen University, graduating in 1988. She then did her teacher training at the Northern College. Next step was teaching at Fraserburgh Academy for 16 years before moving into Aberdeen City to promote music in schools. Anna sees over a thousand children a week, singing, playing games and running choirs. She is also in the Aberdeen and North-East Scotland Festival committee giving children the chance to perform. At EHS Anna sang in choirs, at Burns Suppers and school shows which has continued into university and beyond performing Gilbert and Sullivan operas and musicals. Many starring roles have followed including Eliza in *My Fair Lady* and Yum Yum in *The Mikado*. Anna still sings with Aberdeen Opera Company, she has recently played the aunt of a character she played when she left uni – age is catching up with us! Anna says that EHS gave her a great start and she takes the memories with her.

Hamish Hyndman

Since leaving EHS in 1983 Hamish worked for a short spell offshore before working as a chef for 10 years in various establishments in Elgin. He then drove a baker's van for another 10 years selling cakes and "peeces" to local people. Since then he has been behind bars...currently as the club steward at the New Club in Elgin. Hamish married Janice McKillop – he says he "still can't believe it"...she must be amazing! Hamish still lives in New Elgin, is Dad to two grown up (??) sons, who get fed up being asked all the time if they are Hamish's loons as he "knows everyone"! He also has two younger sons at primary school, one of whom starts at the new Elgin High after the summer.

Hamish left, Ian Jenkins, Yvonne (Mitchell) Tyson and Eric Beattie

Janice (McKillop) Hyndman

Janice left in 1984 with no clue what to do next. She fell into retail, initially at Sinclair's Newsagents in New Elgin before going back to study. After a lot of years of part-time study, she gained a BA Business Administration, finally graduating in 2001. Since then she has been working for the careers service and after completing a post-graduate diploma in Careers Guidance, is the current careers adviser in EHS and, "it's amazing being back there every day". Janice married Hamish in 1990 and has four sons, Kieran (25), Aidan (22), Euan (12) and Lachlan (10) and a mad Springer Spaniel, Millie. Creative activities still play a role in Janice's life as they did in school. She draws, does cake decorating and is the president of Elgin Amateur Dramatic Society – you can see her on stage every December in Elgin's panto....oh yes you can!

Ian Jenkins

Ian started working at Ralph's the bakers when he left school, staying there for twenty-four years...that's a lot of Ralphie's butteries and tattie and bean pies! He then made a move into construction at Robertson's where he still works. Ian has two children, Connor and Madison. Connor started as one of the first S1s in the new Elgin High School, just like his Dad was in the old one.

Janne (Commons) Lawrie

Janne has worked for the Civil Service for he last 32 years. She has a son Joel (23) who she says, "is my world". Janne has a dog Harley and babysits Joel's dog Angos, with an "o", every three weeks. After moving to Hopeman 22 years ago, Janne still lives there. Despite having left EHS many years ago Janne still has fond memories of her school days and the happy times she had there. Her favourite teacher was Mr Dugdale and she loved English so much. Walking dogs and gardening are how Janne likes to spend her spare time...chilling.

Geoffrey Lee

After he left EHS Geoff studied Electronics and Electrical Engineering at the Robert Gordon's Institute of Technology. He has worked for various companies, for the last 26 years with Mentor Graphics, now in sales, which is apparently the "dark side"! Geoff married Maureen in 1993 and they have four children, Matthew (22), Natasha (19), Oliver (17) and Daniel (13). Geoff was part of the first EHS group to go skiing, an activity he still takes part in. He also enjoys snowboarding and plays tennis and badminton competitively, the latter of which was another activity he started in EHS. Geoff also used to row on the coast, sometimes sinking and having to be rescued! Travelling has featured a lot in Geoff's life as part of his work, but it has made him appreciate home more. Geoff likes an active life but it has resulted in a catalogue of injuries!

Dawn (Fraser) Ling

When she first left, Dawn worked for Ralph's the Bakers before starting to train as a nurse – unfortunately she had to stop for health reasons. Dawn married her husband in 1988 at Birnie Kirk and had two sons, and she is looking forward to her first grandchild being born in August. Dawn moved to Ellon, then Suffolk until 1998, when her family moved to Texas USA where she lived for 13 years. They returned to Scotland in 2011 and now live at Troves. Since then Dawn has spent time commuting to Aberdeen where her husband works. He is now retired and Dawn is enjoying getting the chance to have a slower pace of life.

Alan Logan

When Alan left EHS he joined the RAF as a weapons technician, serving for 25 years. He has travelled far and wide with the RAF including USA, Germany, Italy, Kuwait and Afghanistan.

Currently living in Lincolnshire, Alan works for BAE Systems as a maintenance support engineer. He is married to Alison and has three children, Kristie, Garvie and Katie. Outwith work Alan's interests are mostly sport focused, with golf, cycling and football being the main ones. At the time of writing Alan is in training for a Triathlon in June.

Alan Logan, Rodney Badenoch, Neil Shiach, Gregor Milne

Michael MacRae

After leaving EHS, Mike studied at Dundee Institute of technology (now Abertay University) graduating with a BSc Mechanical Engineering. He then moved to Glasgow to undertake a graduate management programme with a timber and building supplier. Mike has continued to work in the construction industry, currently with Harrison Cement, covering Scotland and the Northeast of England. Mike has been married to Vicky for 5 years, having two sons, Daniel and Sean from a previous marriage, and a stepson, Thomas. Completing the MacRae clan are Mike's German Shepherd, Koda and a cat called Kitty.

Angela (Watt) Matchett

Since leaving, Angela has had many jobs including retail manager, waitress, banking adviser and the owner and landlady of a pub/restaurant, to name a few. She is currently working part-time in a call centre and also makes and sells arts and craft items at Quirky Coop. Angela is an aspiring writer of poetry and children's books – two of her poems have been published in anthologies. Angela has lived in Inverurie since marrying Martin in 1988. They have three children, Darren, Liam and Lauren and two granddaughters, Bobbi and Rosie. Angela also has three dogs, one cat, one kakariki, some fish and a tortoise called Fred who is nearly 50! Angela's main claim to fame is staring in TV's Come Dine With Me.

Neil McDonald

After he left, Neil studied Electronic Engineering at the Robert Gordon's Institute of Technology. He then moved to Ipswich to work for BT research labs. After leaving BT Neil had several roles including working at a dot com company and volunteering at a refugee camp in Africa. Neil rejoined BT and is now in a senior technical role, designing security systems. Neil still lives in Ipswich with his partner Katie and son Hayden.

Angus McKinnon

When Angus left he studied History and Politics at Manchester University. He was inspired in his studies by Mr Jim Hamilton, his history teacher and the Modern Studies department. Angus is currently living in Rome reporting for news agency AFP where he has worked since 1990. Angus's career has allowed him to work in London, Paris, Brussels and Hong Kong. He says that everyday he still uses the touch-typing skills he learned in secretarial studies at EHS! Angus lives with Tissy, with whom he has two sons aged five and three, he also has a nineteen year old son. Outwith work Angus still plays football and is planning to resume golf, move to Islay and hopefully work on his beer belly!

Carole (Lawton) Miller

Since leaving in 1983 Carole has lived all over, spending a lot of time travelling abroad to some "far flung places" with her husband Colin on his merchant ships. Carole currently lives on the Isle of Lewis and is working as a supply primary teacher but she also still teaches and performs music,

Paula Aldin-Scott, Stuart Chambers, Shirlene Halbert, Yvonne (Mitchell) Tyson and Shirley (Moir) McWilliam

which was a big part of her time at EHS. She is involved in Big Band, classical and Gaelic choirs. Playing the harp has taken over Carole's life and there is a term in the Miller household, BC which means "before Clarsach (harp)". Carole is currently learning to speak Gaelic.

Julie (Campbell) Moxham

Julie *loved* EHS, and on leaving, her first job was as a junior cashier in the Nationwide Building Society. She worked her way up to branch manager before leaving in 2006 to embark on a new career as a complementary therapist. Currently Julie runs a private clinic and also offers treatments at The Oaks Palliative Care Day Centre. Julie is married to Paul and has three children, Hayley (25), Sam (22) and her "late cherub" Harris (10). Loving life and being active are important to Julie and she takes part in yoga, running, scuba-diving and snow-boarding.

Neil Munro

Neil left EHS when he was 16 and started studying Mechanical Engineering at college. He left before he completed the course and then tried several different jobs. These included farm work, forestry, working for an undertaker, HGV driver and at an outdoor centre before a leg break stopped him skiing. Neil spent time offshore until recently, when he moved to Veolia Water where he currently works. When he was 18, Neil married Debbie and they have two daughters, one son and now, two grandsons. They have recently moved to Cummingston, this was prompted by the sea related hobbies he enjoys. Neil says that he has had many adventures both home and abroad but now it is time to settle down and chill for a while.

Helen (Morrison) Ralston

After leaving EHS, Helen studied at Aberdeen College of Commerce for 2 years to complete an HND in Medical Secretarial Studies. Living in Aberdeen, Helen has worked for 30 years at Aberdeen Royal Infirmary. She has two children, a 19 year old daughter and a 16 year old son. Most of Helen's spare time is spent walking her two dogs, a Scottie cross Border Collie and a rescue Newfoundland cross Labrador.

Lynne (Baxter) Riddoch

For the last 21 years Lynne has worked in the housing sector, currently as an operations manager for a housing association in Norwich. Lynne has two children, Rebecca and Alex and moved to London when Rebecca, now 29, was 1 year old. 13 years ago Lynne moved to Wymondham in Norfolk where she currently lives.

Julie (Turnidge) Robertson

Julie studied Business Studies at Moray College after leaving. This led to various administration jobs including being an area supervisor within the revenues department at Moray Council,

Julie (Campbell) Moxham. And Angela (Watt) Matchett, Janice (McKillop) Hyndman

working in a GP's surgery and now at Dr Gray's Hospital. Julie still lives in Elgin with her partner of 20 years, Philip. They surprised everyone on New Years Eve 2017 by turning up with a registrar at the family BBQ and got married! Julie has two sons, Grant (28) who has his own plumbing business in Elgin and is getting married next year. Ross (26), her younger son, works for Edinburgh City Council and is getting married in 2020. According to Julie, EHS had excellent facilities, she enjoyed getting the chance to do technical and the staff were brilliant. Playing in the school hockey team was something Julie loved. She feels it was great knowing nearly everyone at EHS and she is still in touch with friends she made there.

Neil Shiach

Neil left Elgin in 1985 to join the RAF as an avionics technician. After moving to Norwich, he met and married his wife, Alison on 8/8/88 – a lucky day! Neil then moved to Germany, then back to Norwich, having two daughters along the way – Jessica and Emily. Neil has worked all over the world – 25 countries at the last count! - though usually for short periods and he says that the best part is coming home to his family. His daughters are horse mad, but this is not inherited from their Dad whose experience of horses is being terrified of Heather Gerard's one at the Doocot Park! Neil is still in the RAF as a warrant officer. He loves cycling and walking his dogs on the beach. Neil hopes to retire soon and is planning to spend four years cycling around the world.

Heather (Gerard) Sloan

Heather has fond memories of EHS – school discos, performances and shows, and her pals, though she does admit to "sloping off from school to feed my horse"! When she left school, Heather worked at Arnotts, then moved along the High Street to Templetons. Heather met her husband Ian in 1985 and moved to Germany, in 1989 they moved back to Lossiemouth. Heather then worked in Wm Lows and Tesco till she moved to Saudi in 2004. In Saudi Heather works in schools and spends a lot of time baking and making pies for the compound shop. An especially popular lady on the days she brings a taste of home in the form of butteries.

Nigel Squair

Nigel has been working at Tesco in Elgin for the last 15 years as a manager who has, he says, mastered the art of pancake making. Still living in New Elgin, Nigel married his wife Yvonne in 1991. He has two children, Callum (12) who is one of the new EHS S1s and Lizzie (10). For someone who hated cross country at school, Nigel has run several marathons including an Ultra which is 36.5 miles long. As part of his marathon running Nigel raises money for charity.

Wendy (McGillivray) Toner

Wendy has never strayed far from Elgin and is currently back living in her cosy cottage in New Elgin...for good she says! Wendy has been married to Tommy for over 30 years and has two children, Stacey (29) – also an EHS girl, and Stuart (24). For over 30 years Wendy has been working for community learning and development at Moray Council as a senior youth worker attached to EHS and Elgin Academy. She says she is "way too busy" for interests but when she does get the chance she loves travel, walking with friends in Scotland, politics, socialising and gardening. Wendy still catches up every month with her EHS friends group, she says there is "nothing like old friends"!

Yvonne (Mitchell) Tyson

Yvonne has continued to live in Elgin since leaving EHS. She went on to have two children, Jodie and Scott and is a very proud Granny Von to Ellie, age 8. The pair of them have great fun on their adventures. She loves cats and dogs, having three dogs, Isla, Emmie and Carly. Yvonne currently works for Turning Point Scotland supporting adults with learning difficulties and mental health problems. Prior to that Yvonne worked in Asda as part of the nightshift team. Yvonne enjoys travelling round the world.

October 2017: A last look around the old place before demolition in the company of life-long friends.

Gary Watt

Gary went to college to study Building Construction and worked as a site engineer for ten years. Gary decided on a change and after trying a few ideas started working in the guitar department in Sound and Vision. Music is a big part of Gary's life, he is now a private guitar teacher and he also writes and records his own music. Gary attends lots of gigs and once shook the hand of the late, great BB King. Gary has a 5 year old son, Joseph and being a Dad is now his priority. Gary is a Christian and a big supporter of Mental Health charities – he is currently recording a charity CD. Gary also loves cars and once owned a 1968 Ford Mustang.

John Williamson

John spent only a short time at EHS before moving to Elgin Academy. He does remember Mr Hope though and the school feeling warm and friendly when we all started together on the first day. Studying History, Politics and English at Dundee University followed, but John didn't enjoy the course and left after a year – he still enjoys politics though. John moved back to Yorkshire with his family in 1986 and it took him nearer his beloved Leeds United. After 28 years in the Civil Service, John left to do a job he loved, working with refugees, asylum seekers and migrants. John has two children, Rachel and Ewan. He still visits family in Elgin regularly and watches Elgin City when he can.

Kate (Teenie Cottam) Yeo

After leaving Kate studied for 4 years at Stirling University before moving to London to work. Kate says that she "drifted" into traffic engineering and road safety by accident – but she loves it. Kate currently works for Jacobs (US Engineering firm) in their operational road safety team. Kate was sadly widowed but has a fiancée, a grown-up stepdaughter and a delinquent cat! Kate loves photography, travel and climbing big hills. Kate has climbed some very big hills in Nepal and had all sorts of interesting adventures around the world. These include being held at gunpoint in the Rift Valley for her passport and crashing her jeep and having to spend time in a Tanzanian village until it was dug out.

In Memory

Sadly, as with most year groups that have helped make up the history of EHS, there are some of our classmates that are no longer with us. We have permission from the families to include two of our original S1's classmates. Unfortunately, there are others we have been unable to contact but they will all always be part of our school memories.

Paula Aldin-Scott – provided by brother and sister, Gordon and Beverly

After Paula left EHS she went on to study an HND Business Administration followed by an honours degree in Social and Management Science at Napier University. In 2000 Paula completed a post-graduate diploma in Information Systems, also at Napier. Paula had a range of jobs including customer service manager for Eurocontrol in Brussels and a communication and strategy role for the Edinburgh Youth Social Inclusion Partnership supporting young people, a role Paula relished. With a desire to help people, she worked for organisations supporting people with neurological conditions. During her own battle with cancer Paula spent a lot of time working and campaigning tirelessly in lots of ways, trying to make living with cancer better for others. Paula touched and made a difference to numerous lives before she sadly passed away in October 2017.

Mark Sweeney – provided by Mark's brother Paul

Mark enjoyed his time at EHS and was particularly keen on technical subjects. When he left school, Mark went to Moray College before joining Robertson's as an apprentice engineer. He lived in Ellon for a few years before relocating to London where he became a site surveyor working all over Greater London and the Home Counties. Mark was a keen fisherman and loved motorcycles. Mark sadly passed away after a motorcycle accident. He is survived by his daughter Jordan who has followed in her Dad's footsteps into engineering.

Under 15 hockey players and friends reunited.

Back (l-r) : Angela (Watt) Matchett, Wendy (McGillivray) Toner, Shirlene (Abbott) Halbert, Janice (McKillop) Hyndman, Dawn (Easterling) Phillips, Alison (Farquhar) Semmeling.
Front : Janice McLean, Wendy (Eddie) King, Julie (Turnidge) Robertson, Julie (Campbell) Moxham, Elaine (Hutchison) Ford.
(There is no exact equivalent picture from 1978 but the one below includes some of the same players in our first First Year Team)

Alison Farquhar
from the first
Second Year team

Photos: Nick
Ledingham—see
Champion Teams in
Part One.

First Year Team: Shirlene Abbott (Captain), Aileen McIntosh, Wendy MacGillivray
Kim Spence, Sharon Duroe, Dawn Cooper, Janne Commons.
Front: Brenda Tyson, Julie Turnidge, Elaine Hutcheson, Wendy Murray, Angela Tyson.

Inter House Swimming Galas

Records of Champion Swimmers

Sixteen Swimming Galas were held between 1981 and 1999, at which point because swimming was no longer on the P.E. syllabus, it became increasingly difficult for House reps to raise complete teams for all events. (See PP 132)

The events were first held in the Munro Baths (roughly where the Aldi store now stands) and then in Moray Leisure Centre, which opened in 1993.

In some instances there are two, or three joint champions

Abbreviations

n/a - Not applicable Pupils were not yet old enough to compete in these categories

E—Eagles, F—Falcons, K—Kestrels, O—Ospreys

E—champion house 4 times

F—champion house 4 times

O—champion house 8 times

Year	Junior Boy	Junior Girl	Intermediate Boy	Intermediate Girl
1980-81	Lee Mitchell	Janette Brown Sara Edwards	Brian Ross	Michelle Scott
1981-82	A.Macleod F	Maxine Brechin O	Andrew Elliot O	Emma Campbell O
1982-83	Martin Keil	Michelle McKay	-	Maxine Brechin
		No Galas - staff respect ban on extra-curricular activities		
1987-88	Scott Baillie F	Anne Simmers E	Gavin Dunbar E Donald George F	Catherine Miller K
1988-89	David Sutherland O	Emma Grant E	Gavin Dunbar E	Nicola Gravener E Diane Burgess F
1989-90	Darren Phillips O	Isla Dunbar E	David Sutherland O Paul Menzies E	Jacqu. Phillips O Katie Griffith O Michelle Anderson O
1990-91	Andrew Cobban O Stephen Brands O Barry MacColl E	Susan Sangster F	David Small E Darren Phillips O	Isla Dunbar E
1991-92	Iain Small E	Shona Fraser E	Darren Phillips O	Isla Dunbar E
1992-93	Ross Sangster F	Susan Rodwell K	Keith McKay E	Susan Sangster F
1993-94	Alan Byiers K	Lynsey Buchan F	Ross Sangster F	Paula Main O
1994-95	James Beattie K	Erin Ross O	Ross Sangster F	Louise Reid O Lynsey Buchan F
1995-96	Paul McPhail	Leona Mortimer F Sarah Scott O	Raymond Lyle K	Kirsty Johnstone K
1996-97	Barry Miller K	Rachel King E	David Penny O	Andrea Robertson E Laura Stephen E Leona Mortimer F
1997-98	Andrew Flynn O Gordon Mortimer F	Jacqu. Anderson O	Barry Miller F	Leona Mortimer F
1998-99	Douglas Cameron F	Claire Cameron F	Barry Miller F	Nicky Cramb O
1999-00	Jamie Fraser O Gordon Riddoch F	Sarah James E	Marc Morrison E	Claire Cameron F
2000		*"Gala no more" explanations given*		

Year	Senior Boy	Senior Girl		Details
			Winning House	
1980-81	n/a	n/a	F	PP 18
1981-82	Neil Shiach F	Karen Hawkins K	F	PP 36
1982-83	rawford Robetson	Karen Hawkins K	O	PP 44
1987-88	Tom Griffith O	Laura Robertson O	F	PP 67
		Gillian Collie F		
1988-89	Martin Graham F	Wendy MacRae E	O	PP 71
	Paul Sutherland O			
1989-90	Tom Griffith O	Catherine Miller K	O	PP 77
1990-91	Gavin Dunbar E	Katie Griffith O	O	PP 83
1991-92	Paul Menzies E	Katie Griffith O	E	PP 91
	Paul Fraser F			
1992-93	Darren Phillips O	Katie Griffith O	E	PP 95
1993-94	Darren Phillips O	Isla Dunbar E	O	PP 97
1994-95	Darren Phillips O	Isla Dunbar E	O	PP 102
				PP 103
1995-96	Iain Small E	Lynsey McQuaker F	O	PP 108
1996-97	Iain Small E	Lynsey Buchan F	E	PP 112
1997-98	Ross Sangster F	Lucy Hyland E	F	PP 118
				PP 117
1998-99	Jimmy Beattie E	Lucy Hyland E	E	PP 122
	David Penny O			
	Paul Fyvie E			
1999-00	Barry Miller F	Erin Ross O	O	PP 127
		Leona Mortimer F		

Senior Champion in the late 1980's and later Scottish International Swimmer

Tom Griffith presented the Prizes at our last ever Gala

See PP 127

for details

69

ELGIN HIGH SCHOOL - SWIMMING RECORDS

1.	Junior	Boys	Breast Stroke	'B' Final	David Sutherland	18.0 Secs	1988/89
2.	Junior	Girls	Breast Stroke	'B' Final	Helen Logan	20.5 Secs	1987/88
3.	Inter	Boys	Breast Stroke	'B' Final	Graham Green	20.6 Secs	1987/88
4.	Inter	Girls	Breast Stroke	'B' Final	Helen Logan	18.4 Secs	1988/89
5.	Senior	Boys	Breast Stroke	'B' Final	Donald George	15.1 Secs	1988/89
6.	Senior	Girls	Breast Stroke	'B' Final	Erica Wyllie	18.8 Secs	1988/89
7.	Junior	Boys	Back Stroke	'B' Final	Roddy Sutherland	18.6 Secs	1987/88
8.	Junior	Girls	Back Stroke	'B' Final	Marny Boaler	18.9 Secs	1987/88
9.	Inter	Boys	Back Stroke	'B' Final	Murray Calder	18.1 Secs	1982/83
10.	Inter	Girls	Back Stroke	'B' Final	Nicola Gravener	18.4 Secs	1988/89
11.	Senior	Boys	Back Stroke	'B' Final	Alan Logan	14.7 Secs	1982/83
12.	Senior	Girls	Back Stroke	'B' Final	Emma Campbell	17.5 Secs	1982/83
13.	Junior	Boys	Freestyle	'B' Final	Sean Robertson	17.0 Secs	1981/82
14.	Junior	Girls	Freestyle	'B' Final	Alexia Scott	17.3 Secs	1981/82
15.	Inter	Boys	Freestyle	'B' Final	Colin Gordon	14.8 Secs	1981/82
16.	Inter	Girls	Freestyle	'B' Final	Catherine Miller	13.6 Secs	1987/88
17.	Senior	Boys	Freestyle	'B' Final	Martin Graham	13.2 Secs	1988/89
18.	Senior	Girls	Freestyle	'B' Final	Diane Burgess	16.0 Secs	1987/88
19.	Junior	Boys	Breast Stroke	'A' Final	Paul Menzies	39.0 Secs	1988/89
20.	Junior	Girls	Breast Stroke	'A' Final	Michelle Anderson	42.4 Secs	1987/88
21.	Inter	Boys	Breast Stroke	'A' Final	Gavin Dunbar	33.8 Secs	1988/89
22.	Inter	Girls	Breast Stroke	'A' Final	Michelle Anderson	40.6 Secs	1988/89
23.	Senior	Boys	Breast Stroke	'A' Final	Crawford Robertson	33.8 Secs	1982/83
24.	Senior	Girls	Breast Stroke	'A' Final	Karen Hawkins	45.7 Secs	1982/83
25.	Junior	Boys	Back Stroke	'A' Final	Martin Keil	40.7 Secs	1982/83
26.	Junior	Girls	Back Stroke	'A' Final	Katie Griffith	33.0 Secs	1987/88
27.	Inter	Boys	Back Stroke	'A' Final	David Fraser	40.7 Secs	1981/82
28.	Inter	Girls	Back Stroke	'A' Final	Jacqueline Phillips	37.6 Secs	1988/89
29.	Senior	Boys	Back Stroke	'A' Final	Tom Griffith	23.0 Secs	1987/88
30.	Senior	Girls	Back Stroke	'A' Final	Wendy MacRae	38.1 Secs	1988/89
31.	Junior	Boys	Freestyle	'A' Final	Martin Keil	31.8 Secs	1982/83
32.	Junior	Girls	Freestyle	'A' Final	Jacqueline Phillips	31.5 Secs	1987/88
33.	Inter	Boys	Freestyle	'A' Final	Gavin Dunbar	27.1 Secs	1988/89
34.	Inter	Girls	Freestyle	'A' Final	Katie Griffith	26.3 Secs	1988/89
35.	Senior	Boys	Freestyle	'A' Final	Tom Griffith	22.9 Secs	1988/89
36.	Senior	Girls	Freestyle	'A' Final	Wendy MacRae	31.3 Secs	1987/88
37.	Junior	Boys	Freestyle	Relay	Falcons	71.9 Secs	1988/89
38.	Junior	Girls	Freestyle	Relay	Ospreys	57.9 Secs	1987/88
39.	Inter	Boys	Freestyle	Relay	Ospreys	63.7 Secs	1982/83
40.	Inter	Girls	Freestyle	Relay	Ospreys	56.4 Secs	1988/89
41.	Senior	Boys	Freestyle	Relay	Falcons	51.8 Secs	1982/83
42.	Senior	Girls	Freestyle	Relay	Eagles	71.0 Secs	1987/88
43.	Open	Boys	Medlay	Relay	Ospreys	62.0 Secs	1988/89
44.	Open	Girls	Medlay	Relay	Ospreys	64.5 Secs	1988/89

From PP71 (December 1988)

Inter House Athletics / Sports Day

Records of Champion Athletes

Twenty Six Sports Days were held between 1979 and 2009.

Where more than one pupil is mentioned as champion, they tied on points and were joint champions

Where data are missing or names of the same pupil spelled differently that is how it was recorded in *Pigeon Post.*

Abbreviations

n/a - Not applicable Pupils were not yet old enough to compete in these categories

E—Eagles, F—Falcons, K—Kestrels, O—Ospreys

E—champion house   18 times

F—champion house   3 times

O—champion house   3 times

K—champion house   2 times

Year	Junior Boy	Junior Girl	Intermediate Boy	Intermediate Girl
1979	Ian McDonald E	Sharon Duroe E	Roy Young E	Lynne Beaton F
1980	Neil Proven K	Jill Ellwand F Karen McLennan F	Roy Young E *No Sports Day*	Patricia Ogilvie E *(industrial action)*
1981	Robert Clark O	Rosemary Scott K	Neil Proven K	Sharon Duroe E
1982	Martin Kemp K	K McEwan K	Iain Still O	Rosemary Scott K
1983	Martin Keil E	Gillian Collie F	Gordon Spence K	Janet Stewart
1984	Martin Smith O	Alison Elder F	Stuart Thomson O	Megan Palmer K
1985 1986 1987			*No Sports Day* *No Sports Day* *No Sports Day*	*(industrial action)* *(industrial action)* *(industrial action)*
1988	Neil Whyte O	Gillian Horne K	Steven Wright O	Julie Allan O
1989	Paul Menzies E	Tereza Jefferies E	Gary Burton E	Nichola Grant O
1990	Sean Welch O	Melanie Roddie F	Michael Duncan F	Sarah-Jane Garrow E
1991	Jeffrey Ho F	Fiona Farquhar E	Christopher Wilson K	Sarah-Jane Garrow E
1992	Mark Witkowski K	Suzanne Shanks O	Jeffrey Ho F	Margaret Newlands K
1993	Ian Dobie K	Paula Bonnyman O	Jeffrey Ho F	Lynette Farquhar E
1994	Ryan Witkowski K	Nicola Carleton O	Mark Witkowski K	Stacey Davies O
1995	Johnathan Smith E	Lindsay Ann Collie K	James Butterly E	Fiona Russell F
1996	Scott Witkowski K	Kelly Halbert	Karl Fyvie K	Nicola Carleton O
1997	Gary Barnett F Matthew Davies	Louise Thomson E	Jonathan Smith E	Erin Ross O
1998	Richard Foster F	Jacqueline Anderson O	Scott Witkowski E	Louise Thomson E
1999	Gary Sim O	Laura Chalmers O	Richard Foster F	Rachel King E
2000	Alex Keddie	Jodie Ritchie	Richard Foster F	Laura Chalmers O
2001	Grant Daglish E	Louise Mair F	Bob Bremner O	Laura Chalmers O

2002 *No sports days events as field was having new drainage laid : see page 13, 14 of....PP139*

Year	Senior Boy	Senior Girl	Winning House	Prize Presenter	Details
1979	n/a	n/a	E	Bill Hope	PP 10
1980	n/a *heats results stood*	n/a	E		PP 19
1981	Roy Young E	Patricia Ogilvie E	E		PP 28
1982	Neil Proven K	Carol Johnston F Susan Sutherland K	K		PP 37
1983	Neil Proven K	Sara Edwards O	O		PP 43
1984	Neil Proven K	Lorna Tait O	E		PP 55
1985					PP 59
1986					
1987					PP 60
1988	Kevin Hay E	Lara McDougall K	K		PP 68
1989	Lee Bryson JK	Nicola Gravener E Lynne Grant K	E		PP 74
1990	Steven Duke E	Lynne Grant K	E		PP 80
1991	David Leil E	Nichola Grant O	E		PP 86
1992	Neil Whyte O	Nichola Grant O	E		PP 91 PP 92
1993	Paul Adkins E	Nichola Grant O	E	Bill Hope	PP 95
1994	Jeffrey Ho F	Lynette Farquhar E	O		PP 100 PP 101
1995	Mark Witkowski K	Emma Heron E	E		PP 106
1996	Mark Witkowski K	Fiona Russell F	E	Stuart Anderson	PP 110
1997	Stewart Robertson E	Leigh-Anne Duncan O	E	Angela McCalman	PP 115 PP 116
1998	Paul Fyvie E	Lucy Hyland	E		PP 120
1999	Scott Witkowski E	Jackie Allan O	O	Rev Charles MacMillan	PP 125
2000	Scot Watson	Rachel King E	E	Debbie McDonald	PP 130 PP 131
2001	Richard Foster F	Rachel King E	F	Pat McLennan	PP 136

Year	Junior Boy	Junior Girl	Intermediate Boy	Intermediate Girl
2003	Ryan Daglish E	Jade Longhurst	Grant Daglish E	Louise Mair F
2004	Lee Millar E	Victoria McIntosh F	Alan Turner F	Aime-Jane Byiers E Sarah Stronach F
2005	Dylan Richards	Melissa Longhurst	Lee Millar E	Victoria McIntosh E
2006	Andrew Thomson O	Claire Cameron O Michelle Munro E	Jamie Corbett E	Agnes Neal F
2007	Scott Greig O	Gemma Russell F	Fraser Forbes E	Michelle Munro E
2008	*No sports days events as staff and pupils involved in "We Will Rock You"*			
2009	Robert Campbell	Ellice McCart	Scott Greig O	Tamara Donald

Ex PP 160 re June 2006

A Small Selection of Champions
in traditional post-award pose

Ex PP 150 June 2004

Ex PP 171

18th June 2008

Sports Champions from the early 1980's Mr Roy Young and Mr Neil Proven handed over the trophies to Junior Girl and Boy winners, Ellice McCart and Robert Campbell, Intermediate Champions Tamara Donald and Scott Greig and Senior Champions Lauren Eadie and Fraser Forbes

Year	Senior Boy	Senior Girl	Winning House	Prize Presenter	Details
2003	Stewart Milton	Laura Chalmers O	E	Bill Hope	PP 145
					PP 146
2004	Gordon Riddoch F	Louise Mair F	F	Richard Foster	PP150
				Joyce Marriott	
2005	Ryan Daglish E	Terri Duncan	E	Fraser Bremner	PP 155
2006	Lee Millar E	Victoria McIntosh F	F	Brian Irvine	PP 160
2007	Keiran Stephens O	Agnes Neal F	E	Laura Chalmers	PP 165
2008					PP 170
2009	Fraser Forbes E	Lauren Eadie		Neil Proven	PP 171
				Roy Young	

Athletics Champions—Coming Full Circle

Champions in their own right in the late 70's, Neil Proven (top left)   and Roy Young
presented the prizes in 2009 (PP 171). Laura Chalmers, Champion in her various sections
1999-2003, presented the prizes in 2007. (PP 165)

School Athletics Records at June 1997 (From PP 115)

#	Group	Sex	Event		Name	Result	Date
1	Junior	Boys	Long Jump		Jeffrey Ho	4.95m	13.06.91
2	Inter	Girls	Long Jump		Anne Murray	4.54m	09.06.83
3	Senior	Boys	Long Jump		Roy Young	5.88m	11.06.81
4	Junior	Girls	Long Jump		Anne Murray	4.18m	21.05.81
5	Inter	Boys	High Jump		Douglas Reid	1.63m	08.06.95
6	Junior	Girls	High Jump		Nicola Sundalskliev	1.30m	21.05.81
7	Senior	Boys	High Jump	Gordon Spence	Neil Proven	1.70m	30.05.84
8	Senior	Girls	High Jump		Patricia Ogilvie	1.43m	20.05.81
9	Junior	Boys	Shot		Gordon Anderson	11.66m	15.06.95
10	Inter	Girls	Shot		Nicola Carleton	9.22m	19.06.96
11	Inter	Boys	Shot		Gordon Anderson	12.61m	06.06.97
12	Senior	Girls	Shot		Nicola Carleton	8.21m	10.06.97
13	Junior	Boys	Discus		Martyn Shepherd	27.84m	13.06.91
14	Junior	Girls	Discus		Emma Murdoch	19.24m	04.06.97
15	Inter	Boys	Discus		Roy Young	33.66m	23.05.80
16	Inter	Girls	Discus		Nicola Carleton	19.87m	19.06.96
17	Senior	Boys	Discus		Bruce Shepherd	40.90m	19.06.84
18	Senior	Girls	Discus		Diane Craib	22.96m	20.05.81
19	Junior	Boys	Javelin		Martin Keil	25.18m	01.06.83
20	Junior	Girls	Javelin		Louise Thomson	22.60m	04.06.97
21	Inter	Boys	Javelin		Garry Burton	32.62m	09.06.88
22	Inter	Girls	Javelin		Susan Sutherland	24.93m	25.06.81
23	Senior	Boys	Javelin		Neil Shiach	35.15m	09.06.83
24	Senior	Girls	Javelin		Lorna Tait	24.80m	??.06.84
25	Junior	Boys	Triple Jump		Alan Melrose	8.80m	30.05.84
26	Inter	Boys	Triple Jump		J Gordon Thomson	10.69m	07.06.89
27	Senior	Boys	Triple Jump		Neil Proven	11.70m	07.06.83
28	Junior	Boys	400m		Martin Smith	64.4secs	20.06.84
29	Junior	Girls	400m		Gillian Collie	70.2secs	22.06.83
30	Inter	Boys	400m		Michael Johnstone	59.6secs	23.06.80
31	Inter	Girls	400m		Julie Allan	66.8secs	07.06.88
32	Senior	Boys	400m		Neil Proven	57.4secs	22.06.83
33	Senior	Girls	400m		Janet Stewart	67.8secs	20.06.84
34	Junior	Boys	High Jump		Fraser King	1.44m	19.06.84
35	Senior	Girls	Long Jump		Marny Boaler	4.63m	15.06.90
36	Senior	Boys	Shot		Bruce Shepherd	13.70m	20.06.84
38	Junior	Girls	100m		Karen McEwan	13.3secs	10.06.82
39	Junior	Boys	100m		David Sutherland	13.1secs	16.06.89
40	Inter	Girls	100m		Nyree Boyle	13.6secs	20.06.84
41	Inter	Boys	100m		Ian Still	12.2secs	10.06.82
42	Senior	Girls	100m		Stewart	13.7secs	20.06.84
43	Senior	Boys	100m		Roy Young	11.5secs	03.06.81
44	Junior	Girls	800m		Megan Palmer	2min43.6	02.06.82
45	Junior	Boys	800m		Neil Proven	2min37.3	23.05.80
46	Inter	Girls	800m		Gillian Collie	2min39.9	02.06.84
47	Inter	Boys	800m		Neil Proven	2min19.3	25.06.81
48	Senior	Girls	800m		Nichola Grant	2min47.4	15.06.90
49	Senior	Boys	800m		Neil Proven	2min08.6	02.06.84
50	Junior	Girls	Shot		Samantha Turner	7.89m	16.06.89
51	Inter	Boys	Long Jump		Jeffrey Ho	5.68m	10.06.92
52	Senior	Girls	High Jump		Patricia Ogilvie	1.41m	23.05.80
54	Junior	Boys	200m		David Leil	29.5secs	22.06.88
55	Junior	Girls	200m		Julie Webster	30.3secs	19.06.89
56	Inter	Boys	200m		Ian Still	25.8secs	02.06.82
57	Inter	Girls	200m		Janet Stewart	29.4secs	09.06.83
58	Senior	Boys	200m		Stuart McPherson	25.5secs	19.06.89
59	Senior	Girls	200m		Lynne Grant	29.3secs	19.06.89
60	Junior	Boys	1500m		Kenneth Black	5min38.2	18.06.97
	Inter	Boys	1500m		Paul Stewart	4min57.4	20.06.89
61	Junior	Girls	1500m		Megan Palmer	5min50.0	02.06.82
	Inter	Girls	1500m		Megan Palmer	5min09.7	??.06.84
	Senior	Girls	1500m		Nichola Grant	5min45.1	15.06.90
62	Senior	Boys	1500m		Steven Davies	4min35.4	25.06.81
63	Junior	Girls	4x100m		Kestrels	60.4secs	22.06.83
64	Junior	Boys	4x100m		Ospreys	60.1secs	15.06.88
65	Inter	Girls	4x100m		Ospreys	58.5secs	22.06.83
66	Inter	Boys	4x100m		Falcons	54.5secs	03.06.81
67	Senior	Girls	4x100m		Falcons	60.2secs	22.06.83
68	Senior	Boys	4x100m		Kestrels	52.9secs	22.06.83

School Athletics Records Standing at November 2017 provided by Head of PE Mrs Debbie McDonald

S2 Boys

Event	Name	Record	Date
100m	David Sutherland	13.1secs	16.06.89
1500m	Richard Foster	5m00.9	17.06.98
200m	Ryan Daglish	28.43secs	21.06.03
400m	Grant Daglish	59.0secs	20.06.01
4x100m	Eagles	54.91secs	20.06.01
800m	Keiron Cameron	2.21.0	20.06.01
Discus	Martyn Shepherd	27.84m	13.06.91
High Jump	Fraser King	1.44m	19.06.84
Javelin	Keiron Cameron	25.38m	20.06.01
Long Jump	Jeffrey Ho	4.95m	13.06.91
Shot	Alan Ovens	11.92m	02.06.98
Triple Jump	Richard Foster	9.30m	02.06.98

S2 Girls

Event	Name	Record	Date
Long Jump	Anne Murray	4.18m	21.05.81
100m	Karen McEwan	13.3secs	10.06.82
1500m	Stephanie Reynolds	5min33.2	09.06.99
200m	Jacqueline Anderson	30.2secs	17.06.98
400m	Louise Mair	64.22secs	20.06.01
4x100m	Ospreys	58.98secs	20.06.01
800m	Megan Palmer	2min43.6	02.06.82
Discus	Laura Chalmers	23.72m	09.06.99
High Jump	Laura Chalmers	1.34m	07.06.99
Javelin	Louise Thomson	22.60m	04.06.97
Shot	Samantha Turner	7.89m	16.06.89

S3 Boys

Event	Name	Record	Date
400m	Richard Foster	54.57secs	21.06.00
4x100m	Ospreys	50.90secs	20.06.01
800m	Richard Foster	2min18.9	21.06.00
Discus	Roy Young	33.66m	23.05.80
High Jump	Richard Foster	1.64m	21.06.00
Javelin	Lee Millar	36.27m	08.06.06
Long Jump	Jeffrey Ho	5.68m	10.06.92
Shot	Gordon Anderson	12.61m	06.06.97
Triple Jump	J Gordon Thomson	10.69m	07.06.89

S3 Girls

Event	Name	Record	Date
100m	Steph Reynolds	13.11secs	20.06.01
1500m	Megan Palmer	5min09.7	20.06.84
200m	Steph Reynolds	28.45 secs	20.06.01
400m	Steph Reynolds	55.06secs	20.06.01
4x100m	Ospreys	56.83secs	20.06.01
800m	Steph Reynolds	2min 15	20.06.01
Discus	Laura Chalmers	32.94m	20.06.01
High Jump	Patricia Ogilvie	1.41m	23.05.80
Javelin	Louise Thomson	25.09m	03.06.98
Long Jump	Laura Chalmers	4.60m	20.06.01
Shot	Laura Chalmers	9.22m	20.06.01

S4 Boys	400m	Richard Foster	54.57secs	21.06.00
	4x100m	Ospreys	50.90secs	20.06.01
	800m	Richard Foster	2min18.9	21.06.00
	Discus	Roy Young	33.66m	23.05.80
	High Jump	Richard Foster	1.64m	21.06.00
	Javelin	Lee Millar	36.27m	08.06.06
	Long Jump	Jeffrey Ho	5.68m	10.06.92
	Shot	Gordon Anderson	12.61m	06.06.97
	Triple Jump	J Gordon Thomson	10.69m	07.06.89
S4 Girls	100m	Steph Reynolds	13.11secs	20.06.01
	1500m	Megan Palmer	5min09.7	20.06.84
	200m	Steph Reynolds	28.45 secs	20.06.01
	400m	Steph Reynolds	55.06secs	20.06.01
	4x100m	Ospreys	56.83secs	20.06.01
	800m	Steph Reynolds	2min 15	20.06.01
	Discus	Laura Chalmers	32.94m	20.06.01
	High Jump	Patricia Ogilvie	1.41m	23.05.80
	Javelin	Louise Thomson	25.09m	03.06.98
	Long Jump	Laura Chalmers	4.60m	20.06.01
	Shot	Laura Chalmers	9.22m	20.06.01
Senior Boys	100m	Roy Young	11.9secs	03.06.81
	1500m	Steven Davies	4min35.4	25.06.81
	200m	David Chirashi	24.0secs	17.06.98
	400m	Richard Foster	51.23secs	20.06.03
	4x100m	Eagles	49.2secs	17.06.98
	800m	Ryan Witkowski	2min07.0	17.06.98
	Discus	Bruce Shepherd	40.90m	19.06.84
	High Jump	Neil Proven/Gordon Spence	1.70m	30.05.84
	Javelin	Neil Shiach	35.15m	09.06.83
	Long Jump	Roy Young	5.88m	11.06.81
	Shot	Bruce Shepherd	13.70m	20.06.84
	Triple Jump	Neil Proven	11.70m	07.06.83
Senior Girls	100m	Steph Reynolds	13.07secs	21.06.03
	1500m	Nichola Grant	5min45.1	15.06.90
	200m	Steph Reynolds	27.61secs	21.06.03
	400m	Steph Reynolds	58.28secs	21.06.03
	4x100m	Eagles	57.12secs	21.06.00
	800m	Steph Reynolds	2.20.63Secs	21.06.03
	Discus	Laura Chalmers	33.00m	21.06.03
	High Jump	Laura Chalmers	1.52m	21.06.03
	Javelin	Laura Chalmers	25.49m	21.06.03
	Long Jump	Marny Boaler	4.63m	15.06.90
	Shot	Laura Chalmers	9.88m	21.06.03

Inter-House Competition

Overall Winning House

Points for Sports Days and Swimming Galas contributed towards this and were also awarded for competition in Winter Games, Quizzes, Debating, Indoor Football etc. However, all such events did not take place every year and the award rather petered out at the turn of the century as often Sports Day was the only contributing element. *Pigeon Post* records show little after that.

Session	Winners	Details
1978-9	Falcons	PP10
1979-80	Eagles	PP19
1980-81	Ospreys	PP28
1981-82	Ospreys	PP37
1982-83	Ospreys	PP46
1983-84	Eagles	PP55
(Staff Industrial Action)		
1988-89	Falcons	PP74
1989-90	Eagles	PP80
1990-91	Eagles	PP86
1991-92	Eagles	
1992-93	Eagles	
1993-94	Ospreys	
1994-95	Ospreys	PP105
1995-96	E/O shared	PP110
1996-97	Eagles	PP115
1997-98	Ospreys	PP120
1998-99	Eagles	PP125
1999-2000	Ospreys	PP130

INTER HOUSE ACTIVITIES   43

EAGLES

HOUSE CHAMPIONSHIP FINAL PLACINGS
E 559.5 F 547.5 K 462 O 469

SPORTS EVENTS POINTS
E 132 F 79 K 73 O 68

TRIUMPH!

Sports Day being cancelled through industrial action taken by teachers, the Sports Heats held on Thursday 22nd and Friday 23rd May assumed an unusual importance as Mr. Carstairs decreed that results here should be counted towards the House Championship. The Fun Sports did not take place.

The Junior Girls Championship was shared by Jill Ellwand (F) and Karen McLennan (F) both scoring 10pts. Neil Proven of Kestrels became Junior Boy Champion scoring 21pts with Bruce Shepherd (K) and Ian Still (O) sharing second place with 13pts. Intermediate Girls Champion is Patricia Ogilvie (E) with 17pts, Sharon Duroe (E) being second three points behind. Roy Young (E) outstripped the field to become Intermediate Champion with 27pts. Second was Eagle Michael Johnstone with 10pts. In the 31 events contested 24 new records were set and one equalled.

LAST YEAR'S RESULTS
House Championship E 473 F 508 K 309 O 347   Sports Day E 153 F 123 K 78 O 73
Junior Girl Champion Sharon Duroe (E) 29pts   Junior Boy Champion Ian McDonald (E) 14pts
Interm. Girl Champion Lynne Beaton (F) 16pts Interm. Boy Champion Roy Young (E) 30pts.

Prize Winners

The names of all Prize winners from the 1979—2009 Prize Giving Ceremonies can be found in the final *Pigeon Post* of each academic session, dated either June or July. To access these go to **pigeonpost.info**

However, below are listed some aspects of the Prize Giving that are not always given in those tables through lack of space.

Service to the School

These prizes, of equal value to academic ones, were given to nominees for their work for the general life of the school, for example in supporting *Pigeon Post,* school drama, music and other clubs, providing entertainments, assisting with junior pupils in departments, working as a member of the Pupil Council, raising the positive profile of the school through citizenship achievement and so on. These discretionary awards were not made routinely in absolutely every year.

1979   Sandra Chisholm, Gordon Johnston, Richard Anderson

1980   Fraser Cluness

1981   Ian Wallace

1982   Ian Wallace, Wendy Scott, Robert Linton, Karen Jamieson

1983   Brian Shortreed, Katrina Cottam, Anna Hamilton, Carole Lawton

1984   Elaine Hutcheson

1991   Andrew Cowie, Eleanor Leith

1992   Karen Collins

1993   Grant Jamieson

1994   Lee Butterly, Celia Chan

1996   Pamela Lussier, Lee Butterly, Sarah Dewfall

1997   Rory Mackay

1999   Paul Fyvie, Jacqueline Allan, Mark Smith, Louise Reid, Leigh-Ann Duncan
       Lyndsay Horne, Karen Jamieson

2000   Ross Allan, Tony Green

2001   Nikki Darling

2002   Nikki Darling, Jaclyn Fraser, Kailie Little, Andrew Flynn, Emma Murdoch,
       Lauren Campbell

2003   Bob Bremner, Nikki Darling, Louise Grant, Claire Cameron, Sean Dawson

2004   Bob Bremner, Laura Chalmers, Sean Dawson, Callum Reid, Sarah Leith, Emma
       McInnes, Lynn Gray

2005   Freya McKenzie, Alex Keddie, Gordon Thow, James Wink, Hannah King

2006   Struan Ferguson, Callum Reid, Shelley McDonald, Claire Munro, Jon
       Arbuthnott, Natalie Henderson, Melissa Paterson, Louise Taylor, Amy Coull,
       Laura Kissock, Stacey Toner, Rebecca Scott, Debbie MacDonald, Craig
       Donoghue, Ben Mortimer, Louise Mair, Sandra Pirie

2007   Caitlin Walker, Sean Booth, Sheryl Smith, Hannah Clay

2008   Christopher Haddon, Freya More, Meegan Duncan, Ellen McTavish

2009   Daisy Bruce, Katherine Clare Fischer, Louise Gray, Roseanne Macdonald,
       Victoria McIntosh, Aileen Phillips, Matthew Smith, Graeme Wells, Fraser
       Wilson, Abbie Wright.

Exceptional Service to the School: The Fraser Cluness Award

As explained by the donor of this award in the section "What Elgin High School Did
For Me" these awards were made to pupils whose efforts were outstanding….

1990	Julie Grant	2004	Claire Cameron and Laura Chalmers
1991	Wayne Chisholm	2005	Emma McIntosh
1992	The Pupil Council	2006	Sean Dawson
1993	Josephine Ho	2007	Callum Reid and Struan Ferguson
1999	The Pupil Council	2008	Shelley McDonald and Claire Munro
2000	Jacqueline Allan	2009	Aileen Phillips
2002	Rachel King		
2003	Fraser Bremner		

The Stuart Clark Memorial Award for Success in the Face of Adversity

This was first awarded in 2002 when following the death whilst at school of Stuart Clark, his parents wished to fund an award in his name for pupils who achieved despite great personal challenges.

2002   Lee Denoon

2003   James Smith

2006   Mark McDonald, Gary Ross

2007   Caitlin Walker

2008   Chloe O'Hare

2009   Natalie Fraser

And the Presenter of Tonight's Prizes is....

Always keen to be true to the values it professed from the start, Elgin High invited "local heroes" to be presenters of prizes, rather than seek out better known celebrities with no connection to the school. This meant that often the presenter was the spouse of the Guest of Honour who gave the address to prize winners and audience. Later on when we had some well known former pupils there was a change

1979 Mrs J. Cruickshanks	1993 Mrs Pat Hope
1980 Mrs June Todd	1994 Mrs Ann Lynch
1981 Mrs Bert Laurenson	1995 Mrs Mary-Lynn Schlomkowitz
1982 Mrs Margaret Lawton	1996 Mr Alan Sturrock
1983 Mrs Hilda Brown	1997 Mrs Violet Davidson
1984 Mrs Ronald Torrie	1998 Mr Mike Crossland
1988 Mrs Mary-Ann Wold	1999 Mr Gordon & Mrs Susan Shanks
1989 Mrs Christina McKenzie	2000 Mr John Aitken
1990 Mrs Lena Michie	2001 Mr Gary Robertson (fp)
1991 Mrs Lesley Botley	2002 Dr Andrew Alexander (fp)
1992 Mr Douglas Sinclair	2003 Mrs Pat Hope/Ms Nichola Grant (fp)

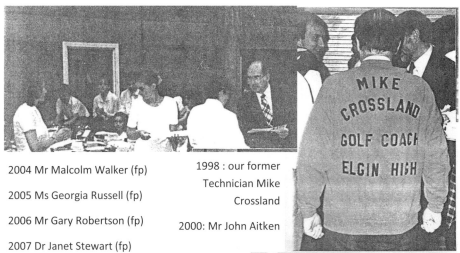

2004 Mr Malcolm Walker (fp)

2005 Ms Georgia Russell (fp)

2006 Mr Gary Robertson (fp)

2007 Dr Janet Stewart (fp)

2008 Insp Ian Wallace (fp)

2009 Mr Garry Collins (fp)

1998 : our former Technician Mike Crossland

2000: Mr John Aitken

2005 Georgia Russell awards Gordon Thow

Jackie Allan (S6)
receives the Fraser Cluness Prize
for Service to the School

2006 Gary Robertson awards as MC Mrs Anne Duncan commentates

2008 Ian Wallace does the honours

Prize Giving 1980 : S3 prize winners

here are shields, cups, certificates, and smiling faces from prize-winning pupils of the newly opened Elgin High School in this photogr taken in 1980.

Reproduced with permission from *Northern Scot* files

This photo represents about a third of the prize winners in 1980, listed on page 45 of PP 19. All the pupils here are from Third Year. When we knew the photographer was coming at short notice we had to get some pupils out of classes, hence the informality of some of the boys.

Back (l-r) Michael Johnston, David Gray, Richard Anderson, Steven Davies, Kevin Walker, Roy Young, Douglas Logan, Brian Ross, Andrew Edwards, Steven Bremner, Gordon Johnston, Colin Fraser, Fraser Cluness, Bobby Hayes, Ian Wallace.

Front: Lynne Craib, Doreen Geddes, Helen Whyte, Julia Hogg, Lorraine Donaldson, Lorna Middler, Hazel Stewart, Pamela Shand, Kim Kerr, Dawn Milne, Lynne Beaton, Lynne Kelly, Wendy Scott, Gillian Murray, Michelle Scott.

Kneeling: Patricia Ogilvie, Alison Farquhar, Mandy Leppard.

Talent Contest Winners

Year	Name	Talent	PP ref re photos etc
1993	Lee Fawbush	Magician	# 95
1994	Malcolm Walker & Pamela Lussier	Musical duo	# 99
1995	Richard Gamba	Comedian	# 104
1996	Gaz 'n' Jaz	Comedy duo	# 108
	(James Butterly & Gary Collins)		
1997	James Butterly & Heather Lawrence	Musical duo	# 114/115
1998	Hollie McBride	Singer	# 119
1999	Louise Masson	Singer	# 124
1999	Mulletville USA	Singers	# 127
2000	Hollie McBride	Singer	# 132
2001	Louise Grant	Singer	# 137
2002	Emma McIntosh & Claire Cameron	Musical Duo	# 142
2003	Debbie & Craig McDonald	Singer & Pianist	# 147
2004	Fraser MacGillivray	Singer	# 152
2005	Emma McDonald	Singer	# 157
2006	Book of Thel	Rock Band	# 162
2007	EHS Staff's "Got Talent"		# 166
2008	Sandra Iwanowicz & Ellice McCart	Comedy duo	# 169

Hollie

McBride

Twice winner

Sandra Iwanowicz
Ellice McCart

1st !

In the trio pictured left
Sandra (extreme left) and
Ellice (right) performed their
winning comedy sketch in
Part Two of the show.

School Concerts etc

Year / Month	Event	PP ref re photos etc
1978 Dec	Carol Concert	# 3 / 4
1980 Feb	Moray Music Festival competition	# 17
1981 March	Café Chantant	# 26

Miss Sheena Cowan conducting her girls choir in the 1981 Café Chantant, with Mr Peter McKay at the piano.

1983 March	Café Chantant	# 45
1984 Feb	Moray Music Festival competition	# 54
1987 Dec	Christmas Concert	# 64 / 65
1988 Feb	Moray Music Festival competition	# 67
1989 June	Summer Sounds Concert	# 74 / 75
1990 Jan	High Notes' New Year Concert	# 77
1994 Dec	High Notes' Concert	# 102
1996 Dec	Christmas Concert	# 112
1998 Dec	Christmas Concert	#123
1999 Mar	Lunchtime (for Cancer Research)	#124
2000 Mar	Moray Music Festival competition	#130

School Concerts continued

2000	Dec	Christmas Concert	# 132
2005	June	Summer Sounds	# 156
2005	Dec	High Time / ASG Concert	#157 (see below)
2006	May	Summer Concert	#160
2006	Dec	Christmas Concert	#163

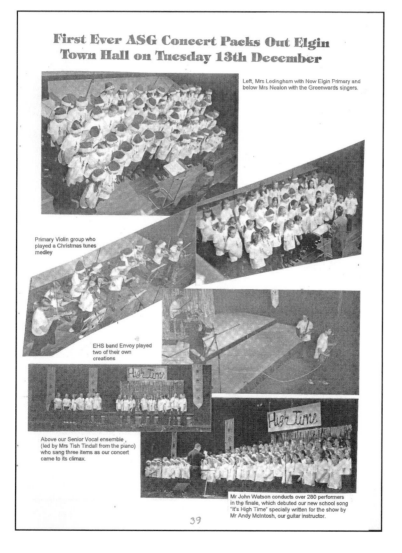

First Ever ASG Concert Packs Out Elgin Town Hall on Tuesday 13th December

Left, Mrs Ledingham with New Elgin Primary and below Mrs Nealon with the Greenwards singers.

Primary Violin group who played a Christmas tunes medley

EHS band Envoy played two of their own creations

Above our Senior Vocal ensemble , (led by Mrs Tish Tindall from the piano) who sang three items as our concert came to its climax.

Mr John Watson conducts over 280 performers in the finale, which debuted our new school song "It's High Time" specially written for the show by Mr Andy McIntosh, our guitar instructor.

39

Excursion Photos

London Theatreland 1997

Playa d'Aro, Spain 1998

Venice 1994

Trip Advisor

A synopsis of the trip reviews (with photos) included in the pages of *Pigeon Post* 1980-2008. See also chapter on Curriculum Innovation.

Destination	When	PP refs	Writer(s)
Paris	May '80	18	Mr Jackson
Leysin, Switzerland	June '81	27	Mr Campbell
Valkenburg	Easter '82	36/37	Janette Brown
London Drama	Sept '82	39	Jacqu. Melrose, Gary Robertson
Italian ski-ing	Spring '83	45	Murray Calder
German Rhineland	Spring '83	45	Tara Stuart
La Plange, France	Jan '84	51	Geoffrey Lee
		52	Charles Grigor, Gary Webster
Austrian Tyrol	Easter '84	54	Gillian Sinclair, Eliz. McCudden

Once Industrial action was over and the TVEI scheme begun, local residential experiences are regular features of the school year from 1987-92

Destination	When	PP refs	Writer(s)
Blois (France)	March '88	66	Mrs Hyde, Wayne Chisholm
Praz sur Arly (Fr.)	Summer 88	69	Sharon Phipps
Valkenburg	May '89	74	Karen Collins
St Valery (Fr.)	July '89	75	Sarah Scott
Dinard (Fr.)	July '90	81	Rachel Sutherland
Rhineland	Easter '91	85	Sandra Dean, Emma Grant
Edinburgh Festival	August '91	88	(photos only)
Edinburgh Galleries	May '92	90	Louise Moore et al
London Culture	May '92	90	Kaye Strachan et al
Inverclyde Residential	May '92	90	Lir Kennelly et al

Destination	When	PP refs	Writer(s)
Loch Morlich Camp	May '92	90	Jane Stuart
Loch Morlich Camp	May '93	95	Ian Leslie, Fiona Russell
Lido di Jesolo	May '93	95	Emma Furness
France	May '93	95	Laura McLean, Jamie Weeden
Inverclyde Residential	May '93	95	Fiona Marshall et al
Lido di Jesolo	May '94	101	(photos only)
Edinburgh Festival	August '94	101	Isla Dunbar
St Filieu, Spain	Easter '95	104/105	Kerry Wares
Edinburgh Festival	August '95	105	(In diary but no report)
London Theatres	Feb '97	113	Catriona Simpson
Loch Morlich Camp	May '97	115	Ryan Gray
Paris—Disney	May '97	116	Karen Gordon, Laura Garden
Edinburgh Festival	August '97	116	Neil Rhind
London Theatre Trip	Feb '98	118	(In diary but no report)
Manchester, and Playa d'Aro		120	
Spain	May 98		Lynne Gardiner
London Theatre Trip	Feb '99	124	Alan Dodd
London Theatre Trip	Feb '00	128	Ross Allan, Rachel King, and Lynne Gardiner
London Theatre Trip	Jan '01	133	Rachel King + 3 others
Miss Saigon, Edinburgh	Oct '02	142	Allan Gray
London Theatre Trip	Jan '03	143	Douglas Cameron
London Theatre Trip	Jan '05	153	Emma McIntosh
Edinburgh Festival	Aug '06	161	Debbie Macdonald, Caitlin Voyzey
Edinburgh Festival	Aug '07	166	Claire Munro

Epilogue
How A New School Rose
Around The Old

A Vision For The Future

Afterword

New Build Pics from Hugh's Camera

How A New School Rose Around the Old

Hugh McCulloch, the school's third Headteacher, who first took on responsibility for the new school build when he was Depute Head, tells the story of how EHS2 came into being...

In September 2012 the Scottish Government announced that Elgin High School was to be included in a programme of new builds through the Scottish **SCOTTISH FUTURES TRUST** Futures Trust. The aim was to have the building ready for summer 2015.

At the start of the school session in August 2012 there was a sense of anticipation of the announcement of funding and in the following weeks an increasingly positive feeling that that Elgin High School would get a new building. However, there was also a realisation that a lot of work had to take place in the next few months if the timescales were to be met.   With a strong commitment from staff, students, parents / carers and the local community the school was well placed to drive the project forward. Although It was several months before any final decisions had to be made, the staff of EHS staff were already thinking about which departments should be adjacent – not only to encourage co-operation and for pupils to recognise the links between subjects, but also to make the best use of resources. As well as subject departments, thought was also being given as to how the pupil support departments could work together and overcome the difficulties of Kestrel House and Support for Learning being at opposite ends of the 1978 building.

February 2013 saw a meeting with various The Moray Council (TMC) officials and the Head Teachers of Greenwards Primary and Elgin High School to look at the issues relating to the traffic both during the construction phase and how the new entrance from Edgar Road would help alleviate some of the difficulties on the roads around both schools at the start and close of the school day. Around this time several EHS staff had also been visiting other new school buildings around Scotland to inform the discussions and decisions, including Lasswade High, Midlothian, (*pictured*

above) which was also being built through the Scottish Futures Trust.

The plans for the new Elgin High School building were for it to be built on the site of the current playing fields. Once the school had moved into the new building, the old structure would be demolished and the playing fields – including an all-weather pitch – would be set out.

The first meeting of TMC Steering Group for the new build was held and this included councillors, council officials and a representative of the Parent Council. The group had the remit of keeping an overview of developments and would link to the "Hubco" which would be responsible for co-ordinating the design, finance and construction of the new build. The timescale for starting in spring 2014 and opening in summer 2015 was then still very much achievable – but tight.

There then followed the completion of the "New Project Request" (NPR) forms which set out the details of the agreement between TMC, Hubco and SFT Head Teacher Andy Simpson and Senior Project Manager Martine Scott travelled to Eastwood Academy in Glasgow to see one of the first schools  build under the SFT process. It was likely that many of the features from that design would be incorporated into our new building.

Towards the end of the spring term 2013 students participated in a feedback exercise to help inform the NPR. Students asked two questions. Firstly, what five features of the current school building would you rate as good? The pupil responses centred around the range of facilities and different department specialist areas. Others picked out specific rooms that they thought were of a good size. The canteen food was given several mentions which is more of tribute to the skills of the kitchen staff! The second part of the survey asked "List the five priorities you would like to see included in our new school building." The answers could have been predicted. Sorting out the heating and ventilation were the top of the list. Toilets were also frequently mentioned as areas that needed improvement as did the narrowness of the corridors. A fitness room was a popular request. Others spoke about the need for all classrooms to be a good size and having "decent" furniture such as "chairs that fit under desks" There were plenty of ideas to think about and to give us a challenge as we moved into more detailed planning.

April 2013 - The Senior Leadership Team of EHS had their first formal meeting with JM Architects. The team had taken the initial ideas from draft NPR forms completed by TMC and

jmarchitects

started thinking about what this might look like and where on the site the construction would take place. Also shared were the designs for Inverness Royal Academy (*artist's image shown*) so that we could learn from their experiences. These were very early days and it was likely plans would change many times before they were agreed. The next stage was to firm up the plans ready to go out to consultation with staff, pupils, parents and the community by the middle of May.

JM Architects also gave a presentation to staff as part of the May in-service day. For the first time staff were able to see the possible design for the school. From this point onwards, we entered into more detailed discussions to see how we could face the challenge of meeting aspirations within the constraints of the tight budget formula.

During May 2013 there was a formal notice from TMC to publicise the consultation "to inform the public about the proposal to erect a new/replacement High School in Elgin..." On Saturday 8th June everyone was welcomed to New Elgin Primary School (10.30-12.30) or Greenwards Primary School (11.00-14.00), on Saturday 22nd June at Mosstowie Primary School (12.00-14.00) or on Monday 24th and Tuesday 25th at Moray College. There was to be a display of plans for the proposed site and other details of the new build. Local Authority staff would be present along with representatives from the architects. Members of the public would be invited to comment on the proposals and identify issues for consideration.

June 2013 - Following a story in the local press, TMC issued the following statement to keep pupils, parents, staff and the local community up to date with developments:

"It became apparent at an early stage that a start date of March 2014 was highly ambitious and while everyone involved is keen to see construction begin as soon as possible, they are even more keen that the project provides a new secondary school that is fit for purpose and will serve the local community well for years to come.

"Issues have emerged in relation to ground conditions on part of the site which require to be investigated further.

"As a result, possible courses of action include repositioning the new building within the overall site and options for that are currently being examined in detail.

"The cost implications of these options cannot be accurately quantified at this stage but all parties are continuing to work closely in an endeavour to keep the project within budget.

"What can be said with certainty is that although the project is currently showing an overspend on the original budget figure, it is nowhere near £4million.

"The project and the council continue to be fully supported by the Scottish Futures Trust, and the funding for the project is thus secure."

Over the summer following several meetings between TMC, Hubco and other partners the NPR we were underway again. Over the weeks and months there were many behind the scenes discussions to overcome the problems of the newly rediscovered underground peat and the affordability gap. We then had until December 2013 to finalise the floor plans with the hope that the contractors would be able to start late summer 2014 with a handover date of spring 2016.

The start of building work was indicated with more site visits by staff from construction firm Balfour Beatty and the utilities companies. In addition to

Balfour Beatty

this TMC had just accepted Option B for the new build, which was as follows:

Option B = Design for 800 pupils, enhanced core (communal) areas for extra cost with future extension capability, plus access road from Edgar Road extension.

August 2013 - Construction workers arrived to start two weeks of ground surveying. They drilled a number of holes to investigate the land on which the new build would be constructed. It was an exciting moment for all as we could at last see works being undertaken on the site. It was also good to welcome a representative of Balfour Beatty to the Guidance department. Steve Petrie joined representatives of the CITB to tell S3 pupils about the wide range of career possibilities in the construction industry.

There was now the significant task of completing the Accommodation Schedule (the list of the number of rooms to be included in the building) which had to be agreed in the near future along with the Room Data Sheets (describing what would be in each room).   Over the next two weeks Senior staff managed to meet with every department to review the proposals and develop draft Room Data Sheets.   These proved to be very encouraging and a number of excellent ideas emerged.   At this time, an educational consultant also checked our projections for room requirements when the roll of EHS would increase.   Thankfully, this proved to be reassuring and we had confidence that the building would be able to cope with a growth in pupil numbers and changes in the curriculum.

Shona Leese was appointed as Senior Project Officer.   She was working in the Designing Better Services section of TMC. The Parent Council also met and agreed that the annual Parent Forum (in September) would be a good occasion to update parents on the plans.

Friday 22nd May was meant to be the day of "financial close" for the project : the day by which the final costs would be agreed and contracts could be signed.   It did not happen.   There were still a few outstanding legal, planning and environmental details to be agreed.   The sad news was that we would not be able to go to financial closure in June.   The problem over "ESA 10" – financial regulation requiring agreement between the Scottish and UK governments and the European Union – was not going to be resolved quickly.   This was not a problem peculiar to EHS, having an impact on a number of other public sector projects across Scotland. As a result, construction on the new build was delayed further.

June 2014 - As we stopped for the summer holidays there was little activity regarding the new build.   An acoustic survey had come and gone and we were waiting for a bat survey to be completed. However, there had been a lot happening elsewhere. Steve Petrie from Balfour Beatty spoke at our annual prize giving. It was good to hear not only about his own career path but also for parents to learn about the ethos of the construction company and their positive aspirations for Elgin High School.   We were assured that the project was still on target with the start of construction scheduled for Monday 5 January 2015.

August 2014 – The new session at Elgin High School started well.   After six weeks holidays, pupils quickly settled into the routine of school life. However, despite the readiness of the plans, the construction companies being ready to go, and the unreserved support of everyone in TMC, there was sadly no positive news about the date for the start of the new build. We, and a number of other projects across Scotland, were still caught in the difficulties relating to the European regulation ESA 10, the interpretation of the Scottish Futures Trust/Hubco model for funding public sector works and the Office for National Statistics.

Students of Elgin High School and of the Parent Council had the opportunity to meet John Swinney MSP, Deputy First Minister of Scotland, *pictured.* He was in Elgin meeting with members of the north of Scotland councils and was able to take time from his schedule. The EHS group were able to ask him about the progress in reaching a resolution to the issues that had stalled the start of work on the new build. They also described the challenges of the current building. Mr Swinney listened  sympathetically. Although he was not able to give a firm date when work could go ahead, he did give reassurances that a resolution was a priority and also of the commitment of the Scottish Government to the project.

November 2014 - after many weeks of waiting, the Scottish Government finally announced the green light for Elgin High School new build and other projects that had been held up.

January 2015 – Following the announcements in November much hard work by staff from TMC, Balfour Beatty, Hubco and SFT had been carried out. There was a sense of optimism that we would reach financial close on 19th February. The target date for hand over and entry to the new build was re-scheduled for October 2017. The optimism allowed us to meet with a colleague from Hubco to start thinking about a date for the turf cutting ceremony! Some senior pupils who are part of school "Events Management Team" were present. They were going to assist with the arrangements and had lots of ideas on how to make it a memorable day.

February 2016 - A text message came through that financial closure had been reached and that the contracts for the construction of the new building had been signed!

Meanwhile, we had met with representatives of Hubco and Balfour Beatty to agree arrangements for the turf cutting ceremony at 12.00pm on Wednesday 16th March. Balfour Beatty were also due start turning the games fields into a building site on Monday 7th March and we could look forward to getting into the new building in October 2017.

Wednesday 16th March 12pm - all the pupils and staff from Elgin High School, along with pupils and staff from Greenwards, Mosstowie and New Elgin Primary Schools gathered to watch the first turf being cut for the new school building. The turf cutters were from the current S4 and P6 classes. When the new building was due to open in October 2017, these students would be in the first

S6 and S1 year groups. The event was followed by a series of speeches and musical items performed by pupils from all four schools. A buffet lunch for the invited guests was finished off with an amazing cake decorated by Annie Davidson our Head Cook. Special thanks went to the S5/6 Events Management Team for all their work in organising the day.

April 2016 - Pupils and staff returned to a very different school site than the one they had left two weeks ago. Very good progress had been made in preparation for the construction of the new build. After school on Tuesday 19th April we provided an opportunity to view the plans for the new build and meet some of the staff involved with the project.

June 2016 – towards the end of term saw another significant landmark with the start of the piling 285 piles into the ground. The first group of EHS pupils to see round the site had a visit. After a full health & safety briefing they moved on to the site and were able to imagine where everything will be. An excellent experience that made everything so real for the students.

September 2016 – Steel structures sprung up over the summer and most of the

roofing sections for the main building had been lifted into place by the crane. Meanwhile, the walls for the changing rooms were well underway in the PE block. Aerial Photographs taken by a drone flying over the site recorded the progress of the building. With the roof now on the PE block everyone was fascinated to watch the giant crane lift the sections along the length of the

building. Meanwhile the frame for the main building continued to grow and was not far from completion.

January 2017 - Over the coming months more detail into the room layout design was required. Detailed discussions with architects, room design companies and mechanical and electrical fitters ensured that the new build was going provide first class facilities for the Elgin High School community.

A teaching wall was selected from a number of designs – this includes integrated drawers and storage spaces with a central location for a 60" Interactive Panel. These units are to be fitted in all teaching areas. Offices, Staff Bases, Teaching Areas and open spaces around the school would also benefit from IT Network access both wired and Wi-Fi. All aspects of these

spaces would be colour co-ordinated to enhance the teaching and learning experience.

Special attention was paid to ensuring huge advancements in the issues relating to the old building. Ventilation, Lighting, Temperature Control, Acoustics and people movement. Teams of specialists continually provided feedback and modification in an effort to ensure all these issues were addressed.

March 2017 - With 30 weeks to go until the opening still scheduled for October

2017, final decisions were taken on the type and colour of all new furniture to be included in the teaching areas. A range of bright colours was used to enhance the teaching and learning environment and provide a co-ordinated feeling around the building. Even the lockers incorporated the school colours!

Construction became increasing busy with over 100 contractors regularly on site and whilst this made it challenging to organise both staff and student visits it was made possible thanks to the support of Balfour Beatty staff.

August 2017 - A strategy was also required to support decant from the old school into the new building. A request was made to the Scottish Government for 'exceptional closure' and four days were granted to allow staff to pack and unpack their equipment. Students benefitted from an extra two days holiday before and after their October Holidays. Whites of Forres were responsible for the removal and provided the school with literally thousands of boxes for the packing of equipment of all shapes and sizes. Staff and students worked extremely hard over a number of weeks prior to the move in ensuring all essential items were packed and labelled for moving into their new room.

September 2017 - As the building developed and photographs of the internal spaces  (such as this) were shared on the school's media including Twitter, Facebook and our on school website, excitement rose. Towards the end of September the school held an opportunity for all former pupils and staff to say Goodbye to the old building. 'A Trip Down Memory Lane' was a huge success with many hundreds of attendees on an evening organised by the S5/6 Events Management Team

Over the days leading up to and over the October Holidays the building was a hive of activity as finishing touches were applied. Staff arrived on Monday 23rd October to experience first-hand the superb facilities now available to them and the young people of Elgin High School. Over the course of the day staff worked feverishly to ensure their teaching areas were ready. S6 students arrived that afternoon and took part in a guided tour in order to familiarise themselves with the layout of the new building – On Wednesday they were to be responsible for orienting younger students around their new school.

25th October 2017 – Elgin High School opened the doors of its new building to students and staff

The excitement was shared by reporters from a number of local newspapers and reported by The Moray Council in the following press release...(beginning on page 103).

"A Trip Down Memory Lane"

...ly of them were very excited to be back at school.

"They shared their stories of their time here and some brought their children along to see where they learned before it goes."

Fellow S6 pupil Gemma Bland said more than 500 people came along to take advantage of the last chance to see EHS.

She said: "There was a good mix of both staff and pupils and people were happy to share stories of how things have changed from their days at school.

"We had quite a few of the very ...

Mr Hope read the school in its first 25 years before Mr Simpson took the helm for the next 13.

Mr Hope said: "Launched in August 1978, EHS has always had the advantage of being an attractive building – rather than being of traditional north-east design it had the looks of a modern hotel.

"However the building maketh not the school and from the start there was a determination to be truly comprehensive.

"A society where every pupil felt of equal value and every achievement was recognised – small and great. It has been a ...

... here.

"The old lady creaked (and leaked) as a building but she never lost her welcoming atmosphere and I am certain that EHS 2 will be a seamless progression.

He added: We wish much luck, much achievement and much fun to all who pass along her new wide corridors."

Above from *The Northern Scot* of 29.9.17

Sisters Michelle Hanna and Sandra Cruickshank neé McGillivray adding their names to the school wall

Former pupils Susan Jones and Yvonne Milton with children Ben and Baillie whilst Hugh McCulloch leads a group of fps on a tour

Right some of the 1978 S1 intake have a last look around. (Photo: Janice McKillop)

"Elgin's new High School opened its doors to delighted pupils and staff today.

The £30million high-tech campus replaces the existing building, and includes a fitness complex, auditorium, library and state-of-the-art catering facilities.

The 600 pupils arrived at the school by year group phases and were addressed by head teacher Hugh McCulloch.

Speaking as the first wave of pupils entered the building, he said: "The look on the pupils' faces has been absolutely fantastic this morning; they are completely and utterly amazed and spellbound by the fact that this is now their new school.

"The outstanding facilities on offer – the performance areas, the sports facilities, the teaching and learning environments are truly outstanding and quite frankly second to none, not just within the authority, but across the nation.

"This is a very proud day for the fantastic staff here, the pupils and me."

"After Mr McCulloch welcomed them to their new school, senior pupils took groups around the school to familiarise them with the layout and facilities. The school bristles with new technology, including equipment for senior students to take advantage of distance learning and smart boards in each classroom.

"Project staff at TMC have been working closely with contractors Balfour Beatty and the procurement body, Hub North Scotland, for the duration of the build.

10 Friday, November 3, 2017 THE NORTHERN SCOT

The Northern Scot

New Elgin High is well fit for the future

IF YOU think moving house is a major, even traumatic experience, then imagine how it must be to flit an entire school. That's the challenge which has been faced, and successfully achieved, by the staff and pupils at the new Elgin High. Just over a week in and already it feels like a home from home.

The replacement for the 1978 building was long awaited and long overdue; indeed, at one time there was a chance that Elgin High would be no more.

A new school was originally earmarked as part of Moray Council's 2001 public partnership proposals, but the plan had to be returned to the drawing board several times because of financial issues and because of a debate as to whether Elgin needed a second secondary. The decision was taken, rightfully, that it did, but it still wasn't plain sailing.

A new high school was dropped from the PPP programme, yet was expected to benefit from a £6.5 million plan for a regional sports centre to operate alongside a refurbished building. However, sufficient cash was not available and the project was shelved.

In the face of complaints about cramped classrooms, leaking roofs, poor access for people with disabilities and an unreliable heating system, it was decided a new school was a must. And here we are, with a magnificent £30 million, high-tech campus that includes a fitness complex, auditorium, library and catering facilities.

It is only what the pupils and staff deserve in this modern era, and it will benefit the generations that follow them.

A building does not make for a great school. Energetic and talented teachers are required, along with committed staff at all levels, supportive parents and a supportive wider community, and, of course, conscientious and hard-working pupils. Elgin High has it all and that is why it is a great school. That it might not have been to pass, is unthinkable.

Well done to all those who made the move happen, well done to those who never lost faith in a new school being built. You have done a great service not just to today's youngsters but youngsters for many years to come.

We should treasure our schools and their roles in our communities, and support the staff who are having to cope with heavy workloads under great pressures.

"The school was funded by the Scottish Futures Trust and Moray Council.

"What remains now is the demolition of the old school building, which will provide space for an all-weather pitch.

"Moray Council's chair of the Children and Young People's Committee, Cllr Tim Eagle, (pictured) said:

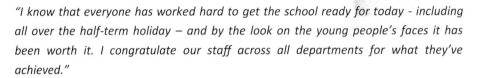

"This is truly a very welcome milestone for Elgin High pupils and staff.

"I know that everyone has worked hard to get the school ready for today - including all over the half-term holiday – and by the look on the young people's faces it has been worth it. I congratulate our staff across all departments for what they've achieved."

At the time of writing (March 2018) the young people and staff of Elgin High School have been in their new building for nearly four months. They have seized the opportunity provided to them with great enthusiasm. The positive ethos, a strongly recognised element of the Elgin High School community has been successfully transferred into the building and the aspiration to continually drive attainment and achievement is very much at the core of our vision and values.

On behalf of all in the Elgin High School community I would like to thank everyone involved with the project from its inception, through the planning and construction phases and its continued completion scheduled for July 2018. Your enthusiasm, commitment and attention to detail has provided a much-deserved facility of the highest standard for a community that richly deserves it.

A Further Selection of Photos from Hugh's Record of the Build

Community Area /
Assembly Hall space

Graph Comm room

Food Technology lab

Open plan Art area

Resistant materials in
Technical Dept

The school kitchen

Double aspect pupil
support room

Toilet construction

The Future

A Vision

Hugh McCulloch concludes our history book by examining where the school is and where it goes from here....

Our school vision "Working Together for Success" captures our aspiration and ambition. We are extremely proud of our open and welcoming school ethos, underpinned by our inclusive and nurturing focus for all of our young people, who will number around 800 in three years' time. This is reflected in the enthusiasm and loyalty of all staff to ensure learner experiences within and beyond the classroom are the best that they can deliver.

Here are, briefly, are some of our strengths and areas for development

Attainment

Over recent years, our results have shown a positive trend in the quality of award gained by pupils. Here's how we plan to keep this improvement going....

Improving Levels of Literacy and Numeracy

Students are tracked and monitored rigorously and set meaningful targets. We have extended options for students to take further literacy based awards such as media studies and finance & statistics

Improving our SQA examination results

Challenging targets are set and our Principal Teachers of Guidance ensure all returning students are sitting the appropriate number and level of qualification.

With the change of curriculum structure our S4 students are now able to sit six national qualifications and there has been an increase in tracking and monitoring for senior phase students. Awards can be gained through additional providers such as Open University modules and National 1 and National 2 courses.

Improving the number of young people going onto a positive and sustained destination

Regular and focussed Pathway planning meetings and a Career management are producing further development of learner pathway opportunities from the Broad General Education (BGE) of S1-3 into the senior phase

Providing Wider Achievement Opportunities, such as..

Activities Days involve S1-S3 Students in May. These long established days are designed to provide a context for learning which is different from the classroom experience.

Student Voice – In line with the United Nations Convention on the Rights of the Child (UNCRC) we have developed our own Groups.

Rights Respecting School – We are committed to being a Rights Respecting School and were the first in Moray to be given a Silver Award, in September 2017.

LGBT+ As a "Stonewall Scotland Champion School" we are looking to promote equality within our immediate and broader communities.

MAD – Making a Difference - All S5/6 students except those doing a course at Moray College are required to participate in an activity during the double period on a Wednesday for example via transition activities and master classes with local primaries, whole school Events Management and Work Experience.

S6 Leadership Team – open to all in the year - organises EHS Charity Events e.g. Jeans for Genes Day, Children in Need, Tickled Pink, Talent Show, Christmas Dances, Final Day Celebration; S6 Year Books, Hoodies and Prom.

House Leadership Teams - Amongst other activities these organise termly house assemblies and inter-house activities across the school.

S6 Students Lessons from Auschwitz Project - two S6 Students represent us at this national project. On returning to school they share their experiences with students from S-S6 and the local community.

Achievement BGE S1-S3 - At the end of the Christmas and Easter Term S1-S3 teachers are given the opportunity to nominate four students from all their classes and electives who have excelled academically and have shown good citizenship.

Whole School Achievement Assembly – End of Summer Term - at the end of the academic school year we celebrate the success of all students sharing their personal achievements.

House Tokens —are given out by all staff within the school (and regularly counted and reported on) to those students who perform well either academically or by being a responsible citizen.

Prize Giving – End of the Year

Duke of Edinburgh Award - is a very successful award run by the Geography Department.   Students work through a variety of activities ranging from volunteering to physical activities, life skills, to expeditions.

Peer Support and Paired Reading – we have a very successful peer support and a paired reading programme exists. Each year after training a large number of senior students provide support in BGE classes.

Social Enterprise – a very successful Social Enterprise projects group continues to run. In session 2016/17 our group was awarded with The North of Scotland School Social Enterprise Award.

Charity Days - throughout the year the school supports various local and national charities, raising, for example over £9K in session 2016/17.

Removing Barriers to Learning - Additional Support Needs (ASN)

ASN supports are catered for over two departments working very closely together. There is the mainstream element of ASN overseen by a PT which works to support many young people in school. There is also the Enhanced Provision non-mainstream department (as with Kestrel House in EHS1) who cater for a group of youngsters who have severe and complex needs.

Developing a Curriculum for the context of Elgin High School

Even with the stall of a projected 33-period week we went ahead with some major changes to the curriculum based on feedback and attainment figures, including the increase from 5 to 6 National Qualifications undertaken in S4; the reduction in the breath of subjects undertaken in S3 to increase the period allocation to 3 for choice subjects to allow for deeper knowledge and skills bases to be developed.

Learning & Teaching

There are several areas of strong practice in learning and teaching within the school and these areas of positive practice will be shared more widely within the school to ensure a consistent learning experience for the students.

Pastoral Care

Pastoral care is an area of key strength within Elgin High School.

Strong and positive relationships exist between students and staff across the whole school and between students and their guidance teachers. Every young person is known well by a key person in the school and they know there is always someone in school they can approach at any time.

To conclude, we are well placed to continue improving outcomes for all young people. The school community has the confidence and capacity to drive forward change. With equal measures of support and challenge young people will be able to reach their full potential. High levels and a range of achievements prepare them fully for their next steps in life.

Report on visit to Zambia – July 2017

The partnership between Mukonchi Secondary School and Elgin High School has existed since 2007. Through continued communication and visits to each other's countries the partnership has now developed further in several ways:

• There is now regular one to one communication between staff and between pupils in both countries through a variety of social media and video conference calls rather than just through senior staff in each school

• Case studies on each specific topic relating to each other's country in a number of subject areas, which this year included 'Crop to Table' and understanding the challenges facing female students in Mukonchi

• Primary schools are including projects on Zambia and a proposed partnership between Mukonchi Basic School and Elgin High Associated Primary Schools

• Regular talks to local community groups (e.g. Rotary, Church Groups and Youth Groups)

• A core group of EHS pupils were 'Highly Commended' in the Moray Young Citizens International Group Award in 2016

• This year a link was made with 'Books Abroad' an organisation which sources educational books in the UK and ships them to Africa. Following a meeting with fellow Head Teachers in the Mukonchi District we are hopeful of making this a much more beneficial arrangement.

Through the visits of pupils and staff from both schools; Mukonchi and Elgin, to each other's countries, we have been able to further develop and embed the partnership. Experiencing a different culture and educational provision has led to a commitment to build and maintain the partnership in both countries. A greater depth of understanding of global citizenship has been developed – not only by those have participated in the visits but also other members of the local communities who have listened to the experiences of the participants or worked together with them on subsequent projects. Another measure of the strength of the partnership is the fact that some previous participants have returned to Africa (and other countries) to carry out voluntary service and many others have committed to service in their communities and beyond. Friendships from Zambia are sustained with both staff and pupils continuing to communicate and talk about their friends in the partner school/ community.

The trip of July 2017 has helped further develop the partnership. The growing trust between the two school communities allowed a deeper sharing on a variety of topics.

Meeting with Mukonchi District Head Teachers to discuss our Global Partnership

Elgin High students visit a local farm as part of the 'Crop to Table' study

The Girls Dormitory at Mukonchi High School. Working on 'Inspiring Purpose' with Elgin High School students

These included:

• Discussions on social pressures on girls – particularly in relation to barriers or challenges facing girls completing their education

• UNICEF Convention on the Rights of the Child

• Staff Continuous Professional Development

• Sustainable development – 'Crop to Table' case study

• The impact of traditional cultural beliefs and values

In addition to leading the trip, I had the opportunity to discuss with Zambian students the Rights Respecting Schools Award scheme, and also deliver the Inspiring Purpose national project (which is part of the S2 RME curriculum in Elgin High School). The programme also allowed all members of the group to spend time exploring the local community and sharing time together.

This was my second trip to Zambia and my first as Head Teacher of Elgin High School. Through leading this visit I now aim to use my knowledge and understanding gained from these experiences to help further develop and embed global citizenship across the curriculum in Elgin High School. The partnership with Mukonchi High School is now widely recognized across not only Elgin High School, but also our Associated Schools Group. This assures me that there are sufficient staff within our community who are motivated and capable to continue building the partnership and develop further the opportunities available to the pupils in both schools in the years to come. I am very grateful to the Trustees of the Dick Bequest Trust for the support that they have given me not only this year but also in 2015 when I first visited Zambia as a Depute Head Teacher. This has made a significant impact not only on my professional development, but also on the lives of pupils and staff in Elgin and Mukonchi. In whatever way is possible, I anticipate continuing to use these experiences and the knowledge I have gained in the future.

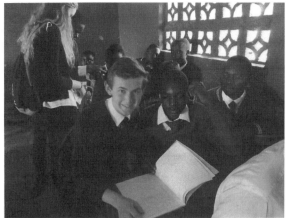

Developing links at Mukonchi Basic Primary School

Enjoying recreational time with new friends

Experiencing a different culture with a visit to Chief Mukonchi's Palace

Afterword

When Jeff Dugdale messaged me from the airport en route to his holiday in Florida last September to ask if I'd be his editor for *The Pigeon Post Years*, it took me all of three seconds to respond with a resounding yes. After all, my stint as Pupil Editor of *Pigeon Post* in 1990-91 had provided the first steps towards a 20-year career in newspaper journalism and I would forever be grateful to Jeff and the school for the invaluable grounding that gave me. However, within days of accepting his offer I feared the book might never see the light of day when I learned that Jeff and his wife Eve were caught up in the devastation of Hurricane Irma, which was at that point wreaking havoc across the supposed "Sunshine State"! Fortunately no hurricane was ever going to be powerful enough to stop Jeff from putting pen to paper and it wasn't long before he was safely back in Scotland with an outline of the book already drafted and eager to get to work.

My enthusiasm for the project was borne largely by a sense of nostalgia stemming from the success of the former pupils' Facebook page which, with Jeff's input, had grown into something of a monster over the second half of last year, its membership increasing from 450 to over 2,500 in the space of a few months. As FPs shared their memories - good, bad and ugly but frequently humorous - the widespread affection with which the school and its staff were held by its alumni became increasingly obvious. It was a joy to witness old friends reconnecting after many years (in some cases decades!) and to share in the affectionate reminiscences stirred by the photographs and old issues of *Pigeon Post* being shared through the digital platform.

Working on this book has been a similar joy and a privilege, albeit at times a somewhat surreal experience to find myself in the unusual position of editing my former English teacher's work! Thankfully my relationship with Jeff has survived the process unscathed and any issues have been worked out more than amicably on the snooker table following our 'editorial meetings'. At times I've been left speechless by Jeff's relentless energy and enthusiasm for the project and his determination to create something truly unique in terms of its scope and content. He and I agreed at the outset that the book should be a collaborative venture featuring contributions from as many former pupils and staff as possible. Elgin High has always been characterised by its strong sense of community and we strived to bring that ethos to the book by making it an inclusive, diverse community project rather than just the reflections of a few.

With that in mind, it's easy to look back on our school days through a mist of rose-tinted nostalgia but it's also equally important to remember that not everybody's memories of that time were happy ones. School isn't always a bed of roses, but then neither is life. Sometimes the real world gets nasty and our school days help to prepare us for that just as they prepare us for so many other things. Some FPs have written candidly within these pages about their experiences of bullying and not fitting in. What shines through in these accounts though is the strength those people have ultimately drawn from their experiences and the way they've used them in a positive way to help shape their attitudes towards others in adult life. I'd like to hope this book has provided those former pupils with a voice, an opportunity to express their feelings in words and, just maybe, some sense of closure.

Witnessing the demolition of the old EHS building unfolding before our eyes, with every hammer-blow documented in photographs posted on Facebook, has been an uncomfortable experience for some. It's seldom satisfying to see a bulldozer being taken to a significant aspect of our past, least of all to a building which housed so many emotion-charged memories from the formative years of our lives. I recall feeling surprisingly emotional when I suddenly realised there was a gaping hole where my former reggie classroom on Z floor used to be - the Business Studies room had literally been gouged out of the end of the building. However, when I met up with the school's founding Rector, the legendary Bill Hope, in February to interview him for this book, he summed the situation up rather perfectly when he told me: "It was a school of its time, just as the new building is a building for *its* time. Everything has to move forward. You can't be sentimental about these things".

It was a characteristically philosophical response from a man renowned for his relentless positivity and he was, of course, entirely correct. Some degree of destruction is always necessary for new growth to take place. You must tear down the old to enable something new to rise like a phoenix from its ashes. Things have to move forward. Whether it's a world, a life, a career or a building, everything has its time. And everything ends sooner or later.

In October 2017 I was among the many alumni who had the pleasure of being given one last tour of the old building prior to its demolition. There had been quite a few changes in the 26 years since I'd left there in 1991 - the blackboards had gone for